Half-Life *of a* Zealot

Swanee Hunt

Half-Life *of a* Zealot

DUKE UNIVERSITY PRESS

DURHAM AND LONDON

2006

4th printing, 2007

DEDICATION IN DOGGEREL

If kids and husbands had the choice
Of mom and wife who raised her voice
Or tended home and darned their socks
Content to think within the box,
They might express constrained remorse
That I've not been a gentler force.
Still, to the quartet I call home
I dedicate this telling tome;
For in between a wink or wince
They've rallied to a dense defense
When I've been dunned by fate or foes
And fortune's ways have yielded woes.
And so dear Teddy, Henry, Lil,
Be sure this author meant no ill
When penning page of love, and life,
Of marbled mom, and worried wife.
Remember precious Granny Ruth
Whose pluck prevailed to transform truth
And share the smile across Charles' face
Despite the tales of Swanee Grace.

Contents

ACKNOWLEDGMENTS

Folks say that when I'm at my best, I'm a wonder. But my zeal in tackling wrongs can render me a difficult boss, as well as an insufferable daughter, sister, or mother. Sometimes I'm insufferable even to myself. In those times, I've been saved by hovering angels who anticipate my missteps, coach and encourage me, help me repair my mischief and blaze new paths.

In my immediate family, our son Henry has wondered what could possibly drive me to be so public about my story, and our son Teddy is sure that this book is yet another example of my unenlightened state. But they have decided not to let it come between us. I owe particular thanks, however, to my husband, Charles, and my daughter, Lillian. Both have allowed difficult moments in their lives to be revealed along with mine. But beyond that generosity, they have been my cheering section throughout these eight years of writing, and I love them for that. As I was crafting this paragraph, Charles appeared with a cup of coffee and a plate of sliced peaches for me; now he's gone downstairs to read through my introduction. And Lillian has called my cell phone almost every day for two weeks with dozens of edits, every one right on target.

My two sisters and brother-in-law—June Hunt, Helen LaKelly Hunt, and Harville Hendrix, all authors themselves—have helped me find facts, tone, and flow. Helen's daughter Kimberly Kreiling has been my companion late at night, sitting on the floor in pajamas, watching family movies. And Caroline Ansbacher, from Charles's side, offered comments. So this chronicling has been a family affair.

Outside and unaware, Senator Hillary Clinton, George Soros, and Queen Noor have inspired my writing and my living. They know the power of privilege and how to spend it for the good of others. But inspiration isn't enough. Friends with talent for making silk purses from sows' ears, to use my grandmother's phrase, have supported me every step of the way on my path to independence. Yet this book doesn't attempt to name many of my most valuable relationships over the course of my life. Some have stretched across decades, growing thick with layer upon layer of joy, hurt, reconciliation, and support. And now one more stratum: gratitude.

As manuscript readers, I owe particular thanks to a legion of friends who told me they wanted to read my book when it was published. "How about now instead?" I begged. So thanks to Hattie Babbitt, Sallie Baker, Naisha Bradley, Barb Brockmeyer, Victoria Budson, Nicole Carter, Debbie Cavin, Jane Ciabattari, Abbie Cyr, Nancy Cyr, Carol Edgar, Jane Elioseff, Christy Fujio, Miki Jacevic, Kathy Jankiewicz, Coral Jenrette, Jim Laurie, Fred Lewis, Sheila Morse, June Page, Fern Portnoy, Marjorie Seawell, Paul Simmons, Chris Taylor, Jane Vennard, Stephanie Warburg, Judi Wagner, and Susan Zimmerman. (I'm *sure* I'm forgetting someone important; please forgive me.) Thanks as well to Julia Appel, Annemarie Brennan, Valerie Gillen, Jan Smith, Chris Vaudo, and Roxane Wilber for help with everything from structural worries to tedious line editing. And, for the final review, Greeley O'Connor spent late night hours sitting with me by the fire, both of us crunching rice crackers to stay awake.

And finally, I'm grateful for a supportive relationship with Valerie Millholland, acquisitions editor at Duke University Press. She's smart, caring, and committed. Who could ask for more?

You've got to serve somebody
You may be an ambassador to England or France
You may like to gamble, you may like to dance
You may be the heavyweight champion of the world
You might be a socialite with a long string of pearls
But you're gonna have to serve somebody, yes indeed
You're gonna have to serve somebody
Well, it may be the devil, or it may be the Lord
But you're gonna have to serve somebody.
—Bob Dylan

Introduction

Over the past years, I've conducted a survey among my friends. Given the choice of having a grown child who spent her time as a "couch potato" watching soap operas, or one fervently caught up in a non-violent but mean-spirited fringe group—which would they choose? Their responses split down the middle. "First, do no harm," replied some; better to be uncommitted than destructive. Others countered, "A life without engagement is the greater curse; the direction can be corrected later."

When they turned the question to me, the answer was obvious. I've always been a zealot, championing causes, waving banners, persuading, cajoling, insisting . . .

This half-told tale of a life was written in my early fifties. Over five decades, history was gradually changing the context; my carefully charted course was diverted by heartbreaking, terrifying, and thrilling experiences. But I've usually managed to keep my balance. And along the way, I've learned to absorb privilege and oppose patriarchy to become an independent woman. Let me be clear: I'm a hard worker but no hero. Gutsy, sometimes almost noble—and always flawed.

My story is laid out in seven chapters with shifting landscapes. It begins with growing up born-again in Dallas, the daughter of an oil magnate. Leaving home, I establish a separate identity, albeit as a Southern Baptist minister's wife, and spend a formative four years away in Germany. Settled in Denver for sixteen years, I immerse myself in grassroots activism, eventually entering the political arena. I step onto the world stage when I join the Clinton administration as ambassador to Austria. In Vienna, my life is almost consumed with concurrent wars: horrific atrocities in the Balkans and mental illness that descends on our family. But even in the chaos, mentors (including my daughter) appear, and my strength grows slowly and steadily.

Why did I write this book? Basically because I had it in me, scratching to get out. This felt more like letting go than a task. Pulling together dozens of loose life strands into one volume has spared me endless hours of psychotherapy. Of course I could have had that benefit if I'd locked the manuscript up in a safe, as one friend urged. But why should you read this book? Some will be drawn to a closer look at my father, H. L. Hunt, who not only was wildly successful as a businessman but also took on the challenge of the unseen, whether oil underground or threats to our national security. Those who love the South may feel warmed by the Southern Baptist scenes, or my mother's honey-sweet drawl. Policy junkies may look for more inside scoop on the Clinton administration. There's some, but rather than a rigorous discourse on domestic or foreign policy, I show how Dad and D.C. taught me how to move through minefields with tap-dancing confidence.

Ultimately, the point of this book is not what someone named Swanee was doing or thinking on any given day. And it's not a peek into lives of the rich and famous. Instead, I have struggles and successes in common with hosts of people I'll never meet. I tell about transforming disappointments into energy rather than encountering them again and again as obstacles along the way. Maybe you'll recognize yourself in these pages and avoid some mistakes I've made. Better yet, I hope you'll savor more fully your own private and public triumphs.

This series of recollections and reflections was written from my perch at the John F. Kennedy School of Government at Harvard, where in November 1997 I helped create the Women and Public Policy Program. As soon as I arrived, students began plying me with questions about life choices that had led to my diplomatic appointment. I developed a two-minute answer, a twenty-minute answer, and a two-hour answer —each progressively riskier. This book is the two-day answer.

Someone suggested that I open my book with a dramatic scene: flying into Sarajevo during the war, staring through the cockpit windshield of a military cargo plane at the shocking destruction below. I decided against the hype, opting instead for a quieter musing on a decidedly unquiet half-life. But the element of risk remains. Frankly, I'm more nervous about writing this book than I ever was about dropping into Bosnia. The battle here is for accurate memories, fair interpretation, and adequate explanation—stretching back half a century.

Given Tallulah Bankhead's quip that "it's the good girls who keep the diaries; the bad girls never have the time," I'm a bit embarrassed to admit that I've been writing toward this book in journals for forty years. Several detailed scenes are lifted from those diaries. I've also used cassette tapes, family movies, scrapbooks, and videos of events. I've rummaged through hundreds of files, press accounts, and interviews. And I've turned to family and friends to corroborate my memories. I loved the process; it made me wish I were a historian.

Still, as I commit words to paper, I know a significant number of them must be wrong. Two recent incidents demonstrate the danger. The first was during my final read-through, when I checked the Internet for the spelling of Justice "Ruth Bader Ginsberg" and found biographical material, famous quotes, and a story in the *New York Times*. Then, on a hunch, I googled "Ruth Bader Gins*burg*" and found an additional ninety thousand entries. Some sources spelled her name both ways in one article—hedging their bets, I suppose. I began to doubt every fact in this book I thought I'd verified.

A second incident shook me up. When I came across a well-known journalist at an airport, I introduced myself, reminding him that we'd met at a White House dinner. No, he replied, he wasn't there.

"But we were both at President Clinton's table," I insisted.

In fact, he retorted grumpily, he'd never been invited to the White House. "Not *once*." Seeing my confusion, he searched his memory, then offered, "I'll tell you where we met. It was Katherine Graham's house. I remember—we were standing in the foyer."

"But I was never invited to her parties," I answered. We both burst out laughing.

I was, in fact, in Kay Graham's home once, for a one-on-one lunch, just before her beautiful autobiography came out. When I mentioned that I was writing my own story, she advised against it, saying I was too young. On the other hand, when I asked what was the most diffi- cult aspect of her book experience, she was quick to answer: "Cutting. I had to take out half." That seemed a compelling reason to start my memoir earlier rather than later.

Kay Graham was right in a different sense: This book would have been easier to write if the other characters weren't still around. Along those lines, friends have warned against describing scenes that aren't favorable to me or others. Yes, some career doors may close and I'll have regrets. But my daughter Lillian, an old soul at fifteen, counseled, "You have to tell the truth, Mom, but not the whole truth." So I've omitted some quite dramatic incidents and generally refrained from exposing people's darker sides, not through naïveté, but because the incremental insight doesn't warrant embarrassing them.

Another serious concern to me as I've written is that I know what it's like to grow up in a fishbowl, with tourists gawking at our home, the press devouring my father or humiliating my mother. I also know how it feels to be constantly on stage. It seems wrong that I'm now putting my own children in the same position. To them, and anyone else who winces in the spotlight I cast, I apologize. I simply don't know how to tell my story without you.

My family members have had the opportunity to offer corrections and critique, and I've mostly conceded. Our three children and I have talked about how memoirs generally focus on extraordinary events and hard times—not the familiar and easy. So the accounts of those three are out of proportion, in part because I describe the courage of Lillian's life with bipolar illness, but also because Henry didn't live with us full time and the main part of this book ends when Teddy is only ten.

As for the Hunts of Hunt Oil Company, I've chosen to say little. Not mentioning my Dallas family and our business would leave too huge a gap, but I've tried to construct the narrowest footbridge possible to cross the topic. The company that my father built and my brother re-built isn't examined. Enough books and articles (some with more fiction than fact) have been written about my family's fortune, and I won't go into detail about what I know only secondhand regarding various family members' forays into markets, industries, and sports. I wasn't a central player, and those stories add little to mine. This book won't satisfy those enamored with money as it explores the relationships between individuality, entitlement, and ethics—and the privileges and pain that grow out of that tangled mix.

Which leads me to my mother, an extraordinary human being, and probably the greatest influence on my life. As I was writing about her unconventional path, I asked her if there was anything she wanted me to be sure and tell—or not tell. She tilted her head, and her eyes moved back and forth as she thought. Then she responded, "No, Honey, my life is an open book; there's nothing about it that isn't already known." I'm sure that's not so, and I'm glad. To live without secrets would be rather flat, and Mother's life was richly textured. At any rate, as I've described her, I've not revealed any secrets. The same is true of Dad, who died thirty years before this book was completed. For the most part, I've only added an inside perspective on what is already public, describing its impact on me.

Mine is a woman's story, and that presents opportunities, but also challenges. First, the decision of how to describe myself. As she writes about her own life, Jill Ker Conway asks how women can authentically describe themselves: "The woman autobiographer . . . cannot depart too dramatically from popularly accepted stereotypes, which affirm the man of action and the suffering or redemptive female. To do so is to risk losing persuasive power." I think she's right. Rather than feel reluctant about showing my vulnerability, I've wondered if it's safe to show my strength. For most people, strength and femininity seem polar opposites. So women like me constantly test the audience, trying to sense whether we're being discounted for being too competent or for being too weak. I don't want to come across as whining, but the truth is, virtually every highly positioned woman I know (and I know many) moans behind closed doors that her actions, however valuable, are discounted because she's operating in a male-oriented world. That's my preamble too, but the rest of my life is the story of how freeing myself from those demeaning situations created mental muscle that I rely on today in my work.

The second challenge relates to story lines. Until I began writing, I didn't understand how the progression of living defies an orderly telling. Keeping events in exact chronology might be easiest for the reader, but not true in a deeper sense, for life isn't lived in absolute and tidy sequence. Teddy runs up to me with a grin, and I experience again the joy of his birth. An old friend calls to exchange the latest news and we both remember, even if we don't say it, a passionate moment at the back gate. I look across the table at my husband and imagine us growing old together. With no loyalty to time, one experience latches onto another.

A third challenge has been choosing voice and style, because in my writings I've developed several. I've spent a year churning out a doctoral dissertation. A full day laboring over a long poem. And many a Saturday morning cranking out a newspaper column. In between have been entries in journals I keep for my children, cables to the State Department, and notes to friends. I may have the odd distinction of being the only author published in *Good Housekeeping* and *Foreign Affairs* in the same year—or ever.

And finally, this book is tough to write because most of my readers will not have a detailed understanding of Central Europe in the 1990s, nor should they. I recall how one day in 1995, as we drove into Vienna from the airport, I tried to explain the Bosnian war to a visiting member of the Clinton cabinet. Like a football coach, I pulled out a legal pad to draw a map of the Balkans, showing the U.S. fleet in the Adriatic, with Xs and arrows marking warring armies and refugee migrations. Having seen how difficult it was for him to grasp the convoluted politics, I'm loath to ask of my readers more than I would of a cabinet member.

I wouldn't have been in that car in Vienna if I hadn't lived a zealous life. For years I've been fascinated by zeal, "ardent and active interest." Where it comes from; how it's nurtured or reined in; why some people have it and others don't; whether it's mostly good, mostly bad, or just neutral. Zeal requires a certain comfort with danger. I recall how in the mid-1950s, in the heat of the Cold War, we first-graders prepared for nuclear attack. When Mrs. Landrum called out, "Duck and cover!" we obediently scurried under wooden desks, crouching with our heads tucked under our little hands until the imagined apocalypse passed. That exercise in fervent futility left its mark. I've been forging into radioactive situations, and occasionally ducking and covering, ever since.

By the time I ended the first quarter of my life, the pattern was clear. When many young adults were tenuously considering the notion of commitment, I'd already thrown myself into a succession of causes: archconservative politics, religious activism, and progressive social organizing. Into each of these movements I plunged, equipped or not, into the thick of the fray. Over time, my inclination has not changed: passion laced with dangers, triumphs, loves, failures, and convictions.

Thank goodness my character has evolved along another track as well. In high school I read *The True Believer*, written by the unschooled but sagacious longshoreman Eric Hoffer, who philosophized on the dangers of blind fanaticism. With some uneasiness, I recognized myself. By nature or nurture, I'm a true believer, with the genes and means to make the most of it. But I try to embrace devotion only in the bright light of self-critique. Studies of theology and psychology have made me more sensitive to others. I've learned to say "I'm sorry," to admit foibles, to realize that we see the world only "through a glass darkly," as the Apostle Paul said.

Despite the shadows, a life of engagement—having clear purpose, making positive change, and acting at full capacity—is worth considerable sacrifice. The results aren't all pretty. Maybe my body is a metaphor. Every morning when I step out of the shower, my soft belly reminds me in its clawed roundness of the stretches that accompany birthing. But as my face has become wrinkled, my arms flabby, and my hair faded, my voice has become stronger, my reach farther, my sense of self more solid. This book is an attempt to understand that development, not as postlogue but prologue. For as Søren Kierkegaard observed, "Life must be understood backwards . . . but it must be lived forwards."

may my mind stroll about hungry and fearless and thirsty and supple
and even if it's sunday may i be wrong
for wherever men are right they are not young
—e. e. cummings

CHAPTER 1

Roots: Rural and Right

Backdrop

"This is a once in a lifetime moment. A room crammed full, and everyone likes me," I laughed before the crowd assembled in Washington for my swearing-in as ambassador to Austria. It was November 1993. A squirmy gaggle of children holding small American and Austrian flags sat cross-legged on a muted rose carpet around a stage. This family-oriented affair was a first for the U.S. State Department, which fancied itself more formally predisposed.

As my eyes scanned the room, I surveyed the characters in the pageant of my life: Aunts and uncles from Oklahoma and Louisiana. A Sunday school teacher at First Baptist Church of Dallas and employees of Hunt Oil Company. My pastor from Fort Worth, friends from the church in Heidelberg, and the rabbi I'd met when I was a seminary student in Denver. Caretakers from our ranch in Colorado, along with grown-up girlfriends who'd rafted the Grand Canyon rapids with me. Board members from the Women's Foundation and Hunt Alternatives Fund, next to members of Congress and the president's cabinet. My sisters, Helen and June. Grade school, high school, and college buddies—they'd aged, even if I hadn't.

I pushed back tears as I shifted my gaze to our three children. They'd reaped some benefits but also borne the burden of my achievement. That wasn't fair, but then what is? They would somehow manage, I thought. No one worried about Henry, dashingly dressed and essentially grown. But Granny would have called our Teddy "knee-high to a grasshopper." And though Lillian was "cute as a button" (Granny, again) as she held her little brother's hand, her first ten years of childhood had been a struggle.

My love for our children blended into the rush of excitement as the ceremony commenced. The occasion was an intense mix of private and public, much as this book, if it's true, must be. Mother, bless her, gazed lovingly up at me as she held the Bible on which my hand rested, while Vice President Gore led me in the oath of office, with Charles, as always, standing close by. I'd worn my only designer suit, a strong cranberry statement, and I felt like She-Ra, Princess of Power, as I turned, grasped both sides of the podium, and leaned into the mike.

Stakes were high. I began by establishing my credentials, saying what I hoped to accomplish in the post. But I couldn't resist remarking to the crowd that Mother must be relieved at not having to explain to my late father why I was hanging out with all these Democrats.

At moments of acclaim, I always wish for my parents, though not my parents as known by the public. My father was described by journalists as the richest man in America. They were probably right. But I remember an early childhood when we weren't so rich. My mother and four children lived in a modest, middle-class brick home five minutes from my father's mansion. He moved us in with him when I was seven. I had a room in his big house, but it took me a couple of decades to figure out where I fit into his legacy.

I've often felt embarrassed about being part of a tribe of zealots: Dynasty builders. Evangelicals. Anti-communist crusaders. Fortune hunters. Pax Americans. While some are stoutheartedly spreading the Gospel, others claim to be rescuing our country from Big Government.

We seem to have it in our blood, the desire to change the world. I've spent much of who I am—time and energy, health and wealth— figuring out how best to help others. But care comes at a cost. It requires courage, a willingness to step out into uncertainty. In my case, that has meant putting myself on the line for my beliefs, sometimes in opposition to members of my family. In particular, I've rejected most of Dad's social and political values, while trying not to reject him.

What does that mean—rejecting his values while not rejecting him? I'd never say *I* exist in a meaningful sense apart from my values, so separating *Dad's* beliefs from his being is a dubious endeavor. But I've worked hard at trying to hold on to my father's best and let the rest slip away. It's been a task worth the trouble. For one thing, relationships always exist in a larger context, affecting other people. And while our father-daughter connection was painfully lacking, he meant the world to my mother, and she meant the world to me.

But there's more. When I step back, I can overlook the pain of my life and be grateful to Dad for resources that have allowed me to lift a bit of burden from others. My brother Ray, a brilliant businessman, restored the wealth that had dissipated by the time of my father's death. It was in the shadows of those two men that my own light grew strong, but it's taken me fifty years to admit that—even to myself.

My inheritance isn't just company stock, but also genes and family lore replete with adventurers exploring new territory, relying on vision and cunning to create institutions and businesses where none existed. Dad's trailblazing probably led to my penchant for striking out into the unknown, taking on intractable societal problems along the way. And my mother's religious devotion inspired my own brand of evangelism: a determination to save others, not from Lucifer's hell but from hell on earth.

When I'm asked how I wound up so different from my parents' conservative ways, I don't fully accept the premise. Sure, my persuasions diverged significantly from theirs. But I've been more surprised by how many of their bedrock attitudes and inclinations are fundamental to my thinking—particularly their insistence that every person is responsible for changing the world. This has nourished my work in the inner city of Denver . . . the imperial halls of Vienna . . . the rubble-strewn streets of Sarajevo. You might say that wherever I've ended up, my folks have come along.

Off the Farm

As a child, I played in a room hung with a picture of my grandfather "Hash" Hunt (Haroldson Lafayette Hunt Sr.) in his Confederate uniform. He enlisted at eighteen, along with his four brothers, in Company F of the 27th Arkansas Infantry, commanded by his father. Hash became sheriff of Fayette County, Illinois, and an affluent farmer. The youngest of eight, my father, Haroldson Lafayette Hunt Jr., was born in 1889 in Ramsey, Illinois, near Vandalia, where Abraham Lincoln started his political career fifty-five years earlier. Dad was called "June," for Junior. He was, by his own account, a genius. And he loved to tell how he started reading at two:

> You see, when we had company, my father would bring me the newspaper and ask me to read the stock quotes. I would straighten my little skirt, then read. So I had to be two, because I started wearing pants when I was three.

Dad was taught by his mother at home. Ella, highly learned, assessed the local school and found it wanting, so she taught her youngest son herself. But at fifteen, itching to see the world, he jumped on a railroad car headed west. His siblings accused him of leaving the farm because he didn't want to work, but there were also tales of my grandfather being violent. Dad claimed he just didn't want to spend the rest of his life behind a mule.

My father wandered from state to state, picking up any sort of job, including stints as a short-order cook and shepherd. I grew up listening to hobo stories, including how as a lumberjack he earned the name "Arizona Slim," because his waist was so trim from bending over a saw. Word went out from some of his co-workers that they had found the Great White Hope, who might knock out the first black world champion boxer, Jack Johnson. Dad was never put to the test. Instead he planted eucalyptus trees, pounded stakes into railroad beds, and, yes, drove an ox plow.

In California he enrolled in college, having never gone to high school. He was there only half a year. The rumor was that he cleaned out the student body in poker. It's not clear whether he chose or was asked to leave. What is clear is that he relished life on the edge. A hundred times I heard him tell how in San Francisco he barely avoided being "shanghaied" by escaping through his hotel window. "Two days later," he would add with a chuckle, "the hotel was demolished in the earthquake of 1906."

In 1911 Hash died, leaving my father the sizable inheritance of $5,000. That was the beginning of his life as a businessman. At twenty-three years of age, he began to buy and sell cotton plantations on the Mississippi Delta until he had amassed "lots of land and lots of liabilities." In 1914 he met and married Lyda Bunker. They had six children over the next eighteen years. By 1919 he'd made a fortune, which he saw disappear in an economic downturn almost immediately thereafter.

Dad then ventured into the rough-and-tumble world of the Arkansas-Louisiana-Texas oil boom. He borrowed $50 for transportation and arrived in El Dorado broke. Early on, he figured out that he could drive into the country and offer a farmer $25 an acre for a lease to drill on the property, drive back to town, sell it to someone else for $35, and pocket the difference.

But that wasn't enough. When Dad didn't have two dimes to rub together, he would ask his foreman how much was needed to meet payroll. Then he'd cross the river to Mississippi and walk into gambling games with a rubber band around a thick roll of one-dollar bills, a hundred-dollar bill on the outside. At the start of the game, he'd take the roll from his pocket, as if estimating how many hundreds he had, and then tuck it back in. But beneath the showmanship was an awesome intellect. I have no reason to think he ever cheated. He didn't need to. Dad was known as a "card counter," calculating from the discards, plus his hand, the mathematical probability that a certain card would be in one place or another. He met payroll.

I obviously wasn't around, but from what I can put together, Dad cut an impressive figure. I have a picture of him from those days: six feet tall and fair, with broad shoulders. He was quite dapper. I've read that his trousers were always pressed and his shirts starched. He smoked a big cigar and wore a spiffy straw hat at a jaunty angle on his head. Even when he was short on cash, my father had the appearance of confidence and affluence.

Adding to his good looks, he was renowned for immense powers of concentration and the ability to formulate a plan, however unconventional. Long after others gave up, he stayed engaged in an enterprise with single-minded determination. And according to my mother, Dad's deals were based on a handshake. The writing could catch up later.

In his early years, half the Hunt wells had parts borrowed from Humble Oil (now Exxon). By 1925, after a string of successful wells,

Dad sold a half-interest in some properties for $600,000. But then, how did he go from being a successful oil man to being an outrageously successful oil man? The story, as I've heard it, is that at forty my father met "Dad Joiner," a colorful oil-patch charlatan who called him "Boy" (an amazing thought). He and Joiner had much in common: neither drank nor used profanity, and both were unusually popular with the ladies.

In 1930 Joiner brought in a well, the Daisy Bradford #3, which drenched the crowd of five thousand hopeful onlookers, including my father, with "black rain." But production was inconsistent. And Joiner, having egregiously oversold shares, faced a slew of lawsuits from investors. Meanwhile, Dad could imagine an underground formation to account for why Joiner's well wasn't as successful as hoped. Intrigued, my father followed progress carefully as more wells were spudded, and he even put a scout on the scene.

Just about dark on November 26, a piece of core came up in a test drill. The scout rubbed it between his fingers and tasted it. He immediately telephoned my father in Dallas, who, that very moment, was negotiating with Joiner. Four hours later, assuming Joiner's legal problems, my father put $30,000 down and pledged $1.3 million from future profits for the discovery well and another five thousand acres of leases. In my home hangs a portrait of Dad with the historic lease in his hand.

His hunch was right. Beneath the red clay farmland was an ocean of oil. Within weeks, Kilgore, population seven hundred, became a wild congregation of ten thousand drillers, desperados, and hookers. By 1932 Hunt Production Company had nine hundred wells in East Texas. A pipeline carried the oil to the eastern seaboard, where it later fed the Allies' war effort.

But tragedy struck in 1937. A leak from a gas pipe that ran from the fields into a local public school caused an explosion that killed about three hundred, mostly children—more than half from Hunt Oil families. Frantic parents tore through the smoking wreckage. As each child's crushed or charred body was found, Dad walked over to the parents, reached into his pocket, and handed them cash for a funeral.

Hearing the story as an adult, I imagined my father doing whatever he could think of to help, yet still somehow emotionally removed.

After the accident, perhaps because of it (who knows?), Dad left the area and moved his wife and children to Dallas. He reinvested his East Texas oil revenues in Louisiana.

My father was an eccentric oil-patch "wildcatter," who drilled for black gold on a hunch and a prayer. It was a wild ride, and his eyes twinkled as he told it later in his laid-back, country-thick voice: "Well, oh, in 1938 . . . perhaps 1940 . . . when I was bringin' in lots of wells, the brokers and speculators and traders developed a saying, 'Follow Hunt and get rich.' And so . . . not long after that, I drilled *ninety-nine* consecutive dry wildcats. So, they began saying, 'Follow Hunt and go broke.'" But then, from 1942 through 1945, Dad's companies produced over sixty million barrels of natural crude—more than all the Axis powers together.

When colleagues ask why I'm so focused—driven, really—I wonder if it's genetic, or if it's from growing up with a drifter who became the largest individual stakeholder in the biggest operating oil field in the world. By the end of the Second World War my father's fame had spread well beyond Texas. His shrewd business sense and gambler's instinct paid off in an era of speculative drilling that predated seismic technology. As his oil wells kept pumping, his income was so high that he calculated it by the minute, at one point joking that he quit cigars because he reckoned the time he spent taking off the wrappers was costing him millions.

When a reporter asked him if it was true that H. L. Hunt had an income of a million dollars a week, Dad answered, with a smile, "I would starve to death with an income of a million dollars a week." Yet money for Dad was just a way of keeping score. I often heard him ruminate, wistfully, that he'd like to wake up stone broke and see if he could do it again.

The Belle of Idabel

Dear Santa Claus,

I am a little girl nine years old. Will you please bring me a pair of skates and a doll stove? Bring my little brother a wagon and my mother wants a box of candy. I do not know what my two big brothers or my sister wants but please bring them something real nice, and don't forget the poor children.

Sincerely yours,
Ruth Ray—<i>Valiant Tribune</i>, December 10, 1926

Mother was born in 1917 and grew up poor in Oklahoma, about the time my father was striking it big in East Texas. Her father, Walter Ray, had moved with her mother Grace by buggy and wagon from Arkansas to the new state created out of "Indian Territory." Walter was elected the initial county clerk and helped organize First Methodist Church of Idabel.

Granny told me that even though her husband "couldn't carry a tune in a bucket," he belted out hymns on Sunday, earning the nickname "Sing." All her life, Mother cherished the memory of her father, who succumbed to tuberculosis in the curative dry climate of Colorado Springs when she was three. Mom described Walter's last visit to their rental house near the sanitarium. Her eyes sparkled as she recounted how her weak and gaunt father rolled a newspaper into hats and trumpets, which the children proudly turned into a marching band, parading around his wheelchair in a scene straight out of Norman Rockwell. Large crowds gathered at the train station when his casket came home.

Life was hard when the family of seven, missing Walter as its breadwinner, returned to my grandmother's white frame house in Idabel. The owner of the general store gave Mom a little pair of red shoes— "the most beautiful shoes in the world," she told me. At first she refused the gift, but he insisted, saying "You'll be advertising for me." She was naïve, of course, to believe his kind pretext. But maybe innocence was in order, for in the Great Depression jobs were scarce, and Grace was selling off Walter's property bit by bit to get by.

Even so, Mother's tales from that time were thick with succulent nostalgia. The aroma of bread baking on Fridays, the children kneeling next to the fireplace for prayers, my mother crawling into *her* mother's bed—the bed in which she was born—or walking the mile to school. She was in the same schoolroom as two of her older brothers. Her first day, the teacher asked her name. "I'm Sis," she piped back politely.

"What's your real name?"

"Sis," she repeated, puzzled. The teacher turned to her brothers.

"Yep. It's just 'Sis,'" they insisted. The teacher gave up and told her to find out her name when she went home for lunch.

Like my dad, Mother (her name, she discovered, was Ruth Eileen Ray) was the youngest, but girls weren't raised with the same freedom as boys to forge their way in the world. Her poems, dotted with homespun expressions like "Gee Whiz" and "No Siree," were published regularly in the *McCurtain County Gazette*. Though she didn't realize it, by later standards she herself was one of "the poor children" Santa sometimes forgot. She did eventually receive the skates, but the family couldn't afford her dream of piano lessons.

As a teenager, Mom taught herself to type, volunteering long hours at the courthouse for her big brother, who'd been elected county clerk in his father's footsteps. With several of the older children working and sending money home, one of the younger siblings could go to college. Mom had been class president and a straight-A student, so she was chosen. But, she told me, she couldn't bear the thought of the tuition at Oklahoma State University draining family income, so she left after a year and found a job as a secretary, moving in with her only sister, Swann, in Shreveport, Louisiana.

Swann, whose nickname was Swannee, was fifteen years Mom's senior. As her namesake, I see myself in her: hardworking, bossy, and dedicated to her family. Her husband, Charlie Lake, was a small, jolly man with whom she seemed to share little affection. His name, however, was irresistible to my aunt, never shy of the dramatic twist. Long after Charlie died, she'd introduce herself, in a thick Southern drawl: "Hah thaya. Mah name is—are you ready for this?—Mah name is *Swann . . . Lake*. It *really is!*"

Up to this point, telling my family's story is easy. But I have conflicted feelings about going further, as if I'm exposing a closeted skeleton. On the other hand, my family history is no secret. In three minutes of research anyone discovers that my father and mother had a lengthy relationship out of wedlock.

That story is generally repeated by people who weren't there and didn't know Mother or Dad. I heard Mom's version, and I witnessed their relationship with my own eyes. So I'll tell my mother's story with the respect she deserves, but not glossing over the truth. In later years, she was a role model and an inspiration to thousands. But her saintly spirit was more likely *because* of her mistakes, not despite them. She often said her faith grew out of her belief that she had no options but to "live on her knees." She, more than anyone I've been close to, understood the concept of the grace and mercy of God, which she discovered because of a sharp turn in her life in her mid-twenties.

After she moved in with Swann, Mother began working for the law firm that represented H. L. Hunt's oil interests in Louisiana. He met my mom, a brunette beauty, in the hallway of the law office. My father was twenty-nine years her senior and married, with six children—one older than she. But she didn't know all that in the beginning.

Swann told me simply that one day her sister didn't come home from work. Swann was worried sick. The next months are unaccounted for. Mom told me only that she ended up for about a year in an apartment on the Upper West Side of New York City. This was a period she talked about with sad, even imploring, eyes. It was impossible not to feel her fear as she divulged to me how she went alone to a hospital on April 6, 1943, to give birth in the anonymity of the big city.

Family in Oklahoma didn't know her situation. Piety was at the core of Mother's identity, and in her last years she said that was the most difficult period in her life. She visited Idabel with her infant son and a fabricated story about a husband off in the Foreign Service. "One lie led to another," she told me.

It would be many years before her family learned the truth. Meanwhile, my father brought his "Ruthie" and her new baby to Dallas, setting them up in an unassuming three-bedroom house on Meadowlake Drive, a few minutes from his mansion. My sister June was born two years after Ray. Patrick was born with a faulty heart and lived only a few days. Mother was once again alone; she panicked when they didn't bring her baby for a feeding.

Helen was next, and I was born fifteen months later, when Dad was sixty-one. My life unfolded against a backdrop of political drama. The day of my birth, May Day 1950, a U.S. Navy patrol bomber was shot down near or over Latvia. "Lesser incidents than these, if anyone wanted war, could obviously provoke one," *Time* magazine noted. Secretary of State Dean Acheson said, "We must not forget that it is we, the American people, who have been picked out as the principal target of Soviet Communists." On the other side of the world, Chinese troops crossed the Manchurian border, launching the Korean War.

As the "communist menace" grew, Americans elected General Dwight Eisenhower president. The country was swinging toward conservatism and virtuous living. I try to imagine how my mom, a devout Christian, coped with "living in sin," the single mother of four children under the age of eight. She told me she found a large Methodist church and sat in a different part of the sanctuary each Sunday, hoping she wouldn't be recognized by members who might ask embarrassing questions. Meanwhile, I wondered why I didn't have a daddy like the children next door, one who would come home at the end of the day, toss me in the air, and carry me on his shoulders.

My mother, who had grown up fatherless, had inadvertently recreated that loss for her own children. During my preschool years, I have only faint memories of Dad's visits to our home on Thursday nights, when his wife, Lyda, was out with her bridge club. I recall him as rather soft-spoken, with a large frame and big, gnarled hands. The hours he was in our home we had to act differently. Mother wore fancy shoes. She dressed Helen and me in matching pastel party dresses and pinned small silk flowers in our hair. Those nights we had candlelight, duckling, and scalloped oysters. Dad must have been there one morning for breakfast, because I remember asking Mother, who was unusually excited, why we had to eat our bacon with a fork and knife.

Mom, I learned later, was completely dependent on my father. She had no outside income. He owned the house and supplied cash for groceries and clothes. And he paid the salary for Frances Betik (we called her "Franny"), a diminutive Czech woman brought in to help when Helen was born. Our family never ate out or traveled, except by car to Idabel or Franny's farm in central Texas. In short, during my first seven years, life was simple. Mother's life, on the other hand, was complicated. She did tell June, who was six years older than I, that "Partner," as she called him, was our daddy, making up a story about their marrying in the Little Church Around the Corner in New York City. But Mom's relationship with Dad was as secret from me as it was from Dad's wife and six children.

Mother never met Lyda Hunt but told me, "She must have been a great lady. After all, she was married to *him*." That esteem didn't stop

Mom from accompanying Dad on trips abroad, to New York, or else-where. "No one would notice us there," she told me.

Mother was excruciatingly sensitive to any hint of being judged by others. When our Meadowlake neighbors moved away, she supposed it was because of her. Her whole life with Dad, she was in awe of him. But their relationship came at a huge price; throughout her life she remained convinced, wrongly, that she was an embarrassment to her children.

As a young girl, I was completely unaware of my mother's anguish, in part because Franny was a stabilizing presence, and in part because Mother filled our home with joy. She taught us to sing and dance our way into the hearts of others. With her daughters gathered around the piano, she'd stretch her thin, red-manicured fingers over the keys, her foot holding the sustaining pedal down forgetfully through a series of chord changes across a dozen measures, until the tones blended in a melodic soup.

Meanwhile, in the dining room, preteen Ray practiced his trumpet as Lucky, our faithful black-and-white fox terrier, sat at his feet howl-ing. Helen, June, and I scurried by, our shoulders hunched and faces scrunched, covering our ears with our palms as Lucky let out with an-other "Oooooooooouw" in B♭.

We were a most artistic bunch—Lucky aside. June organized living-room productions, directing the neighbor children and her little sis-ters. For "The Cobbler's New Shoes," Helen and I were thrilled to pieces to be cast and costumed as elves. When dark fell suddenly upon the cobbler's workshop, we popped up excitedly from behind our audi-ence on the sofa. Fingers to lips and hammers in hand, we tiptoed out onto the beige rug that served as our stage. While the cobbler and his wife dreamed, we tap tap tapped and stitched through the night, turn-ing pieces of leather into the finest shoes in all the land.

We shared other magical moments as well. When Mother was away with Dad, Franny took us to her big Catholic church, by bus since she didn't drive. We walked with her into the cathedral and stood at the back, staring wide-eyed at the painted statues that seemed like so many giant dolls. "Now children, you can each light a candle." Turn-ing to one of us at a time, she guided our hands toward the slim white tapers, standing like stalagmites in the tray of sand. "Look. See how the smoke is going up into the air. It's on its way to heaven."

"You girls bow your heads and close your eyes and pray for someone you love. And if you really believe, God the Father will hear your prayers as long as the smoke is going up to Him." Compared to other stories Franny told us, like the one about a clever fox giving children rides on his wide bushy tail, this one seemed rather believable. But we would have believed her if she'd told us the clouds were raining lemon drops. In a willing suspension of disbelief, I passed on the secret of the candles to my children and never gave up the practice, or the hope.

Franny and Helen were my companions almost every waking hour. They were my constants. Rituals also created stability. Sunday nights meant stopping for Southern Maid doughnuts on the way home from church. With the sweet, tantalizing smell of chocolate and vanilla glaze filling our car, it took all the will power we could muster to stay out of the big white box the final ten minutes until we got home. After the last drop of milk was drunk and the last finger licked, Helen and I went upstairs and put on our matching flannel pajamas. Then, as Granny had in Idabel, Mother lined up Ray, June, Helen, and me in a row at her bedside. I pressed my folded hands against my forehead and leaned against the peach satiny covers of her bed, waiting my turn to mumble words of gratitude for the love of my family and Bambi, our tiny gray poodle. We ended in unison with "Our Father, which art in heaven, hallowed be Thy name . . ." With the final "Amen," Ray went off to his room. June crawled in with Mother. Helen and I slipped into our twin beds painted with pink roses, at the foot of which, we were sure, angels stood guard.

During my first five years, my father continued to live with Lyda in the home where their kids had grown into young adulthood. In the era of "Ozzie and Harriet" and "Leave It to Beaver," with cookie-cutter family constellations, ours was a bizarre exception. My mother lived with the fictitious last name of her fictitious husband, Ray Wright. (She said Dad chose the name because their relationship was *right*.) So I was Swanee Wright. Of course, my memories of that time are selective. I recall the bright blue wind-up plastic swimmer in my bathtub. I can see the miniature carousel with lights that glowed as it turned. But I can't remember exactly when I found out that the white-haired man who came to dinner on Thursdays was our father.

Dallas was a patchwork of billboards, asphalt, and traffic. But twenty minutes northwest of downtown, a country lane led into a retreat from the urban bustle. Mt. Vernon was a replica of George Washington's Virginia home, with the requisite white pillars and long green shutters. The estate was separated from the civic cacophony by its sheer size: ten acres, with bright St. Augustine grass carpeting a sloping front yard that spilled graciously into White Rock Lake. That scenic lake park offered something for everyone in the city: a tranquil view, for my folks rocking on the front porch; fishing, for black men with a picnic box at their sides; a course for multihued sailboats racing on Sundays; and a late-night destination for young lovers seeking a deliciously secluded spot to go necking.

In May 1955, after a season of cancer, Lyda Hunt died. Two years later, on my first day at Mt. Vernon, I got lost wandering through the house. I'd never been anyplace where the first and second floors were connected by three stairways plus an elevator. As I roamed, amazed, from one room to another, I came across Dad in the foyer. He stopped me and, with a satisfied chuckle, asked, "Now, which one are *you*?"

Mother's room was down the hall, next to Dad's. Franny's was right by mine. She brought me a rosary to hold on sleepless nights, teaching me to say Hail Marys for each bead, until repetition finally conquered fears of the darkness. I adopted other nightly rituals, gathering every baby doll, Teddy bear, or plastic horse and putting them on a bed in the guest room. The largest went between the sheets, with their heads on a plumped pillow and a blanket tucked snugly under their chins. The others I lay carefully in rows across the bed, covered with scarves and dishtowels I'd scrounged. "There you go, Dear. Now you'll be warm," I said, patting each one.

I was putting two and two together. The man who'd visited Meadowlake was my father, and his first wife had died. But I was still confused. One day, standing in my swimming suit in the small breakfast room, I asked the cook to tell me about Dad's divorce from Lyda. She answered casually, "Honey, they were never divorced." That moment is etched in my memory. Her voice, the cream wallpaper with petite flowers, the Dresden figurines. That's when I found out I was—a word I'd learn later—illegitimate.

One afternoon, about a year after we moved, I remember Mom and Dad getting ready to go out. Mother was dressed up. She seemed excited. Before they left the house, she asked someone to take a picture. (I don't remember who, but I have the photograph.) It was a normal day, and Helen and I did normal things, watching TV, playing paper dolls. When our parents returned, we learned they'd been married in a private ceremony. An oil industry associate was at my father's side, and my mother brought my first-grade teacher as a witness. I imagine each hoped to fill a need. For him, youthful companionship. For her, the fathering she'd missed and security for her children.

At school the next day, the teachers rewrote our names on the class list. Instead of Swanee Wright, I learned that I was Swanee Hunt. The teacher who'd been Mother's witness said she wanted to see me during recess. She took me into the school's tiny restroom and latched the door. "If the children say anything to you about your name, you hold your head up," she leaned over and whispered. "You've nothing to be ashamed of."

I don't remember if anyone did say anything. Frankly, almost any slight or jab would have seemed anticlimactic, after the hush of Mrs. Willard's voice, and the intensity of her look. Thinking back, it's remarkable that Mom asked my teacher to be the witness. Frances Willard was not a close friend. But I imagine that having her standing there was Mom's way of bringing us children into the moment that would change our lives forever.

Over the years, Dad's children by Lyda had discovered that their father was in a relationship with my mother. Each has his or her own story about finding out, just as I do. Lamar, the youngest, was only eighteen when I was born. Were the tables turned, I don't know if I could be as gracious as he and his siblings were to me. Herbert, twenty-one years older than I, taught Helen and me to swim along with his children in the long, rectangular pool at Mt. Vernon. Caroline delighted us with ornate jewelry boxes from a trip to Europe. Sadly, Dad's first daughter, Margaret, found opportunities to slight Mom. But I really couldn't blame her. She was a year older than her new step-mother. At least she didn't know that two unwanted half-sisters, Helen and I, clandestinely played dress-up with her deceased mother's costume jewelry, left behind in a dresser.

Stepping back, I can only imagine how raw it must have been for them to see the five of us suddenly in their home, or, for that matter, how scared Mother must have been the first time Dad's older children came over for an afternoon. For me, the situation was more odd than painful. When Dad's family gathered for his birthday, Helen and I sat in the foyer at the children's tables, with our newly discovered half-nieces and -nephews. They were our age, and after lunch we all went outside to pitch a football and play badminton. We were seemingly a relaxed, all-American family.

At that time, Mt. Vernon had no gate to keep out the curious. Each afternoon a city tour bus pulled over at the base of our lawn, and tourists piled out to take pictures of the mansion of H. L. Hunt. Sometimes Helen and I were outside playing. "Hello! Hello there!" we'd call out with a wide wave to the sightseers in the distance. I imagine we offered a rush of interest to the visitors—two stupendously rich girls running pell-mell across the yard barefoot, in matching shorts and tops.

Although our new home looked grand, the interior wasn't opulent. The twenty-plus rooms had white walls, Venetian blinds but no drapes, and worn oriental rugs on hardwood floors. More important, that physical austerity was matched with emotional severity. The contrast between the carefree life that the outside world imagined and our life as I experienced it was striking. I'm sure Dad wasn't intentionally distant. In fact, he was proud to show us off to his attorney, whom he summoned to Mt. Vernon one Sunday afternoon. As always, my father was in a suit; I don't believe he even owned a sports shirt. On that day his young companion, Ruthie, stood beaming by his side; the snug waist of her cotton sundress made the most of her hourglass figure. "Now you cause the children to come here to the porch," he said.

Once we were gathered, he instructed us to sing, starting with the eldest. "Yes, Sir," Ray said, pushing past his teenaged embarrassment to accommodate our father. In a callow baritone he belted out the theme song from the new movie *Giant*, about our beloved Texas. "Just like a sleepin' giant sprawlin' in the sun . . ." Our parents and guest applauded eagerly.

Then it was June's turn. She planted her feet solidly, clasped her hands in front of her, and took a deep breath. "When you walk through a storm, hold your head up high," my sister crooned, "and don't be afraid of the dark . . ." Dad smiled approvingly at her rich contralto voice, lifting both his eyebrows with delight at his attorney. "She don't need voice lessons," he said with pride. "She's plum good enough. *Professional* quality."

"Now you, little girls," he looked toward Helen and me. "Come here and sing your songs." Helen stepped forward obediently. But I said "No!" and stuck out my lower lip. After two or three attempts, Dad gave up.

"I was mighty proud of you," the attorney told me four decades later. That story struck me as nearly unbelievable when I heard it, as I gathered material for this memoir. Acts of defiance were almost unheard of in our new home. The price was far too high.

Dad was intent on never being alone. He wanted his new wife to be at his side every minute he was home. As a result, Franny became all the more important to me as Mother reluctantly abandoned bedside prayers and goodnight stories. The best Mom could do was excuse herself to go to the restroom and then rush past our four bedrooms with a quick "I love you" before hurrying back downstairs. She slowed her step as she walked back into the library, to resume her place on the sofa beside his large armchair, to wait for his commands. "Get me a pencil!" he'd bark, and she'd spring up. Surely there must have been tender moments, but I never saw them kiss.

Rather than gain security from the move and marriage, my mother found herself in a gilded cage. She liked to sing, "You've got to ac-cen-tuate the positive / E-li-minate the negative . . . Don't mess with Mr. In-Between." But Mother's life was lived in-between. Between a husband with a wandering eye and children who needed her. Between her rigid upbringing and the compromises of our messy family situation. Between idealized memories of rural simplicity and a compelling desire for precious acquisitions. Between her sunny disposition and the spells of sadness that kept her confined to her room for days at a time.

My recollections of those confusing years, the early sixties, are filtered through a child's understanding. No doubt many of our happy moments have been overshadowed in my memory by the stressful times. I could never forget the anguished episodes—Mom shouting the name of one of Dad's girlfriends as she threw her clothes into a suitcase. But she never left, at least never for long.

Ray seems to have a whole different set of memories of Dad, and he speaks about our father with only the highest accolades. But we three sisters developed a deep resentment of the man who'd taken our mother from us. Our unhappiness only added to Mother's burden. "You should feel sorry for him," she urged, with a worried look. "He just doesn't know how to show love."

But we hated how he treated her. One evening, when Dad was involved with a woman named Ginger (I wasn't privy to the details), instead of the usual stewed fruit for dessert the cook brought in a platter of brown squares of cake. We never, ever had cake, except at birthdays.

"What's this?" Mother asked the cook, in a quiet voice.

"Mr. Hunt asked for *ginger*bread."

Mom looked startled, then rushed from the table in tears. Dad continued eating. I sat there, miserable, not knowing where to go or what to say.

In turn, I wonder how lonely Dad must have been. Although we lived in the same house for ten years, Helen and I had little meaningful interaction with him. Sometimes when I heard his slow, heavy step, I'd duck behind a door, holding my breath until he walked by. Mostly, I bounced through my days or had an occasional tantrum, wearing my feelings on my sleeve. Helen, on the other hand, suffered in silence.

One evening, when we were eleven and twelve, Dad came down the hallway, past the stairway, toward Helen's room. He knocked at the door. When he saw Helen, a half-smile crossed my father's face. It was an unfamiliar look, an uncomfortable, unpracticed look. Helen stood there shyly, not knowing what to do.

"You're the only one who likes me," he said, holding out his hand. There was something in it. Engraved in gold with "HLH" (Helen's initials too), it was a brown leather wallet—a man's wallet. Dad was unschooled at generosity or affection; that's the only personal gift I recall him giving to any of us. But even though it was a strikingly ungirlish present, it was probably more from the heart than a pink music box with a twirling ballerina could have been.

As far as I knew, my father had only two close friends. One was H. L. Williford, an adorable old southern gentleman who faithfully brought us girls dainty Neiman Marcus handkerchief dolls. He was a sweetheart of a fellow. "He's squandered several fortunes," Dad would chortle, saying how his friend tipped a maitre d' $100.

His other friend was Ray Ryan, a wheeler-dealer and gambler, from whom my mother had borrowed the name "Partner." Summer nights, I lay on my bed with the window open, while "Uncle Ray," rocking on the porch with Dad, whistled lyrical melodies that floated up through the magnolia and live oak trees in our front lawn. He brought us elephant tail bracelets from his Mt. Kenya Safari Club. I didn't ask what took him to Africa.

Dad had given up gambling. He said he couldn't find enough tough stud poker competition at his level, and winning all the time "was too much like cheating." But Uncle Ray, it turns out, had gotten himself into a mess. I'm not sure anyone knows the exact whys and wherefores, but soon after his visit (I learned later, through U.S. Supreme Court records), the Chicago crime syndicate demanded $60,000. When he refused, they followed him to Las Vegas and beat him up. After he testified against the Mob, he was a marked man. Kenya, it seems, was his hideout. I'm glad Dad wasn't still alive when Uncle Ray, upon his return to Illinois, was killed by a dynamite bomb when he started his car.

For the most part, Mom was great company for Dad too. Nicknamed "Bubbles" in high school, she was witty, clever, and quick. If her expressions of affection were sometimes sappy, her sense of humor could be deliciously dry: When an elderly friend departed on a transatlantic cruise, instead of sending the predictable bouquet, Mother had a push lawnmower delivered to her tiny stateroom.

Just as she'd been a school cheerleader in Idabel, she was the cheerleader in our family, looking for the silver lining in the clouds that frequently darkened our lives. One year, the night before Easter, teenaged June chemically straightened Mother's hair. Problem was, Mom's hair had recently been frosted and then dyed dark again before she even left the salon, because she was afraid that Dad wouldn't approve.

June's chemicals were too much. Every strand broke off an inch from Mom's scalp.

The next morning, when believers gathered at Mt. Vernon for a sunrise worship service, Mrs. H. L. Hunt emerged in the predawn dark, wearing an elegant suit and an oversized floral hat worthy of Irving Berlin's "Easter Parade." The enormous hat stayed on throughout the religious service and all morning long. Concocting an instant tradition, she sat down to midday dinner, still hatted. In a slow southern drawl, she spun out for any and all to hear: "Ah jus' *love* Eastuh Sunday, 'cause ah can wear mah hat all . . . day . . . *long*."

The next day a thick wig arrived, concealed in an imposing hatbox. Mom dubbed the contents "Matilda." "You can't tell it's a wig, can you?" she asked us kids worriedly.

"No, Mom, really. Not at all," we assured her, with an artless air. But for months we hummed "Waltzing Matilda" whenever she, and her hairpiece, strolled into the room.

We children introduced fresh life into the mansion. A ping-pong table appeared on the sun porch, a swing set and refrigerated Coke chest near the pool, basketball hoop above the three-car garage, tether ball, croquet, and bikes. Mom sprinkled psychological comfort throughout the house with sayings embroidered on pillows: "When friends meet, hearts warm," "Sit long, talk much," and, perhaps in tribute to her father, "If you can't sing good, sing loud." Yet another ode to zeal.

In my early teens, Mom let me pick out wall-to-wall carpet and blue flocked wallpaper for my bedroom. I was overjoyed to have a space that was really, really mine. Throughout the house, with Dad usually not noticing, Mom added silk drapes, fountains with Grecian figures, and antique sofas. Such refined taste, in a rural Oklahoma girl, testified to the power of romance.

Ever Mom's best friend, June found a beautiful copy of Raphael's *Madonna of the Chair*, as well as a large romantic canvas, *The Proposal*—themes understandably dear to Mother's heart. Mom declared herself "tickled pink," but Dad was gruffly opposed. In the weeks that followed, Mom prevailed on various people whom her husband admired to come over and ooh and ah their approval. "These paintings are a true credit to Mt. Vernon," one of them declared. Dad never agreed, but he stopped disagreeing. The paintings stayed on the walls.

In contrast to Dad, Mother was consistently and spontaneously generous. Guests to Mt. Vernon rarely left empty-handed. There were storybooks for the children, *Ideals* magazines for the grownups. When my girlfriends came to spend the night, they found a gift-wrapped porcelain box or an inspirational booklet inscribed by her on their pillow.

But Mom's baroque decorating and charming gifts could only wrap a bow around the difficulty of life with Dad. She told me later that she felt guilty for putting her children in the path of his irritability. Few parents in those times communicated frankly with their kids, and professional counseling was highly stigmatized and rare. So for the most part we were left to find our way in our dramatically new family structure without even an explanation from Mother. Perhaps she compensated by overlooking bedtimes, curfews, homework, and other typical parental boundaries. Or maybe she was just preoccupied with trying to survive. At any rate, Mom gave us bountiful infusions of love when our paths crossed, but for the most part we were pretty much left to raise ourselves.

When I was thirteen I worked several summer weeks at Hunt Oil Company. The women at the office, all secretaries, took charge of me, teaching me to type. They gave me a seat and a headset so I could maneuver the plugs and toggles when the old-fashioned switchboard lit up. That office work experience gave me a wonderful sense of achievement.

Those mornings I rode with my father to work, just the two of us in his car. As he drove, we listened to the radio, or he talked about the communists. One day, I summoned my courage to confront Dad. The minutes slipped by as we drove away from downtown. Finally, as we were rounding a bend in the lake near our home, I screwed up my fortitude and blurted out, "I have a question. Why do you go out with other women?" Much as I tried to sound strong, I'm sure my voice was shaking. Dad's large hands gripped the wheel, and he stared straight ahead, into the harsh sun reflecting up from the road. "You're married to my mother. That's not right. You shouldn't do that," I added, pedantically.

I waited tensely for an explosion, but he just looked over at me and arched his eyebrows. Then he said, in a gruff voice, "Well, now, you don't know what you're talking about. King Solomon had seven hundred wives. And that's in the *Bible*." That was the only time I ever heard

Dad reference the Bible. We pulled up to the house. I got out of the car and stomped in. Dad followed. He was really cross. But he didn't take it out on me. He took it out on Mother.

I've never understood the need that drove my father to keep siring children beyond his first family. He had ten children before he met my mother. Why did he need more? Creating progeny may have given him pleasure, but it seemed cruel. When I pushed Mom for an explanation, she had little to say except that she had prayed constantly about her relationship with Dad, because she didn't want to hurt anyone. I guess her guilty feelings were so overpowering that she couldn't hear how insufficient her response was. But as for what she said, I believed her.

Maybe we weren't sure how to be real with each other, but we sure knew stage cues. Even as Dad had read stock quotes for guests as a young child, seven decades later he wanted us to perform so that the world could applaud his talented offspring. At Mt. Vernon, our formerly carefree musical productions became command performances. Helen and I developed a sweet song-and-dance show with a dozen selections, replete with elaborate costumes and complex choreography. "Alice Blue Gown," "Que Sera, Sera," "Play Gypsies" . . . We could go on for hours.

And we did, night after night, for a constant stream of high-level guests like General A. C. Wedemeyer, Attorney General Ramsey Clark, the teen crooner Pat Boone, and the opera diva Lily Pons. Whoever was meeting with Dad at the office that day was a likely audience member, with Dad as impresario and director. From his chair, he waved his arms stiffly back and forth, calling out "Use both hands!" as he tried to inspire us to give our animated best.

Unhappily, Helen and I were also issued corny anticommunist lyrics to half a dozen popular tunes. Even the venerable "Take Me Out to the Ballgame" was transformed: "Let's go out to the people / Let's go out to the crowd / Tell them our country is on the rocks / I don't care if they get a big shock / for it's root, root, root for our freedom / If we don't work it's a shame / If the Reds take over we're out of the / old ballgame!"

We sang at any and every occasion Dad could arrange, including the intermission of the Dallas Opera, where we paled, I fear, in comparison. But we also performed at promotional events for Dad's books, which he published himself. "How much is that *book* in the window . . ." (displacing one disappointed doggy).

One day, as a surprise, we added to our robust repertoire, from *South Pacific*, "I'm in love, I'm in love, I'm in love, I'm in love . . . I'm in *love* with a *won*derful *guy*." Ending the song, cheek to cheek we cupped our outer hands around our mouths, and tacked on, *sotto voce*, "Mainly Popsy"! Dad's pleasure knew no bounds. "Call me 'Popsy' from now on," he ordered. We refused. His emotional clumsiness had spoiled our gift. Mom, as she did so often, stepped in to save the situation. He became "Popsy" to her. In a way, the shift fit reality. Perhaps she'd found a father. We most certainly had not.

We coped with the family strain as kids often do—with play. Mom had the habit of slipping off her fashionable spiked heels under the dinner table. One evening, Helen ducked down, ostensibly for a fallen napkin, stole her shoes, and wrapped them in her napkin. After we'd dutifully provided Dad's guests with tableside songs, my sister and I excused ourselves with a curtsy and left the room, our bounty behind our backs. A few minutes later, Mom was about to suggest that, as always, the dinner ensemble "retire to the library." She felt around with her feet. Just flat carpet. Flat, and more flat. Extending the conversation, her toes tap-danced across every square inch under her end of the table. Eventually she had no choice but to bend down and look under the table. Still no shoes.

Baffled, Mom pressed the hidden buzzer beneath the table edge and asked a maid to retrieve another pair, then figure out some way to bring them to her. The maid went upstairs, selected more shoes, and slipped them to Mom wrapped in a linen napkin. When Mom and Dad walked into the paneled library with their guests, her high heels were dangling from the chandelier.

No one today can remember who the fancy visitors were. But we all remember how Mother laughed every time she told and retold the story. As far as I know, Dad never knew that anything had happened.

Some of our surprises weren't nearly so pleasant, like when I remarked to June how much our visiting cousin Hugh looked like our eldest half-brother. "Don't you know?" she asked. Hugh wasn't a cousin at all, but yet another half-brother by yet another mother. He was one of my father's four children by Frania Tye Lee. Those births were interspersed with those of Dad's six children by Lyda.

Plenty of books and articles have speculated on the scintillating details of "the three families of H. L. Hunt." Most I've left unread. Their research wouldn't explain the pain blighting a family tree that resembled a weeping willow.

When I look back on Mt. Vernon, I see a life both privileged and bizarre. In our kitchen was a key holder with a saying, "Our home is just a little house, but God knows where it is." "Just a little house" had a basement with three freezers and a walk-in cool room filled with food. But as I turned on any of a number of TVs, I saw "colored people" protesting for the right to eat in restaurants with white people, and children in Biafra with hunger-bloated stomachs. I longed for a happier family life, but even in my sadness, I understood that I was a "have" in a world with painfully many "have-nots."

I felt guilt more than gratitude and resonated with a more socialist truth rooted in the New Testament writing of Luke: "For unto whom much is given, of him much is required." But like so many wealthy children, my sense of privilege included an assumption that I was entitled to succeed. "Entitlement" is usually a pejorative word, attached to people who think they deserve more than their share. But my sense of entitlement convinced me that I could, and therefore should, wrestle the world's problems. Consciously or unconsciously, I was inspired and burdened every morning that I woke up in a four-poster bed in the replica of the home of an American hero.

As Much as Salt

As a young child, my strongest emotional tie wasn't so much with Mother as Franny. I remember Mom as often not around. But Franny was. "I love you as much as salt," she said every night, alluding to the theme in our favorite story. It was the tale of a spunky princess who tells her father she loves him like salt, instead of the gold, silver, and jewels that her sisters name. The king is insulted, and she's banished—until salt disappears from the realm and its true value is clear. She returns to the arms of her repentant father, who realizes that value may not be where it seems. I especially loved imagining the final scene, the delicate daughter with her head buried in her father's barrel chest.

Franny, who never married, lit up when strangers asked about Helen and me: "Are those your little girls?" She was never our "governess" or "nanny." She was family. I couldn't imagine what she had to tell the priest at confession, except the time she asked for forgiveness because I had said, with a child's candor, that I loved her more than my mother.

When Mom was traveling with Dad, we three girls often spent weeks at the farm of Franny's family. She gave us our own giant, beige burlap sacks to lug through the cotton fields, till it was time to weigh our "pickins." Back in the farmhouse kitchen, Franny taught us how to grind poppy seeds to make a sweet filling for pastries. She took us to the old barn, where we collected eggs and milked cows, braving turkeys as big as we were. We used both hands to cradle mugs of coffee, with hot milk and sugar. And we drank our warm brew sitting on board benches against the kitchen wall after a magical evening of folk dances in the basement of the small-town Catholic church. The conversation moved in and out of Czech and English, but laughter was a language of its own. When the thick Slavic accents made our heads nod, we took one last trip before bed. Out the creaky screen door, along the wooden walk past the water well, through the farmyard, to the outhouse. Then back inside, where Franny brought colorful patchwork quilts down from the attic. Tucked in under layers of covers, we'd fall fast asleep.

Franny's farm was a respite but not a shelter from an unhappy home. The summer I was ten, Dad sent June, Helen, and me away to camp in Colorado. "You're a bad influence on your mother," he accused. Helen was miserable, missing home. I was in heaven, grooming the horses in the stables and drinking in the smell of pine needles on the rocky trails. One day at mail call June received a letter from Dad. The names of each person on staff at Mt. Vernon were listed. June was asked to rate each, 1 to 10. She gave Franny a shining 10.

Soon after we returned, as I was going outside to play, I noticed Franny walking out the back door of the house. Her curly thin hair was, as always, pinned back on each side with a single bobby pin. But she was wearing street clothes instead of her white uniform, and carrying a brown leather suitcase. Her step was hurried, as if she were trying to leave without being seen. "Where are you going?" I called out, alarmed.

She turned reluctantly, and her face softened as she said, "Swanee, I'm going away for awhile." Then she hugged me, hard. Franny was crying. I'd never seen her cry.

I ran upstairs to Mother's room. "Franny's going on vacation," Mother said, through tears. I wandered out of her room and down the long staircase. There was no one to ask what was really going on. Weeks went by, but Franny never walked back in the door. Her small room next to mine was empty.

June finally told me that during a quarrel with Mother, Dad accused Franny of taking sides against him. A more likely scenario is that my father, in angry suspicion, demanded that Mother fire the person who'd been at her side for a decade. The person she was devoted to. The person I loved more than salt. That was the greatest loss of my life. I don't know that I ever fully recovered.

I once believed I had the saddest life any kid could have. It was an ignorant thought. As we age, our lives include joy beyond what we as children could envisage, and pain beyond what we thought we could endure. I didn't know about the terror and hardship of other children in the world. But I remember lying across that four-poster bed, sobbing, not because of any one disappointment, but just because of all the pain in the air. My greatest consolation, especially after Franny was gone, was our black maids.

Celestine was my favorite. She was young, tall and willowy, with honey-colored skin. Her hair was pulled back under a crisp white cap, which matched her apron. I followed her like a puppy dog as she moved through the house in her pale pink uniform, pulling the Hoover (I much later learned the words "vacuum cleaner"), or making slow circles on the furniture with her dust rag. "On a hill, far away, stood an old rugged cross, the emblem of suffering and shame," her voice floated through the air, in a high, sweet soprano. I trailed behind, in one hand a yellow aerosol bottle of furniture polish, in the other my own soft cloth.

"And I love that old cross, where the dearest and best, for a world of lost sinners, was slain." At "sinners," Celestine's voice, already miraculously high, lifted another six notes over every care in the world—hers or mine. I felt a glow inside whenever we were together, though no one else in our family seemed to have the same attachment as I did. So Mother was surprised that I was so distressed when she quit. I have no idea what the problem was, but to Mom's credit, she put aside whatever unhappy feelings she had, got into her car alone one night, and drove into the Dallas slums to urge Celestine to come back. My companion returned, although for only a short while. Then she was gone for good.

Three plus One

Growing up at Mt. Vernon, I also had Ray, June, and Helen. Mother described her toddler Ray as a fair-haired "little judge," with a cheery disposition and keen mind. Preteen, Ray was already man of the house. "Mom, sometimes I just get girl-sick," he told her, understandably, given his role watching over his mother and sisters. In the absence of an engaged father, Ray made a few inept attempts to discipline me, which created a dynamic that was hard to shake in later years; but I was ready to burst with pride listening to my brother sing solos in the church choir or play his sax at the high school concert.

My brother must have felt an enormous responsibility as he tried to hold the family together. I never saw him lose his temper with Dad. In fact, the challenges of our home life seemed to blend in an alloy with Ray's intelligence, talents, and energy. My brother grew into a young man of enormous capability, whether in football, photography, student governance, debate, or gourmet cooking. His leadership was so dominant that when he graduated from St. Mark's prep school, a rule was established limiting the number of presidencies that one student could hold.

Ray spent summers in the oil fields as a roustabout, experiencing firsthand the labor of rough-and-ready workers who years later would refer to him as "Mr. Hunt." True to our father's form, he called that experience more valuable than any master's degree in business might have been.

I was eleven when Ray went off to Southern Methodist University. He'd wanted to go to Stanford, but Dad said all colleges were controlled by the communists; at least at SMU, midway between Mt. Vernon and the Hunt Oil office, we kids would be close enough for him to keep an eye on us. One consolation was that in his freshman Western Civ class, Hunt was seated next to Nancy Ann Hunter—a beautiful young woman from Kansas City. On their first date, Ray told Nancy Ann his father was in the food business. It wasn't a lie; Dad had bought a processing plant to sponsor his anticommunist activity. But she assumed he was a grocer. Soon her new boyfriend brought her home to Mt. Vernon. No grocer's house, this. Excited that Ray had a girl, I came running down the stairs in my slip to meet her. Embarrassed, he snapped at me to go put on some clothes.

June was one year behind Ray in school. As a young girl with long, blond braids and a scrappy personality, she seemed more natural in jeans than a dress. Dad said that any female who would wear pants was mentally ill, but she was Mother's ally, having shared her bedroom, her hopes, and her hurts in the close quarters on Meadowlake. When we moved to Mt. Vernon, as difficult as life with Dad was for the other three of us kids, it was most difficult for my twelve-year-old sister. Tensions at home exacted their toll on her at school, but June took great interest in Helen and me. She had us stand with our toes lined up at the free-throw line as she coached us in shooting baskets. And she was my mentor in music, teaching me to play guitar and sing harmony, with a hymnal or by ear.

She also turned on the record player and taught Helen and me to jitterbug to Elvis's "Blue Suede Shoes." Taking both my hands, she patiently moved me through the motions, chanting, "Side . . . , Side . . . , Back . . . , Front. Side . . . , Side . . . , Back . . . , Front. Now *sliiiiiiiide*!" We cranked up the volume and then yanked and swayed, twirled and twisted, with eyes wide and ear-to-ear grins.

My sister was a performer through and through, and even Dad was impressed with June on stage. One of my few positive memories of their relationship is his declaring the high school rendition of *Brigadoon* on a par with Broadway. I remember him recounting repeatedly to whoever our dinner guests were on a given evening how "Junie" bounded up the stairs in the chase scene.

While Ray carried my Mother's maiden name, June was named after my father, who was Haroldson Lafayette Hunt Jr. but was called simply "June" or "Junie" by his Illinois family. As much as she might wince at the thought, my sister was much like the parent for whom she was named. Her thinking was single-focused and brooked no compromise. For June, right was right. That was all there was to it.

June badly wanted to go to Baylor University, but Dad wouldn't allow it. At SMU she studied music, eventually becoming a pleasing singer and adept guitarist, talents she used in her Christian ministry.

She was devoted and tireless, dedicating her life to "God's truth for today's problems," as she later put it.

My most intimate sibling relationship was with Helen. Our lives were intertwined from the beginning, as we slept in our crib with arms and legs draped limply over each other's. To our elders, we were "the babies," who grew, only much belatedly, into "the girls."

As toddlers, we parroted the nomenclature. "Come in here, Baby," I'd call.

"I'm coming, Baby," she'd chirp back.

Since we were dressed alike, people on the street often stopped to ask if we were twins. But the likeness ended with dresses. Helen was brunette and curly-haired, with careful demeanor. I was barrel-chested, with a boxy "Buster Brown" hairstyle and personality to match. Mother said she never worried about me, such an extrovert that I bounced into a room without a care in the world. But her heart went out to Helen, who entered tentatively behind.

My advantage reversed during teenage years, when Helen evolved into a slender beauty, and her occasional shyness became an allure to young men. We wandered the adolescent identity labyrinth on divergent paths. I felt chagrined as the phone rang off the hook, with boys lining up dates with my sister.

"Hunts' residence," I answered the phone cheerfully, only to discover yet another Romeo. Once or twice I covered my jealousy by clowning. If he was unaware that Helen had a sister with exactly the same voice, I continued, "This is Helen. . . . Oh, I'd *love* to go. . . . Sure. . . . But tell me the truth, why are you asking me out? What about me made you call?"

Somehow, Helen found it in her heart to forgive my vicarious enjoyment of her beaus' proclamations of devotion, and my perverse laughter at their subsequent embarrassment.

Our home included one other sibling. My father's eldest son, Haroldson Lafayette Hunt III, was called Hassie. The same age as my mother, he was Dad's look-alike, with fair hair and skin, blue eyes, and a tall, sturdy frame. As an adolescent, Hassie was brilliant but difficult. As a result, he was sent to Culver Military Academy, but even that rigor couldn't prevent his psychotic break. In his early twenties he was diagnosed paranoid schizophrenic. After years in physical restraints, with countless insulin and shock treatments, my father's firstborn son and heir apparent was lobotomized.

The state-of-the-art frontal lobe surgery to quell aggression was performed on eighteen thousand Americans during the 1940s, since psychotropic drugs that would transform the care of psychotic patients weren't discovered until a few years later. The procedure left Hassie less violent, but he still clenched his fists and snarled as he muttered angrily to himself about "vicious killers" lurking around him.

Soon after we moved to Mt. Vernon, Dad took us, his new instant family, to visit Hassie in a private hospital in upstate New York. Mother's heart broke when we met him at that institution, despite the red brick buildings and manicured lawns. She urged Dad to "bring Hassie home." And so Hassie moved in, along with a male nurse strong enough to handle his outbursts. We were already reeling from the loss of time with Mother and the presence of an ill-tempered father. Now we needed to adjust to life with a psychotic brother.

Hassie was tormented by internal demons that he often projected onto his surroundings—although, given the shock treatments, his fear that our oriental carpets were wired made some sense. At dinner, we took our places at the long, graciously carved table in a room with walls covered in painted scenes from American history. For the next quarter of an hour, we'd hear the hallway floorboards creak with an occasional step. Then Hassie's hefty form would appear in the arched dining-room entry. There he'd hesitate, his eyes moving from side to side as he looked at us silently. "Hello, Hassie," one of us would say. "Dinner's ready. Come on in."

His thin lips would curl in a grimace of acknowledgment that doubled for a smile. Abruptly, he'd extend his leg in an awkward motion, with his toe pointed as he stretched across a dangerous piece of rug, his arms out for balance. A lunge forward. He was unharmed. He'd steady and straighten himself. After a few more strategic but clumsy movements, he'd set himself down safely in his chair on Dad's right, across from Helen and me. There he'd stare at his place setting, occasionally mumbling under his breath.

Hassie seemed to have an uncanny ability to read our thoughts. When he was "feeling well," he played a mind game with us, inquiring politely if the time at that very moment might be precisely a certain minute after a certain hour. He was almost invariably right, although he never looked at his watch. Other times, he seemed to reach into my thoughts, asking timidly, for example, if my new sixth-grade teacher (whom I'd never mentioned but was thinking about) was Egyptian or German. I explained that she was Jewish but had left Germany and lived in Egypt before coming to the United States.

Someday someone explaining that phenomenon will win the Nobel Prize for physics. I've experienced with a few close people such an intensified intuition, as if ideas are moving from one of us to the other, mind to mind. That discovery will explain the evening I turned Hassie's extrasensory perception against him. I sat at the table, silently saying hateful words, until he abruptly pushed his chair back and stood, his fists clenched in anger, muttering epithets as his stare bored through me. Though the table was between us, I backed off my thoughts.

Hassie loomed large in our family, as the tragedy always in our midst that no financial fortune could fix. Our father dictated memos instructing his son not to urinate in the shrubs and addressing other points of etiquette. Always seeking a cure, Dad enlisted Jeanne Dixon, a popular futurist, but even that star of the *National Enquirer* couldn't help. My father was left with only his own occasional assertions to acquaintances that "Hassie is well now," as if saying so could make it true. But visitors discovered otherwise when Hassie didn't respond to an offered handshake, keeping his arm firmly at his side as he mouthed whispered warnings to the intruder.

With no professional help to interpret his illness, Mother and we four kids just tried to treat him like one of the family. But who could deny that he was different? In more than a decade of living under the same roof, I don't remember ever touching my half-brother, although Mother later described her astonished appreciation as one day she found me kneeling at his feet, tying his shoelaces.

Who was this imposing figure, appearing occasionally like a third parent in our annual Christmas card family portrait? Hassie was an embarrassment to be explained to my girlfriends who came to spend the night. Hassie was the strong, angry man standing around the corner, whom I feared. Hassie was a hounded refugee from pernicious, evil delusions I couldn't imagine, even in my worst nightmares. Hassie was a predictor of genetic predisposition to mental illness that I might carry. Hassie was my brother, whom I cared for, but with precious few moments of believing that care could be returned.

The Mistaken Enemies of Freedom

Outside the family sphere, Dad had been wildly successful, building Hunt Oil Company into the nation's largest privately owned independent oil and gas producer. But he also reigned over the near-demise of that business empire when he diverted his attention, throwing himself into championing what he called "the Republic USA."

Dallas was conservative, but Dad's political views were on the right edge, almost falling off the continuum. Appalled at the power that President Franklin Roosevelt amassed and at his election to a tradition-breaking third term in 1940, my father avidly campaigned for the Twenty-second Amendment to the Constitution, limiting presidents to two terms. The amendment was ratified in '51, a success that must have encouraged Dad in his political pursuits.

Subsequently he produced a radio program, "Facts Forum." The format was political debate, although guests matching Dad's views always seemed to prevail. Eleanor Roosevelt, U.S. ambassador to the United Nations, took him to task for his strong criticism of that new body. I found the correspondence between them in archives, with his letter responding that she must have been ill-informed, since his program always presented two sides to any issue.

In 1960, Dad was greatly disappointed when an oil concession he'd been negotiating for six months in Kuwait went to the Japanese (with a bribe, he believed). From that point his interest in oil and gas dried up. But for my father, the Cold War was hot. The strength of the company steadily declined as he devoted his concentration to saving our nation rather than replacing depleted oil reserves.

After "Facts Forum," Dad developed "Life Line," which aired on hundreds of radio stations across the South. He put a large radio on the dining room table. At 6:00 we were all in our seats, listening in silence. After the first fifteen-minute commentary, Dad turned the dial until he found a second "Life Line" program, with a different script, on another station. Conversation about a school test or softball game was preempted by warnings of the Red infestation of the State Department. Even discussion about the broadcast was hazardous. When I picked up on a name from the program and asked who Alger Hiss was, Dad was outraged. My ignorance about the spy proved I was being duped by pinko sympathizers at school.

One evening at dinner, Dad passed around a letter he'd received addressed simply to "H. L. Hunt, USA." He smiled, proud of his nationwide reputation. Still, his patriotic crusade was lonely. Though many Americans were fueling the anticommunist movement, he considered few his peers. Besides, he insisted, rather than being "anti-" anything, he was "*pro*-freedom." "There's not a conservative bone in my body," I heard him tell reporters. A conservative would still have been back in Illinois, pushing a plow. Instead, he was a "constructive." No one, he argued, could be too constructive.

To promote his political philosophy, Dad became a writer, with a daily newspaper column and a string of books. *Alpaca* was his utopian novel describing a government with voting privileges in proportion to wealth. My father expressed no awareness of social injustice. He figured that anyone could accomplish what he'd accomplished financially, since everyone in our great country was free. It didn't dawn on him that just by being white and male, he had started life privileged.

A more predictable person might have pursued his aims through a political party, but my maverick father eschewed affiliations. He attended both political party conventions in each election year. In 1952 he warned, "With Ike, we'll have more of the same." Mother glowed as she recounted how my father lifted the flag from its pedestal on the stage and led an impromptu march on the floor of the Republican Convention, promoting the nomination of General Douglas MacArthur. A dozen years later, he floated the idea of promoting the evangelist Billy Graham for president. Graham dismissed the prospect, but Dad received supportive correspondence from across the country.

As a teenager, I was thrilled to go along with Mom, Dad, and Ray to the 1964 Republican Convention at the Cow Palace in San Francisco. I was a sign-carrying Goldwater Girl, but I was also along to do Dad's bidding; he sent me out to slip propaganda under delegates' hotel room doors early each morning. But Dad was more than a financier or dogmatic idealist. I wasn't attuned to his personal charm, but I didn't miss Mother's sharp reaction when Ike's ambassador to Italy,

Clare Boothe Luce, cooed to my father on an elevator, "Hello, Baby Blue Eyes."

Mother seemed to enjoy being at Dad's side on those occasions. Though less fervent, she was in general agreement with his political views. Like my father, she was a product of her rural roots. When she walked through a room and found me watching a speech by Martin Luther King Jr., she switched off the TV with a terse, "You're *not* going to watch *that*."

My father was convinced that King was a communist agitator, bent on destroying our country by breaking down law and order. In later years, I found in his files a picture of the civil rights leader at "a training school for communists" and a memo from 1966 alleging that J. Edgar Hoover's FBI had pictures of King involved in sexual exploits while in Sweden to receive the Nobel Peace Prize. I don't how or why my father had those files.

Prejudice is an attitude more than a taxonomy. Helen and I were prohibited from playing with the only other child in walking distance of Mt. Vernon. It was irrelevant that her father was a neurosurgeon and her mother had a social work degree from Columbia, that they welcomed us girls to their home, that they showed multiple kindnesses to my mother. They were Jews. And as part of Dad's sanction against aiding and abetting communists, our family was prohibited from shopping at Neiman Marcus, because Jews owned the store. Even Dad's devotion to free market economics took second place to his firebrand politics.

I was only ten when Dad drafted me into his crusade to "save the Republic USA from the mistaken enemies of freedom." For several years we appeared in tandem to support his causes. In the early 1960s Dad established Youth Freedom Speakers, a corps of cheery, clean-cut young people sent out to propagate warnings against the communists. I was the prototype, booked on Art Linkletter's TV show, on stage at Knott's Berry Farm near Disneyland, or anywhere else Dad could arrange a venue.

Making speeches with my father was the closest to a meaningful relationship we ever had. But even though we spent hundreds of hours together, I could never tell him if I was tired, scared, or even happy. I could only submissively listen to him talk about communists. If his ideas seemed harebrained to me, how could I say so? It wasn't a sense of duty that kept me in line, but the fear that if I disobeyed my father, he would punish my mother, saying she hadn't raised us right.

In October 1965 Dad wanted me to give a speech beside him at the discovery well of the East Texas oil fields. Mother taped our practice session at home. My voice was young and energetic, spread wide with a Texas twang that was an odd match for the gravity of the three-minute speech I'd memorized. But Dad was thrilled. "Now I wish we could jar that, because that is just plenty, plenty good! *Plenty good!*" Then he paused. "You're fifteen years old, aren't you?"

"Yes, Sir."

"Well, I think you should say that specifically in your speech," he coached.

Now it was Dad's turn to practice. He began reading, in a down-home, country drawl: "I think of East Texas as the finest place to be . . . and the people as fine as the land in which they live." (My mother began clapping, enthusiastically.) Dad went on to give a fascinating firsthand account of the area's oil history, replete with wildcat wells, down-dip reserves, sand sections—and of course his dealings with Dad Joiner. But midway through he abruptly switched topics, describing the failure of Karl Marx's economic theory, and how recent American food shipments had prevented the communists from starving. "The Soviet Union was on the verge of collapse when given diplomatic recognition by the United States in 1933. A billion human beings have since fallen into communist domination in the past thirty-two years . . ."

As if to defend his concern, he added, "We must realize that the truth is no longer popular. . . . . An atmosphere has been created that those who oppose communism are considered divisive and much more dangerous than communists themselves. Without apology either major political party welcomes the support of any communist front organization and procommunist worker. . . . The public is primed daily to oppose any spirit of nationalism in the United States. But we have the facts on our side." (Once again, Mother burst into applause.)

A clear glimpse of my zealous roots comes near the conclusion of Dad's speech. "Many people ask, 'What can I, one person, do?'" Dad answered the question, laying out his vision that young people's revolutionary tendencies be channeled into combating communism.

Youth are "another chance for salvation." "Two million crusaders could be activated to convert one other person in the fight for freedom—an 'each one teach one' crusade. In one month there would be four million, in two months eight million . . . in six months, 128 million, and in seven months communism would be out." But that's not all. Members of the crusade would pledge that they wouldn't go to sleep at night without spending ten minutes a day for freedom. "Ten minutes may seem little, but with two-thirds of the population, that ten minutes becomes twenty million hours for freedom. And this is opposition which communism cannot survive."

On the day of the speeches, I was surrounded with people for whom H. L. Hunt was a hero, one of their own who'd made it to the pinnacle of power. I took my place on the outdoor stage with Dad and delivered the warning I'd painstakingly practiced:

"You see, I'm worried because we are scheduled to be slaves when we grow up. Khrushchev said so and now Kosygin backs him up. . . . Some adults dismiss us and say political affairs is not a child's game. Mussolini and Hitler thought differently; they placed guns, real guns, in the hands of fourteen-year-olds. Now in Cuba there is an organization for seven- to thirteen-year-olds called 'Union of Rebel Pioneers.' All over the world in different uprisings the communists and atheists are using youth to stir up rebellions and work against the United States. But we can really have good fun working to save our liberty. They can't beat a person who knows what he is talking about and has the truth. And someone who is not silent, silly, or sentimental about it. Someone who isn't worried about hurting the communists' feelings. . . . Come on in, the water's fine!"

As inflammatory as his—or our—ideas may have been, Dad maintained an almost endearingly naïve modus operandi. After taking me to Washington to lobby Senators Strom Thurmond, Mark Hatfield, and Ed Muskie, he brought me to the Louisiana State Fair to stand next to him, handing out tracts to awestruck browsers who'd come for cotton candy and to check out the hogs. Hand-scrawled signs urged "FREE SAMPLE. HLH CAKES" and "Books by H. L. HUNT," but to ensure success my father decided to press the flesh in front of neat shelves lined with HLH-brand ketchup and pinto beans. That appeal to common folk didn't, however, replace his weekly political memos in the late 1960s to his "Near Nixon" list of Washington powerbrokers.

But as thoroughly planned as they were, Dad's tactics were so peculiar that in an interview Hugh Hefner, the *Playboy* mogul, once called him "an irritating enigma. . . . No one, not even his own family, professes to understand him; no one, not even the partners he's made rich, seems to have any idea what drove him to amass his vast fortune; and no one, not even Hunt himself, seems able to explain just what he is trying to accomplish in the political arena." "No one" included me.

As I got older I chafed at being expected to appear here or there with Dad who, by his mid-seventies, was so out of touch that I could generally avoid being in his sight and therefore, it seemed, his mind. When he wanted to send me off on a patriotic speaking tour during school, I hid from my father for a week, having dinner in my bedroom until his passion moved on to his next idea.

But June was more reluctant to say no, since the blame would fall on Mother. And so with no preparation and only the charge from Dad to "go to Chicago and win converts to the pro-freedom cause," my older sister arrived at O'Hare Airport with no one to contact and no plan. She says now that those experiences taught her independence, but they made an already tense father-daughter relationship even more difficult.

Dad expected all his children to line up for his cause, and some became converts, or at least loyal soldiers. In particular, Lyda's son Bunker was a major funder of archconservative organizations. But even being in earshot of Dad was high risk, for he might press anyone into service at any time. In later years I felt sad for my elderly father, when I heard scuttlebutt at the Hunt Oil office that his sons Herbert and Bunker avoided him, almost never walking down the hall to stick their heads in his office.

Lamar, on the other hand, frequently stopped in to see his father. That took some courage, since Dad's and Lyda's youngest was intent on starting the decidedly nonpolitical Dallas Texans (later Kansas City Chiefs) and the American Football League, while Dad was intent on keeping him out of sports. My father's attorney told me that Dad, despite his disapproval and unbeknown to Lamar, quietly gave the bankers an unlimited guarantee for all of his son's debts, allowing him to build his sports empire. I took from that story that my father was capable of caring feelings that I, as a teenager, couldn't imagine him having. I was too caught up in needing his validation and feeling bitterly disappointed. That said, he was a provider. My father set up trusts for each of his kids: all fourteen of us.

It's sadly ironic that someone who could provide so handsomely was impoverished when it came to social capital—the currency of trust, reciprocity, and relationship. Despite our having lived together for more than ten years under the same roof, Dad knew little about me. I wish he'd asked, even once, "How are you?" Instead he'd call on the phone, give an instruction, then hang up. I wondered if he was aware of, let alone distressed by, the distance between us. He either didn't know how to inquire or didn't care to. I couldn't bring myself to ask.

As I mentioned earlier, Dad had a secret set of four children, which we called the "third family" even though they were chronologically his second. They lived in Atlanta, although one, Hugh, came to Dallas from time to time to visit his father. After Dad's death, I found among his papers a lengthy piece entitled "Unified Theory of Human Existence," a product of Hugh's "Constructive Foundation." In it, Hugh proposed eliminating government handouts, by which he meant foreign aid and domestic welfare programs.

The piece struck me as a thinly veiled plea for his father's approval. It didn't work. I flinched one day when I heard Dad grumble that Hugh was mentally ill. Maybe he was. Maybe not. But whether dealing with sickness or health, my father was unequipped for intimacy. So I wasn't really surprised by the formal tone on a mailing I found from Hugh— a brochure of a school in Atlanta. "Dear Sir," he inscribed on the cover, "I pointed out with red arrows your grandchildren."

November 22, 1963

As unengaged as my father was personally, he was passionate politically. In 1960 Dad had shocked his associates by supporting the presidential bid of Senator John F. Kennedy of Massachusetts. I've heard three reasons: his disdain for Richard Nixon, whom he considered soft on communists; his conviction that Jack's father, Joe, would ensure his son's "pro-freedom" orientation; and his relationship with Senator Lyndon Johnson of Texas, Kennedy's running mate. But ardent anti-Kennedy sentiment was common in Dallas; my schoolmates sang as they played tetherball, "We'll have a World War Three / We elected

Kennedy." Soon my father also expressed great disappointment in the president's politics, ruminating that Harvard communists must have ruined him.

Virulent dislike of the president extended far beyond schoolyards. When JFK was scheduled to visit Dallas, an ad appeared in our paper bearing the caption "Wanted for Treason" beneath what looked like police mug shots of the president. (The Warren Commission later found that Bunker had been a sponsor of the ad.) That November day, even middle-schoolers felt ferment in the air. I remember the mix of tension and excitement as I milled around with my friends during our mid-morning milk break. I wasn't feeling well. I had an unfamiliar pain in my lower abdomen, but I didn't say anything to anyone.

The bell rang, and we went back into the building and upstairs to class. It was science period, and I was in the lab when an announcement came over the loudspeaker. Passing in their open motorcade through downtown, President Kennedy and Governor Connally had been shot.

The eyes of the world were riveted on Dallas. Connally survived, but the president, who'd been welcomed by cheering crowds at the airport, was pronounced dead shortly after he arrived at Parkland Hospital. On TVs across the nation, Walter Cronkite choked back tears as he announced the news. Word swept through the school. My friend Susie Strauss, whose father was a friend of the governor, began sobbing. Noticing that my teacher's face was ashen, I filled a beaker with some water and brought it over to her. Just then the principal came to my classroom. He beckoned for me to come out. Helen was already waiting in the hall. He told us the police had arrived to pick us up. We gathered our books and sweaters and piled into the back of the squad car, with no sense of what was going on. The police car pulled up in front of the home of casual church friends.

Later, a member of Congress declared, "If anyone is responsible, it's H. L. Hunt and the fanatical right-wing radio broadcast he sponsors." Turned out that others shared that belief. In the whirlwind that followed, we Hunt kids were in the eye of a storm. My father's combination of far-right views, political activism, and financial wherewithal made him suspect.

Danger seemed to be swirling around us. Every hour brought new rumors, and I felt anxious as I tried to do my homework, study for tests, and just keep chugging along through everyday life. Aunt Swann revealed that before the shooting she'd seen someone at Mt. Vernon's back door who looked suspiciously like the assassin, Lee Harvey Oswald. She whispered this to me, hunched over, with a sinister look on her face and her hands curved like claws as she portrayed the would-be intruder. Threatening phone calls came to Mt. Vernon. Helen and I were instructed to tell no one where we were staying. Each morning we were fetched by Mt. Vernon staff coming directly from their own houses (thus more difficult to tail) and taken to school. At SMU, a kind professor insisted that June move into her home. Ray stayed close to the Phi Delta Theta house.

We eventually learned that Mom and Dad had immediately left town under assumed names, disguised with sunglasses. Meanwhile, a surreal series of events was unfolding: the shooting of Police Officer Tippit, the swearing-in of President Johnson, the apprehension of Oswald, the murder of Oswald in the jail hallway by Jack Ruby, and the funeral of Kennedy. Dallas was the center of the universe, as television stations carried little other programming, to the exasperation of our conservative hideaway hosts. We didn't hear from our parents for weeks. Helen feared that they were dead.

It took years for Dallas to return to normal, and a decade before the world would associate our city with anything but the killing. At a personal level, the Kennedy assassination haunts me. I was caught off guard when, a decade later while watching a movie storyline unfold, I realized that the cigar-smoking Dallas businessman bankrolling the Kennedy killing was based on my father. Soon after seeing that movie, I was stunned by news over the radio: a Florida man had killed himself after claiming that he'd served as Oswald's and Dad's go-between. A purported note from Oswald to a "Mr. Hunt" fueled such theories. The link to my family faded but did not die: I saw it forty years later on a classroom poster outlining assassination theories. And the speculation still surfaces unexpectedly in conversations with strangers as I travel. I haven't had any inside information, although I've gone so far as to raise the question in a private meeting with Dad's attorney. He firmly denied the rumor I'd read in conspiracy annals, that Ruby visited Dad's office the day before the assassination.

I remember November 22, 1963, for three reasons: the drama of our unceremonious exit from school, the sense of awesome political upheaval, and the beginning of my womanhood that evening. I was too embarrassed to ask our church friend what to do about the bleeding that had started. I just sneaked into her bathroom and stole some supplies.

Just Plain Folks

It strikes me that Dad was also open to suspicion partly because he was iconoclastic and conspicuously unaware of others' expectations. Even as he knew few bounds in his campaign to save the world from communists and flouted ethical rules in his familial relationships, he also defied societal norms with his parsimonious tastes. He was a self-made man with little polish who dressed in a signature blue suit, blue shirt, and blue bow tie, when no one, but no one, wore a blue shirt, and bow ties were far out of favor. Dad's vocabulary was extensive, but he spoke with remnants of rural syntax. My parents didn't watch TV and weren't plugged into any world of ideas beyond his patriotic zeal and her religious fervor. I never saw Dad hold a book, except one of the many he'd written and self-published.

Dad expressed his patriotism through rituals. Each day he raised and lowered an American flag on the front lawn, often with Helen or me to help fold. And he was like a kid when parades wound through downtown Dallas. He'd invite the family or anyone else he could find to his top-floor office and hurry eagerly from one window to the next, leaning out over the marching bands and clowns.

Our family's social needs were minimal, which was a good thing, since given the history of their relationship, my parents were blackballed from the country-club scene. Dad was essentially a homebody, staying in probably nineteen evenings out of twenty. His idea of high-class entertainment was inviting the families of Hunt Oil employees to Mt. Vernon once a year. Dozens of children roamed the grounds with paper sacks, gathering pecans, and a prize was given to whoever found the shell with a red painted "H."

Our guests often supped on country fare: cabbage and cornbread. For New Year's Day, Mom served hog jowls, turnip greens, and black-eyed peas. She was such a teetotaler that in the middle of the night she poured down the drain the gallon jug of fruit I'd been fermenting for ice cream topping. But otherwise, on the rare occasions when Dad was away, mother let the cook indulge us with fried chicken and banana pudding. After all, Granny, bless her, had advised her daughter, "Now Sis, there'll be plenty of times you'll have to say 'No.' You'd better just say 'Yes' every chance you get."

"Yes" at Mt. Vernon meant a secret drawer in the kitchen (low, so Dad would be less likely to open it), filled with Oreos and Hostess Twinkies. Long before the rest of the nation caught on, Dad was enamored with health foods. "The whiter the bread, the sooner you're dead," he repeated, lauding his "Deaf Smith County Wheat," ground right there in our kitchen. The Central Asian Hunzas, he told anyone who would listen, played polo at the age of 100 and lived to be 120. And so like them we ate the soft pits of apricot seeds, bitter with a touch of cyanide.

A reporter quizzed my father about his frugal lifestyle. "Why don't you spend more of your money? As they say, 'You can't take it with you.'"

Dad gave him a puzzled look and answered, "I don't intend to go."

One far-out idea followed another. Adding fluoride to the public drinking water supply was part of a communist plot. "Creeping and crawling" on his hands and knees around the dining room table would strengthen his mind. And plastering our cars top to bottom, front to back, with orange and black Gastro Magic bumper stickers was a sure-fire way to attract customers for his new antacid. I don't think anyone who saw those cars was attracted to the product, but I can vouch that Dad's advertising antics were enough to give his wife and children heartburn.

Dad also loved visiting his Texas cattle ranch and huge pecan grove. When one interviewer asked his profession, he answered, "Farmer." I guess that's right. Mom and Dad were farm folk plunked down in a mansion. In the late 1940s my father had even developed a plan to create training colleges on farms and ranches, where young people could study scientific agricultural methods—but he added pointedly, they wouldn't have so much education that they lost their common sense.

As a girl, I often saw my father outside, wandering through the vegetable garden and corn patch, or strolling through our back acres to talk with his pet deer and goats. "Here, Sweetie. Come Sweetie. Have a bite," he'd call, his crackly voice rising to a caressing treble. Watching him there in his business suit and polished dress shoes, with grain in his extended palm, I felt a stab of regret. He could offer those animals a tender attention he couldn't give to me.

When asked the secret of his success, "hard work and frugality" was always Dad's answer. A candid picture in *Life* magazine from 1948, captioned "World's Richest Man," showed him standing on a street corner in New York. Unnoted was that he was holding pecans, cracking them as if he were out in a field. But the world's richest man couldn't bear to see the hotel bill after his stay at the Waldorf Astoria. And even years later, when he was mistakenly shown the $3 million invoice for the company's jet, he turned ashen. "Take that down to my lawyer," he said, "'cause I don't have authority to spend money like that."

At the same time, maybe as a throwback to his oil field days, Dad always wanted "walking-around money" in his pocket—three or four thousand dollars in hundred-dollar bills. Though none of us, including Mother, received an allowance, we had free use of a charge card. So Helen and I developed an adolescent money-laundering scheme, buying record albums for friends who paid us back in cash that we could spend on a milkshake.

One of the few times I did ask Dad for money was for a movie. He pulled out his rubber-banded roll and handed me a bill. It was hard to find a place where an eleven-year-old could break a hundred. That memory is such an anomaly, since Dad shunned the trappings of wealth. When he agreed (after many requests) to an interview on "60 Minutes," a production crew spread out across our living room to film Dad playing a game of checkers with Mother's brother, Uncle Pat. The producer, Joe Wershba, was taken with Mom, whom he dubbed "Magnolia." When he discovered me as ambassador in Vienna nearly thirty years later, he reminisced with affection about how she clandestinely asked him to lobby Dad for a new car for her.

Mike Wallace captured this tight-fisted streak in Dad beautifully: "Possessing almost everything, he insists on a spartan way of life." The chairs in his office weren't just old. They weren't just worn. The brown leather was cracked, with stuffing showing through wide splits. "The Hunts live on a level of comfortable frugality—at least for a billionaire," said Wallace.

My father was such a mix. On the one hand, he chuckled as he told

Wallace, "Well now, there are deals made in this office that may involve the outlay of as much as ten million dollars, and they don't even go to the trouble of askin' me about them." On the other hand, he hated Cadillacs, considered Packards the epitome of indulgence, and rejected Fords because the Ford Foundation supported "anti-freedom causes."

For years, Dad drove a relatively modest Oldsmobile, but eventually, he graduated to blue Continentals. (We weren't to say "Lincoln Continental," since he had an aversion to expensive Lincolns.) Riding with Dad was often harrowing. His driving was the real-life version of a child in command of a video game for the first time. He'd head right into a city bus and force it up onto the curb, create a central lane where there was none, or sideswipe cars in a daring dash to the airport. On one hellish ride, Dad was racing recklessly to catch a plane. Mother sat gripping the leather, her lips pinched together; she knew a word from her could make a terrible situation worse. Terrified, I lay down on the floor of the back seat, covered my head with my arms, and squeezed my eyes shut, bracing myself for the head-on crash we somehow avoided.

Dad's driving was so calamitous that an aide at his office arranged to have an identical car in stock at the dealer, so when my father arrived in one that was banged up, without a word it was replaced by a new one in his parking space. Fearing a tragedy at an intersection where Dad consistently ignored a light, the aide added to the company payroll an off-duty policeman whose only job was to watch for my father's blue Continental each morning and blow his whistle like mad to clear pedestrians out of the path.

It was difficult to anticipate any actions of my father, the quintessential entrepreneur with a disregard for social rules. That being said, he had many classic virtues, such as everyday honesty and idealism, and he avoided many vices. In addition to being fastidious about his eating, I never saw my father with an alcoholic drink. That discipline makes all the more enjoyable the story of his deposition by a lawyer for the opposition, named "Whisky Bill."

During depositions, rather than answer the other lawyer's questions, Dad generally talked about whatever he wanted. But for his session with Whisky Bill, he filled up twenty-four small bottles with clear Aloe Vera gel, a potion he regularly drank even though it was meant for topical use. After every question from Whisky Bill, Dad pulled a full bottle from his pocket, chugged the contents, and nonchalantly threw the empty over his shoulder into a corner. By all appearances, this elderly man was downing an awesome amount of vodka, but he seemed to be getting stronger. According to Dad's attorney, "Mr. Hunt sensed he had Whisky Bill on the run. Then he got ferocious." Dad had won the battle of nerves.

Mike Wallace got the same treatment. Sitting on our blue sofa, Wallace would ask one of his barbed questions and then listen to Dad talk about whatever he wanted—almost always the communists. At one point Wallace pushed on the question of giving back to the society from which Dad had benefited so much: "One writer said about you, 'When it comes to philanthropic works, H. L. Hunt is only about six cents more open-handed than Scrooge.' What's your reaction to that?"

"Well, now, he used a very fancy expression which I don't know what it means."

"I mean compared to big philanthropists like the Rockefellers, or . . ."

"Well now, now, I could not . . . I would turn over many times in my grave, you see, if I were Carnegie and John D. Rockefeller and so forth, you see, with the people running their foundations that are running their foundations . . ."

"Why? What's wrong with their foundations?"

"Oh, you know as well as I, and the public knows as well as I, everyone that knows any anticommunists at all, why they very well know, you see, that those foundations are influenced by and pretty much operated for the benefit of the people that are trying to destroy our nation . . . And my philosophy is that I would like to *save* our republic just as long as it can be saved."

"Do you have any notion, though, about what the majority of Americans feel about you or think about you, *if* they think about you?"

"I don't have any persecution complex whatsoever, but there are foundations that will advance writers to write adverse stories about me, and I wish I could hire one of those writers sometime. And I think if I was right smart I could, because they're so much better writers than anyone I've ever heard tryin' to say anything from my side. There's no comparison."

"Well, why would somebody want to write nasty things about H. L. Hunt?" Wallace was drilling straight down to bedrock. "What is the significance of H. L. Hunt?"

"Well, I am a product of the individual initiative and the profit-motive system and the profit-motive system has, we'll say, created or generated the greatest nation on earth."

The show ended with an aerial view of our mansion, swimming pool, guesthouse, and yawning expanse of manicured green lawn. The voice-over is Mom and Dad singing their favorite song, about a simple elderly couple visiting their pompous son in his "mansion in the city." The son is embarrassed, surrounded by rich friends "who'd often heard him speak of 'home so grand.'" I'm not sure Wallace, with his penchant for social satire, understood how unambiguously true the words were as Mom and Dad sang: "We are just plain folks, your mother and me / Just plain folks, like our own folks used to be / We are sadly out of place here, 'cause we're just plain folks."

Mom and Dad holding hands, singing, is a beautiful memory. One to cherish. As in most families, there were some terrible ones on the other side. One of the most difficult for all of us kids was Mother's panic when Dad tried to force her to take Hassie's anti-psychotics and threatened to have her committed to an asylum. We four were a phalanx determined to protect our mother. "She's not crazy!" we rallied in her defense. It was easy to blame Dad for her distress, seeing how she was beaten down by his dictates and deceits. We, after all, knew nothing about mental illness.

But despite difficult patches, Mom always managed to bounce back. "Life is what you make it" was her mantra. If we weren't happy, we should still act happy. Despite, or perhaps because of, the spells of sadness that plagued her, she defined character by one's ability, and willingness, to play the hand dealt . . . with a smile.

Mom's philosophy of "bloom where you're planted" had roots in Oklahoma. Two decades after she left Idabel, we kids passed the hot, mosquito-thick summers there. By the time I was old enough to remember, my grandmother Grace (from whom I received my middle name) had spread to a robust size and depended on a cane as she tended her exquisite irises.

She was a chuckling, plainspoken, card-playing granny, impatiently drumming her fingers on the fold-up table in an unsubtle "Hurry up" to her grandchildren, who were, she allowed, "as slow as molasses in January" when deciding on a discard. Granny's language was filled with colloquialisms. "She told him how the cow ate the cabbage" was Idabelese for "She gave him a piece of her mind." Words that today could invoke a race riot were tossed around without a thought.

Idabel was Ku Klux Klan territory. An affable uncle and cousin were reputed members; both were avid churchgoers and high-ranking Freemasons. Racial prejudice was as natural to them as sweat in July, even though a beloved elderly Negro man was occasionally featured in family stories. Those prejudices reappeared when my aunt heard me talking with my father's black cook and reprimanded me, "Don't you say 'Ma'am' to her."

Still, for all the shortcomings, Idabel was a place where I belonged. We passed slow, sultry hours stirring up a breeze on the squeaky porch swing. There Granny sang me the lullaby she'd sung to my mother before me, a popular song written in 1893 by Hattie Starr, part of the ragtime genre of "coon songs." I had no idea the lullaby had racial overtones.

Lilted comfort drenched me as we swayed in the dusky air, night after night on the porch swing. Granny's weight made the swing creak in time. She crooned in a low voice that sounded as if she always had phlegm in the back of her throat:

> This here little Alabama Coon,
> Ain't been born very long;
> I 'member seein' a great big round moon,
> And hearin' one sweet song.
> When dey tote me down to de cotton patch
> An' I roll and I tumble in de sun;
> An' my daddy picked de cotton, while my mammy watched me grow,
> And dis am de song she sung:
> Go to sleep, my little pickaninny,
> Brer' Fox 'll catch you if you don't;
> Slumber on de bosom of yo' ole Mammy Jinny,
> Mammy's gwine to swat yo' if you won't.
> *Lu-la, lu-la lu-la lu-la lu!*
> Underneaf de silver Southern moon;

Rockaby, hushaby, Mammy's little baby,
I'm my mammy's little Alabama Coon.

Granny's dying in 1968 was hard for us all, even Dad, who would take a tongue-lashing from her about how he was treating her baby Sis —a scolding that he wouldn't tolerate from anyone else. Maybe he did that because Granny's life was simple, and my father, like my mother, yearned for simpler times.

In an Idabel way, nothing had changed. Work boots still crunched on the gravel path outside. Wasps still circled near her window. And her bathroom still smelled of damp talcum powder and old brushes. But Granny hadn't responded to anyone for days. Instead she lay almost motionless on her bed, in the room in which my mother had been born. We all knew the ultimate change was imminent. The hour came for me to leave, to go back to college. I leaned over her bed and sang our lullaby, one final time. As I finished the last line, she took a deep breath and pursed her lips. Without opening her eyes, she forced out a plaintive, "'Cooooooooon."

Faith of Our Fathers

In the buckle of the Bible belt, a church for "just plain folks" was on almost every corner. When we moved into Mt. Vernon, my parents decided we would change churches, even as we changed names, to make a clean break. Mom looked for a congregation that hearkened back to her rural roots. Dad had his ambitions too: a pulpit for his anticommunist crusade. They looked for a lowbrow but influential house of worship.

A solid 25 percent of Dallasites were Baptists. First Baptist Church, the largest property owner downtown, became the center of gravity for my family's faith. When I was nine, Mother, Helen, and I sat on the velvet sofa in our capacious living room as leaders of the children's programs at First Baptist asked if we knew the Lord. We nodded our heads, and they invited us to Sunday school. Soon we discovered that at First Baptist, thousands gathered not just Sundays, but every day, for a smorgasbord of activities. In time I came to spend twelve to eighteen hours a week at church, and not out of obligation. Church was a haven, filled with born-again believers who greeted strangers with hugs rather than handshakes.

We soaked up that warmth. I longed for the predictable middle-class life of my best friend, Carol Edgar, at First Baptist. We shared girdles and curlers, but also lofty ideas and secret hopes. Ours was an all-service church, determined to be an oasis to keep kids out of the clutches of Satan; Carol and I not only studied the Word and wept as we prayed. We also held hands as we roller-skated, and kept score for each other as we bowled—all at the church gym. We sat together on the bleachers, and when we weren't whispering about boys, we marveled as celebrities like the Yo-Yo Champion of the World offered us everything from self-confidence to salvation.

Services were decidedly "low church," meaning that reverential demeanor took a back seat to down-home friendliness. Before and after services, the cavernous sanctuary filled with friends catching up on news, their chatter competing with the swells of the organ. Prayers were spontaneous, never read, for prayer was conversation with God led by a man (always a man) kneeling at the altar, pouring out his heart. Each service ended with an "invitation," as congregation members moved by the Spirit walked forward to announce to the whole assembly a momentous decision: accepting Jesus as Savior, joining the church, or coming for baptism.

These moments of conversion were dramatic, intense, and life-changing. Although I no longer hold many of the beliefs that I did then, Christian fundamentalism was as important an influence as my family. Hymns assuring me of God's love eased the hurt of life with my father. Years of Bible study introduced me to Jesus, the social revolutionary. Hot summers at our rustic church camp taught me to love people, not comforts. Tithing ingrained in me that I was only a steward of possessions and wealth, not the owner. And soul winning on Tuesday nights—approaching strangers with the good news of salvation—gave me a sense of messianic mission.

Baptists made much of having direct access to the Lord. We didn't observe sacred rites, unlike Catholics (who we, with all earnestness, prayed might become Christians). But I particularly loved our tradition of a monthly "Lord's Supper," when round silver trays filled with tiny cups of grape juice and morsels of unleavened bread were distributed by dozens of church deacons (again, all men), who fanned out across the congregation in a careful, intricate choreography. The ceremony ended with us all holding hands, singing about the blest tie that binds our hearts in Christian love.

No ecclesiastical ceremony, however, matched the drama of "believer's baptism" (as opposed to the infant baptism practiced in other churches). The new family of H. L. Hunt joining the church and being baptized as a six-some was an undeniable coup for W. A. Criswell, the winsome pastor who dunked us, in succession, before the congregation.

But only later did I kneel alone by my bed one night after a moving church service and pray for Jesus to "come into my heart." Even now this moment is fresh. I was in the same bedroom in which I went to sleep every night, but the spiritual presence surrounding me was palpable. The following morning, I didn't tell anyone what I'd experienced. But I came forward during the invitation hymn of the next church service. Convinced that my baptism with my family was invalid because I hadn't been "saved" at the time, I asked for "rebaptism."

Soon after, on a Sunday evening, I went to a small dressing room behind the sanctuary and donned a white, ankle-length robe. A passage from the room led into the baptistery. My heart was beating faster as I stepped down into the water. Across from me, Dr. Criswell, also in a robe, entered the giant tub. The water, visible to the congregation through the glass front, came up to my chest. Stage lighting left the congregation dim, but our virtual Jordan River aglow. The organ played softly, hymns of the faithful.

As instructed, I crossed my arms over my chest and tucked my feet under a metal bar for stability. The pastor put one hand between my shoulders and with the other gently pinched my nose as he tilted me back. "I baptize you, my sister, in the name of the Father, Son, and Holy Spirit. Buried in the likeness of His death"—he dipped me under the water—"raised to walk in newness of life."

I blinked as I came up, my hair dripping, the robe clinging to my upper body. This was my first big moment apart from my family unit, but I wasn't thinking in those terms. I stepped gingerly out of the baptistery, "happy in the Lord."

Baptism was a one-time symbol, but the Scripture was our ongoing sustenance. Before I could read, I loved the colorful pictures of Moses in the bulrushes in our huge family Bible, always out on a table in the living room. Later, I read each evening from my own King James Version, sitting in bed, just before turning off the lights. Sundays, we carried our well-worn Bibles to church to take notes in the margins. I can still pull those lyrical scriptures out of my memory for instruction or comfort in times of distress.

But to us the Bible wasn't only wisdom poetically phrased or a metaphorical guidebook. It was the Word of God. We knew every jot and tittle was to be taken literally—because the Bible said so. The scriptures were, as the Apostle Paul wrote, "the sword of the Spirit," slashing through apathy and evil alike, penetrating the hard of heart: people who didn't see things our way.

Dallas public schools gave credit for Old Testament and New Testament courses taught at church during our high school years. And in vacation Bible school, Carol and I memorized a score of verses each day for two weeks. But no historical overview or rote learning could approach the "sword drills," Bible-toting Baptists' version of the spelling bee. As we lined up with other children to hone our prowess, we were ensuring that we were ready for the ultimate spiritual battle.

Our commander was a jovial, middle-aged volunteer, who sold insurance when he wasn't training troops. "Attention!" his voice rang out. A dozen swashbuckling eleven-year-olds stood expectantly in a row, our backs arched and our chins high as we held black, white, or pink leather Bibles at our sides.

"Draw Swords!" We shifted position, our Bibles now flat and waist-high, with left hand beneath, right hand on top. Nervous smiles spread across our faces.

"First Timothy 4," he paused, letting the suspense build, "verse 12."

First Timothy! A mere four and a half pages out of some fourteen hundred! Tension was reaching fever pitch as we stood motionless, each trying to visualize the exact position of that Pauline letter relative to the other sixty-five sacred books between the leather covers.

"Charge!"

Heads down, we frantically flipped open our Bibles and raced breathlessly through the silk-thin pages. Within a few seconds, a book worm with horn-rimmed glasses stepped forward, his lanky finger pinned on the page in an accusatory pose, too much white showing in his eyes wide with pleasure: "Don't let anyone look down on you because you are young," he said, in a squeaky voice. This was his chance to shine—and shine he did, like a glistening, polished blade.

The Biblical injunction to go out and teach all nations, which drove our evangelism, was based on the doctrine that only believers like us would be spared eternal damnation. Looking back, I realize that I was inside the general's tent as a theological war was evolving into the Religious Right political movement. In this battle for the soul of America, our strategic advantage was enormous. Liberal theologians taught universal tolerance, while evangelicals like us preached salvation only through Christ. But evangelicals prevailed, for our cause was more urgent. It was a matter of life or death.

Proselytizing was an expression of our love for others, and no setting was more loving than our annual Revival Week. Carol and I always sat together, savoring the nightly services, with bountiful music and energetic preaching. The revivalists were dramatic men, able to break into songs, sobs, or snickers as a story demanded or mood struck. One went too far, I thought, when he asked everyone to rise, then instructed born-again believers to sit down and pray for those left standing. The unsaved were uncomfortable, I'm sure, although not as uncomfortable as they would be in eternal torment.

But no revival preacher outshone Angel Martinez, appearing in a different bright-colored suit each night at the sawdust-strewn livestock coliseum. Angel had memorized the entire Bible. He told how he'd been drawn to church as a boy by free snow cones. I walked out into the summer night, feeling more burdened than relieved, as I pondered how I might entice others to Jesus.

My most powerful experience at church was Chapel Choir, a chorus of high schoolers led by the witty and handsome Lee Roy Till, more effective than a thousand preachers in lighting the evangelical fire within us kids. More than one hundred of us woke at 6:30 on Sunday mornings to sing for the early morning service. For Mr. Till, we endured the pastor's preaching verse by verse through the entire Bible, including some extraordinarily arid patches. In rehearsal, Mr. Till talked with us about the texts of our pieces—from Negro Spirituals to Handel—which we memorized so that we could commit ourselves, without distraction, to his direction.

The choir toured places that most of the singers would otherwise never visit. We gloried in London's grandeur as we performed in the Royal Albert Hall. And we squealed when Italian boys pinched us as we climbed the bleachers in the Piazza San Marco. But much more important was the sense of purpose we derived after we waited long hours at the East German border before being released to drive into West Berlin, where we sang before grateful crowds. They saw in us not only the gift of God's grace, but also political freedom. This was a history lesson no book could teach and a view of communism that my father's tirades could never convey. Staring for two hours into the faces of people who'd lived through hell, with passionate innocence we promised them a piece of heaven.

Truth is, we would have gone anywhere with Mr. Till. With vulnerability our parents rarely witnessed, we entrusted ourselves to him, singing our hearts out. As he led us through texts of conversion and commitment, tears rolled down his face. His nose turned red as he took deep breaths to keep from sobbing. And his arms pulled from us every ounce of earnestness while our voices and spirits climbed, step by step, the hill called Calvary.

At fourteen, Carol and I joined two boys from the choir to form a Christian folk group, the Lively Ones. For three years we carried our message in music to youth retreats and church services. We even sang at a Billy Graham revival. Gentle melodies of Peter, Paul, and Mary or Pete Seeger led into contemporary evangelic tunes. On stage in our matching red, white, and blue outfits, we looked out on a sea of up-turned faces, eager to be not only entertained but inspired. We were songsters with a mission: to win the lost to Christ. And we had a glorious time coming up with our own arrangements and harmonies, without bothering to write down a note, trading off guitars, banjo, tambourine, string bass, and vocals. Carol and I took turns on soprano and alto—and tenor for that matter. Decades later, I listened to our recording in awe of our musicality and, frankly, gumption.

Deep and Wide

Social messages in folk songs of the sixties equipped me for ministering in parts of town unknown to my school friends, even those from politically liberal families. Public housing projects lay in the shadow of First Baptist Church. My civic conscience was forged during sweltering summer weeks in ghettos with names like Little Mexico.

Our vivacious youth director drove slowly through inner-city streets, honking her horn, with us sitting on the hood holding onto windshield wipers and each other, calling out at the top of our lungs, "Come to vacation Bible school!" We recruited children who looked nothing like us into a neighborhood churchyard where, in 102 humid degrees, I toiled away at a portable pump organ. Little boys ran around in circles while a few little girls with dozens of short pigtails held by bright barrettes learned religious ditties. "Deep and wide. Deep and wide. There's a fountain flowing deep and wide . . ." they sang out gleefully, proud of their accompanying new hand motions.

When my legs weren't pumping, I held toddlers on my lap and placed cut-out figures on a felt board to teach the stories of Zaccheus the tax collector, the woman at the well, and the widow's mite. As the morning slowly simmered, Jesus turned the social order on its head, accusing religious leaders of hypocrisy, befriending women and outcasts, crossing barriers of tribe and class.

To be fair, almost no church I know of was racially integrated in the 1960s. Through that lens, ours was progressive, our summer activities shared with minority kids. Still, back at church, I asked a deacon, "Why do we need a separate Sunday service in a side chapel for people bussed in from housing projects?"

"Because they wouldn't feel comfortable in our regular service." I wondered *who* wouldn't feel comfortable. Looking back, it's easy to see how First Baptist offered solidly middle-class, rank-and-file parishioners psychological relief from the discord of that decade. But eventually the segregation wall fissured. The first African American enrolled in our "special education" department. A mentally retarded child was as much as we Christian soldiers could risk, but even that onward move came with a price. A deacon's wife explained to me her version of the dilemma. "The colored child is welcome, but the parents of the special ed kids used to gather socially. Now, of course, they can't."

I'm not saying our church was made up of bad people. But most of us had blind spots. We reflected a fractured American culture. I don't remember race ever being mentioned from the pulpit, but it would have stunned the congregation had a black person walked in and slipped into a pew in the main sanctuary.

June, who was on staff at the church, had heard Dr. King speak at SMU. She insisted that the Bible didn't relegate blacks to the back of any bus. June's stand against racism was the strongest cry for social conscience within our family. That was in contrast to the aunt who showed me a poster with face shots of apes and African American men. "Do you see the resemblance?" she probed—and she wasn't arguing in favor of the theory of evolution.

First Baptist was one of the strongest institutions of a South in the throes of political change. Even so, Dad was dissatisfied that the pastor didn't turn over his pulpit as a forum for anticommunism. Feeling spurned, my father forbade our going to church on Sunday nights. Helen and I sneaked out as if we were frequenting a speakeasy. Rebels, Southern Baptist–style.

On the other hand, our congregation led the national movement that joined church doctrine to a political agenda—known popularly as the Religious Right. This development was ironic, since the Baptist denomination was originally founded by religious refugees fleeing state-sponsored persecution in Europe. We had learned the earthly "separation of church and state" in the same breath as the divine "God is love." Of course, sermonizing with political overtones also had strong roots in American history. But in my teen years, that tradition was expanded so that we were warned from the pulpit of the evils not only of licentious living, but also of class struggle.

I didn't naturally identify with oppressed groups demanding their rights. As a child at the Texas State Fair, I'd drunk from water fountains labeled "WHITES ONLY," and I'd grown up with obliging gardeners called "yard boys." But I began to feel torn between the idealism of hymn-singing freedom marchers organizing in Mississippi and the devotion of faithful members filing into First Baptist. As the church was shifting right, I started slowly to shift left. Ever so slowly. My conversion to Jesus as Savior was instant, but my conversion to his teachings would be gradual.

It's no surprise that given my preoccupation with adolescent insecurities and a home often heavy with hurt, I directed my zeal toward a faith that offered up answers. I could rely on belief in the virgin birth, salvation through the blood of the Lamb, the priesthood of all believers—doctrines that I could recite without thinking. "Without thinking," in fact, turned out to be necessary. When I raised my hand in

Sunday school and asked why a loving God would condemn to eternal hell people in Africa who'd never heard of Him, our teacher told me to write my question down and we'd get to it at the end of class. We ran out of time.

Beyond First Baptist, Helen and I became involved in another evangelical organization, Youth for Christ, which was a significant distraction from my schoolwork, but as powerful a magnet as gangs were for others. Helen's and my need for fathering was transparent; she and I called the warm and vivacious leader "Daddy Don."

In addition, the club director, Mark Meeks, was a young man of strong intellect and conscience. He was a straight-A student, a talented quarterback in a football-crazed society, and president of his public school senior class. A "preacher boy," Mark was raised in a religious tradition that labeled Billy Graham "liberal." He began preaching revivals at thirteen. Family friends said how impressed they were when he would pound his Bible on the lectern and shout his message of salvation.

I first laid eyes on Mark when he was eighteen and I was fourteen. I'd brought my school friend Cathy to a rally in a large auditorium, praying that she might be won to Christ. As I sat in the second row, my thoughts moved between concern for Cathy's immortal soul and whether my hair would look better with a headband.

Broad-shouldered and handsome, Mark came on stage and welcomed everyone. He talked about why we all should be part of Youth for Christ. His broad smile lit up the whole auditorium, and he spoke with a voice that was at the same time earnest and energetic. I straightened up in my seat and looked around, wondering if anyone could tell what I was feeling. Sitting there, literally at his feet, I was enraptured. He seemed the embodiment of authority and stability.

Hockaday Heathens

Back when Mom married Dad, we three sisters got not only a new father, new home, new name, and new church, but a new school as well: the Ella Hockaday School for Girls. A wide chasm stretched between school and church. For ten years, the teachers at Hockaday encouraged me to question. I was the only Baptist in my class, since Baptists generally didn't have the money for secular private education. My church friends only dreamed of shopping in the stores, investing in the companies, or working in the political offices that bore the names of my schoolmates' fathers.

It was also difficult to bridge the gap between school and home. At first June, Helen, and I all attended the prep school as day students. But as June increasingly came to Mother's defense with defiant words and a flash of anger in her eyes, Dad responded by making her board for a semester, even though the campus was only fifteen minutes away and Helen and I were driven there each day. We learned a lesson. Shut up or be shut out. June says she shut down.

Despite the strains of our family life and the pull of religious passion, I managed to hold my own in the rigorous academic sphere. That wasn't because of my parents. It never dawned on them to quiz us about our homework, much less help with it. In fact, in the "60 Minutes" interview Dad told Mike Wallace, "I didn't go to high school, and I didn't go to grade school either. Education, I think, is for refinement and is probably a liability when it comes to making money."

I had a showdown with my father when he insisted that I should move through school as quickly as possible—by skipping fourth grade, for starters. "You can make me take the test, but you can't make me pass it," I pouted. I'd had a great time with the tutoring he'd wanted me to do that summer. But alone in the small lower school library, after whipping through several pages of the exam, I paused. At the rate I was going, I realized, I'd have to move into Helen's class. Sitting at the long wooden table, chewing on one of my yellow pencils, I decided to sabotage the test. I began circling nouns when asked for verbs, writing in wrong numbers in the arithmetic section. Even at eight I had some power, I realized.

Fourth grade was saved, but moving between Hockaday and Mt. Vernon was its own feat. At school, Franklin Roosevelt was one of our greatest presidents. At home he was a communist sympathizer. Hockaday was regarded as élite. (Where else would one discuss character flaws by studying Latin roots? *Sine nobilite* . . . snob.) In reality, school wasn't a liberal bastion. We were all white girls, though an occasional foreign exchange student came in exotic mellow brown. Even the assassinations of Robert Kennedy and Martin Luther King Jr. barely registered. But what we didn't have in social awareness, we made up for in academic acuity. At Hockaday I developed a great love of learning. I begged my incredulous mother for a set of the *World Book Encyclopedia* instead of jewelry for my thirteenth birthday, and then spent hours lost in those volumes, reading whatever entry I opened to when I was supposed to be looking up a specific topic.

If anything, being a Hunt at Hockaday was a negative. I felt devastated to learn that I'd been described at a faculty meeting as "a tin-type" of my father. It seemed so unfair, given how disconnected I felt from him and his extremism. I wanted to offer a warm family environment to my friends who were boarders, but coming home with me was more like a field trip to the circus.

Of course there were moments of high drama at school as well. I trembled before the venerable Miss Grow. She was in a class by herself, a white-haired, stooped relic. About five feet tall, she towered psychologically over our small group of resolute Latin students. To bring Caesar's Gallic victory into the classroom, she pulled two chairs side by side and climbed onto the seats. With a foot on each, her legs bent like a wishbone, she drove us into battle on the back of her chariot with a loud "Whoop!" No other teacher called us at home if we managed to make a perfect score on a test. No other brought us to tears if we dared come to class without our homework. That woman understood power, and she knew how to wield it.

Not I. I always felt on the margins. Granted, I dutifully conformed to Hockaday's strict dress code (green and white uniforms with saddle oxfords, no makeup or jewelry, skirts touching the floor when we kneeled). But so did everyone else. Though I was generally liked, I never really felt that I belonged. Perversely, one of my Hockaday highlights came when a teacher called me in for a stern tête-à-tête. A classmate, she told me, felt hurt by the way some of my friends were treating her. "I know you're the ringleader," said my teacher. I had two reactions: First, I'd been sadly maligned. Second, I was thrilled to be even wrongly suspected of being a leader.

We had ample opportunities for leadership, not needing airhead twitter for fear that a boy might be scared off by a too-competent girl. All the while, though, I never understood why my name didn't pop into the same sentence as the word "president." And I was equally clueless as to what to do about it.

Hockaday had an outstanding sports program, with a giant pool, state-of-the-art gym, softball and hockey fields. My closest friends leaped and sprinted like gazelles on varsity teams. I repeatedly tried out but didn't make the cut. The coaches graciously let me be the manager. Instead of shooting and spiking, I spent my time kneeling— wrapping my friends' shins with tight bandages.

The one area in which I should have led was music. Given latitude to miss study halls because of my good grades, I often holed away for hours in a cramped practice room with an upright piano, transposing "The Old Rugged Cross" from one key to another—unlikely corridor music for highbrow Hockaday. And I created a jazzy a cappella trio of spirituals for our school talent show in the spacious new auditorium.

But my stage career was cut short when I reached size fourteen and age fourteen at the same time. So I was shunted into roles of middle-aged characters like Wendy's mother in *Peter Pan* and a matronly nun in *The Sound of Music*. Still, I felt wounded that despite my musical aptitude, my classmates didn't cast me as president of the Glee Club.

I only managed to be appointed assembly chair in our senior year. It was probably the most inappropriate position possible. I rarely attended school on Mondays, the day of assemblies, being drained by the church activities of the weekend. (The blurb under my yearbook picture read, "For Swanee, the earth was created on Tuesday.") I dragged myself out of bed to introduce the physicist Edward Teller, but non-nuclear notables were left for the vice-chair to handle.

Likewise in academics, I wasn't at the top. Teachers took me aside to express concern because I fell asleep in class, exhausted by my religious overload. Still, I was usually in advanced sections, where I worked hard but earned mostly B's.

At the end of our senior year, the entire upper school gathered for the awards assembly. My friends filed up to the stage, one after another, as praise was heaped upon virtue. No one was surprised when the names of the first six of seven cum laude graduates were read out. These were excellent students, and their names met with supportive applause. But when my name was announced, one of my best friends bellowed, "No *way!*" The sound seemed to bounce eternally off the tall, gray auditorium walls as I slinked up to the stage to receive my pin.

Everyone at Hockaday knew I was no leader, athlete, or scholar. Nor saint, it turned out. I felt pulled between the emotional nurturance of church and the intellectual demands of school. Academia didn't compel me to try to influence my church, but I spent significant energy at school trying to figure out how to fulfill my promise to win over the lost to Christ. I longed to be one of the gang—even if it were made up of heathens (by Southern Baptist standards). Still, I had no excuse for not practicing the soul-winning methods I'd learned at church.

"Beach witnessing" during First Baptist choir tours, I had approached strangers lying unsuspectingly on striped towels in the sun; but those anonymous situations were easy compared to school, where I would continue to share Cokes and study notes with unbelievers who rejected my appeal for their immortal souls. Standing in line in the lunchroom, I frequently tried to arouse the fortitude to tell the girl in front of me that Jesus was her Savior—before we reached the grilled cheese sandwiches.

My last big opportunity came the spring of my senior year, when as a rotund Aunt Nettie in *Carousel* I would sing "You'll Never Walk Alone." In rehearsals I delivered the song as written. But in secret at home, I practiced over and over, replacing "hope" with "Christ" in the text: "Walk on, walk on with *Christ* in your heart, and you'll never walk alone . . ."

The evening of the performance arrived. I'd been hooked and snapped into a pale green checked frock, with my hair pulled back into an old-fashioned crocheted snood. Standing in the wings by the light board, I silently prayed for courage. Then I walked onto the stage, determined to publicly witness for the Lord.

Staring over the footlights, beyond the director in the pit and out into the audience, I built up to the climax of the song. Then I lost my nerve. I sang the lyrics as written, delivering inspiration rather than salvation. My high G on "never" was a success. My voice didn't crack. But I couldn't appreciate the applause. As my family gathered 'round, Ray told me I was the best singer in the show. Only the Lord and I were aware of my failure as I walked out of the school building, into the night.

My graduation from Hockaday was in the spring of 1968. Franny came, and I wept. She did too. It was the first time I'd seen her in years. It seemed to me she had shrunk. Mark Meeks came too. My life was changing. I was changing. I was breaking with the political traditions and social assumptions of my parents, as well as with fundamental-ism. And I was heading into a new world that would test my bonds with family, friends, and church. I wasn't sure where I was going, who I'd be when I arrived, or what would be left if I needed to return. I just knew it was time.

I'm a little lamb who's lost in the wood
I know I could
always be good
to one who'll watch over me.
—*George and Ira Gershwin*

CHAPTER 2

Two Steps Forward

Bridge over Troubled Water

One night when I was seventeen, I drove my car into a torrential Texas thunderstorm. I was going nowhere, trying to navigate both the slick highways and the treacherous transition from adolescence to womanhood. With the ranks of protective forces thinned, home was no haven. June and Ray were grown, and Helen had moved to the SMU campus, ten minutes from Mt. Vernon. For the first time in my life, I was alone, sitting at the long table with my parents at dinner each evening. It wasn't safe to discuss my day. Society was lurching forward, pulled by the new relativism of the sixties, but my father's anticommunist crusade and my mother's evangelical religion declared unchanging truths. I was confused. I needed traction.

The windshield wipers were slapping back and forth as I began to pray aloud, confident that God was listening in the darkness. My thoughts drifted to Mark, standing on a stage, leading the Youth for Christ rally. He'd made the scriptures come alive. He was funny but earnest as he talked about God's love in spite of our sin. I felt he was speaking just to me. I wasn't so presumptuous as to hope that his attention would actually fall on me, but even watching him from afar gave me a sense of possibility. "Dear Lord," I said, "I know it won't be Mark himself, but could You please find someone for me as much like Mark as possible?"

I had no vision of how my life could turn out to be one I would want to live. My dream had been to go to Radcliffe, Harvard's sister school, but my father was immovable. The Ivy League was a training ground for the enemy.

Dad would have been disturbed to learn what dangers lurked even at Southern Methodist University, which was the only option I was given. One instructor, a dear theology graduate student named Bill Fox, introduced me to *Man's Search for Meaning*, by the Holocaust survivor Viktor Frankl: "We who lived in the concentration camps can remember the men who walked through the huts comforting others, giving away their last piece of bread. They may have been few in number, but they offered sufficient proof that everything can be taken from a man but one thing: The last of his freedoms—to choose one's attitude in any given set of circumstances, to choose one's own way." Frankl's existentialism helped me claim the strengths and foibles, wonders and failures that made me who I was. I was becoming more secure, more convinced that a meaningful life was mine to create.

Living on campus, I began to stretch, to enjoy differences and look for possibilities. My Italian professor expressed her sympathies with the emerging women's movement by wearing a button that read: "Rape is inconsiderate." Maybe I needed to lighten up, I realized. Meanwhile, I stunned my professor of Biblical studies (Johannine Literature) by laying out a literalist interpretation of the Book of Revelation, delineating the schematic I'd learned at First Baptist of the series of world events that would lead to Armageddon, the battle that would herald the return of Christ. The professor was incredulous when I told him I'd been a true believer only a few years earlier.

I wasn't a neat fit at SMU. In fact, I wasn't a neat fit. I was twenty pounds overweight, my clothes weren't preppy, and my hairstyle wasn't cool. After ten years at an all-girls school, I felt self-conscious even walking across campus. Should I carry my books in my arms, or rest them on one hip? I stole glances at women in miniskirts and Pappagallo shoes, laughing as they teased the men I found intimidating. In the dorms I made friends, but I particularly hated "rush," the frantic popularity contest that decided which freshmen were invited, or not invited, to sorority parties. I wasn't in a hurry to join the Greeks, and they weren't in a hurry to have me join.

I occasionally had a chance to be with Mark but realized from comments he made to me that he yearned to be with Helen. I knew she felt the same way, but their melodrama ended in frustration, with each afraid to pursue the other. Truth to tell, I had little interest in helping Helen's relationship with Mark flourish. Instead, I waited in the wings. When Mark was shy about declaring his love, Helen, disappointed by his silence, announced she'd marry a handsome law student after her sophomore year.

Mark's hopes with Helen dashed, he asked me out. My sister was a Julie Andrews look-alike, as kind and intelligent as she was beautiful. I knew I wasn't as attractive in any sense, but I was thrilled to play her stand-in. I was eighteen; Mark was twenty-two.

Being with this heroic fellow was a dream come true. Even his parents welcomed me into their life. They were short on cash and long on love. Fred was a baker; Lillie worked the assembly line at the Texas Instruments factory. Mark went to the University of Texas at Arlington. He couldn't afford to live on campus, so he lived at home.

Sitting around the kitchen table with his folks was so different from the formality of Mt. Vernon. After dinner, his father read or watched TV history programs while his mother knitted. In the next room, I would chatter with Mark about everything that had happened that day: every new insight, every slight that cut me to the quick, every grand dream destroyed. Finally, I was in a home where someone wanted to hear what I had to say, be it a hilarious gaffe or flash of indignant anger. I spent every hour I could at the Meekses, my college textbooks open across the living-room sofa. When you grow up in a bizarre household, a sense of normalcy is a thrill.

Mark himself was far better than normal. He was a rapt listener, knowing when to engage, when to disagree, and when to hold back so I could vent. He'd sit next to me, letting me go on and on—not just about my mother misunderstanding me, or my father barking at the world, but also about politics, social issues, and religious reform.

My new boyfriend was much more aware of what was happening in the world than I was: who was running for the Senate, what church leaders were speaking out against Vietnam, or why land values in his parents' neighborhood had plummeted when a black family moved in down the block. His doubts awakened mine as he railed against injustice in the world. Our conversations unveiled a whole new level of sin and redemption, heaven and hell right here on earth. This was the kind of life I wanted. He was the partner of my prayers.

Soon we were talking about marriage, and I was ecstatic. So as not to crowd Helen's wedding, we agreed to wait a year. I didn't dare talk with Mark about his feelings toward my sister, and I wasn't mature enough to talk with Helen about our triangle. In a nutshell, I couldn't believe my good fortune and didn't want to screw it up.

With the comfort I was finding at Mark's, I became more critical toward my parents. I was unappreciative of the privileges that my father's wealth afforded, acutely aware of the inconsistencies in my mother's values, and self-righteous in Mark's and my budding liberalism.

We weren't alone in our discontent. The country was in turmoil. Mark had a draft deferment because of his seminary studies, but most men his age were facing mandatory military service. Vietnam was incinerating tens of thousands of them. Many others were returning to their families maimed, physically or mentally. But another battle was raging: the battle for racial equality. Although major civil rights victories had been won in the courts, discrimination was constant and dangerous. Victims of urban poverty were torching their neighborhoods. Attempts to put a lid on their rage resulted in more violence, with riot police sometimes shooting to kill. I wasn't yet confident enough to be a full participant in the movements of the sixties, nor was I part of the drug scene, which was more prevalent on the coasts than in Dallas. Still I identified with, and occasionally aided and abetted, cohorts who sat in, sat out, scrapped ties, scrapped bras, dropped acid, dropped out, burned bridges, and then burned out.

At least I had Mark, which ought to have been bliss. Training to be a Southern Baptist preacher, he could have been a perfect new addition for my family. But his credentials were tarnished when he supported Hubert Humphrey for president. Even more troubling was his being spotted flouting social norms by tossing a football with a son of one of our black maids. In Dallas in the sixties, that made my fiancé one of "those agitators."

Mom opposed our union. She felt that Mark was pulling me away from First Baptist. As weeks went by, our conflict grew way out of proportion. When I typed a college paper for him, she warned that he would make me his slave—this from the mother who'd devoted her life to Dad and taught me that my highest calling would be to make a husband happy. Taking a more rational approach, Ray, working at Hunt Oil Company, invited me to lunch downtown, a first in our relationship. Over a chef's salad and iced tea, he took out a ballpoint pen and scribbled on a white paper napkin divorce statistics for couples that marry young. I was impressed by his logic but left more stubbornly determined to heed my heart, feeling challenged to defy the odds.

I shouldn't have told Mark about Mother's and Ray's attempts to thwart our union. Of course he was hurt and insulted. But he tried to put aside those feelings and was always polite to every member of my family. I wasn't nearly so good. I wrote Mom a letter telling her everything she'd ever done that I resented. Now that I have three kids of my own, I'm triply sorry to remember that flaming hot letter. Somehow she managed to keep her reaction to herself.

My biggest worry was Dad's reaction. For months he was kept in the dark. I think Mother hoped that my relationship with Mark wouldn't last, and we'd never have to tell Dad. When it was time for invitations to go out, she decided to "ac-cen-tuate the positive" as she broke the news. Expecting an explosion, I waited anxiously outside the library, where Mom and Dad were talking after dinner. Their words were muffled and I couldn't make out who was saying what to whom.

Finally, the suspense was more than I could bear. I pushed back the heavy pocket doors and walked in, just in time to hear Dad say, "I think they ought to start having babies right away." Then he turned and left. Almost eighty, Dad was keen on seeing his dynasty grow. He was also nearing his date with eternity and enjoyed the thought of having a minister in the family.

Mark's father, meanwhile, faced a different challenge. At the bakery, a co-worker wondered with amazement, "Is it true your son is going to marry H. L. Hunt's daughter?"

"No," replied Fred, "She's going to marry my son."

I walked down the aisle on May 23, 1970, as soon as my sophomore year was finished and three weeks after my twentieth birthday. The ceremony was in a small chapel at First Baptist. I'd made life miserable for poor Mother, disagreeing with her about almost every detail of the wedding. She was distressed that Carol Edgar, my maid of honor, was singing Simon and Garfunkel's "Bridge over Troubled Water." "All people will hear is *trouble*," Mom said. I was upset by her florist's proposed extravaganza, which cost the same as a year of college tuition. We compromised, with only greenery in the chapel. But I gave in on a larger reception, where Mother's friends picked up their lemonade (no champagne) at a table groaning beneath a five-foot tall, three-tiered floral arrangement.

Lamar, Bunker, and Caroline, three of Dad's children by Lyda, came to the wedding. So did Franny. She had a homespun look, in her simple white dress with a green, hand-crocheted jacket. At the reception she carried the long-stemmed red rose I'd handed to her as I walked down the aisle.

I hadn't seen Franny for two years, since my Hockaday graduation, although she lived only a few minutes from SMU. Somehow I couldn't bring myself to visit the home where she was taking care of other children. I wanted to preserve her where she'd been ten years earlier: at the very center of my life.

I felt a muddle of sadness and indebtedness when I hugged her at the reception. That was such a meager, fleeting gesture, with a hundred people lined up behind her. As full as the beautiful evening was, at that moment I felt empty. My childhood was over. No future experience could be inserted to make my past more complete.

Cowtown

If I'd been single in the late sixties, I might have jumped into the social movements of the times, for both meaning and companionship. But I wasn't really independent, having walked out of my father's house on the arm of another man.

We are who we are not just because of genetic predisposition or the times in which we live. We're shaped also by those we encounter at just the right split-second. Victor Hugo writes a saintly priest into the story of the escaped Jean Valjean, and a thief is transformed into a godly mayor helping *les misérables* of pre-Revolutionary France. No one can imagine the effect she has on others to whom she offers advice, encouragement, or warning, without even knowing that the moment was ripe. Likewise, I can't take credit for any triumph without appreciating those who supported, cajoled, or inspired me at a pivotal juncture.

Mark was my escort at the crossroad as I decided, though the youngest of Dad's children, to be the first to move away from Dallas—to another town, then another state, then another continent. I never completely abandoned my rural and religious roots, but I was delighted to escape what I perceived as the charm and charade of life as a "steel magnolia"—the familiar southern belle who drapes delicate manners over her immutable core.

When we moved to Fort Worth, an hour from Dallas, my new husband was in seminary. There my life as Swanee Meeks was punctuated with lessons about privilege and class. Although the right-wing takeover of the Southern Baptist denomination had already been launched at First Baptist Dallas, it would be several years before moderate congregations felt forced to conform or withdraw. Having left fundamentalism behind, Mark and I found a spiritual home at the more liberal Broadway Baptist Church, refreshingly upfront compared to our upbringing.

I had a modicum of anonymity, which was a mixed blessing when we visited Sunday school at our new church. We went into a classroom with about fourteen "young marrieds." The teacher asked for anyone sitting in the circle to create a modern setting for Jesus's "parable of the rich young ruler." We all opened our Bibles and read the passage from Matthew 19: "A wealthy man came to Jesus and asked him how he could have eternal life . . ." After a few minutes of creative thinking, someone in our group offered: "H. L. Hunt came to Jesus and said 'I want to follow you.' Jesus said, 'Sell all your oil wells and give the money to the poor.' Old Man Hunt's eyes got big, then he walked away, frustrated." Blood rushed to my cheeks; however anonymous, I hated being a bit player in that story. And I wondered what effect it had on Mark, having my family's wealth shoved into his face.

White flight to the suburbs had left the beautiful downtown church surrounded by impoverished citizens. I not only joined the choir but also put together a weekly music club for inner-city kids. Mark was committed to social justice, not just theoretically but in everyday action. He and I informally adopted a family on welfare, headed by an obese, mentally retarded woman with six children. We spent time in their chaotic home, getting to know the kids and helping with a variety of needs. The family had no car, so we drove them out of the state for excursions, to give the kids a sense of the larger world.

Standing in line with the mother at a grocery store, helping her count out food stamps, I tried gently advising, "Why don't we replace some of the potato chips and Cokes with something more nutritious, like fruit?"

"I can't do that," she said. "My kids go through that fruit as fast as I can buy it." I felt appalled, then ashamed. Of myself, not her. I'd been seeing this family through the lens of privilege. But fretting about vitamin content wasn't in the index of their survival handbook.

The push-pull of money is an issue in every family—just in different forms. Mark and I were trying to be financially independent from my father, and the first two years we were married, we received no cash support, just the use of a gas charge card. That was a great help, since almost every weekend we drove to Dallas to see our parents. Fortunately, it was an hour's drive from one world to the other; it took that long for me to gear up or gear down.

More and more, I was determined to be a risk taker, but as a daughter of vast wealth I had neither the danger nor the privilege of real risk. I could walk a tightrope, pretending I was brave, but I always had a thick, wall-to-wall safety net. In a way I regretted that protection, but only a spoiled brat would complain. Poor little rich girl, indeed.

Class was emerging as a nettlesome problem between Mark and me. I had memories of my family's love and laughter, but he didn't have many happy associations with Mt. Vernon, especially since he'd been rejected by my mother. Of course after we married, different family members tried to make him feel comfortable, but their efforts were often stymied. One Christmas we invited the Meeks family over for gifts. Mark opened a robust red toolbox from my mother and father. Then he opened another package: a smaller, gray version from his parents. "That will be perfect for our car," I offered, in a cheery voice. But I knew Mark was hurt for his parents.

Over the years, I had no way to measure the effect of our family wealth on him, or on us as a couple, but I imagine that for every gift from my parents, my marriage paid a price.

Mark's and my first home was a duplex off Seminary Drive. Rent was $60 a month. Formerly used as military housing during the Second World War, it was a far cry from the excesses of Mt. Vernon. Monotonous rows of gray structures exactly like ours lay exposed on a flat stretch of ground. I dubbed our neighborhood "Sparse Forest Estates," since no pesky trees blocked the view of wide-sky Texas sunsets. Nor did we have to worry about lawn care, since, water as we might, the grass burned up in the summer.

Mark and I were able students. But I also relished setting up house, making tables out of piles of books for guests whom I relegated to the floor and then served with our fancy wedding gifts: dainty Bavarian china and Gorham silver. In the backyard was a communal laundry, where I hauled a big, red plastic basket, brimming with damp sheets, jeans, and plaid shirts. Like every other seminary wife, I hung our underwear on the long clotheslines we shared with the other couples.

Though he was a full-time student, Mark had two jobs: nighttime janitor at the children's hospital and salesman at Sears. My colorblind husband was advising unwary customers about which tie worked with which shirt. (Trade secret.) Given classes and jobs, we didn't see a lot of each other. Still, my first overnight away from Mark felt traumatic. I don't remember the circumstances, but I was at Mt. Vernon without a car. As evening wore on, I became anxious without him, so much so that Mom offered to drive me to Fort Worth. I hesitated and then said no, since Mark would be pushing the floor polisher at the hospital anyway. But I was remarkably miserable. Back in Fort Worth the next day, I caught from a comment Mark made to someone else that he hadn't gone to work at all the night before. I looked at him, puzzled, but he offered no explanation.

It seems now like such a small exchange, but at the time I was hurt by his distance. I was also afraid to press. I didn't want to seem controlling, and I wasn't sure I could handle the answer. In fact, I never found out what he did that night.

Despite my self-doubts, those two years were a relatively sunny period in my life. I loved playing homemaker—gathering wild, tart muscadine grapes from the roadside to make our own jelly; setting my home-stitched kitchen curtain on fire in an attempt at bananas flambé when Ray and Nancy Ann visited. I didn't mind that we budgeted down to the penny, with $40 a month for groceries, enough for meat once a week. Brimming with a newlywed's idealism, I insisted on contributing to our joint money jar and found a job as a clerk in the children's section of a department store. But by the last day of the two-week training, the novelty had worn off, and I dropped out. (I still feel guilty for whatever the store spent training me.) Instead, I took up teaching piano in our home, at $10 a lesson.

I rode my bike a few miles to Texas Christian University to complete my junior and senior years. Dallasites called Fort Worth "cowtown," and even university mascots betrayed the discrepancy. Who wouldn't rally around an SMU mustang rather than a TCU horned frog? Still, I was at home in the philosophy department, where a Swedish-American professor told boyhood stories of standing on street corners, preaching fundamentalist Lutheran salvation. Gus Ferre introduced me to the writings of Søren Kierkegaard, who stirred my conscience.

At exactly my age, Kierkegaard had taken a respite from his studies, tormented by questions of identity. "What I really need is to come to terms with myself about what I am to do, not about what I am to know. . . . What counts is to find a truth, which is true for me, to find that idea for which I will live and die." I'd never read someone who spoke my mind so well. The class-consciousness I was feeling in my new life as a Meeks and my disenchantment with fundamentalism were fueled by Kierkegaard's insistence that "to ignore is no escape." From that point on, I vowed, I would look issues head on. In addition to the privileges of Dallas, the tragedies of the world were mine, like it or not. Hungry children on another continent were my children. Mexican emigrants wading across the Rio Grande to find work were risking their lives for me. I was responsible for black women too old and arthritic to lift a vacuum cleaner. The jungle hut hit with napalm was my home.

It wasn't easy to build a life that stretched across the totality demanded by Christian existentialism. While Mark and I were skimping to buy coffee beans, Dad and Mom flew us to New York and surprised us with $200 scalped tickets for a Broadway revival of the 1940s musical *No, No, Nanette.* We groaned thinking of what we could do with $400—almost seven months' rent. For me, this was another moment of family oddity. For Mark, it was the rumble of social injustice.

Back home, around every corner we bumped into signs of our incongruent worlds. Two elderly, wealthy live wires in the Fort Worth social scene adopted us. I imagine they were pleased to have H. L. Hunt's youngest daughter in their circle. I instinctively liked the wife, who told me gleefully that she "collected" people. One evening we were among a large and eclectic array she'd invited to dinner before a new musical, *Man of La Mancha.* "What do you do?" asked the wife of a young dentist, sitting across the table from Mark and me. I introduced us not only as students but also as salesman-janitor and piano teacher. The face of the young woman softened. "Isn't it wonderful that you're here?" she whispered. I smiled, not needing to correct her perception that such an outing would be a rare treat.

Midway through the dinner, a waiter came to replace my teapot. I told him no thanks. "Let him give you some hot water," the housewife coached. "My palette's not that refined," I tossed out. A shadow crossed my new friend's face. "Oh, I didn't mean *that*!" she said quickly, trying to undo any offense. Now that I was an untitled member of hoi polloi, I realized, what would have been eccentricity for a wealthy woman could be perceived as a commoner's gaffe.

During our two years in Fort Worth, I moved frequently between my two worlds. Mother's health was poor; and Dad, in his early eighties, had slowed considerably. He still insisted on constant attention. Mark and I spent hours on the porch in the old, white wicker rocking chairs, looking out across the lawn, listening to Dad reminisce. That gave Mom a break. Dad had mellowed; he rarely barked orders or made cutting remarks. He even occasionally expressed poignant feelings: "I'd give up all this to have Hassie as he used to be, before he got sick."

Sometimes Mark's parents drove over. They were great company for my father. Fred and Dad were both self-educated, and they exchanged stories for hours. This meant that Mom and I could go upstairs, where I would put away endless stacks of gifts she'd purchased and then piled on the floor of her office.

As much as I reached back into my parents' world, I rarely had the sense of their stepping a foot into mine, which was consistent with parenting in those times. I'm positive that my own three children have their versions of times when I've let them down, but I remember with particular pain one Sunday afternoon at Mt. Vernon. To set the scene: Mark and I, trying to educate ourselves, had bought classical record albums for each other, and on one of them was the most beautiful musical piece I'd ever heard. I set a distant goal. For nine months, I was at the keyboard, until at last I had "in my fingers" Chopin's Fantasie Impromptu. My parents were unaware of the hundreds of hours it took for me to master the piece. I simply told Mother I had a surprise for Dad and her.

Mom welcomed Mark and me that afternoon with her usual, bubbly "Hi there, Precious! Hello there, Markie!" At my request, Dad came in from the front porch. I felt excited as the four of us proceeded into the living room. Mom, Dad, and Mark took their seats in the cream-and-gold upholstered chairs I'd pulled around to face the cherry-wood baby grand. I told my parents I'd worked all semester on this gift, then announced the piece, sat down, and adjusted the bench.

The Chopin is a five-minute composition. A few measures into the frenzy of the first section, my mother, who had unthinkingly slipped into hostess mode, left the room. I barreled on, trying not to notice her footsteps behind me as she crossed the foyer and walked down the hall.

After a pause I poured myself into the second section, which was dominated by the lyrical melody that had brought tears to my eyes the first time I heard it. My parents weren't familiar with classical music, but I figured they would recognize the theme as "I'm Always Chasing Rainbows," and I played with every ounce of sensitivity I could muster.

Mother had still not returned when I began the third section, a fiery presto building to a stormy climax, with the romantic slow melody recalled in the bass before the piece resolves into calm.

I never reached the calm. Midway through the third section, my father stood up and cleared his throat. "I've heard enough," he announced as he walked out of the room, passing my mother, who was just then coming from the kitchen, balancing a small silver tray carefully arranged with white linen embroidered cocktail napkins and crystal glasses filled with grape juice.

I stopped playing and closed the keyboard cover. Mark was consoling. Dad was oblivious. Mother was regretful. Everyone was in character.

Actually, our characters were continuing to evolve. A serious conflict had developed between Mark's increasingly liberal beliefs and the year's worth of required fundamentalist courses that he faced at Southwestern Baptist Seminary. After I graduated from TCU, he was eager to transfer to Southern Baptist Theological Seminary—not much difference in name, but a big difference in theological tone. Being at my husband's side was more important to me than choosing my own education path. I was content to trail along, first for a summer in Denver where I took psychology courses while he underwent chaplaincy training, supervised by an effervescent psychiatric nurse named Jessica. Then on to Louisville, where a Baptist could be politically liberal and not ostracized. The move would mean more distance from Dallas, where we no longer thrived. In 1972 we created our new Kentucky home.

As we were trying to figure out where to live, I called Ray. I had almost no sense of the scope of my Dallas wealth or how to access it. No one had explained our family finances to me, and I'd never asked. But I knew Ray was the person I should go to if I needed something.

"A house? That's no problem," he assured me. Ray arranged financing for me to buy a home: two-bedroom, red brick, in a quiet neighborhood with huge trees. My big brother also produced (it seemed out of thin air) a modest monthly allowance, which meant that Mark didn't need to get a side job as he finished his last year of seminary.

That action marked a colossal shift in our circumstances. Having extraordinary privileges can be lonely. There was no one with whom to discuss how, with one phone conversation, I could transform Mark and me from humble students to members of the middle class. I didn't deserve that power or place, and I knew it. Or perhaps a better way to think of it is that every person deserves such a life, but precious few have it.

Although moving from Texas was a big step, I wasn't anywhere close to Kierkegaard's quest of finding a truth for which to live and die. In that pursuit, I decided to take some seminary courses. At registration, the admissions clerk couldn't find my file. Eventually we discovered my application—in Mark's file. I suggested, insisted, and then demanded that I have my own file. And no, she shouldn't list me as studying religious education so that I could teach Sunday school like most women students. I knew Baptists refused to ordain women, but I was studying theology, dammit.

In several classes, including Christian Ethics and Sexuality, I was the only woman. For a presentation, I chose the novels of D. H. Lawrence, musing that his regard for simultaneous orgasm seemed exaggerated. That comment may have been typical counterculture fare at the time, but most Southern Baptists had managed to miss the 1960s. A few years later our professor, Paul Simmons, would be forced out during the crackdown by fundamentalists. At that time, however, political liberalism was alive among faculty and students, the majority of whom supported George McGovern for president.

Even we liberals were woefully inconsistent. As we played bridge with our best friends, Debbie complained that John never helped around the house. "Women's work," he said disdainfully. I thought he was kidding and waited for the smile that never came. Like many others, John was a promising theologian, excellent listener, and worldly thinker. How could one part of his psyche be so out of kilter with the rest?

The lesson wasn't John's ignorance, but the bias regarding women's limitations. Women were spoken of as "girls," just as black men were "boys." Children's grammar books illustrated nouns and verbs with two pictures, a boy with pliers bent over a lamp and a girl reading in a chair, under the lamp. The caption: "Boys make things. Girls use things boys make." Some women bravely identified themselves as "feminist" and took the flak of being on the front lines. I wasn't in the vanguard; I was following far behind women much more resolute than I.

What once seemed radical is eventually woven into society person by person and year by year. Also, publication by publication. When the first regular issue of *Ms*. hit the newsstands in the summer of 1972, the TV network anchor Harry Reasoner challenged, "I'll give it six months before they run out of things to say." They didn't, and I was heartened, knowing that other women were sharing my frustration. I felt more determined than ever to break open the social institutions that were boxing me in.

Nothing during that Kentucky year tore open my own neatly packaged assumptions like the "urban plunge" that I signed up for. Each student would spend twenty-four hours alone in downtown Louisville to get a taste of life on the streets. The organizers debated whether to let a woman participate. After much arguing, I prevailed.

The experience started at midday. I was twenty-two, with long, wavy, blond hair and John Lennon glasses, wearing a green sweatshirt and jeans and, as instructed, carrying nothing but one dollar. For hours I wandered the streets, feeling self-conscious and out of place, with no one to talk to and no justification for walking into a store. By evening I was hungry. I sauntered into a cheap cafe and looked over the menu. I couldn't afford anything, so like the Fort Worth welfare mother whom I'd taken grocery shopping, I bought a candy bar and Coke to take the edge off my hunger. My dollar was gone.

It was dark outside when, back on the streets, I walked by a theater where the rock pianist Leon Russell would be performing. As I stood looking at the poster, a young man in line on the sidewalk asked if I was going in. "I don't have a ticket," I said, "But I wish I did."

My advocate put his arm around my shoulders, took off his baseball cap, and held it out to people we passed as he walked me up and down the line. "My mother needs an abortion," he pleaded. People smiled. Someone dropped in an extra ticket.

In the crowded concert hall, I handed joints from left to right as they were passed among strangers. This was exotic territory for me, but mostly I felt relieved and grateful to have been adopted into the group, no questions asked. At 10 p.m. I was to check in with the seminary adviser. Reluctantly, I left the theater. After a rendezvous with the other students, where I assured our faculty sponsor that I was okay, we scattered again. My next challenge was finding a safe place to spend the night. I roamed the streets looking for a brightly lit space. At the bus station, I self-consciously curled up on an uncomfortable chair and tried to doze. A security guard spotted me. "No sleeping allowed," he said curtly.

"But I . . ."

"No sleeping allowed," he insisted impatiently.

Sitting up, I waited until his back was turned and sneaked behind the concession stand where I wouldn't be seen. The linoleum floor was cold and dirty, but I lay down and tried to sleep. Knowing I wasn't welcome, I couldn't nod off. Outside again, I wandered into the night.

Near the station I found a bar, went in, and sat down at a table. One of the "regulars," a middle-aged black man, had launched into an animated conversation with a young, blond soldier from Fort Knox. The GI bought me a Pepsi. Once again, I belonged. I enthusiastically joined the discussion, which drifted from politics to the meaning of life. Around 3 a.m. the bartender was ready to close.

"Would you like to share a motel room with me?" the soldier said. "I promise, nothing will happen."

Declining, I went out yet again, walking the streets, thanking God it wasn't raining, and waiting impatiently for the first light of morning. How many people do this every day, I wondered. With daybreak, I found a triangle of grass surrounded by rush hour traffic. In the safety of a totally public space, with cars and busses whizzing by, I lay down and went to sleep.

For those twenty-four hours I was cold, hungry, nervous, and lonely; but that was one of my most profound experiences ever. In one day, on one dollar, my life had doubled in scope.

While my world was widening, my husband's was narrowing. Our lives had intersected for a moment, but they were diverging. Forever an extrovert, I was becoming more consistently self-confident. Despite Mark's natural kindness, strong conscience, and sharp intellect, he was becoming more withdrawn. He felt pushed by me and read my efforts to get help for us as my wanting to change him. I felt that he was trying to avoid dealing with reality. Only two years into our marriage, we were in trouble.

At church, we'd listened to our pastor exhort, "Choose your pain: the pain of loving or the pain of not loving." Soon that preacher left his wife of many years. I wondered if love had to be so painful. Penning emotional diary entries and composing pathos-filled poems, I searched for a way to rekindle the flame between Mark and me. One day at seminary, a professor of pastoral care asked us to come by his office. Perhaps he'd noticed that in the cafeteria I was usually with a group, laughing and carrying forth, while Mark sat far apart, his head buried in a book. "How are you two doing?" the professor asked.

"Doin' fine," Mark said.

Hearing his response, my spirit sank. "We're far from fine," I muttered.

The professor probed a bit, then concluded, "Let me know if I can help." But we left without answers.

Best-sellers of the time added to our confusion. *Situation Ethics: The New Morality* urged a reexamination of legalistic norms that preclude loving actions. And *Open Marriage* introduced the notion of healthy romantic forays that defied the moral strictures we associated with our parents' age, repressed as we were sure it was. I knew how I *didn't* want to be: bound by convention. It was harder to figure out how I *did* want to be.

Searching, I signed up for a Quaker weekend retreat dealing with sexuality in contemporary society. I listened to a range of panelists — those in traditional unions, some with romances outside their marriages, and gay people in committed relationships or not.

Meanwhile, my body had begun to scream. Small blisters developed on my left hand, around my wedding ring. I repeatedly felt sick at the doorway coming home. The idea of seeing a psychiatrist was foreign to my upbringing. But going to church was not. So I made an appointment with a kind pastoral counselor who'd led a group of us seminary students in a ministry to elderly shut-ins. He was a man of extraordinary depth, well-educated, trusted. He was not only a respected church leader who held the hands of the dying. He was also a wonderfully empathetic listener.

Looking back three decades at myself, barely out of college and in an unfamiliar setting, it's obvious how emotionally vulnerable I was. After a few sessions of talking privately with him, I felt as if I'd lifted the lid off a poisoned well. I began to count the hours before I'd be walking in through the back of the church, knocking on his door, then sitting in a chair in his dark paneled private office, pouring out my desolation. His pale blue eyes welled with tears as I wept. He helped me put words to the heart-ripping pain that I felt over my father. Then he helped me see how that longing fueled my fears about my marriage. I'll always be grateful for that confessional space, where I finally felt known.

One day the pastoral counselor made an awkward admission. He wished he could hold my hand.

"Then why don't you?" I asked. I was, after all, my mother's daughter, externally bubbly, internally needy. For hours we sat together, our fingers intertwined, as I continued to energetically divulge one story after another, trying to deconstruct the hurt so that I could reconstruct the whole. Soon my counselor, troubled about his own marriage, was seeking comfort from me. We were becoming enmeshed. He adopted a pet name for me: Heidi, a reminder of the resilient internal strength of an orphaned mountain girl. We met several times a week and even dared hold hands in public, marching in an anti-Vietnam demonstration downtown. On my twenty-third birthday, he whispered with satisfaction that he'd never again be twice my age. We never did more than kiss, but it was consummate drama.

My Louisville love story ended with a sudden jolt when his wife discovered that trust had evolved into tryst. Instead of healing, the relationship was a stinging disappointment. Looking back, I realize how that failure is as much a part of me as any grand success. It was one of those hard life lessons that crash unceremoniously into my carefully constructed self-image of competence and kindness. At my best, I've learned from such incongruity, from those awful moments when I've said or done something I thought I was beyond. More often I suppose I operate in self-deception, unable to admit that I don't live up to my own standards—forget the standards of critics.

From a distance, the pastoral counselor and I were one more rendition of the tired duet that has entertained psychologists for decades: my search for a good father, his midlife crisis. But I was also betraying my new feminist ideals, by finding an older man to lean on.

His violation was even more serious. He breached fundamental professional ethics as a minister sliding into romantic territory with a needy parishioner. But I was too caught up in what felt good to realize how wrong his advances were.

With a heavy conscience, I confessed to Mark that the counselor and I loved each other.

"I trust you both," was my husband's response.

I appreciated his confidence, but I also realized he didn't want to fight for me. Mother, on the other hand, dissolved into tears of concern. She vowed that she would live on her knees, holding me in her prayers. Mom was a great confidante for many, but I shouldn't have gone to her with a situation so close to her own. Word was immediately out among her sister and nieces, to whom she turned for prayer support.

I felt guilty about taking emotional energy away from my marriage. And I felt guilty about whatever I did that led my counselor into a crisis with his wife. Both reactions, however, strike me now as a woman's response. After all, we apologize when it rains at picnics.

Having grown up pained by others' complicated romances, I also worried that I was following in my parents' wandering steps. But I'd felt thrilled and fulfilled, and when the relationship broke apart I grieved for months. I wasn't good at goodbye.

Shortly thereafter Mark graduated, and it was time to leave Kentucky. In a surprising and supportive gesture, my family flew to Louisville for the occasion. Mark and I painted the house, planted a new tree in the front yard, and prepared a sumptuous feast to welcome them and introduce them to our best friends, students, and professors. I played my new harp, and we all sang "Amazing Grace." Mom was beaming and sweet. Dad handed out anticommunist leaflets. Mark and Helen reconnected. Ray and June wished us well as we embarked on our next adventure.

Weep No More, My Lady

"Ich hab mein Hertz in Heidelberg verloren," crooned a popular singer. "I lost my heart in Heidelberg." With great luck, Mark had come across a job announcement on a seminary bulletin board about a church in need of a Baptist pastor—not in the conservative hinterlands of rural Arkansas or Mississippi, but in a medieval city of enchanted charm in the center of West Germany. I was thrilled.

One year might have been an excellent educational experience. But we stayed four, long enough for me to develop an identity truly separate from Dallas. We were removed from the expectations of family and the need to conform to American society. In postwar Germany, stark Bauhaus construction rose obtrusively in front of quiet vineyards and cobblestone roads. I lived a similar mosaic as a bold preacher's wife, critical student, impromptu homemaker, but ever and always a soft southern soul.

I thought that as Swanee Meeks, I'd at least be anonymous. Far away from Texas, I'd be spared my embarrassment in Fort Worth, hearing my father talked about with either reverence or disdain. But in the car leaving the Frankfurt airport, the church deacon who met our plane told a story about his friend Randy in Kerrville, Texas. "I think my sister June knows him," I said, nonchalantly.

"June *Hunt*? Is your sister June *Hunt*?"

"Yes," I said, groaning inside. I should have realized that if a Texan knew a Hunt, he'd let that claim to fame be known far and wide. No matter what, my parentage was part of me. That was a lesson I needed to learn time and again. Nevertheless, life in Heidelberg was in many ways idyllic, played out against a backdrop of centuries-old castles bedecked with coats of arms. Every day, Mark spent hours reflecting as he walked our white sled dog, Dostoyevsky, through the woods. Evenings, we shared wiener schnitzel with friends at the lively Red Ox, crowded with students who carved their names on heavy wooden tables.

Mark, at twenty-eight, was the pastor of Grace Baptist Church. Our congregation was English-speaking: American military, Canadian opera singers, New Zealander physicists, American and British students living abroad. As my husband prepared his sermon each week, I ran off church programs on a mimeograph machine. He was an articulate, talented preacher, and I was proud of him. I threw myself into the role of minister's wife, playing my harp, guitar, or piano for services and teaching a Sunday school class entitled "Controversial Issues in Contemporary Society."

In four years we were invited only twice into a German home. That social distance was reinforced by grammar. Only near the end of our stay was I permitted to use the first name and familiar form of "you" with the seventy-year-old woman who cleaned our house twice a week. She and I celebrated by drinking a traditional toast with interlocked elbows.

My years in choirs paid off when I auditioned for the large community Bach Chor. The ebullient director proclaimed with great enthusiasm (if not linguistic acumen), "You vill become a letter from me!" ("bekommen" being the unlikely German for "receive"). The letter arrived, and I did become . . . a member of not only the large chorus but also his élite Heidelberger Kantorei. That group of about twenty was mostly lawyers and doctors; in Germany, singing was serious business.

The Kantorei performed Baroque a cappella works in churches across Germany. I found those concerts intensely spiritual as I delved into an interpretation of the masters—on their own turf and on their own terms. Consequently, I knew the German for "praise" and "sin" before "plays" or "grin."

I loved that even in the early 1970s, Mark and I shared the home-making, including shopping, which was a daily ritual. Bread from the baker, cheese from a stall, sausage from the butcher, flowers from a cart. Life was simple. But in other ways it seemed complex, as I ferried women's lib across the ocean.

At a European Baptist convention in Interlaken, Switzerland, each minister couple in the huge auditorium came up to the microphone for introductions. I'm John Doe, the minister would say, pastor of Any-where Baptist Church. And this is my wife. "My wife" nodded her head obediently and followed her man offstage. I rolled my eyes at Mark, who was sitting next to Greg and DeeLee Burk, old friends and our counterparts at the church in Mannheim, Germany. DeeLee and I were both working hard with our congregations, but we prickled at the assumption that we were appendages of the pastor.

When our turn came at the podium, Mark and I broke ranks. "I'm Mark Meeks at Grace Baptist Church in Heidelberg," he said, and moved aside.

I stepped up to the mike. "I'm Swanee Meeks, and I'm working as a music therapist on the U.S. Army base." We'd cracked open the door. Now a hurricane blew through.

"I'm Greg Burk . . . and my wife can speak for herself."

"I'm DeeLee Burk," she declared, "and I teach at the high school in Heidelberg, where I've been for three years. My courses are English and social studies, and I feel I've been able to have a meaningful impact in the lives of kids in transient military families who move in and out. It's a real pleasure to be here with you today."

The members of the audience shifted uncomfortably in their seats. I loved it.

Following the plenary service were breakout groups. I'd signed up to facilitate a discussion entitled "Women's Changing Roles in Church and Society." At twenty-four, I found this an exciting leadership mo-ment. One of my first. I took for granted that Mark would be part of the group, and throughout the hour I kept waiting for him to come in. He didn't. It seemed Mark wasn't eager to be part of my congregation.

As my life was opening before me, my father's life was closing. Dad's trip to Mark's graduation in Louisville was the last time I saw him up and about. In his eighties, he continued to haunt his office six days a week and worked on Sundays at home. But in the fall of his eighty-sixth year, he went to the hospital directly from Hunt Oil Company. He never came home. Colon cancer had spread to his liver.

I flew back twice as he was dying, the first time when the diagnosis was made, the second a few weeks later when I received a call saying he'd probably not make it through the night because of an infection. The doctors gave him a massive dose of antibiotics. When I arrived from the airport, I was told that "thank God" the crisis was averted.

I found Dad twisting restlessly on his hospital bed, fighting the tubes attached to his body. In addition to the family stress, I was frustrated by the hospital's seemingly mindless preoccupation with medical procedures and disregard for death with dignity. I was just a visitor, an outsider to my family, having moved away. My role was limited. But as Dad thrashed and turned, I began to sing for him, old songs from Helen's and my childhood performances. Dad would become completely still, but only as long as I was singing. Over the next days, I spent tender hours at the hospital, serenading my father—one of the few times in my life I felt useful to him in a direct way. I wasn't doing his bidding for some off-the-wall political effort. Just offering a dose of human kindness. As days stretched on, Dad lapsed further from consciousness. The doctors couldn't say how many days he would live. In fact, they seemed determined to stretch his dying out as long as possible.

After weeks in Dallas, I decided to resume my life in Germany until my father's funeral. With that decision, I was opting never to see him again. Before I left his hospital room for the last time, I leaned over his bed. This was my opportunity. Now I could finally say words that others might normally say to fathers—words I couldn't say before because I knew he would ruin the moment:

"You know, Dad, I remember when you asked me to come one Saturday to the Texas State Fair to hand out leaflets. I developed a migraine, and you saw me lying in a massage chair at the Jacuzzi exhibit nearby. Then on Monday, a big truck pulled up to our tiny Fort Worth duplex, delivering a huge recliner just like the one that had helped with my headache. That was an important moment, because I came to understand that you've done your best. But you know, the truth is, we haven't had much of a relationship. I guess we've both made mistakes. I'm sorry for my part, and I hope you'll forgive me. You've not been much of a father, but maybe you didn't know how to be. So I forgive you."

That was the most satisfying "conversation" we ever had. Dad lay on his bed, unable to respond. I could say whatever I wanted, pretending he could not only hear, but also comprehend. He said nothing about the pinko menace or Hassie being well or my mother being crazy. Maybe, just maybe, if he could have spoken, he would have said all the things I'd been waiting to hear for twenty-four years. In my magical thinking, I could pretend that my walking out of his hospital room had ended forever my chance for the father-daughter bond I'd longed for all my life. It hurt less, I think, for me to end our relationship by going back to Heidelberg. At least my father couldn't reject me one more time.

November 29, 1974. A news commentator flippantly remarked, "Today two impossibilities happened: the Baylor football team won a place in the Cotton Bowl, and H. L. Hunt died." But Dad was, and still is, revered by many at the company, who nonetheless had their own stories of his idiosyncrasies.

In Dallas once again, I walked into the First Baptist Church parlor across the street from the sanctuary. Scores of us had gathered from his three families, the fullest array ever. We smiled tensely as we shook hands, then stood around trying to make small talk. Eventually it was time for the service. The family lined up to move across the street. Mother led the entourage, with June on her right, Ray on her left, past a dozen photographers and TV crewmen.

The youngest, I moved to the back of the group as we entered the huge auditorium, which was packed with employees, church members, family friends, and the curious. A section was reserved for family in the front, but as Dad's many children and *their* children filed in, the pews filled. For a moment I was left standing in the aisle. My half-brother Lamar whispered, "Make room for Swanee." I've always loved him for that.

One family member had entered before we did. That was Hassie. A reporter wrote that the congregation gasped when a man who looked almost identical to my father walked in by a side door, approached the casket, and raised his arm. Instead of striking he saluted, and then, with his nurse, slowly made his way to a pew for the rest of the service.

The organist stopped playing. A beloved employee gave an oration about the long shadow that Dad had cast. The soprano sang a high C.

Then Dr. Criswell came up to the pulpit, where he eulogized H. L. Hunt as "the good father." I was sitting among children and grandchildren who'd grown up not knowing who their real father was, or reeling from the discovery that he had other families, or believing that he didn't really know them. The absurdity was harsh.

At Mt. Vernon, family and friends streamed in for post-funeral greetings. A young man approached Helen and me. "I wanted to meet you. I'm Helen's son," he said.

I paused, confused, and then did the math. His mother must have been the half-sister we'd never met, who'd died in a plane crash when I was fourteen and my sister fifteen. "Thanks for coming," I said, putting out my hand.

But Helen stared at him blankly, as if hearing for the first time that she was only one of my father's two Helens. Suddenly her composure melted. She turned and ran, sobbing, up the stairs. In that split-second, seeing the raw suffering on her contorted face, I realized how we'd become accustomed to defending ourselves from painful realities. And I realized the extent of our father's oblivious unkindness.

Lost in the Wood

After a week in Dallas, I returned to Heidelberg, where once more I shifted into student gear, learning German at one of the oldest universities in Europe and signing up for Russian through a community program. I'd become interested in psychotherapy, so I drove two nights a week to the U.S. Air Force base near Frankfurt to complete a master's in counseling psychology through an extension program of Ball State

University in Muncie, Indiana. One evening, my professor asked for a volunteer to role-play. I agreed to be the client in a counseling situation, in love with my therapist. I blushed afterward at the aplomb with which I performed. The teacher handled the simulation masterfully, as the supposed therapist thanking me for the great compliment, saying how warm it made him feel, but explaining why a romance couldn't work. I was amazed at my sense of self-worth, even as he was saying no.

I wish my Kentucky counselor had learned that part. I'd looked for help and found more hurt. Now my marriage to the man of my prayers had gone up in smoke. Mark was rarely unkind to me, but shallow passivity is deadening. I stayed up all night sometimes, thinking, What can I do to win him back? I never reached the point of blaming him but would always turn on myself. Maybe I was insensitive. Maybe I talked too much. Maybe losing weight would help—I'd been chunky for years, but now I'd gained two dress sizes. Of course my weight was just a sign of something far deeper. I was yearning for love, impatient with societal expectations, and determined not to let life just blow by.

Even so, I wanted to strengthen our marriage, not leave it. I frequently slipped into cathedrals to remind God that He had, after all, created a most imperfect world. In one ancient stone church after another, I sat alone for hours on empty wooden pews, trying to sort through the conundrums of my life. I remembered what I'd learned from Franny, and always lit a votive candle to carry my petition heavenward.

One gray wintry day, sitting in the splendid dimness of Strasbourg Cathedral, I stared at the long white taper I'd pushed into a sandy base below a sad-eyed Mary, who gazed down on me with solace. For half an hour, footsteps of a few tourists were the only sound as I silently prayed, wiping away tears. Then an elderly janitor in a deep blue smock shuffled over to the candle stand. Tidying up, he unceremoniously turned my candle upside down and snuffed it in the sand. "So that's how it is," I thought.

Young adulthood was to be a thrilling, distressing age. I was wise and foolish beyond my years—wise enough to quest, but sometimes foolish in my search. I'm hesitant now, in my relatively conservative middle years, to put words to my naïve desire for closeness. I'm sure that shrewd detractors or dull admirers can take a moment that's precious and make it ugly or, worse, mundane. But my mistakes, and I made many, were never wanton. They drew from the same source, the same longing for connection that in later years compelled me to help others. My future was shaped as I learned the rough-and-tumble lessons of love, not just for myself or another, but for people I'll never know by name.

From that time I learned that even as happiness is never unalloyed, pain rarely travels unaccompanied by joy. One friendship during my Heidelberg years was so abundant that it spilled over into the hollow of disappointment left by my marriage. Joe Maw taught drama at the U.S. Army high school. I met him when he was adding his energetic tenor to the Army chapel production of Menotti's *Amahl and the Night Visitors*. The first night I showed up to join the chorus, he and I ended the evening standing on a street corner in a lazy-flake snow, caroling in the dark for all of sleepy Heidelberg.

A few days later, I invited myself along on a New Year's trip to Paris that he was planning. Mark said it was fine with him. Joe would visit his friends, I would see the city, and we'd go to a party. The drive was enchanted, along roadways lined with glimmering iced trees. The two of us crooned one tune after another, with glorious harmony, as the kilometers rolled by. We knew all the same hymns; Joe had been raised by missionary parents in Congo. But he had an Ivy League education, and we could talk about any subject under the low French sun. I was in heaven.

In Paris, Joe greeted his friends, Copper and Rob, as I moved into my $7 room at the nearby Hotel Minerve. I walked the streets, drinking in the bristling bustle of the Left Bank. Honking horns crowded the air as I stood staring at honey-dripping North African pastries the likes of which Dallas had never seen. A few hours later, back in my tiny hotel room, I heard Joe's knock. I was dressed and ready for the party. He came into my room and, with a worried look, shut the door behind him, saying we needed to talk. "I should have told you, but I didn't know how," he stammered. "Copper and Rob are homosexual. So am I. This isn't the kind of party you think."

"Are you saying you don't want me to go?" I asked.

He looked a bit startled. "Well, no, but you'd probably be the only woman there."

I took a deep breath. "I get it. Well, let's go."

Joe was right. It wasn't the kind of party I'd expected. Neither was our relationship. When I returned from Paris, I told Mark about the whole trip. He had no aversion to homosexuality, and he liked Joe. He didn't seem to mind that the bond between us was so strong. For the most part, Joe and I were spared the man-woman power struggle, and free to love each other at a level not limited by physicality. But like all things untested, our relationship was unpredictable, dangerous. A gay man, a married woman, both fundamentalist-bred. But the risk was well worth it, for in Joe's eyes I saw my best reflected. As we talked, I could embrace my worst.

We shared favorite poems, read each other's diaries, told secrets. Joe made me want to dance—literally. For each of us as kids, dancing had been taboo as a perilous pathway to carnal knowledge. In clubs across Europe we made up for lost time, creating new steps, laughing, gesturing, twisting, and twirling. Even in our most glorious moments on a sun-drenched Greek island or in the recklessly vibrant tulip gardens of Holland, we knew our friendship would be strained when we returned to our regular lives. Joe's difficulty would be explaining me to the men in his life. My difficulty would be explaining Joe to the men in my life. But those worries didn't prevent us from trading off at the piano, bringing in friends to sing with us at the top of our lungs: "Try to Remember," "Younger than Springtime." I learned by heart Edith Piaf's *"Je Ne Regrette Rien."* Like the husky-voiced chanteuse, I would regret nothing.

From time to time the deacons of the church fretted to learn that Joe and I were off on yet another jaunt. But I figured that their ecclesiastical responsibilities didn't include granting me permission to be with my friend. They would hardly have been placated had Mark informed them that Joe was gay. In my absence one Sunday night, Mark responded to their worries with a sermon describing himself and me as the sun and the moon, in individual orbits. If he could accept Joe, I rationalized, that should be enough. But it wasn't lost on me that he offered no resistance to my leaving town with another man. Was he relieved that I'd be away? I wondered.

I discovered that Joe, Mark, and I weren't the only factors in our equation when I came across exorbitant telephone bills for Mark's calls to a close friend of mine. He was indeed head over heels in love, but not with me. Now his frosty distance made sense. Seeing his anguish when I confronted him, I offered him a divorce. Instead he found an American psychiatrist living in Heidelberg, Curt Judd, to help him sort through his choices.

After several sessions, Mark announced that Dr. Judd wanted to meet with me as well. I walked up to his second-floor office, on a small side-street near the river. A tall bouquet of flowers stood in a vase in the waiting room, offering a moment of silent grace to anxious patients. When the doctor appeared, I was surprised by his Hollywood hand-some looks: collar-length auburn hair that matched his eyes, a turtle-neck sweater and jeans, and platform-heeled boots. He led me into his office and offered me a place on his sofa, with the obligatory box of tissues nearby.

I poured out my concerns about our marriage to Dr. Judd, who was lounging in a cocoa-brown leather chair. At the end of the appoint-ment, he opined that Mark and I needed several years of therapy, sev-eral times a week. Mark should come alone and for group sessions, and I needed separate appointments. I was alarmed by his grave as-sessment, but what was most important was that my husband get the help he needed.

During my second appointment, I was completely taken off guard when Dr. Judd asked bluntly, "Would you like to be my lover?"

I managed to quip: "Not if I'm paying." After that stunning breach of professional ethics, I didn't pursue therapy with Dr. Judd. But in the coming year, Mark expressed no objection to having Curt come over late in the evening to sit on the sofa, talking with me. As soon as Curt arrived, my husband would go off to bed to read.

Curt's attachment to me waxed hot and cold. He was an inveter-ate liar, and our relationship was riddled with unexplained, unneces-sary disappointments. I passed long hours of the dark northern winter waiting for him in my candle-lit living room, reading classics like *Tess of the D'Urbervilles* and the poetry of Gerard Manley Hopkins, with the lyrics of Joni Mitchell and Neil Diamond working their 1970s magic. Some people have a power, a charisma, that can draw others to them as if they're on a leash. I churned inside, waiting for the faint rumble of Curt's midnight blue Mercedes pulling up to the curb, the creak of our wooden gate, and his heavy step on the grate outside the door. He seemed attracted to me, but that thrill had a steep cost. I developed debilitating migraine headaches. Curt would bring an injection that had me floating above the pain within seconds.

A couple of months after he and I met, Curt's wife, Ingeborg, called and asked me to meet. I walked an hour up the road past the medieval monastery where Benedictine monks sang vespers, tended their apple orchards, and sold us still-warm unpasteurized milk. As I crossed the yellow-blanketed meadow beyond, I rehearsed what I would say to Inge about the time her husband was spending with me. The walk through the forest, along the fern-lined Philosopher's Way, was calming. Eventually I crossed the ancient bridge over the Neckar River and made my way to the pedestrian mall running through the center of the Altstadt—the old town.

Inge was waiting for me at a pastry shop. We sat at a small table, taking each other in, as marzipan animal figures stared at us through the glass display cases. She described her husband's drug addiction and how, when she'd tried to shake her own habit, she would wake in the morning and find a fix and syringe next to her bed.

Inge also warned me that he was attracted to women of note. I winced when she said he had described me to her as "H. L. Hunt's daughter," with the same relish she'd heard in his voice when he introduced her to others as an Olympic diver. I believed everything Inge told me, but I was too enmeshed with Curt to pull away. She understood, and before she left the café she gave me a small silver charm: a dog with a butterfly on its nose.

The whole scene felt as surreal as that fanciful butterfly landing. But it was real. All too real, I discovered one day, when Dr. Judd made his intentions clear. "I'd like us to work together. I'd like you to fund my clinic."

"I don't have that kind of money," I stuttered.

"Then you should ask Ray," he pushed.

"No. I'm not going to let my wealth complicate our relationship," I insisted, aware even then that our relationship was probably over. Soon after, I found myself stranded after a late-night class at the air force base, an hour up the highway. Rain was pelting down as I stood in a phone booth, calling Curt at home to ask if he would pick me up. He said he was too tired. I hung up and began to cry, then flagged down a stranger for a lift to the train station. The other passengers in the train compartment averted their eyes as tears streamed down my face, kilometer after kilometer.

That was one of the last times we spoke. Like my futile relationship with the pastoral counselor in Louisville, this botched liaison was a powerfully instructive experience, but only later. I sank into a severe depression that lasted weeks. I've never again fallen into such despair, but having had the experience once has given me empathy for those who battle the demon of depression.

In my melancholy, it seemed that at twenty-four I was seeing clearly for the first time, and everything that once gave me meaning was shallow. I was convinced that all existence was a sham, an insipid pretense. My attention became funneled inward. Intellect was no help, and nothing anyone said was useful. As I peeled back outer layers of aspirations and order, all I found was a mushy, rotten core.

Despairing one night while Mark was out, I searched for a bottle of pills to end my life. I was furious that Mark had hidden them and confronted him angrily when he returned home. He opened the drawer. They were where they'd always been—and where I'd looked an hour earlier. The part of my mind that wanted me to live had prevailed.

The depression went on for weeks until, at a Gestalt therapy conference in Switzerland, I volunteered for a training demonstration. The teaching therapist had me bid farewell to my father in an imaginary casket. Looking back, I realize that my disillusionment with Curt had elicited a much deeper sadness about my relationship with my father. That dramatic exercise produced an extraordinary moment of healing, and my depression lifted.

But I found no such closure with Curt. One day, my heart caught in my throat when I saw his convertible parked in front of our church, which he'd never visited before. I entered the sanctuary and looked around. He wasn't there. Turns out he'd loaned his car to one of my closest friends, a woman he'd met through me. Next I knew, they were off for a week in the Virgin Islands. How fitting.

It was time to get on with my life. Impressed by the power of my experience at the conference, I signed up for a four-week summer session in transactional analysis and Gestalt therapy in California. We trainees sat facing an empty chair, addressing our thoughts to an imaginary friend or foe. Then we switched positions, answering as the other person. The insights stunned me, as one-dimensional characters assumed full form. I was still relieved from my depression, but I wanted more conversations with Dad. As I played his part, he was not only a tyrant. He also felt inadequate in relationships and was frustrated because he couldn't make the world fit his conception of right. I knew because he told me. Or *I* told me.

The next day, I carried the exercise further. I imagined Curt in the empty chair and bombarded him with my disappointment. Then I went off by myself, addressed an envelope, and wrote him an angry letter. It felt cleansing to put the words on paper. I left the letter in my bedroom to reread when I was cooler. The next day I searched but couldn't find the envelope. I never found out if it was thrown away or mailed.

Summer drew to a close. I returned to Heidelberg and began leading women's consciousness-raising groups on the U.S. Army base. One afternoon our pastor colleague Greg Burk telephoned. He'd just learned that Curt had died of an overdose. I held the phone, staring out our plate-glass window overlooking the river, speechless.

Late the next night, Inge called. She'd found Curt's journal and thought I should see it. Would I come over? I sat on her floor, reading page after page that traced our relationship, first extolling my warmth, later cursing my demands. Inge's friend Gert, a man I'd never met, sat with us in the dimly lit room. I began to heave with sobs, wallowing in a confused pulp of anger and self-pity. I don't know why, but Gert suddenly slapped me across the face, hard. Blood whirled through my veins as the slap pulled me back into the room. A few minutes later, I mumbled my thanks to Gert, embraced Inge, and left.

Over the next few days, Inge called me with two last requests. We agreed that Mark would deliver the memorial service. And as a favor to Curt's mother, I would sing her favorite hymn: "God Be with You Till We Meet Again."

Home at Last

Mark and I rounded off four years in Western Europe, taking the eastward route home. I did the planning for the ambitious three-month backpacking trip, which included climbing in the Tatras of Czechoslovakia, crossing Hungary on horseback, fourteen days and nights on the Trans-Siberian Express, and hiking in a Japanese national park. Midway through, for respite from communist privation, we dropped into Vienna, a bit of the Free World surrounded on three sides by Eastern Europe.

Several weeks with a group from the Sierra Club provided my first exposure to Yugoslavia, a country of relative prosperity in the communist world. Despite his harshly autocratic style, Marshall Tito, leader of the Nazi-resisting Partisans, was being supported by the United States because he had thumbed his nose at the Soviets. Our guide joked, "This country has seven neighbors, six republics, five languages, four religions, three rail systems, two alphabets, and one wish: that the Russians will never come here." Urban Yugoslavs were highly educated and had sophisticated artistic taste. The rural people we encountered were friendly, with passions watered by the national brew, slibovic, which burned its way down gullets into guts. The society was clearly much more open than the rest of Eastern Europe. In Belgrade I was surprised to find an issue of *Time* magazine for sale, then even more surprised that it had an article about Ray's business ventures, entitled, aptly, "The Nice Hunt."

I had worked hard to get in shape for the mountain hiking portions of our trip, which I hoped would mean a lot to Mark. In the Julian Alps of Slovenia, I strained as I gripped steel cables, pulling my heavy body up steep, rocky trails that connected picturesque huts for hikers. Farther south, we passed colorful gypsies whose pots and pans were hung from the wooden saddles of their horses. Our road wound into the Dumitor Alps of Montenegro, from where we could see the mountains of Albania. Mark climbed the glacial-carved bowl above timberline, while I stayed at the base camp, spinning out thoughts in a journal.

As I sat by a stream, a tall woman dressed in black appeared on the bank above. A little girl, around three, was tucked in the folds of her skirt. The woman motioned to me. Curious, I followed her, walking a distance behind as she went over a hill, past her tethered calf, to a one-room stone cottage. She motioned again, this time for me to come in. The floor was dirt, and I sat on a stool near the small wood-burning stove. Magazine pictures were tacked to the walls. A communal bed, wide planks covered with straw and blanket, took up most of the space. A pregnant woman my age woke, embarrassed, and bade me, *"Dobra dan.*" Then she rose and began grinding beans for our morning coffee. Off the shelf came sheep cheese stored in olive oil, fresh yogurt, and of course the ubiquitous slibovic.

After an hour, grandfather came home, and even more slibovic flowed. I sat with the little girl on my lap, tying her shoelaces and stroking her hair. With hand gestures and my few words of Russian, I learned that all seven lived in the one room from May through September. I later learned that the average annual income of these mountain people was $150. Yet I envied their generosity, openness, and simplicity. Franny would have fit in here just fine. I guess that's why I felt at home.

I returned to the hut at six the next morning with candy for the children. My new friends insisted that I come in for hot sheep milk, with a sprinkling of coffee grounds. As I left, I suggested that they write down their address so I could send them a photograph, but they owned no pen or pencil. A few hours later, filing out of the base camp with my fellow hikers, I looked up on the ridge. The entire family was lined up, waving goodbye. Sixteen years later, I'd remember that bucolic encounter as I reentered the Balkans at war.

Our trip continued with a week in a cheap dive above a noisy fruit market in Istanbul, two weeks chugging across Asia on the Trans-Siberian Express, and hiking in Nikko National Park in Japan, from which we almost didn't emerge since we couldn't read any of the trail signs. At the end of the summer of 1977, with Heidelberg already a fading memory, we returned to the United States.

We had chosen Denver as our new home, since it was a thriving city (for me), near mountains (for Mark), and near enough to and far enough from Dallas (for our families). Another draw was our fondness for Jessica Stone, the smart, kind psychiatric nurse—twenty years my senior, I was glad to learn—who had been Mark's supervisor five years earlier. I enrolled in the Iliff School of Theology; Mark continued his independent theological studies as we concentrated on getting settled. Once again I sought out Ray to help me buy a property, this time in a turn-of-the-century neighborhood in the process of being gentrified, three blocks from a blighted urban strip. Jessica was my house-hunting companion. Mark and I imagined we'd have people flowing in and out of our home and our lives, but Jessica rolled her eyes when I chose a once-grand brick house that had been divided into separately rented apartments. I laughed that we now had six kitchens and I didn't even like to cook.

We replaced twenty-two broken windows, and Mark and I spent endless hours steaming and scraping off wallpaper thirteen layers thick. When we weren't up to our elbows in paint stripper, our two furry dogs with congenital smiles ran alongside as we skied, hiked, and biked, lacing urban life with mountain sports. With Mark not drawing a salary, we lived off the allowance that Ray provided from Dallas. My husband and I weren't close enough anymore to talk about the effect of this role reversal on his sense of ambition. But apart from his self-directed studying, he didn't seem willing to take risks. In contrast, I became accustomed to setting a high bar and taking a leap. It was a personality I'd seen in Mark in high school but decreasingly ever since. Looking back, I wonder if I was the reason. We still shared our social and political idealism, but maybe our family could only accommodate one zealot.

We had invited Joe to move with us from Heidelberg. Mark had misgivings but seemed relieved that we were a threesome, so that I had someone else for emotional support. For five years Joe lived on our third floor. We were all immersed in community life, volunteering for groups like the Clean Air Coalition and Amnesty International. I played piano for a neighborhood rhythm-and-blues group, and Joe and I sang in a madrigal quintet, both of which rehearsed in our living room.

Our home was a center of activity. Long before the Americans with Disabilities Act we made our front entrance wheelchair-accessible. One evening Joe was hosting an organizing meeting in the dining room for a Gay Pride Parade, while Mark was leading a Bible study in the living room. I answered the doorbell to find two guests: a man in flamboyant drag, standing next to our neighbor Esther, a white-haired, retired secretary for the FBI. "Come on in," I smiled, directing each to a meeting as we all pretended not to notice the unusual pairing.

As Joe and I lived in the same house, our friendship faded. I feared that our relationship would lose its magic as he met exciting new men in Denver; he experienced my anxiety as pressure. At the same time, Joe understood my insecurities and wanted to protect me. When, while Mark was away, Joe also went off for a week, he left behind a pile of envelopes, one for me to open each day, with a poem we had shared or a protestation of his devotion laid out in whimsical colors across the pages. The friend he was with derided him for "babysitting" me. Perhaps.

All was not well in Dallas. As Dad's life had wound down, and after his death, a host of difficulties emerged: a company in financial distress, a passel of lawsuits, and venomous feelings among several of my father's children. Two of Dad's lieutenants were accused by family members of being undercover agents for the FBI and the IRS, assigned to infiltrate Dad's circle. Though my half-brothers Herbert and Bunker admitted to wiretapping the employees' phones, a federal offense, they were acquitted by a Texas jury.

Ray bore the burden of that period. In a dramatic signal of Dad's confidence, he had designated my brother, his eleventh child, as executor of his estate—an awesome responsibility for a man in his early thirties. Surely Dad had not anticipated the implications of that decision.

In 1978 I flew to Shreveport, Louisiana, where all the children (except for Hassie) from Dad's two acknowledged families had gathered for a trial. (Mother stayed home, taken to her bed.) Prodded by her son Hugh, Frania Tye Lee had sued Ray for half of Dad's estate. She claimed to have married my father in 1925; but even if that couldn't be proved, she said she was to be his "putative wife" because she had been his common-law partner of many years. It was excruciating to listen to accounts of our father's deceits and betrayals and to hear love songs recited by Frania on the stand, songs that we thought Dad had written for Mom. As pain mounted upon pain, Ray settled the case out of court, although variations on the suit would ripple out for another ten years.

That family drama was set against an even greater public spectacle. In 1973 Herbert and Bunker began buying silver, initially as a hedge against inflation. Six years later, together with Lamar and some wealthy Arabs, they had amassed more than 200 million ounces, half the world's deliverable supply. In one year the price multiplied tenfold, to the low $50s per ounce.

Silver, it turned out, was used for dozens of everyday purposes, from scientific processes to dental fillings. Photographers had trouble buying the products they needed in their darkrooms. Household burglaries increased dramatically, and women began hiding their forks, knives, and spoons, which had soared in value. Directly and indirectly, everyday citizens were being affected.

As my brothers were cornering the market, speculators joined the chase. Suddenly, a combination of changed trading rules on the New York Metals Market and the intervention of the Federal Reserve put an end to their venture. The price plummeted on March 27, 1980, dropping from $21.62 to $10.80.

I had zero interest in commodities trading or any other form of wealth accumulation, and so the front-page story facing me when I picked up the newspaper day after day had no allure. The notoriety yielded only embarrassment. Some of my friends were naturally curious. I'm sure they didn't realize how mortified I felt when, for example, a woman at church, whose husband had just died of cancer, told me bitterly that upon opening his safe deposit box she found the devalued silver he'd left her. He thought, she added with a rueful look, that he had provided handsomely for her future.

The historic market collapse meant enormous losses for multitudes of small investors as well as the speculators: most of all Herbert and Bunker, who several years later declared bankruptcy, having plunged from a net worth of multi-billions. Magazine stories recounted their secret deals with the Saudis, their accusations that they were the target of East Coast socialist conspiracies, and exposés of our interfamilial tensions. The name Hunt was once more "out there" in the public consciousness.

I rarely tune in to tittle-tattle about what has motivated Dad's children, most of whom have had dramatically ambitious careers. Observers have hypothesized that we're driven by a need to prove our worth to a father consumed by obsessions. Over the years I've asked several of my siblings if they ever wished for a Dad who could participate in their worlds, even as he wanted us to support his crusade. Some seemed to be able to accept that a bond with him would always be on his terms. Others, like me, ached for a mutual father-child relationship. One of his closest associates told me, "Your father's business career would read as fiction. A Hollywood script would never do justice to the true story." Dad was a star in a drama of a rural American swept up into the vortex of global power and prestige. Still, it took me years to appreciate the adventure of his life and look beyond the man whom I knew in his winter, holding frozen in his gnarled hands the validation that fathers should bestow on daughters.

I read one lengthy article (later a book) about my family by an eager author, Harry Hurt. Tantalized by the high-flying silver calamity on the heels of a juicy trial, he collected sensational tales and historical facts that had only been rumored. Hurt delved into the recesses of Dad's private life, exposing details about business trips, closed board meetings, private conversations, and the secret set of children fathered with Frania in the 1930s and 1940s. The piece appeared in *Texas Monthly* as the cover story.

Unfortunately, the edition hit the stands the opening day of the Hyatt Hotel in downtown Dallas, which marked Ray's début as a businessman to be reckoned with. He was immensely proud of the hotel's geodesic dome that had instantly changed the Dallas skyline and become the city's signature. The project was owned by all four of us siblings; but the development was conceived and executed solely under Ray's direction, without input from his three sisters.

To accompany Mother, Mark and I had flown down for the black-tie affair. My husband with reluctance rented a tux while I helped Mom put on her diamonds to dress up her elegant best. From the moment we entered the mirrored magic of the new hotel complex, the management was solicitous, anticipating her every wish. I was dismayed, then, as we walked by the gift shop to see a prominent display of *Texas Monthly* depicting my father at an altar with three brides tearing at his tuxedo. I was afraid that Mother would see the degrading image, and so I boldly asked the surprised store clerk to put the magazines away, at least for that evening. Ray undid my censorship, no doubt concerned that my action might create another story for the next Harry Hurt. When I learned that he'd reversed what I'd done, I felt embarrassed, but also frustrated. It seemed that by trying to protect Mom, I'd become the problem.

As this melodrama was unfolding, we all kept flashing our smiles. All except Mark, who told me, midway through the evening, that he was taking a cab to his parents' home to spend the night. I asked, "What's wrong? Are you okay?" He'd had all the glitz and glamour he could abide. After years of being exposed to my family's wealth, he'd become more sensitive, rather than more accustomed, to the trappings. "I'm getting out of here before I hate your mother," he said abruptly, heading for the exit.

Later, just before bed, I read the *Texas Monthly* article. I was stunned by the level of detail about my family. That night, I dreamed I was gang raped.

Passing

All four of us kids were affected by not knowing when we'd pick up a magazine and find a story about our family. But the shared hardship and happiness of early childhood forged strong bonds among Helen, June, Ray, and me, ties that withstood the years. My sisters and brother nurtured, corrected, endured, instructed, and loved me. Because our family ethic was based on unity rather than individuality, in the course of forging my own identity I put each of them through considerable grief. They listened to my complaints but longed for my compliance.

Like Ray and June, Helen was given no choice but SMU. Upon graduation she taught senior English in an all-black high school in Dallas. During the first half of class, she led her students through the required *Romeo and Juliet*; during the second half she taught them how to read. Closest to Mom's looks, Helen seemed also to be closest to Mother's hopes during our young adult years; after her teaching stint, she settled into baby making and cake baking. But she also earned a master's in liberal arts. Her marriage produced two beautiful daughters and a lasting friendship: Helen's consistent thoughtfulness toward her husband after their divorce was an example that I took to heart.

I was in awe of Helen's mothering. She had a wonderful sense of what was important. During an elegant lunch she was giving in my honor on her brick patio, her one-year-old Kathryn, who was crawling on the floor, spilled a tall glass of iced tea. I jumped up to get a paper towel to sop up the mess. "Just leave it," Helen said. "Let her play in the puddle. She's already wet." New definition of tea party. After that epiphany, when raising my own children I frequently asked myself, "What would my sister do in this situation?"

We were connected with a pull so powerful it felt involuntary. One day when we were in our mid-twenties, my sister cut her waist-long hair to a pixie length. "Oh no!" I cried, when I saw her.

"What's wrong?" she asked, with a look of concern.

"I really liked my hair long," I answered. We both laughed. Sure enough, within a couple of months my Goldilocks tresses lay on the beauty salon floor.

With an inner eye, we tracked each other. Soon after I left Dallas, Helen struck out for New York, forging a new life as a single mother. She was taking courses in art history, so of course I gathered friends in a weekly arts appreciation group. I studied theology; she later followed. She started a women's foundation in Dallas; I would emulate her in Colorado.

In contrast to the tag team that Helen and I lived, my sister June delved more deeply into the church world I was rejecting. Our discussions were often heated, ending in hurt. It was a sad turn of events for my big sister, who'd spent her teenage years trying to protect me from the harshness of life with Dad and her twenties trying to protect Mother from my frosty adolescent rebellion.

June was the family gamester, and we were as likely to find her playing pool or charades as studying her Bible. She needed to be a great sport, since for years Mom subtly and not so subtly urged her eldest daughter to find a husband. Saint June invariably smiled graciously. Unlike me, she didn't pull back in frustration but maintained closeness to Mother that prevailed over the years in an extraordinary partnership. June shared Mom's core value: service to others. She devoted almost every waking hour and many that shouldn't have been waking to helping friends and strangers deal with emotional trauma. In doing so she reminded herself (and us) that while our fathering may have been inadequate, many suffered much more than we.

Ray, who had become a respected and influential civic leader, was keen on family harmony. His unease with me would become a troubling theme in the years ahead. Upon my return from Germany, I enlisted Helen and June to impress upon Ray that as beneficial owners we should receive basic information about Hunt Oil Company. I suggested quarterly meetings. Ray objected that this would take too much employee time. However, when Helen asked for meetings every three months, the idea suddenly became palatable. We got the meetings. I got the picture. It seemed that my brother was allergic to me.

Although Ray and I were more alike than any of the other siblings, differences at an identity level didn't bode well for future collaboration. Ray started college in 1961. I entered in 1968. Those seven years that separated us could have been seventy, judging by the change in the social views of the students. Ray had learned from the TV actor Robert Young that "father knows best." I had learned from the feminist iconoclast Gloria Steinem to call myself "Ms." There's nothing older than an older brother. Ray was a natural leader, but I was no natural follower. We had basic disagreements in the way we saw the world.

Given these differences in our perceptions and values, transitions from the quarterly Dallas meetings, where we reviewed budgets in the hundreds of millions of dollars and listened to reports of company operations, boggled not only my mind but also my conscience. I'd followed Mark out into the wilderness, camping among bears and mountain lions to help chart land for federal protection. Decades later, the company would adopt a more progressive statement about environmental policy, but I was appalled when my brother's new manager for mining said wilderness should be the designation "for land without mineral value."

Once, returning to Denver, I got out of my cab, and before going inside our house sat rocking in a chair on our front porch. I was living with one toe in a towering office building where success was tabulated in profits or replaced oil reserves; but the rest of me was in a community where success could be an "A" on a course paper, the smile of a mentally ill friend, or a bumper crop of zucchini. I'd bought the empty lot next to our house and organized our neighbors, who'd been gardening there for years. They could have their plots beside ours, and I also planted a sign on the corner, "Leeks, Meeks, Etc." These were my Earth Mother years. We grew our own vegetables and baked our own bread, listening faithfully to Garrison Keillor's "Prairie Home Companion" on Saturday evenings—as close as I could get to Franny's farm.

One afternoon, I was thinking back on Franny and Meadowlake. I felt again my uncontrolled joy as Helen and I ran, our arms out and fingers spread wide, through the sweeping branches of an effusive willow near the bus stop. Out of the blue, I called information and tried half a dozen telephone numbers till I ferreted out Mary, Franny's sister, in Ennis, Texas. I called her to find out where Franny was living. To my delight, Mary handed Franny the phone. "Little Swanee!" she said, as she began talking rapidly in Czech.

I heard her sister in the background: "Speak English! English!"

"No," Franny insisted, "It's my Swanee. She understands me."

Mary took the phone to explain that Franny's mind was going. "It's so great you remembered her birthday," she added. In fact I'd never known my nanny's birthday. At least I didn't know I knew.

Franny died soon after. I was the only member of our family at her funeral. And the only one around Mary's kitchen table afterward, reminiscing over strong coffee and kolaches stuffed with sweetened poppy-seed paste, the poppy seeds we'd ground as children. Back in Denver, outside our kitchen window, I planted a weeping willow in Franny's memory.

My backyard became a collection of secrets that others walked by unaware every day. From a branch of our tall elm, I hung a luxuriously long swing, a reminder of afternoons in Idabel when Helen and I draped ourselves through the center of a tire hanging from the grandiose tree at Granny's. But most secret of all was the grapevine I planted to remember my first child.

Even though I'd stopped taking the Pill, I didn't know I was pregnant in 1980 when I went roaming through France with my childhood friend from Dallas, Carol Edgar. After France, Mark and I met up for a visit to Heidelberg. There, to my surprise, a drugstore pregnancy test came out positive. I was thrilled. Mark and I celebrated by spending the good part of an afternoon looking through a display of the classic perambulators used by German matrons as they stroll their children along sidewalks, often with shopping bags hanging from the handles. Mark and I picked out a large, chocolate brown pram to be shipped to Denver.

When we arrived home, I bought a small library to learn everything I could about exercise and nutrition during pregnancy: Walking is important. So is lots of spinach for folic acid. Almost every day I tracked the development of our child, reading aloud to Mark the details of what organs were forming, excitedly spreading books in front of him that showed the miraculous pictures made possible by new inter-uterine photography. Every breath I took was for the new child growing inside me. I could think of nothing else.

At a meeting in Dallas a few weeks later, my family celebrated the news of our coming addition with a decorated cake and presents. A couple of days later, as I was sitting in a management course at a hotel in downtown Denver, I turned to the two women behind me and asked if either had ever been pregnant. One said yes. "Is it okay if I'm cramping?"

"Happens all the time," she said, "but maybe you should call your doctor." I went out to the hall and tried to get through to his office. It was lunchtime and I reached someone at an answering service who told me to call again later.

Back in the seminar, I soon realized that blood was beginning to flow between my legs. Snatching up my note binder and briefcase, I headed for the restroom. "Come with me!" I begged a woman sitting at the registration table in the hall. Startled, she followed; then, realizing what was happening, she called an ambulance. Meanwhile, inside the toilet stall, I was crying hysterically as I reached into the basin with my right hand and pulled out the curled-up form of my child. I stared at it, heaving sobs. It didn't look like the pictures I'd been worshipping. The head seemed so oversized, and it was so small, far too small for 11 weeks. "Is this my baby?" I heard myself cry out as I cradled the fetus in my hand.

I don't remember how I ended up on a stretcher. But I do remember that after I was rolled outside, the two metal doors were slammed shut. As the ambulance sped to the hospital, a gentle medic asked what I had in my hand. I said nothing. He asked again. I trusted him and slowly stretched out my palm, and then watched incredulously as he carefully took from me my beginnings of a baby and put it in a small plastic bag.

At the hospital, I was wheeled into an emergency room and shifted onto another table. As I lay on my back, someone picked up my legs and put my heels into metal stirrups. I endured the painful internal scraping procedure that was routine to the doctors. As I stared at the white ceiling, trying to calm myself, I noticed a movement on my right. I turned my head to see a nurse toss a small plastic bag onto the counter, next to the antiseptic soap dispenser. I was afraid to ask but finally choked out, "What was that?"

"That's the tissue. We send it to pathology for analysis," she answered casually. I've never forgiven her.

Mother was on the next plane, without my asking. I was deeply depressed as I tried to relive every moment of the eleven weeks, to figure out what had gone so terribly wrong. I blamed myself, imagining every glass of French wine as poison, not understanding how common miscarriage is to women across cultures. The pram arrived a few months later. It sat in its shipment crate in our backyard, an unwelcome guest, until Mark and I went out one afternoon and lifted it onto a high shelf in the garage.

Unto the Least of These

In the late 1970s the global gulf between rich and poor was growing. My studies at Iliff, a liberal Methodist seminary, put front and center the distrust of wealth I'd wrestled with for years. Vietnam and Watergate had led to metastasized cynicism toward government, big business, and organized religion. Although I was something of a flower child, Iliff didn't allow me to escape the mainstream but instead confronted me with inconsistencies in my life.

As part of my pastoral care and ethics curriculum, I took a summer course on world hunger, taught by the head of an activist nonprofit organization in New York. Given the news coverage of the silver scandal, I shouldn't have been shocked when a student raised the question for classroom discussion: "Do you think a Hunt can be a Christian?" My heart began to pound; as in the Sunday school class in Fort Worth, I felt my cheeks turn red while I sat meekly, wishing for the bell to hurry up and ring.

Two elements of my faith were colliding. The first had been inculcated in me during fervent revival meetings at First Baptist. Jesus was my personal savior. "And he walks with me, and he talks with me, and he tells me I am his own . . ." In fact, our relationship was so personal as to be exclusively ours: "and the joy we share as we tarry there, none other has ever known." That, of course, was "In the Garden," as Granny's favorite hymn was called.

But at Iliff I met students and faculty who believed in the "social gospel," a notion I'd been warned about back in Dallas. That theology did not consider any one person's relationship with the Lord the primary focus of faith. As the disciple Matthew quoted Jesus, "Inasmuch as you have done it unto the least of these, you have done it unto me." This meant that loving God required caring for the poor, orphaned, and imprisoned. Who I was in the community had ultimate significance.

My professor of Christian ethics listened patiently as I talked over options. Should I follow the compelling example of St. Francis of Assisi, give away all my inheritance from my father, and live a life of utmost simplicity away from the distorting influence of wealth? Eventually I decided I wasn't that pure. Instead I would try to use my privilege for the poor. Still a nagging voice inside warned, "Power corrupts."

At first, Mark and I didn't have much power to corrupt us. We built a life in Denver that was oriented around people who were most vulnerable. Before arriving, we'd thought that Mark might start his own house church. Instead we took on leadership roles in Capital Heights Presbyterian Church, just around the corner from our home. Mark was the preacher and I was the minister for pastoral care in the small parish, which shared its building with a Catholic community and a gay congregation.

Likewise, instead of creating a home-based initiative, we'd become directors at Karis Community, a converted convent a block down the street. The couple who'd started an urban retreat center there were ready to move on just at the time we arrived in the neighborhood. So we took over, shifting the emphasis more to a halfway house for mentally fragile young adults.

We gathered talented friends to help us. Our mainstay was Jessica, who'd left Fort Logan Mental Health Center, where Mark had done his chaplaincy training years before. Jessica had decades of experience as a psychiatric nurse. Her mantra was that people who were schizophrenic or brain-damaged were still responsible for their behavior. She turned the traditional clinical model on its head. Rather than focus on negatives, Jessica suggested that we let people stay at Karis as long as they were improving. For some, that meant years. Our community included a concert pianist and the daughter of a national TV commentator, but most were everyday folk who, with different brain chemistry, would have been able to negotiate society.

As at Mt. Vernon, I shared meals with people often lost in a world inside their heads that I could only imagine. One was Donna, a brilliant young woman who, during a psychotic episode, had jumped off a roof. After years of treatment, her leg was to be amputated. I found her in bed one afternoon, with covers pulled over her head. She was hallucinating and terrified.

"Come on out," I insisted. "I'm taking you to the hospital."

"No. Go away," she wailed pitifully.

Despite Donna's protests, I pulled her out, got her into my car, and headed for the emergency room at Denver General. But for all her determination not to capitulate to her illness, another side of Donna recognized how badly she needed help. When I stopped at a red light she pointed to the left, and offered helpfully, "Turn here, it's faster."

At Karis, in addition to the clinical challenges, for the first time in my life I was a manager. Mark and I led the staff mostly by intuition. Morale was high, with exceptions. One resident coordinator, a bright theology student, had an eloquent way with words, referring to me as a "rich bitch pseudo-psychologist." I took that to mean she was resigning. She left her position—with a chunk of my confidence.

Jessica was always there to help me learn from those tough moments. In addition, I met with a supervisor at a mental hospital. In a weekly meeting, six of us analyzed each other's written-up verbatim accounts of our therapist-patient interactions. I was fascinated by those conversations, ready to decipher subtexts and interpret motivations. But my responses outpaced others, and some in the group resented my frequent contributions. I tried to pull back, tone down, and count to ten after I had a thought.

In the end, I vowed that I would avoid groups where I had to backpedal. I preferred to spend my effort on the wards, where one drug-damaged patient shuffled by another strapped into his chair, sitting across from still another wearing a helmet to protect him from his own head-banging. The power dynamics in our relationships were wretchedly skewed, but at least they were overt.

Whatever I learned, and whomever I helped, the experience at Karis was most valuable to me because of time with Jessica. I trusted her completely, and we shared secrets past and present. When my sky was falling in, she was nearby to pick up the pieces. "What are your options?" she would ask matter-of-factly, and instead of having tenacious fears, I'd see the world open up before me.

I asked Jessica to come to Dallas to meet Hassie, knowing that she'd tell me the truth about his condition. We went to the estate adjoining Mt. Vernon, where my half-brother was now living with round-the-clock nurses. Hassie's older sister, his guardian, resented my mother, and since Dad's death had ordered the gate connecting the two properties to be locked. But I noticed that Hassie had worn a path from his kitchen door to the locked gate, and I wanted to tell him that Mother still cared for him and wasn't trying to keep him away.

Jessica and I rang the doorbell. A nurse let us in. We were shown into the large living room where Hassie was sitting stiffly in a wingchair beneath a huge photograph of Dad's six children by Lyda. He was wearing a blue suit, staring straight ahead. "Eyes can kill," he muttered, as we sat down.

"This is my friend, Jessica," I said, hoping against hope that the two of them might have some sort of interaction that would break through forty years of isolation.

"Hello, Hassie," she said in her deep, solid voice. Then she tried to strike up a conversation.

"Be careful. She may be looking at you, but she may have a knife behind her back," Hassie murmured through a half-smile that seemed tense and angry.

After half an hour of such non sequiturs, my friend and I said goodbye, drove down to the lake, parked, and walked out on an empty pier. We sat for awhile, watching the sun sparkle, like glitter sprayed across the water. The air was heavy as ducks moved silently in and out of the reeds. Finally Jessica broke the silence. "He's very, very sick. There's nothing you can do to make him well." I began to cry. My sadness blended with relief.

A Brave Girl in Ireland

A decade into my marriage, I was feeling more and more that my identity was rooted in our partnership, not in an unshakable sense of who I was as an individual. Looking back, it's no surprise. Marrying so young, I'd never been a single woman. Granted, I probably couldn't have taken such a dramatic step away from my Dallas family had I been alone. Although I drew enormous comfort from my relationship with Mark, by linking myself at so early an age to a husband (and a man, four years older), I'd forfeited self-confidence that others gain when they carve out an independent life.

That tension between coming into my own and being in partnership is probably the reason that in my studies, I was drawn to the German existentialist theologian Paul Tillich, who argued for balance between knowing ourselves as unique individuals and knowing ourselves as parts of a whole. Looking at my life through his lens, I could see how I'd summoned my courage to leave my conservative upbringing by joining Mark and a wave of young people pulling away from the Establishment. But although I may have reveled in my uniqueness vis-à-vis the Hunt family, becoming part of a movement didn't constitute a real act of individuality.

My feelings were exacerbated by the women's liberation movement coursing through American culture. Building on the civil rights struggle, the movement raised the possibility of my earning rights and responsibilities that were rare only a decade earlier. Marches for reproductive rights, protests against male-only schools, and demands for equal pay fueled my own pursuits.

Just before my thirtieth birthday, I had a dream set at Mt. Vernon, with animals striding by. A monkey, a horse, a dog. I interacted with each but didn't really engage. Then a lioness appeared, with sinewy muscles rippling under her thin blond coat. She was power incarnate, but when I stooped to run my hand across her back, she lay down and rolled over. Her claws withdrawn, she swatted at me playfully with soft paws.

I took the dream as a message not to be afraid of my power. With some trepidation, the next day I spoke to Mark: "I want to spend the summer away."

He listened carefully and expressed no resistance. "What does this mean in terms of our marriage?" he asked.

"Nothing at all," I insisted. I spent the first month exploring New York City, camped out at Helen's apartment on the Upper East Side. At a performance of *Annie*, I was the only person in the theater sobbing when kind, strong Daddy Warbucks adopted the little orphan girl. Watching the two of them dance a soft-shoe arm in arm wasn't just a sweet scene to me, but the enactment of my greatest longing. I was alarmed by how uncontrollable my grief was and determined to return from my summer more whole.

To that end, I made my way one Sunday to St. Thomas Episcopal Church on Fifth Avenue. There I encountered one male after another, as either an emissary from or a conduit to the Father, Son, and Holy Ghost. Altar boys led the procession, a layman read the scripture, the choirmaster directed his singers, after which the priest ascended to his pulpit to deliver his sermon. His, his, his. I studied the carvings behind the altar. Christ . . . Saint Augustine . . . Savonarola . . . John Wesley . . . George Washington. George Washington? Dozens of men stared down beneficently on me. I guess I was supposed to feel grateful. Instead, I felt cheated.

At the communion rail, I imitated my neighbor, kneeling, waiting passively for the priest to come by. "This is my body," he said softly, putting a wafer on my extended tongue. I felt like a panting dog. A second priest came by. "This is my blood," he said. He held the cup to my lips and tilted it, then took it away. The wine never made it to my mouth. I walked back to my pew and out of the church, profoundly aware of my thirst.

I was going on to Scotland for eight weeks. Helen sweetly insisted on giving me a farewell party. Not strong on geography, my sister told her friends that I was headed for Ireland. Several came with guidebooks to the Emerald Isle. Footloose and fancy-free, I changed my plans to fit my new library.

Arriving at the ferry port of Rosslare, I walked up to the big yellow Hertz sign and rented a car. "Now, could you recommend a road?" I asked the woman behind the desk, trying to seem nonchalant.

She stared at me in disbelief, looking for a clue. I gave her my best Mona Lisa smile. She offered with a musical lilt, "Well, Love, there's a strawberry fair at Enniscorthy, just up the road. Why don't you drop in?"

I named my car "Annie," determined to transform the orphan inside me. This Annie could withstand any storm, I laughed to myself. Heeding my Hertz consultant, I wound through the narrow streets of sleepy Enniscorthy, pulling up to a rock-and-stucco house with a "bed and breakfast" sign. I tried to look purposeful as I spoke with the owner, but I felt nervous and self-conscious as I brought my bags into the small room. After unpacking my clothes, I looked around the house. By a phone in the hall was a list of places of worship, including a Quaker meeting house. "How Irish," I thought, not realizing that Quakers are as English as fish 'n' chips.

Next morning I sat on a pew among twenty Quakers, who remained remarkably silent almost an hour, waiting for the inner Light to inspire a message for the entire group. Finally, a man with a strong, lusty voice launched into "Amazing Grace." I couldn't resist adding a touch of harmony.

At the back of the room sat a strapping Kennedy look-alike. I was interested in him; his mother and aunt were interested in me. Ann and Ethel, both in their seventies, were the matriarchs of RockSpring Farm, nestled within a labyrinth of stone hedges. I joined the family for three weeks as cook and farmhand. Sweet Ethel supervised as I cut the large lawn with an ancient push mower, gathered hay, and painted urns in the garden so that they would look even older than they were. But Ann was more mannish than her sister. I marveled as she plunged her arm inside the end of a cow to tie a rope around the unborn calf's ankles. She showed me how to run the tractor, to pull the calf out. We both cried when that calf didn't make it.

Leaving my new friends at RockSpring, I continued my search. In pubs I adopted a fictitious name, home, and occupation, stripping away externals that so easily defined me not only to others but also to myself. I wrote short stories, essays, and poems to describe what I was seeing, but also to try to make sense of the pastoral care—or lack thereof—that had left me more wounded than well.

Sonnet of the Dance

Her flow was youth, and every moment spring
Every move more supple and more bold
With impassioned dance her heart would sing
For into her form she poured her soul
His ground was safety, posed with planted feet
In the sturdy strength of balanced stance
Years informed his steps as he'd repeat
Steady patterns of his studied dance
Then he took her hands into his own
Clasping in that grasp her youth-kissed charms

Such protection she had never known
And she tried to dance within his arms

When the music stopped, they were apart
She a tangled heap, he a mute heart.

My next verse in Ireland was my journey by ferry to treeless Inish-more, the largest of the three Aran Islands. At the post office I in-quired about the Hernon residence, where I'd arranged to stay. The clerk laughed. "Half the people on this island are Hernon." Eventually connecting with my hosts, I fell, like Alice through the looking glass, into an Ireland of ages past, saturated with the soggy history of fisher-men now lying in cemeteries, their beds marked by Celtic crosses peer-ing through tall grass. Nora and Colman Hernon's remote abode was a simple, whitewashed home near the ruins of a seventh-century mon-astery. My tiny room, whittled out of the attic, was an Irish version of Van Gogh's in Arles. After depositing my bags, I dragged the small table and desk to the window for view and light. Then I went down to the kitchen for a cup of tea and heavy soda bread with butter.

Nora asked about my situation. "Your parents?"

"My father is dead . . ."

"Lord rest him."

". . . and my mother is in Dallas . . ."

"God keep her."

"My husband is in Denver holding down the fort while I'm travel-ing on my own."

"Good Girl. Lord bless you. Traveling by yourself! You could be pulled over and have your car stolen by IRA thugs. You're a brave girl, you are!"

Bravery or bravado? Or both? It's astonishing how within one per-son strength lives alongside insecurity. How in a split-second hands on hips become hands politely folded. How glowering eyes suddenly are cast downward and a raucous belly laugh is reduced to a piteous whimper. But strength without a vestige of vulnerability often leads to abuse. Knowing that, instead of being distressed by inconsistencies we should probably accept them in ourselves and others. Even be-friend them. But that's easier said than done. Even though I was push-ing through one adventure after another, I didn't feel so brave when

I called Mark once a week, to check in. I would begin crying when I heard his voice. It was as if Mark's relationship was with only the insecure, incompetent part of me.

Nora, on the other hand, seemed like a graying tower of strength. I admired her scrambling nimbly over the meadow walls, or dismantling then replacing the heavy stones to create gaps for the cattle. After we milked each cow, she dipped her thumb in the bucket and spread a frothy cross on its hide. She talked to them and me with comparable terms of endearment.

My strong-framed, robust host was in his sixties. Every day he wore the same gray flannel pants and green knit sweater. His cap had created a dramatic sun-line, dividing his face and balding head. Since his recent stroke he could speak only with a severe stutter. Nora was clearly pained by Colman's frustration and tried to encourage him. "Just talk slowly, Colee, and the words will come." Then she proceeded to finish his every sentence. But the stroke didn't affect his rich, full baritone. In the evenings, as we sat by the peat fire, Colman's Gaelic ballads filled not only the cottage but the caverns of my heart.

Before retiring, the couple knelt on the cold cement kitchen floor, their forearms leaning on the seats of their chairs. They prayed the rosary before a picture of Jesus, a red light burning before his bleeding heart. But piety had its limits. One day Colman drove me in his horse-drawn carriage. We pulled over and set out afoot, crossing meadows until we looked down on waves crashing against the cliffs far below. Here nature was expansive and intimate. The abstract questions that had so preoccupied me seemed far away. Suddenly Colman pressed his big hands against my breasts and started to kiss me, with burly desire. Startled, I said no and pushed him away.

The night before, I'd lain in my narrow bed reading Oscar Wilde's prison opus *De Profundis*, in which the Irishman reflects on his sexual passions indulged at great expense. While I felt repulsed by Colman's advances, I could empathize with his longing for intimacy.

For my return, Mark offered to pick me up at the airport. I said I'd take a cab. I wanted to complete the trip on my own. My emotions were running high as the taxi drove up to the house. I was coming back stronger, with more understanding of the world and my place in it. My mind was racing with anticipation. I imagined Mark's was too.

As the driver pulled up, I saw my husband walking briskly up the sidewalk, coming home from a meeting at the church. If I'd arrived five minutes earlier, I would have walked into an empty home.

It must have been terrible for Mark to have me drop back into his sphere after three months spared of my pressuring, criticizing, and disturbing. But in addition to that adjustment, the basic equation of our relationship had changed. At least in our early years he could balance the mismatch of my extroversion and his love of quiet with a sense of himself as my rescuer of sorts. It wasn't a role that he'd really bid for. More one that we'd fallen into. A dozen years earlier, in high school, I'd sprawled across my canopy bed at Mt. Vernon, indulging in our long, late-night phone calls. I'd brought to him my griefs, confusion, disappointment. He'd listened patiently, compassionately. On rare occasions he'd let me in on his own turmoil, his battles and temptations, his personal struggle with good and evil. But from the beginning the balance was tilted toward me as needy parishioner and him as pastor.

The summer of 1980 was a turning point. I'd gone exploring on my own. My return wasn't rocky. It was barren. In the days of my reentry we walked around the house in silence, the air heavy with unspoken resentment. Finally, I took the plunge. "What's going on? There's something on your mind."

"You don't need me," my husband responded.

"No, but I choose you. Isn't that better?"

Mark looked at me somewhat confused but didn't really answer.

Hunting for Alternatives

I've always had a place in my heart for torch singers: those slim women who drape themselves across a piano, sliding a chiffon scarf through their fingers, bemoaning the man who got away. I didn't have the willowy figure, but I had the scarf and the scars. Even after Ireland, where I'd developed a deeper sense of myself, I was still searching for someone to watch over me. At least I was more aware of it.

Fortunately my rough times were interspersed with splendid moments, and most of the men with whom I became infatuated over the years ultimately remained friends. But one told me, "I've never known anyone whose strength and weakness are so close." At the same time that I was pushing away from my patriarchal heritage, I was writing tender entries in my journal because *he* didn't call when he said he would. Our relationships weren't about companionship. Nor sex. To me they felt like life-or-death. Fill my cup, and I had a whole reservoir at my disposal. But I feared that without a steady stream of care I would dry up inside.

Franny used to tell me about a contest between the wind and sun: Which could make the man walking down the road take off his coat? As the wind blew and blew, the man down below clutched his coat tighter. The clever sun was the victor. In my marriage, I was the wind. I couldn't force Mark to share his thoughts or feelings with me, although glimpses of his rich inner life through his sermons prolonged our marriage. But when we were alone, I had no idea what to do, so I blew and blustered even more, trying to thaw our relationship.

Of course it didn't work. Mark loved sensitive solitude. He confessed that my fears were right—that he was relieved when I left town. My Sturm und Drang way of being intruded on him. At times he tried to find the love he once felt. Reading a sweet inscription in a book he gave me for my birthday, I blurted out, confused, "Do you really believe this?"

The relationship was so broken that I finally told him I would find love where I could. He said he understood. As it turned out, he understood all too well—but that's his story, not mine. Quite apart from too-easy scorekeeping about who injured the other first, our marriage was failing because neither of us knew how to break out of our fear, how to deal openly with disappointments, or how to coach the other across the chasm that separated us.

In the next couple of years, as I tried to keep some embers of romance alive inside myself, my attentions were dramatically misdirected, including toward one man who mumbled a lame excuse when I discovered Helen's telephone number on his office speed dial. That was the last straw. I realized just what a mess I'd become. Once and for all, I needed to change this destructive pattern. I found a new therapist. In our first hour, I described how too much of the energy I wanted to spend making the world a better place was instead channeled into my need for fathering. Could he help me? "Are you sure you want therapy?" he asked bluntly. "Maybe you just want to come in here and say, 'Let's screw.'"

On one level, I appreciated his honesty. I was also outraged at his crassness; disappointed at his betrayal of professional standards. And thrilled. Homeless passion is dangerously defiant. It grows unnoticed, then emerges from a dark corner and latches onto circumstances, overwhelming the careful priorities and solid values we determine in calmer, more rational moments. Each romantic attraction in my early years of womanhood taught me a valuable lesson, destroyed a false hope, and left me better able to father myself. Still, I confessed to my erstwhile therapist that I felt like a parasite. "Think of the beauty you've brought into the lives of a few lucky men," he countered. Absolution—and perhaps the kindest thing anyone has ever said to me.

I'm not sure if becoming less focused on my personal yearnings allowed me to think more about helping others, or if turning outward made me less preoccupied with my own needs. But the two developments coincided. My training in service had started early. As a girl singing at a nursing home, I was disturbed when an old woman thought I was her daughter, until I realized that in that role I could comfort her much more. As a college freshman, my own eyes were opened when I read textbooks aloud for an aspiring and inspiring blind law student. For my child psychology class, I spent hours rocking an autistic toddler. When we moved to Fort Worth, I organized young adults to "Adopt a Granny," linking them with elderly shut-ins. And in Denver, Mark and I took Lao refugees and Eritrean torture victims into our home for months at a time as they made the transition from refugee camps to America.

Our society, then as now, was riddled with inconsistencies. The Me Generation was turned inward, while unskilled young people, mainly minorities, were dropping out of chaotic schools, signing onto welfare rolls, or taking dead-end jobs. Our burgeoning class was the working poor. Politicians railed against "welfare queens," claiming that women were getting pregnant to wangle a bigger check; but they excused businessmen whose greed or incompetence cost $150 billion in a bailout of the savings and loan industry. Despite President Reagan's trickle-down rhetoric about balanced budgets, he stacked up a national debt in the trillions.

Becoming more comfortable with personal power, I decided to use my family name as well as fortune to leverage social justice. I went to the courthouse and became Swanee Hunt Meeks. After several strangers thought I was a law firm, I decided to abandon Meeks. "I'm keeping the husband but dropping the name," I assured one and all. Mark said he didn't mind. That was probably true, in part because he had so little investment in our relationship by then.

I was starting to think hard about . . . how can I say this without sounding trite? I actually spent hours trying to imagine how I might do the greatest possible good for the world. It was a naïve question, and a profound one. I had discovered how one kindness leads to another, creating a habit of the heart. A life turned out toward others, I realized, would be worth living. Helen was in the same place. Although our relationship had gone through some rough times, I trusted her vision, common sense, and most of all, compassion. I told her that through Amnesty International I'd met a New Yorker named Vincent McGee, who called himself a "fund-lowerer," helping wealthy people figure out how to set up their philanthropy. Out of the blue, I called Vinny, suggesting that we get together next time he was in Denver. "Put your proposal in writing and send it to me," he said, somewhat abruptly.

"You don't understand," I insisted. "I'm not asking for money. I'm from Dallas, and my name is Hunt." The conversation took a quick turn.

I'll always be grateful to Vinny for helping Helen and me become partners after a fifteen-year uneasiness. We three fashioned a private foundation and stayed together for years as its trustees. It's clear to me now how Helen and I brought with us our father's disregard for limits and our mother's heart for those forgotten. We decided that I would focus on Denver, Helen on New York and Dallas. And given our experience as women in our own family, we would devote half our incomes to creating opportunity and access to those relegated to the margins.

Our new alliance almost broke apart when we needed to choose a name. We didn't want to use "Hunt," given our family's infamous right-wing politics. We almost agreed on the Mustard Seed Fund, but our associates outside the Bible Belt missed the allusion. A friend wryly suggested Hunts Catch Up. Eventually, we decided we'd try to change what Hunt stood for, and chose the name Hunt Alternatives Fund. Whether that meant we funded alternative strategies or were alternative Hunts, we'd let others decide.

From our earliest upbringing, Helen and I had been taught that there is wealth beyond money. But now in our thirties, as we spent time in neighborhoods where people were barely scraping by, we realized in a fresh way how wealth isn't concentrated among a few with high incomes. It's dispersed among all people with generous hearts, exciting ideas, willing hands, and a longing to work with others to build a healthier community. Unlike money, that wealth is without limits.

We came face to face with such wealth every day when we decided to start working with direct services like soup kitchens, where we could get to know providers and clients up close. I often learned more about their work from an expression on their faces as they talked with their staff or clients than I did from a written grant proposal.

Our first Denver grantee was Safehouse for Battered Women. We promised to provide the last portion of their funding drive; the organizers went on the air, announcing that they had the last chunk, contingent on others' sending the rest. When contributions flooded in, we realized our leverage. Soon we were expanding our influence, finagling appointments with elected and appointed officials to represent our grantees.

The most eloquent advocates were those directly affected by problems, so we funded leadership training in poor and distressed neighborhoods. You could say that we intentionally walked into trouble— in a living room filled with angry people, in an inner-city school, at a crowded rally. But in the middle of the problems, we began to find the beginnings of solutions. Even when those solutions weren't polished and perfect, we pushed ahead, believing that the *process* of social change could be as important as the *product*.

Eyes open only to models they've seen in the past might not recognize the creative ways that communities in crisis help themselves. But ears trained to listen beyond apathy and anger can often detect the slightly off-key resonance of a transformational idea. The fund became so closely identified with unusual approaches that when we supported a Girl Scouts program to work with prison inmates, the director thanked us for taking a chance on such a traditional organization.

In most foundations, we discovered, trustees tried to adhere to the desires of a deceased funder, who obviously can't evolve with the times. They were also reluctant to take risks. We reasoned, like venture capitalists, that if all our grantees were around three years later, we hadn't gone far enough out on a limb. Bending in the breeze, we didn't realize that as we were promoting change, we were the ones changing.

On the Ropes

Relationships aren't static. As Mark and I had moved in tandem from Dallas, adventured together in exotic places, and set up households in four consecutive cities, outsiders admired us as partners in values and mission. But our marriage drifted as it moved further into its second decade.

Still I longed to have a child. With careful planning, we became pregnant in early 1982, two years after my miscarriage. Granted, one reason Mark and I had stayed together was the pressure-valve effect of relationships outside our marriage. But now I begged him for a fresh start, with a firm commitment. "Just you and me and the baby makes three." He agreed. But the afternoon before I went into labor, six days overdue, I spent a distraught hour in the arms of Jessica, knowing that Mark was at the home of his current love, our church pianist.

It was a tough night before we went to the hospital for the birth, early the next morning. After my twelve-hour labor and delivery, Mark kissed my forehead and said simply, "Good work, Gracie." Reminded of how rare kisses were in those days, I felt tears roll down my face. We left the hospital within a few hours. At home, I walked up the stairs and climbed into bed. We ordered a pizza, then slept with our new baby between us. I wanted to name her Jessica; but Mark's new love already had a daughter by that name, and I couldn't risk repeating the hurt my sister had endured with our father having two Helens.

The next day, Lillian Helen Hunt-Meeks wailed inconsolably. My secretary, a mother of six, insisted that the problem was onions in the pizza, passed on through my milk. "This is going to be more complicated than I thought," I said to myself. I had no idea. A few days later, as I was carrying my tiny pink bundle through a doorway, her foot hit the frame. She began screaming. My heart started racing. I calmed myself, saying out loud, "Well, Honey, that's not the last time I'll hurt you. And I'm sorry."

Soon after Lillian was born I bought a ranch, seventy miles southwest of Denver in the Kenosha Mountains. Mark and I dubbed it the Columbine, after the delicate blue-and-white state flower—although not one grew on our eleven hundred acres. The ranch was steeped in history and legend. The Utes had used the site for protection from fierce winter storms. For teepees and clothes they hunted buffalo, on horses stolen from Spanish explorers. The U.S. government, in turn, stole *their* land, moving them to reservations in the mid-1800s. In 1861 a bone-jarring stage road carried travelers between boomtown Denver and the mining community of Leadville. Eighteen years later, when tracks were laid across our future property (the stage stop became our ranch house) a car brought Denverites out and back for daylong excursions. Passengers included Walt Whitman, whose journal described the breathtaking sight. I wondered what stories our walls would tell of weary travelers, heartbroken lovers, and hopeful pioneers.

Mark was at home in the wild. He became a mountain man, with his full brown beard, Russian fur hat, and plaid shirt. I loved watching him strap on snowshoes to go out and chop wood. On New Year's Eve, braving a dramatic snowstorm, we cross-country skied into the ranch, my husband wearing our baby in a Snugli fastened to his chest. Friends joined us that evening, and we sat in a circle around the fireplace sipping hot mulled wine, with the wind howling outside.

I asked everyone how they would rate their past year, with ten as highest. As we went around the circle, Mark came before me. I was thinking of how this had been one of the most difficult periods of my life, but he gave the year an 8. Hearing his answer, my heart sank. Clearly, we hadn't shared even the pain of the deterioration of our marriage.

My husband had once seemed to find satisfaction as my companion or comforter; now we didn't even hold hands. Moments of delight weren't shared; when friends filled our home with music and laughter, I sometimes found him upstairs watching TV. He took to getting up each morning at 5:00 to read theology before I awoke, the only time he could be undisturbed, he said.

It was my turn. Resentfully, I muttered, "I was going to say 5, but hearing Mark's answer, I'll lower it to 4." Our friends stared awkwardly into the fire.

Back in town, in a last attempt to save our marriage, I persuaded Mark to see a therapist with me. It was an idea I'd suggested before but hadn't been smart enough to insist on. Now it was too late. Mark told the counselor we were beyond help.

"When did you realize you'd made a mistake by marrying Swanee?"

"After the first couple of months."

In my mind, I reached back fifteen years, to that time he hadn't gone into work and I didn't ask why. Maybe if we had been more open from the start. . . . Now I felt livid and appreciative, realizing he'd waited fifteen years until I was strong enough for him to leave.

Neither of us could imagine ourselves divorced. After all, we were the people others came to for answers. But we had failed. I guess it was natural that I felt troubled—no, furious, really, when he stayed in his relationship with Debbie, the pretty, gentle, and wildly talented church pianist, who'd actually been my friend before becoming his. She was sensitive, with an almost saintly persona. Still, it wasn't lost on me that their relationship had gelled when she was going through an extremely difficult personal patch in her own life. I imagined that Mark had slipped into the same role of rescuer with her that we had known earlier, when I was less independent.

I suppose to bring my competition down a notch (and preserve some sense of self-respect, albeit as a loser), I explained to Debbie rather harshly that she was the occasion, not the cause, of our breakup. On the other hand, the better part of my nature was happy for my husband; his new partner seemed much more suited to his temperament. But I wasn't a quitter, and I hurt till I thought my heart would split open. Rocking with our small child in my arms, day after day I wept, realizing that our family was irreparably broken.

Even in my sorrow, I never believed that marrying Mark was a mistake. As much hurt as we caused each other, we created more good. He was a diligently hard worker and an outspoken champion of social justice. I look back over thousands of exquisitely beautiful times, remembering his twinkling eyes, his wise words. And thank God I never had to wonder for a minute if Mark had designs on my family fortune. That wasn't our problem. During our brief divorce negotiations, I asked what financial settlement he wanted. Characteristically, he named a modest amount. I just doubled it. No contest. That's how it was between us.

Not long after, I learned from a minister friend that he would be marrying Mark and Debbie in their living room the next Saturday. "That's Lillian's birthday," I cried. "There are 364 other days they could choose. That day is *taken*. It ought to be preserved as *ours*." My friend shifted the date. But the next spring Mark's new daughter was born on our wedding anniversary. It seemed our lives would remain intertwined, whether we wanted them to or not.

During those darkest days, even as I was trying to keep my balance emotionally, I kept up my hectic professional schedule. That included visiting the base camp of Outward Bound, which Hunt Alternatives had funded to take mentally ill people on whitewater rafting trips, rape victims for solo time in the wilderness, and inner-city kids to the top of the Rocky Mountains.

I joined several foundation executives to observe a training session for rough-and-ready instructors. That included a ropes course: walking on a log that spanned about twenty feet between two trees, swinging like Tarzan from one platform to another, and crossing above a roaring river on a swaying rope bridge. The intrepid trainee wore a halter attached to a slack line connected to a higher cable. In case of misstep, he or she would hang suspended above the ground. Death was not an option. Terror was.

We stood below with our necks craned, watching the bronzed and muscled apprentices move through the course or freeze in fright. Suddenly a genial instructor called out, "Come on up, Swanee!" We all laughed. My laugh sounded least sincere. The very idea made my knees weak.

Then I thought: Why shouldn't I? Why is it *they* can do it, and *I* can't? "Sure!" I yelled.

Amused, the staff harnessed me before I could change my mind. To my colleagues' amazement, I began climbing the rope net into the trees. For a non-athlete, even that start was difficult. The rough hemp hurt my hands, and I felt like a baboon, my rear end sticking up in the air as I hauled my body up the net.

What on earth am I doing here? I chided myself. A groundless answer popped into my head: If I can make it through this course, I can make it through my divorce. I raced from one tree platform to another, to another, never stopping long enough to feel my fear, and never dreaming what lay ahead.

My dapper father when
I was born

Our Meadowlake fivesome

In my sweet little Alice-blue gown

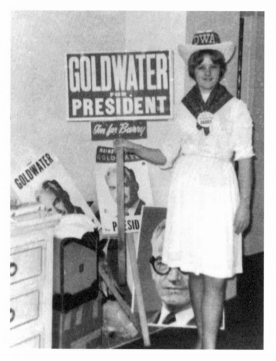

Goldwater Girl—who'd
'a thunk it?

Dancing with
Dad

Helen and Hassie

Pushing pastry and propaganda at the Louisiana State Fair

United with Mark, reunited with Franny

Mom and me

Baby Lillian on the Mount Vernon lawn

Wedding doubts at the
Boboli Garden

South Park rancher—that's my
story and I'm stickin' to it

Onward and upward in Nepal

Navigating the Shelikof
Straits of Alaska

Marathon training with
Katherine Archuleta

The only tyrant I accept in this world
is the still voice within.
— Mahatma Gandhi

CHAPTER 3

Finding My Voice

Courage to Be

I was learning a lot about courage, what it means and how to find it. In my theological studies, Paul Tillich defined "the courage to be" as faith that includes the acceptance of despair. I found comfort in that paradox. It seemed truer than the easier idea that in some grand plan tragedy is justified. In other words, there is no despair to accept. Of course lessons embedded in hardship are useful. But try as I might, I can't imagine a divine plan that stretches wide enough to include the former concentration camps I visited in Germany or the gross inequities worldwide that leave children starved.

Mother, speaking of her relationship with Dad used to assure me, "You know, Precious Lamb, the Lord gives us difficulties to make us stronger." Most of the people I knew would agree with her.

"But Mom," I countered, "It's still a bad deal. If life weren't so hard, we wouldn't have to be so strong. And besides, tragedy as exercise would be a rash gamble on God's part, since many people don't end up stronger. They're left psychologically maimed. Or they kill themselves."

Mother just shook her head, with a sad look that always made me feel guilty.

I could accept a loving God who didn't have control. But a God who ordained, or even permitted, the pain I witnessed was not a God I would worship. In the rejection of God's power as omnipotent, my faith changed. No longer did I imagine a heavenly father, beneficently doling out well-being like a weekly allowance. Instead, God is the context in which I am living, what Tillich called "the ground of being." Faith is not belief in the unbelievable, but acceptance of a source of strength—strength forged every day in my relationships and in my work. As I moved to this new theological place, the old hymns and scriptures still had meaning for me, but as metaphors, as descriptions of the writer's relationship to the ground of being, not a prescription I needed to follow. Their meaning was changing as I was changing.

One afternoon at Karis, as I passed around little cups of grape juice and plates of chocolate cake to the mothers and children clustered around me, I made a point of not staring at Donna. On her lap she held her son, letting him play with her long, blond hair.

We'd gathered for a farewell party, given by a mothers' group, but not just any mothers' group. A local researcher trying to understand the roots of mental illness was tracking the young children of schizophrenic mothers. The genetic link was well established, but he wanted to determine why, as they grew up, some children develop psychosis (hallucinations, paranoia, etc.) and others don't. I'd organized this group at his request. Week after week, while the toddlers played tag or napped in the chapel, the mothers talked in the Karis living room.

One mother wondered how she could allow her son to go play next door during times when she was convinced that spies were lurking around her home. Another asked, what if the angry, mocking voices she heard goaded her into hurting her child?

Sometimes a mother decided she didn't trust herself to provide the care her darling deserved, so she gave him up for adoption. I was excruciatingly sensitive to separation, especially between mothers and their children. As the farewell party drew to a close, I looked out the window with a sense of dread. A car from an agency was waiting to fetch the little boy, who was about to lose the most important person in his life.

I remembered my last glimpse of Franny, as she walked out of our Mt. Vernon kitchen with her suitcase. That sweet child would feel devastated at first. The very foundation of his world would tremble. Then, over time, hurt would mellow into a constant, sorrowful ache. I knew. I'd been there.

As the young boy was delivered to the adoption officials in the car, a chunk of my heart went with him. Yes, my work with those who were hurting felt personal. But that wasn't obvious to others. When my sister Helen and I announced in 1981 that our new Hunt Alternatives Fund would focus on marginalized people like the mentally ill, another foundation president told us, "I'm surprised you'd get into anything so *political*!" I was baffled by his remark until I delved deeper and discovered that during the Kennedy administration, a well-intended but doomed policy of "deinstitutionalization" had been launched. In twenty-five years, the population of asylums had shrunk by 75 percent. The intention was right: With new psychotropic medications, most patients could live in less confined settings. But the projected community-based support wasn't forthcoming from state legislatures, and from that time on huge numbers of mentally ill Americans have ended up untreated, on the streets.

The number swelled during the Reagan years as budget watchers, in their keenness to slash spending, encouraged cuts in programs for the disabled. If mentally ill people didn't answer the officials' inquiries correctly, the government threw them off the rolls. The result was unconscionable hardship and a rise in suicides; the sicker a person was, the less likely he was to get help.

Monthly payments weren't their only loss. In his inaugural address, Reagan declared, "Government is not the solution. Government is the problem." Hundreds of public policies trickled down: among them, support for low-income housing was reduced by 80 percent and addiction programs curtailed. These disastrous cuts weren't only the result of economic miscalculation but also of insensitivity and even mean-spiritedness. I was stunned but not surprised when a highly respected business leader in Dallas muttered to me: "Texas should cut out all social benefits so 'those people' will move to Oregon."

Colorado, my adopted home, was rather progressive. Without enormous state hospitals or powerful unions, our tax dollars were more likely to follow a patient in or out of an institution. But only a fraction of our mentally ill received help. Working with Jessica at Karis, I'd pieced together the mosaic of our clients' needs. Theirs weren't so different from mine, really. Not just medications, but also school, a job, friends, and a home. Obviously, all this was impossibly complicated for a person paralyzed by fears or lost in grandiose delusions.

Even as we were trying to help those people be heard, the fund was becoming a megaphone for my voice, and for values I'd learned from growing up with Hassie. The first project of Hunt Alternatives Fund was to contract with my neighbor and great friend, Dr. Jean Demmler, to compile a directory of organizations serving persons with mental illness near Denver. To our amazement, she found over seventy.

One was a visitors' program for homebound elderly people released after decades in mental hospitals. Another was a social club, with popcorn and card tables, for schizophrenic young adults who stepped up to an open mike as practice for stepping into the mainstream. "Sheltered workshops," designed with extra staff support and pared down expectations, allowed workers to keep earning wages even when they were so disoriented that they could hardly dress themselves. Still another offered long-term therapy for refugees traumatized in Cambodia's killing fields. All these organizations ended up competing with each other for funding until we put together a new nonprofit, Support Systems Consolidated, enabling them to coordinate their message to legislators and funders.

Across the mental health field, I found, the personal and the professional were unusually intertwined. Even as I'd been drawn to this issue because of Hassie, many clinicians had mental illness running through their family. The director of Denver Social Services had a schizophrenic brother, who disappeared for months at a time. She founded and we funded the Colorado Alliance for the Mentally Ill, offering support groups for family members. Kindness traveled in a circle. A dozen years later, our family would be calling for meeting times.

With all this exposure to the world of mental illness, I witnessed how even the most attentive family members were sometimes unable to care for their sick relative, who might run away, wander off, or become so belligerent that other family members weren't safe. I could relate, remembering my father's efforts, however inept, to care for Hassie. Dad's inability to make Hassie well was failure heaped on tragedy. Seeing the limits of what was possible with my half-brother helped me to empathize with Jack and Jo Ann Hinckley, who asked me to serve on the board of their American Mental Health Fund after their son John tried to kill President Reagan.

One afternoon I visited ward 18 of the city-county jail, which held psychotic people accused of breaking the law. Moving from cell to cell, seeing the miserable inmates rocking themselves in a fetal position or clutching the bars, I felt outraged that our society wasn't providing better alternatives. But if I was honest, I knew I was part of the problem. People like me were gentrifying the city, converting apartment houses back into single-family dwellings at the same time that low-cost single-room-occupancy hotels were disappearing. And in a similar contradiction, the fund supported grassroots organizations like Capitol Hill United Neighbors, even though part of CHUN's mission was to keep our part of town from becoming a "dumping ground," with halfway houses like Karis.

In other words, I was complicit. I remembered Viktor Frankl, whom I'd studied at SMU and who would become a mentor to me almost thirty years later. As he described "man's search for meaning," he insisted on action in the face of inconsistencies. That action-oriented brand of existentialism fit my disposition more than Mother's notion that "God must have a plan." I vowed not to let the perfect become the enemy of the good. Instead, when I discovered wrongs I would try to make things right, even though my role and my motives were never pure.

Crazy Politics

My experience at Karis plus my activist inclination led me into the life of a social reformer. I'd worked with a divided public system that had rigid boundaries, in which a patient lost his therapists if he moved to another part of town. That policy can be deadly, since unlike with other maladies, the more psychotic or depressed a person is, the less likely she is to get herself to a doctor, especially one she doesn't know.

We simply had to change the system, so I took a deep breath and plunged into my first attempt at professional leadership. We needed to integrate the city's four mental health "catchments." It would be tough: each of the quasi-private centers had its own administration, board of directors (often with state legislators and civic leaders), and program specialties. Turf battles were legendary. Two reform attempts had already failed.

At thirty-two, and with guidance from wise mentors, I designed a campaign. On a yellow legal pad, I mapped the current mental health system and listed probable allies or detractors. The page resembled a stringy Jackson Pollock canvas more than a working structure.

Jeanie Demmler and I then made appointments with about thirty stakeholders, some of whom might lose their jobs if we accomplished the reform. We included people who were respected by the community, such as a wonderfully crotchety Kentucky-born investor named Rex Morgan. "I care about this because my family is full of drunks," he scowled. "How about yours?"

"Yeah, our family's kinda crazy," I answered. That was a liberating moment. I could create something sane from the craziness.

Another pearl was handed to me by an older leader of the psychiatric community, who'd watched reformers come and go for twenty years. Genteel and wise, he offered me advice as important as any in my life: "Never ascribe to maliciousness what could be explained by incompetence." Those words kept me from becoming paranoid as I faced one bewildering obstacle after another.

Over a three-year period our ambitious reform succeeded: in part because I was a gutsy, idealistic young woman out to change the world; and in part because I had many wonderful people helping every step of the way. But let's be honest, in a field with declining resources, I was a funder. When we needed fresh ideas for stale problems, I paid for two government officials to travel with me to observe model systems across the country. Next, we made grants to dozens of mental health organizations that needed to be integrated into one system, to bring them to the table.

As we met more and more resistance, I realized that we had to find some dramatic way to break through the distrust. We designed a Colorado Outward Bound raft trip with twenty key players whose names were in boxes on my yellow pad. Some of them had never met, much less collaborated. Suddenly they were plotting a course through dangerous whitewater, yelling out instructions and sharing the rush of adrenaline at the base of a rapid. Around the fire, revisiting the day, competitors were partners.

That mental health reform launched me into politics when the fund sponsored a forum for Denver mayoral candidates. We sent out Jeanie's twenty-page briefing describing the current system, or lack of one. As the moderator, I would grill each candidate on his commitment to the mentally ill. A little-known state legislator with a first name I couldn't pronounce called me at home for more background information. He went on to become mayor, U.S. secretary of transportation, and secretary of energy. But far from the halls of political power, my relationship with Federico Peña was born in a packed church basement, as he faced a crowd of psychotic constituents and their families.

As mayor, Peña turned to me to create the Denver Community Mental Health Commission. I'd given several years of my life and a large portion of my income to get us to that point. So it was no surprise that the other commissioners asked me to be the chair. The surprise was that I didn't have the courage. From high school to Heidelberg, I'd never been president of any group. As assertive as I was in so many ways, I was also typical of the majority of women across time and cultures who are both hard-wired and socialized not to step forward or speak out. The men around me didn't show the same trepidation. They displayed what psychologists term a "positive illusion" that they were clever, wise, and wonderful; in contrast, most women underestimate their own capability. Unless we thrust past nature and nurture, it's easy to surrender to an "imposter syndrome," with an internal voice chiding, "You're not really up to this job."

"Chair? No, I'll work from the wings," I responded. But when we eventually realized our goal of an integrated city system, the key players and I knew it was primarily my accomplishment, despite my low public profile. The next mayor, Wellington Webb, issued a proclamation, preceded by a string a "whereases," that since "Ms. Hunt has made a life's work of finding opportunity in crisis and empowerment from suffering . . . I do hereby officially proclaim Tuesday, November 23, 1993, Swanee Hunt Mental Health Awareness Day in the City and County of Denver."

That public policy success was my first taste of the satisfaction my father must have derived from campaigning for the Twenty-second

Amendment to the Constitution, or lobbying Strom Thurmond. Maybe Dad and I were more alike than I'd thought.

My work had become more meaningful, but also more demanding. So too had home life. I'd agreed to shared custody of Lillian, not just out of love for Mark, but because I wanted to be damn sure my daughter had the fathering I'd missed. But that choice came at a high price. Every week, Lillian spent three days with her father. Although they adored each other, she often screamed nonstop as she went from my care to his. It was gut-wrenching for all of us. But given my worries about whether I was being a good enough mother, her yelling left me limp.

For the days she was with me, I found delightful young women to share in the parenting. They were more like family members than nannies for Lillian and Anna Marie, Jeanie's daughter, who came over every day. Lillian loved our helpers, but even as a toddler she was so intuitive, I felt as if she could read "GUILTY" written across my forehead every time I walked out the door for a meeting.

My daughter's reaction was more than typical separation anxiety. I knew she was imaginative, with a super memory. (At two and a half, she rattled off a ten-minute version of Romeo and Juliet, correcting me impatiently when I confused the houses Montague and Capulet.) But I knew nothing about neurotransmitters and brain chemicals that modulate or magnify emotions. Only later would I realize that her anxiety spilled into terror, her disappointment into despair. Meanwhile, I was trying to be the best parent I knew how. Mark was doing the same. And Lillian, bless her, was just trying not to drown in her emotions.

One morning, already half an hour late to a board meeting, I was trying unsuccessfully to calm my daughter. Thinking she'd quiet down when I was gone, I asked a neighbor to take her in and then drop her by the preschool with her son. I abandoned everyone in that household to Lillian's unabated screams. For years after, the neighbor refused to speak to me.

On the other end of the day, bedtime stretched into hours as my child resisted slumber. She became more hysterical if I left her to cry herself to sleep. So night after night I read to her for hours before she succumbed. Around 10 p.m. I could return to my desk.

I wondered how much of Lillian's hyper-emotionality was a result of my distress when she was in utero. I'd been fastidiously careful about how what I ate and drank might affect my baby. But what chemicals coursed through my body when I confronted Mark after he returned from being with his true love? Joe, as well, had left during my pregnancy, heading off to California with Al, *his* true love. I'd helped pack his moving van, but when he called from a gas station in Utah, we were both crying so hard neither of us could talk.

Had those experiences been imprinted on the daughter developing inside me? I empathized with Lillian's fear of abandonment, but I didn't know how to allay it. Sometimes I tried to fulfill my little girl's needs with an infusion of constant, undivided attention. But even after days devoted to her alone, if I tried to walk across the street to speak to Jeanie, she could become panic-stricken. I couldn't give enough, or be enough, for her.

Courting a Maestro

Single and thirty-five, I wasn't as independent as I appeared. I felt uneasy walking downstairs at night to turn off the lights and lock the doors. When I climbed into bed, I often let Lillian snuggle up with me for comfort—hers and mine. But day by day I was becoming stronger. I was on my own and excited, even if afraid.

Determined not to latch onto one more father figure, I remarked to a lesbian friend, "Maybe I should try women." She counseled that as much as she admired me, I was "hopelessly heterosexual." "Are you sure?" I wheedled. "Positive," she said. I countered that I might then emulate the mournful Parisian chanteuse Edith Piaf and find a nineteen-year-old amour.

Enter Charles, six feet tall, seven years older than I, who'd spent his life onstage, commanding an orchestra and acknowledging applauding fans. Not so far from my old script, but this time with a happier ending. We met in the offices of the head of the Piton Foundation, Fern Portnoy. This was my first board meeting of the Public Education Coalition, which linked businesses and schools. Although I was going out with several men, ever the multi-tasker, I let my eyes survey the table for an eligible companion. After a few minutes, I jotted a note to my neighbor, "Who's that guy?" and nodded toward the lanky, bespectacled fellow across from us.

"Charles Ansbacher. Conductor of the Colorado Springs Symphony," he scrawled back.

"Married?"

"No."

"Gay?"

"No."

The meeting ended. In a burst of boldness, I walked over and gave Charles three telephone numbers in case he wanted to be in touch. He did. For our first date Charles drove the hour and a half up to Denver. He accommodated my suggestion that we lounge in a park, listening to gospel music. I loved the poignant melodies from my past, but Charles wasn't keen, so we headed up into the mountains for a summer symphony concert. "What's that black instrument next to the clarinets?" I asked.

"An oboe," he replied patiently.

Over dinner at a Wild West restaurant called the Fort, my date leaned forward in his chair and gazed into my eyes as he listened. I had a headache, and when the waiter was slow to bring water for my aspirin, Charles gallantly walked over to the bar, to get it himself. Funny how a slight act can pack such robust meaning. I took notice.

Over Rocky Mountain oysters (fried bull testicles, no less), we talked about our divorces, my young daughter, and his teenaged son. Our conversation moved from Charles's civic experience and time as a White House Fellow—the only artist in the program's twelve years—to my mental health organizing. He was clearly attracted by my multiple accomplishments. I, meanwhile, was earnestly searching for his soul.

"What's your favorite song?" I fished.

"Aaron Copland's 'Simple Gifts.' I've performed it recently with solo and orchestra. It's beautifully lyrical."

"No kidding! I've composed a piano arrangement of the piece and sung it for two weddings, accompanying myself on harp!" The gods were giving us a sign.

Other serendipitous connections emerged. I realized midway though my trout meunière just why the name Ansbacher was so familiar: I was using *The Individual Psychology of Alfred Adler*, edited by Heinz and Rowena Ansbacher, for my doctoral dissertation. So we were both the youngest child of famous parents, we were both musicians, we had both led major civic initiatives. We each had one child from a first marriage. I was intrigued by the coincidences.

When we pulled up to my house after the late dinner, I invited him in. Little Lillian had refused to go to sleep and was waiting up for me. She wasn't as enthusiastic about this new element in my life. Charles was, at best, bemused.

On our next date, lest he get too interested, I told him that I had three requirements for my next partner. He needed to be culturally and intellectually stimulating, to like the kind of woman I was, and to adore me 70 percent of the time. The first, Charles met in spades. He was versed in culture, politics, and finance more than anyone within my sphere. As for the second, he was clearly drawn to the intrepid part of my personality, wanting to hear every detail about the initiatives I was spearheading.

And adoration? He promised he could. I wasn't convinced.

I suppose asking for adoration was a bit brazen. But then Charles was no shrinking violet. Fifteen years earlier, he'd arrived as an energetic twenty-seven-year-old in Colorado Springs, a community in search of a cultural leader. He'd built the local orchestra from a season of five performances in a high school to more than sixty in the Pikes Peak Center, the large arts complex that he conceived and promoted.

Charles was eager to have me see his world, so a few weeks after we met he invited me to come for a concert. I agreed, although by now I had strong reservations about whether he was right for me. He'd been calling twice a day. Why so often? I wondered, concluding that he probably didn't have the ego strength I needed in a mate.

A blizzard hit Denver, but Charles assured me that the streets in the Springs were fine. Three hours before curtain, I began inching through the snow. My car was sliding precariously on the ice beneath, and I hoped against hope that the storm would lighten as I traveled south.

Reaching the Interstate, I went ahead only because I didn't want to turn back into the weather behind me. On both sides of the road, dozens of vehicles were angled into snow banks. Twenty feet ahead I could make out red brake lights, my only orientation, which I didn't dare let out of my sight. I followed my unknown guide until Monument Hill, the weather divider along the Front Range. I looked out on the Springs with relief. The road ahead was clear.

At the Pikes Peak Center box office, I found a ticket in a card from Charles, with a sweet thanks to me for coming. Quietly entering the balcony ring, I sank thankfully into my seat in time for the last dozen fiery bars of the Tchaikovsky violin concerto, delivered with exultation by the hotshot Nadja Salerno-Sonnenberg, wearing black leather pants.

In that moment, Charles was transformed from supplicant to master, with authority I could never have imagined. As he punched the air with his baton, the swells of the orchestra filled the hall. With his last triumphant chord, the crowd rose, cheering. I joined in the ovation, staring in wonder at the tousled man bowing to the audience. He looked up at my seat and smiled.

After Charles's four curtain calls, I found the way to backstage, where I knew he would be waiting for me. His strikingly beautiful "significant other" of many years—with whom he'd recently parted ways— was waiting as well. "So you're the 'pretty philanthropist,'" she said, quoting a newspaper gossip column conjecturing Charles's involvement with a Denverite. I tried to smile as I shook her hand.

Soon my new beau emerged in dry clothes, and we headed out for dinner. At the restaurant, he walked ahead of me, looking carefully left and right as we made our way to a small table in the back corner. He seemed apprehensive. Rightly so. After we sat down, his former partner, accompanied by a friend, walked in and unceremoniously joined us. They stayed for the duration of the extraordinarily awkward meal.

It was midnight when we left the restaurant. As we walked out, I said to Charles's ex, "I know this is hard. I'm sorry."

"Just remember," she replied, "You'll be sleeping in my bed tonight." Charles looked embarrassed but said nothing unkind to her or about her, then or ever.

A few days later, the manager of the orchestra took me out to lunch, to welcome me. She recounted over squash soup how Charles had been in love with other women, but his feelings hadn't endured. (Of course, she was telling me as a friend.)

Undaunted, a week or so later I hosted a birthday dinner in his home. One of the dozen guests took me aside and whispered a warning: "You seem to be quite taken with him. Be careful. He has lots of irons in the fire."

I walked back into the room. "You're white as a ghost," Charles worried. I smiled, weakly.

Despite the warnings, I waded deeper. Charles continued to call several times a day just to check in, and we agreed to alternate weekends seeing each other in Denver and the Springs. His home was only a few blocks from where, more than sixty years earlier, my mother's family had lived as my grandfather was dying of tuberculosis. That bit of sweet nostalgia kept me company when Charles was preoccupied and nervous about an impending concert. Still, he was usually a focused, intentional suitor. He cleared a desk where I could work on my dissertation, moved a grand piano out of symphony storage into his living room for my composing, and week after week had a large bouquet of flowers to welcome me. Adoration in action.

After three months, we received our first invitation as a couple: a Christmas party at the Garden of the Gods, given by a wealthy businessman and his wife. I would be stepping into a risky arena, where Hunts were better known than in Denver. The resort was owned by my father's eldest child, Margaret, who had locked the gate between Hassie and Mother.

As Charles and I dressed for the black-tie dinner, I realized I'd forgotten to pack shoes. I rummaged through his closet and found the white, shiny patent-leather pumps I'd left in September. We were already late, so I asked Charles for some black shoe polish and hurriedly smeared it on. Smeared. And then smeared some more. "How's this?" I said, holding out the blotchy mess. He raised his eyebrows. "Sort of like rattlesnake skin," I offered meekly, "At any rate, can't be fixed, let's just pretend they're the hottest New York fashion."

To my relief, Charles wasn't any more uptight than I. Half an hour later he was twirling me around on the dance floor, both of us trying not to look at my feet.

I was feeling adventurous, entering my new lover's territory and encountering his colleagues and calling. As a sidekick to the maestro, I tried to make all of Charles's performances. That meant four shows in four days, and with each repetition my brain recognized more musical themes. By the last performance, I found the complex beauty of a piece transporting. Over time, I came to understand Charles's music as sustenance for those needing a taste of an existence beyond the niggling imperfections or tragedies of their everyday lives.

For all the glamour of the footlights, life backstage was another world: dog-eared and worn scores marked up over years of performances; shirts and even jackets drenched with sweat; a supply of batons, to replace those broken on the edge of the music stand. On concert days, Charles's passion was for his music. I was little more than second fiddle, but that vicissitude was well worth the privilege of being so close to this man. I loved the "take charge" in his personality, as dozens of people on and off stage looked to him for cues. And I loved the reach in his thinking. His Christmas "Pops on Ice" drew twenty thousand to watch the world's skating stars. And his summer concert series attracted seventy thousand picnickers on the Fourth of July.

After shows I waited around, trying to be useful in the post-concert glow, greeting well-wishers and collecting bouquets. I asked Charles if he didn't find the people who gathered around him a nuisance. "Not at all," he explained. "Artists worry about the day no one will want to come backstage." He, in turn, appreciated his audience: the families who came to his Young People's Series and the "blue rinse set," who favored Sunday afternoon. Often before lifting his baton, he turned and addressed the crowd, telling biographical details about the composer or giving clues about interesting moments coming up in one section or another.

I asked if it bothered him when someone mistakenly applauded between movements of a symphony, "No! That was someone who's never been to a concert before. I'm glad they were there." I liked this man.

At after-concert dinners, I took my place beside Charles as he hosted guest soloists for shop talk about which halls had the truest acoustics and the virtues of one tempo over another in whatever movement of whichever symphony. One pianist I found particularly winsome. He turned his head to the audience and beamed with a dreamy, beatific smile as he played Rachmaninoff's *Variations on a Theme by Paganini*. I'd be in New York in a couple of weeks, I told him over our dinner with Charles. Maybe we could get together. After all, I reminded myself, I hadn't offered exclusive companionship to anyone.

In New York, I purchased two tickets for Andrew Lloyd Webber's *Song and Dance*, a perfect coincidence, since it was based on Lloyd Webber's variations on the same Paganini theme. I'd be staying at Helen's. My pianist said he would pick me up at her apartment.

When the doorbell rang, I answered with considerable anticipation. "How thoughtful!" I exclaimed, taking two dozen yellow roses from his arms.

His face fell. "They're actually from Charles." Surprised, I took a step back. "He had them delivered to my apartment, with a note that I should bring them to you." My date had been bested by one of the best.

Eventually I felt accepted by Charles's Colorado Springs world as more than an interloper. (Most of) his colleagues told me they'd never seen him happier. I wasn't in love, but given my experience with Mark, I no longer trusted "in love."

One passionate February afternoon, I proposed. Charles was stunned. With eyes wide, he spluttered, "Well, uh, yes!" I suggested he think it over carefully.

An hour later, we were at a Denver Symphony performance of Beethoven's Fifth. Sitting in the enormous hall, I felt overwhelmed by the significance of the decision we were making. I looked at Charles's face. He was staring straight ahead, with an almost brooding intensity. I took his hand in mine, knowing he must be overcome by questions, by possibilities, by apprehension. We were standing at a juncture that could sculpt our lives forever. Suddenly, I felt his thumb begin pulsing with the music, I looked again at his face. He was staring at the second-hand of his watch, calculating the conductor's tempo. My spirits fell.

In fact, I was extremely sensitive and frequently disappointed by Charles. Of course I also disappointed him—and not just him but also the manager of his orchestra. Under no circumstances, I told her, would I be a financial contributor to my future husband's employer. Charles completely understood that decision. On the other hand, he was rather taken aback with my insistence on a prenuptial agreement ("advance divorce planning," I called it).

But the real test of wills came one evening as we talked about our future together. From some comment Charles made, I realized he was thinking I'd be changing my name to his. "No way," I said, definitively.

He pushed back, "There are plenty of women who would gladly become 'Mrs. Ansbacher.'"

"So marry one of them."

"We'll have a constant hassle at airports and hotels. And how will people we meet know we're together?"

"That's their problem," I retorted. After a long silence, I told my fiancé I'd consider changing my name if he promised he would be equally willing to change his to "Hunt." That established, we could come up with criteria for the decision making, such as order in the alphabet, or ease of spelling. That was our last conversation on the subject.

Civil Ceremony

My life was changing dramatically, in many ways. In 1986 the National Mental Health Association named me Volunteer of the Year. Mother came up for the fancy ballroom dinner in Washington. Charles was conducting in Colorado that night, but from his experience as a White House Fellow, he knew how to arrange a letter of congratulations from President Reagan, which was read aloud at the reception. Given the cuts to social services resulting from the president's anti-government policies, the juxtaposition was bizarre. But to hell with politics. I loved that my suitor cared enough to pull strings for me. It was a far cry from a year earlier, when I was given an award from the Colorado Mental Health Association. Newly divorced and acutely alone, after my acceptance speech I'd gone to my hotel room and lain across my bed, in tears.

I didn't want to move to the Springs, only seventy miles south but politically a pole apart. Given that the city was home to the Air Force Academy, the North American Air Defense Command, Fort Carson, and Peterson Field, it was small wonder that large numbers of military retirees formed a strong conservative constituency. Further, some city leaders had tried to stimulate the economy by supporting the relocation of Christian fundamentalist organizations from all over the country. As I was entering the scene, so were some seventy groups reminiscent of my early days such as Youth for Christ, Young Life, and Focus on the Family. Colorado Springs was quickly becoming a nerve center of the Religious Right.

For me, that conservative culture was Dallas revisited. So was Charles's notoriety. That took me back to my teenage years when store clerks, seeing my credit card, would ask if I was related to "*the* Hunts." In Colorado Springs, Charles had led the World Affairs Council, was vice president of the Urban League, taught at the local campus of the

University of Colorado, worked on political campaigns, and appeared frequently on television. His name was recognized at 7-Eleven checkouts and country clubs alike. I found that his expansive ideas fit the wide-open spaces and western flavor of the Springs. He wouldn't feel intimidated by me, I decided, which meant he probably wouldn't try to hold me back.

Soon after I proposed, it was time to break the news to Mother. Given her unhappiness with Mark even though he was a Baptist, I fretted about how she would regard Charles, who was an agnostic Jew, raised Unitarian. "Her first question will be what church you belong to," I mused aloud to him.

"Just tell her that because of my work I visit lots of churches, to hear different musicians," he coached naïvely.

"She'll ask where your membership is," I said flatly. Charles looked at me puzzled. But I knew this territory, he didn't.

I flew to Dallas and took Mom out to a quiet little French bistro. Over bubbling onion soup and Bible Belt iced tea, I felt a surge of expectant bliss as I told her how happy I was with my newfound beau. "Honey Lamb, if *you're* happy, *I'm* happy," she said, with a generous smile. Then she leaned forward, tilted her head and got down to business. "Now, what church does he attend?"

"Well, as a conductor, he visits *lots* of churches, to hear different musicians," I tried.

"But where is his *membership*?" she asked, on cue.

I decided to pass right over the Jewish and agnostic descriptors. "He's not actually a *member* anywhere," I said, with a slight quiver in my voice. Seeing her face fall, I pulled out the least of three evils. "He was raised Unitarian."

She leaned forward even more, until she was pressing against the table. "Oh, that poor dear," she whispered, her eyes soft with pity, "You know, Unitarians are *very cold*." Compassion had trumped dogma.

Charles, in turn, introduced me to his parents. I found Rowena, ten years into Alzheimer's, dear and darling, like my mother. But Professor Heinz Ansbacher suffered no fools; he pulled me aside to assert that he'd heard I was studying theology and wanted me to know that *his* family didn't need a crutch like religion. I thus braced myself when I met Charles's siblings, who happily gave me a thumbs-up and became (as Heinz did eventually) lifelong friends. Approval followed from Ray,

June, and Helen. Charles liked them as well, although he assured me that he had the "pick of the litter." I was grateful . . . I think.

My close friends Carol, Vinny, Jessica, and Joe were supportive. I explained to them that this relationship was sooner after my divorce than I wished, but what was the likelihood of coming across another man right for me? "You're one in a million," I gushed to Charles. "You think there are a hundred others in this country who could be married to you?" he retorted. To my and Charles's relief, I found I didn't need to look further. Perhaps I'd grown into the calm of middle-age conservatism. Perhaps I was learning that I was strong enough to take care of myself. Regardless of the reason, my maneuvering for attention from men receded. I skated close to the edge a few times but learned that I could keep a healthy distance while marveling, smiling appreciatively at overtures, and exchanging innuendoes. I was relieved to be past the emotional maelstrom of earlier years, but I was happy that the intensity of those episodes was part of my past.

Meeting Charles was a watershed. For the first time in my life, I had a partner who found my assertiveness attractive. He urged me to develop my strengths rather than apologize for them. That affirmation was catalytic, shaping my future to an extent I couldn't then imagine.

In many ways we were a fit, in other ways pathetically incompatible. I loved the heroic, iconoclastic, and outrageous in him. But for the most part my psyche was out of reach for Charles. I'd known hurt, and instead of disabling me, the disappointments in my life had scooped out a chunk of my interior world, leaving a hollow space. That space became capacity, allowing me to feel more deeply, to hold the hurt of others. For all he could connect to my strength, Charles didn't share the full range of my sensitivity. If I talked about a weighty feeling, he often changed the subject. When I tried to speak of some experience I'd had, he often became preoccupied with the accuracy of a detail and missed the larger point. Distraught over his inability to connect to a poignant moment, I would storm out of the house, sometimes driving into the hills to cool off.

Not surprisingly, my companion rarely expressed fears or joys. Did he even experience those feelings? I asked Chuck Lobitz, a therapist. How could I even ask him? It was like asking if the yellow he saw was the same yellow I saw. Speaking of colors, walking out of the movie theater one night, I was telling my date how moved I was by *The Color*

Purple. "The score had too much flute," he complained. I just sighed. Our marriage would be a constant negotiation of disparate perceptions, values, and sensibilities.

Ironically, measuring just how different we were was a help. When Chuck had us take the Myers Briggs personality test, we discovered that in most categories, neither of us fell within the normal range—and we were polar opposites, not even in shouting distance. I asked Chuck what that meant in terms of our staying together. "I'd say your level of difficulty is at 90 percent; but your chance of breaking up is about 10 percent, because you two are both so stubborn." So *there.*

I wasn't the only one having trouble adjusting. Lillian resented Charles terribly, although even at three, she watched him on stage, transfixed, through several Mahler symphony performances in one weekend. Frostiness is typical in blended families, but it was rough. In a circle of negativity, he grimaced as she screamed while I combed her hair before school. I shot him dark looks across the breakfast table, irritated at his impatience.

Sadly, Charles also missed out on the fun. As the youngest of four boys and the father of a son, he found barrettes, Tinker Bell crowns, and sparkly fingernail polish silly on her part and indulgent on mine. Lillian intuitively picked up on his disdain, and I resented Charles for not trying harder to enjoy my daughter, tutus and all.

Several times I called off our marriage plans. But Charles was so gentle and so patient. Every time I despaired, he drew me back to his side. Finally, ten months after we met, we decided to wed during an upcoming trip to Italy. Looking into arrangements, we discovered that our each being divorced created an obstacle in that Catholic country. So we improvised. As I was finishing up another meeting at the Piton Foundation, where we'd first met, my friend Fern asked what the rest of my day looked like.

"Charles is going to try to get away from the office and drive up from the Springs in time to get married."

Fern's voice rose five pitches as she pressed: "What about flowers? What are you going to wear? Who are your witnesses?"

"I don't know, Fern," I said impatiently. "I guess Lillian's nanny, Karla, will come along. Wanna join us? You could bring flowers for Lil to carry."

Three hours later she met us at the City and County Building to witness our marriage, with a bouquet for my three-year-old flower girl. Lil held the nosegay with both hands and La la la'd "Here Comes the Bride" as the five of us trooped down the wide hallways to the office of whatever judge was on duty at the moment.

Making Room

We would still have a simple, private ceremony of our own design in Florence, followed by a honeymoon. To informally officiate, we were joined for the day by Helen (her ten-year-old daughter, Kimberly, in tow) and Charles's brother. Max generously took time off to fly over just for the day.

On our wedding morning, I conversed with my future brother-in-law over breakfast in the stone courtyard of an ancient villa. Charles's brother was a Yale Law School graduate, respected author of books on finance, and savvy investment manager. Over coffee, he commented on the stock market. I took that as an opportunity to move the conversation to the discrepancy between rich and poor in America. That reminded unsuspecting Max of a favorite Ansbacher story about his mother's discovering, when she brought supplies to an impoverished family, that their table had real butter, which was more expensive than margarine. "*Real butter,*" Max repeated. "We had *margarine* in *our* home, and *they* had *real butter.*"

The conversation careened from bad to worse when I described my work in impoverished neighborhoods. "Don't you think you're throwing your money down a rat hole?" Max asked. My answer seemed obvious, so I left my croissant and went to lick my wounds instead.

"What am I doing, marrying into this family?" I fumed to myself back in our room, as I began to dress for the ceremony. To honor our wedding, I'd given Charles two oriental rugs, but he'd given me nothing. That oversight now had a larger context of family parsimony.

There were other perceived slights, I reminded myself. I had of course thought long and hard about what I would wear: pink silk dress, matching earrings and sandal heels. But that morning, when I'd asked Charles what he would be wearing, he'd walked over to the closet and started casually pulling out whatever tie or shirt his hands landed on. I crumpled. "Didn't you think about this before?"

After a few minutes, another jab. "And do you have plans for after the ceremony?" I'd asked, testily.

"I figured we'd go out to a restaurant somewhere," he'd explained. No reservations had been made. But I was beginning to have some of my own. I took a deep breath and tried to stay calm, but as the minutes went by I was churning.

At last, as we walked up the gravel path of the lovely Boboli Gardens, I stopped. Ahead, we could hear the street flutist whom Helen had hired to play with his boom-box accompaniment. As he patiently tooted and re-tooted his Bach, out of earshot I was protesting to Charles that this was a dreadful mistake.

"Please," my perplexed groom urged, his voice pleading but strong. "Let's keep going. I'm sure we can work things out later. I know I've disappointed you, but this will pass. Come on now, let's keep walking."

"I don't think so." I resisted, standing with my back against a gray, moss-covered wall. "This feels like a mistake."

I looked at Charles's face. His brow was furrowed. His eyes had a longing look, tender with vulnerability. Eventually I gave into his assurances and stepped back onto the path. We walked on to where our family members were worriedly waiting. With Kimberly holding a broken tape recorder to (not) capture the moment, we stood in front of Max and Helen as they delivered the scriptures and blessings they'd prepared. I watched a bird soaring overhead. That's my spirit, up there, not here, I said to myself, thinking wistfully of other loves. Just then the celebrated Ansbacher family orator pronounced us "man and wife."

"Man and *what*?" I shouted at Max. I thought of the seminary registrar who insisted I was Mark's appendage; the parade of clueless pastors and dutiful wives at the European Baptist convention; and Charles's unhappiness that I was keeping my name.

"Why not 'man and *cow*'?"

Poor Max was flustered. "What should I say?"

"How about 'man and woman,' or 'husband and wife'?" I suggested impatiently. After we'd made it through the ceremony, I suggested that my new husband go on to our wedding lunch with his brother, not me. Charles gave me some space but soon came back, searching the labyrinthine garden, calling my name. I heard him but didn't answer. Eventually he found me sitting on a rock on the steep path, glumly staring down on the broken, red-tiled roof of a garden shed. I was barefoot, holding the dress sandals that had rubbed blisters on my heels. My apprehension had changed to despondence, and I still refused to go with him. Rebuffed, Charles left.

Helen and Kim found me hours later in the back of a small church, crying. My sister put her arm around me. "We don't have to tell anyone this even happened. We'll just go back home and have your marriage annulled."

But Charles, when he found us, had a different idea. Taking me aside, he begged, "Let's just wipe these last hours off the slate, and start the day over." When I didn't respond, he went on. "Good morning, Love. Did you sleep well?"

It was such a creative notion and he was so earnest that I felt a smile returning. Then I remembered the vows I'd composed for us to recite: we'd promised to meet disappointment with humor. I'd broken that vow before it even left my lips, I confessed.

Over the next days, in the exquisite company of Raphael's angels and Giotto's madonnas, I regained a sense of tranquility and confidence. Charles and I had never spent so much time together, and with each conversation we trusted each other more. A week later, holding hands as we strolled on the breezy, sun-kissed bluffs above the harbor of Portofino, my new husband stopped and turned to me. "I've never believed in a God," he confessed. "But being with you makes me want to have a creator to whom to be grateful." Of all the traditional holy words that celebrate nuptial union, I found that blessing the most profound.

Given those ups and downs, to ensure that we didn't retreat, we threw parties in five cities, letting everyone know what we'd committed. As time wore on, I commented to Charles that our marriage seemed to be getting better. "Considering where we started, that's not saying much," he rejoined dryly.

Slowly, I was learning to trust that we were both smart and well intentioned. If we disagreed, I should remember that we were seeing a complex situation from different angles. Having a relationship strong enough to allow for my anger was a great gift. Charles could be annoying and grouchy, but he was wonderfully patient when I was upset, listening intently rather than escalating in return. In spite of, or perhaps because of, conflict with Charles, I grew stronger, walking away from our disagreements either more certain about why I was correct, or allowing, dammit, that he might be right.

We were both so headstrong that even after we married neither of us was willing to move. Instead each of us enlarged our home. He built an office for me, and I built one for him. Most people live together before getting married. Not us. Even after Italy, we commuted for a year and a half before we tried living together.

Henry stepped in as an older brother to Lillian, who was having an increasingly difficult time emotionally. The power of his commitment to her became clear to me one evening after Lil ran upstairs in a fury. From below, I heard his voice, soothing her: "Listen, Lillian. Listen to me. Stop crying now. It's going to be okay. Stop crying. You don't have to come out. But stop crying so we can talk." I stepped quietly up the stairs and found him sitting on the hallway floor. For an hour he talked to his new sister through the keyhole of her door until she calmed down and let him in.

The men in my life were certain I was the source of Lillian's problems: My poor mothering had created the clinging, the insecurity, the neediness. Mark insisted that I provoked our daughter by being too demanding, while Charles insisted that I didn't set enough limits. I tried to think back on what could have gone wrong. When I was pregnant with her, I'd feared the new little one growing inside me might suffer the mental illnesses that appeared throughout our family tree. Now I was not only worried but also distressed, thinking of how torn up she was inside. And what did this say about me? I desperately wanted to give my daughter a beautiful childhood, and I was failing. I read books, talked with other mothers, conferred with psychologists. Time was passing, but the tantrums weren't.

Other Performances

I'd met Charles near the end of nine years of part-time theological studies at Iliff, where I'd specialized in pastoral care and counseling, applying the lessons of psychological theorists like Freud and Erikson to the needs of the church. My adviser, Larry Graham, had pushed me hard, personally and academically. I was respected as an active doctoral student, coming up with new concepts that synthesized old ones, and writing polished works. Several of my papers were published in professional journals. Three dealt with women: the motherhood of God as a symbol for pastoral care; an analysis of Carl Jung's gender bias; and pastoral care for coping with miscarriage. I was thriving.

My confidence in my analytic skills had grown. But I borrowed against that confidence when after two years of doctoral work I took my comprehensive exams, entrée to the dissertation phase. That was back when I was eight months pregnant with Lillian and my marriage to Mark was suffering. Although I studied for months, I still felt nervous. When I sat down for the written exam, adrenaline coursed not just through me but through my unborn daughter. For six hours, she squirmed and turned inside me.

I felt fine about my answers. The next day, I was poised as I walked into Larry's office to meet with three professors for my oral exams. So I was stunned when they told me I'd failed my written tests, but they would give me a chance to redeem myself in the orals. I stared at Larry. He looked horribly worried. As the hours unfolded, I could tell from his face that I wasn't pulling myself up to the expectations of my questioners. I waited in the hall as they conferred. Larry emerged to tell me that my overall exam result was still a failure.

Neither of us had an explanation. I felt like an idiot, not even knowing what I didn't know. With tears of humiliation burning my cheeks, I drove home. I wanted to slink down beneath the steering column, imagining every pedestrian and driver I passed gawking at me. I'd known disappointment. I'd known failure. This was different. I felt ashamed.

The doctoral committee was in a conundrum. They told me that the comps were designed to demonstrate proficiency to write a dissertation, but they already had that proof in my published articles. To stop me now seemed wrongheaded. The committee assigned me a substitute for the exams: a major paper integrating the works of an ethicist, a psychotherapist, and a social critic. The hundred-page tome took a year to complete. It was a struggle to focus—with a new baby, a marriage in shambles, a foundation to run, and the mental health system reform I was steering. But I managed, and the school waved me on to the last hurdle, my dissertation.

"The Socio-Ethical Dimensions of Empathy: Robert Coles as Paradigmatic to Ministry" was my imposing title, as I described how a psychoanalytically trained social critic moved from examining the inner workings of the psyche to inveighing against injustice. That study fueled my interest in social change, helping me make the connection between the workings of a person and the workings of society. It provided the theoretical framework for the grantmaking of Hunt Alternatives Fund. Still, I hated curtailing my hours *in* the community so that I could sit by myself and write *about* the community.

I squeezed time out of already packed days to write at the long table in my bedroom on which I'd spread my materials. Lillian would crawl into my lap, wanting to play with me as I tried to work. Often I stopped. Sometimes not. Always I was torn, wanting to give my child the fullness of every moment, but feeling distracted and depleted by the labor of a dissertation. I loved my little girl with all my heart, and I wanted to be a great mother. Any time I chose to work on my doctorate instead of play with her felt like a betrayal.

Despite the pulls in other directions, eventually my attempt at a magnum opus was completed. Receiving my doctoral degree was a momentous passage, representing not only years of study but also coming into my own as a thinker. The Th.D. (doctor of theology) was a rigorous degree, which was discontinued after I received mine, and converted into a Ph.D. I had to show proficiency in German and French, as well as the ability to research and articulate new ideas. I was one of the few women, maybe the only one, to have received that degree from the school.

To my surprise, when graduation day arrived, I found myself wishing that Dad could be there. I imagined that he would be enormously proud. It was a more mature thought than usual toward my father, and an emotional place I wish I'd been able to reach while he was still alive.

Mother flew up for the ceremony, with a comically long congratulatory poem she'd composed, and which she read with flourish. Not to be outdone, in the car, as Charles drove Mom, Lillian, and me to the ceremony, my little daughter added to my big day her *coup de grâce*. "I don't think mommies should do distations 'cause they can't let their little girls in their laps." I cringed. Charles threw me a sidelong glance. If Mother heard, she didn't let on.

Quickly changing the subject, I asked Lillian, "Idn't it great Granny Ruth could be here?"

"What did you say, Love?" Charles asked.

Thinking he hadn't heard me, I repeated, "Idn't it great Granny Ruth could be here?"

"How do you spell 'Idn't'?" asked Charles, grinning.

"I-s-n-apostrophe-t." I responded, then hearing myself, and laughed. We were all just plain folks, after all. And no passel of education could change that.

As if we didn't already have our hands full, half a year into our marriage Charles and I decided to have another child. At thirty-six I thought we should get right to it. I would not, however, compete with a symphony in this production, so we consulted a calendar. August was the only month my husband wouldn't be conducting: we had to get pregnant in November. Like clockwork, we accomplished our mission. I was sick as a dog for seven months, but never mind. Our son would be worth it in the end. "The end" was projected as August 11, 1987.

It was nearing time for Teddy to be born, and we still hadn't joined our households. Charles made the difficult decision; he would leave the Colorado Springs orchestra with the title of "conductor laureate" and move to Denver. Governor Romer appointed him chair of the Colorado Council on the Arts and Humanities. Still, I worried that I'd pulled him away from the career of his calling. Life would be simpler, but would it be as fulfilling for him or for me?

In April, Charles rang up with good news. The Colorado Springs Symphony had been asked to perform in Vail at the Gerald Ford Amphitheater. It would be one of his last engagements with the orchestra. As at the first concert I ever heard Charles conduct, Nadja Salerno-Sonnenberg would be the violinist. I was delighted for my husband.

"When's the concert?"

"August 9th."

"But we have a birth planned, remember?"

"Yes, but that's not until the 11th." A tense conversation ensued, as I rattled off statistics about the very small percentage of births that occur on the due date, recounted the importance of this occasion, and reiterated my unwillingness to have a performance compete with a sacrosanct personal moment.

Charles promised to arrange for an understudy. "I wouldn't miss this birth. This will be one of the most important days of our lives.

I'll be right there with you at the hospital," he insisted. I relented. He was giving up the orchestra to come live with me. This was the least I could do.

Weeks passed. "This is like lying next to an aircraft carrier," my husband joked one night. Kidding aside, I reminded Charles again and again of his promise to get an understudy, my anxiety growing along with my belly. "Of course I'll be with you at the hospital," he insisted, now without enthusiasm. "But anyway, the baby's not coming on August 9th."

Finally, we were within two days of the concert. Charles was past the study period and deep into rehearsals. Not only had he not arranged a substitute conductor, he hadn't even rehearsed the concertmaster as a stand-in. He was clearly irritated when I raised the issue yet again.

The evening of August 8, I asked one more time, "What will happen if the baby comes tomorrow?" But it was far too late. After weeks poring over his scores, he was enslaved to the muse. No amount of ranting on my part penetrated. After a stormy exchange, Charles walked out of the living room, leaving me crying. My sobs quieted as I lay on the sofa—all 204 pounds of me. Then through the air conditioning vent, I heard him dialing the phone of his office in the basement below. At last, I thought gratefully.

"Nadja? Let's go over the tempo of the cadenza one more time." Charles was lost to me. I collected my thoughts and then called down on the intercom, asking him to come back upstairs. He walked in rather sheepishly.

"Let's bury the hatchet," I proposed. My husband was amazed and appreciative. In fact, his gratitude led to an amorous encounter— which induced labor. At five the next morning, August 9, I was awakened by contractions, which I timed for the next hour. Every six minutes. But I figured I had some time. I awakened Charles.

"Let's get to the hospital," he said solicitously.

"I have a different plan." I knew that Charles couldn't conduct his concert if we went to a Denver hospital. "Let's drive to Vail. They must have some sort of clinic or hospital there."

"Are you sure, Love?"

"Positive." I pulled from my shelves *Our Bodies Ourselves*, a flower-child holdover that had once shocked me in its frank discussion of women's physiology. Turning to instructions for home birth, I read aloud the checklist of what we needed for a roadside delivery: paper towels, a knife, shoe strings to tie the umbilical cord, a towel to wrap the baby . . .

Thus equipped, Charles and I made it to Vail Valley Medical Center, climbing three thousand feet in altitude, with me clocking contractions the whole way. We walked into the clinic around 7:30. The receptionist asked me our address.

"No, not your Denver home, your Vail address."

"We don't have a Vail address."

"Where did you spend last night?"

"In Denver; we just drove up this morning to have our baby."

"Who's your doctor?"

"Who's on call?" She was not amused.

The concert was scheduled for 2 p.m. I tried, to no avail, to persuade the baby to keep coming. Eventually, it was time for Charles to rehearse the orchestra. We called Fern, who was in the mountains for the weekend, and asked if she could help out. She was flustered; I was calm. "Breathe," I told her. "Keep breathing."

Charles went off to his rehearsal, leaving Fern with instructions to call when he should return for the grand finale. Now I was trying to keep the baby *inside* until Charles could rejoin me. I had as much success in that effort as I'd had earlier in trying to make him come out. The labor became more and more intense. I was moaning, constantly changing positions, trying to ease an excruciating pain in my back. Finally, in tears, I turned to Fern, "Tell him he's gotta come *now*."

She called the backstage pay phone number Charles had left. He had stationed a young man by the phone, with our car keys in hand. "I hear clapping! They're between pieces!" Fern reported excitedly back to me as I groaned. "He says he's giving Charles the sign! Oh *no*! The music has started again!" Missing the all-important wave, Charles had launched into an encore: fittingly, the William Tell Overture. Then, seeing the stagehand signal, he picked up the tempo. The Lone Ranger never made better time.

Without waiting for bows, the maestro sprinted off the stage, grabbed his keys, jumped into his car, and raced to the clinic. He burst into my room in his tuxedo, stripped off his jacket as the nurse covered his sweaty shirt with a green gown. Teddy made his appearance, and

Charles was there to catch him. I figured we all gave grand performances that day.

Of all the new challenges that Charles introduced in my life, I was most nervous about his bringing a teenaged boy into our family. I dubbed Henry "young Adonis," but to my friends only. Charles blanched whenever anyone commented on his son's handsome features, determined that Henry not be overly impressed with his appearance.

Henry's mother was Barbara Kimball Ansbacher, a talented and attractive musicologist in Massachusetts. Soon after we decided to marry, Charles had introduced me to his former wife over the phone. I liked her immediately and over the next months we compared notes on Henry, who was smart, sensitive, and kind, albeit rather knotted up in an adolescent way. She seemed genuinely happy to hear how when he came out to the Springs for spring break a year after we married, Henry stretched across the bed, talking for hours with me about identity, meaning in life, and relationships—including with her.

A few weeks later Barbara learned that she had terminal cancer. She was forty-four. I got on the next plane, so she could meet me face to face. Lying in her hospital bed, she asked if I "could make room for Henry." I promised her that I would consider him my own.

Most of that visit I spent with Henry. We talked about how his recent unhappiness toward his mother was normal for a teenager and would probably shift in a few years. He had to leapfrog over his resentment. "You just have to pretend you're twenty-one," I pushed. To help, I put a few hundred dollars in the bank for him to spend on his mother: a bed jacket, a dinner, or a bouquet, maybe. He protested that he'd never done those things and she would think it was fake.

Some weeks later, Barbara called: "You won't believe what just happened! Henry took me out to dinner, and"—she began to cry—"he even gave me flowers!"

While she still had enough strength, Barbara and her second husband came out to Colorado, giving Henry a few days of united parents and letting Barbara experience the home that would become her son's. Her abdomen was swollen, so I took her shopping at a maternity store. I was so enormous with Teddy that when we walked into the store, the clerk looked at me and said, "I'm sorry, we don't have anything your size."

"It's OK. We're here for my friend," I laughed. That evening Barbara grinned like a kid as she modeled her new outfits for us all.

Henry went back home with his mother. But within a few weeks he called, his voice full of fear. Charles and I caught the next plane east. We found Henry at home, holding a paper cup with morphine for his mother to sip. I was sitting by Barbara's bed, reading psalms aloud, when the hospice worker said the end was imminent. Charles and I stood in the next room as Barbara, with grace and dignity, died. Being in her life even those short months was a gift to me. My gift to her was to love her son, knowing full well I would never take her place. Henry finished his senior year of high school and then moved out west to attend Colorado College and be near us.

The Columbine

I'd become a risk taker. And that wild side of my personality had room to roam on the high alpine meadow of South Park, stretched out before wayfarers emerging over the pass. The rugged terrain and physical demands of life at ten thousand feet spurred an adventurousness otherwise confined by city culture. Every time I drove away from my ranch I felt stronger, not only physically, but with my spirit toned as well.

The ranch included a dilapidated blacksmith's shop, which I shored up as a cabin. To the west and south were some of the highest peaks of the Rockies, but a long barn obscured my view of the Continental Divide. We couldn't move the mountains, so I moved the barn, allowing us to watch a sheet of rain creeping up the plain for an hour before we felt a drop. Evenings we gawked at the sky bursting into flames in a maddeningly glorious backdrop to the purple mountains.

I'd wanted horses ever since Helen and I played Annie Oakley and Dale Evans, mounted on brooms as we skipped through Granny's woods in Oklahoma. As a camper, I'd tumbled head over heels in love with riding, but twenty years passed before I had my own horse, Shoshone. By cowboy standards she was a joke—a small, sway-backed, ignominious Paint. I was the only rider safe (relatively) on her. Half a dozen times I landed on my backside, but we eventually worked out the kinks in our relationship. She had a trot as smooth as pudding, which compensated for the clenched rein I had to keep most of the time. Shoshone and I explored trails below and above timberline, bushwhacking through terrain so steep and rocky that other horses balked. During long rides, our minds seemed to merge. Rather than whisper the gait I wanted her to take, I'd just think it and off we'd go. Inspiring endurance. Tough to handle. Shoshone and I understood each other, because we were alike.

I'll never forget Charles's introduction to the ranch, just a month after we met. He described with relish his five-day-long riding stints with civic leaders in Colorado Springs.

"How fast did you move?" I asked.

"We walked the whole way."

"My horses don't do much walking," I commented.

Down at the corral, we saddled up Shoshone and Wemenuche, her spunky offspring, who'd sent a friend to the hospital with a broken arm a few months earlier. "I wouldn't wear that hat if I were you," I warned.

"I always wear this hat when I ride," Charles answered in a half-convincing drawl.

"Shoshone's pretty calm, but Wem spooks. I wouldn't wear *that* hat on *that* horse," I repeated. He wore the hat.

About three miles out from the ranch, we paused after a long canter for the horses to catch their breath. I was thinking how great it was that my guy could sit a saddle so well. Just then, Charles reached up with one hand and adjusted his Stetson. With a loud whinny, Wemenuche reared high in the air. Cowboy Charlie landed on the ground. I left him sitting in the road as Shoshone and I raced after Wem, circling and cutting him off before he headed back to the barn.

Over the years, I was wrangler and rancher, but also camp counselor, hosting half a dozen girls for several summers. Lillian was too fearful to go to a regular camp, so we created our own. In addition to sleepouts, nature walks, and horse shows, the girls wrote musicals featuring Native Americans confronting murderous hags, lost loves, and an occasional Spanish conquistador. Neighboring ranchers and families of the actresses watched the show, perched on bales in the hay barn.

Teddy made his début at two, joining a war dance with a flimsy rabbit skin around his loins but parting from the script, tearfully demanding an arrow to waggle with the girls. By three, he'd graduated to a speaking line. "Off with the savages!" he passionately rendered, "Off with the *cabbages*!"

With Henry too, the ranch provided a backdrop for bonding. When he was fifteen and brand new to my life. I asked him to take a walk along the gravel road to establish, as it were, our rules of engagement. "We're going to have some great adventures," I said, "but there'll be times I'll get under your skin. Let me know so we can talk it out."

"I can't do that."

"Then you've gotta learn, just like right now."

Soon after, Henry became exasperated with me over some matter I no longer recall. Hearing his complaints, Charles, ever the careful listener, promised his son that I was "high maintenance but high yield." Henry had plenty of practice in maintenance. Eventually he could take the lead, asking what unhappiness I was harboring. We'd end up sitting on a log, sorting through our problems.

Even as they develop along broad themes, relationships crystallize in specific moments. Those memories stay with us forever. One of mine is the day Henry walked hesitantly out to the porch where I was talking a blue streak, gesticulating angrily at his father. His teenage brow was furrowed as he held out two cups of coffee. Surprised, I stopped my diatribe and looked up at him. Taking the cup, I sipped the coffee, which he'd fixed with hot skim milk and half a package of sweetener, exactly as I liked it ever since my childhood visits to Franny's farm. From someone who didn't choose me but inherited me through tragedy, that coffee was an eloquent gesture of acceptance.

Vision. For better or worse, I suppose that more than most, I operate with a vision of the way things ought to be. Myself, or a family, or the world. But also a ranch. Caught up in the romance of the West, I decided to do my part to return Great American Bison to land they'd roamed by the uncountable thousands. Over the years, my ten cows and one bull grew into a herd of seventy-six.

Four hooves and bad breath were about all they had in common with cattle. They purportedly could out-jump a deer and out-race a thoroughbred. But they seemed to me more like a column of tanks as they trampled fences into flattened heaps of barbed wire. We had to swallow our pride and ask angry neighbors if we might open their gates and on horseback drive our herd back across their already insulted property. As we pushed the buffalo toward the opening, the leader would suddenly pivot 180 degrees, and the whole herd would rush toward us. We'd wheel our horses around to escape the stampede, the thunder of hooves matching the pounding of my heart. Suddenly the herd would stop, and the brutes would lower their heads and start munching grass as if we were out for a Sunday picnic. We'd turn our horses and start coaxing again until the leader finally found the way out.

After one bison had a blind date with a porcupine, we confined her in a metal "squeeze" while Charles and I pulled quills from her lips and nose with pliers. A week later she was dead; a quill had worked its way into her bloodstream and punctured her lung. I imagined she had died of humiliation. Death was never far from buffalo life, as we slaughtered one beast a year to stock our freezers. Our friends adjusted to buffalo burgers, buffalo meat loaf, buffalo steaks . . .

Finally, one day, before dawn, the yet-again-escaped herd stood on the highway in a thick fog. A semi and a Toyota truck hit them from each direction. Several buffs were killed, but miraculously no people were hurt. Romance faded into reality. I sold the herd.

Rounding up errant buffalo, galloping across meadows, and hiking up peaks, I developed an appreciation of what I could do, as opposed to just how I looked. That was a major shift for me. As a child, I'd memorized verses about the body as "the temple of God," not to be profaned. But I'd never been inspired to worship when I looked at myself nude in the mirror. Like most of my friends, as a teenager I compared my form with those on the cover of *Seventeen*. Even as an adult, in grocery lines my hand wandered over to the magazines; I surreptitiously tucked an issue on "tummy flattening" between the broccoli and the guacamole. Then in the kitchen, I'd snatch up the telltale magazine and take it upstairs, where it waited in a stagnant pile to inspire or instruct me the next time I noticed, in dismay, that my undressed body called to mind not so much a firm, shapely pear as a plate heaped with Jell-O.

In my twenties, Mark, a jock, had been a good sport—literally and figuratively—taking me with him on mountain treks and ski trips. Still, I felt like an extra burden that he had to lug along, and I was more concerned with keeping up than enjoying myself. If we were skating, my ankles gave out. If we were skiing, my feet cramped. But the Columbine was my territory. Beyond pretty, there I had to be strong. For my new role as rancher, I needed a new body. Before I met Charles I lost thirty pounds, and while never slim, I was delighted to finally buy clothes from a "normal" store.

But more than the activities at the ranch or the relationships built there, the Columbine was a spiritual retreat. Away from the trappings of my office, the hum of traffic, and the intrusion of passers-by, I gave myself long hours surrounded by only nature, hours that turned my thoughts to the mysteries of creation. I dubbed a magnificent aspen grove the Cathedral, where white bark branches reached to blue sky with Gothic grandeur. My closest friends and family understood: This was where my ashes should be spread.

The Women's Foundation

At the same time that the ranch was providing me a haven, my work to create the Women's Foundation of Colorado was pulling me deeper into the community. That saga began when two activists, impatient with the status quo that kept women struggling for an equal voice, dropped by my Denver home for a backyard visit. After the usual "ain't it a shame" warm-up came what I thought was the punch line: "We think it's time to organize some way to address the pressing needs of women and girls. Are you interested?"

"Count me in," I declared, proud of my decisiveness. "When you're ready to start, I'll contribute $10,000."

There was an awkward pause. "We were actually thinking *you* should start it" was the real punch line. "We've tried this from the grassroots, looking for a thousand women to send ten dollars a month. It's a killer. We need leadership among power players."

I laughed to myself. I was hardly acquainted with, much less integral to, Colorado's power set. But why not? Thinking they wouldn't say yes, I wrote to several influential women, including Fern and Colorado's First Lady, Dottie Lamm, promising that the project wouldn't take much time. Maybe we'd each host an event along the way. That turned out to be an egregious understatement. It took six weeks for us to find a meeting date, after which my course was set for the next six years.

The need was clear. Policy reports announced "the feminization of poverty," caused by an increase in unskilled teenage mothers, deadbeat dads not paying child support, divorced homemakers un-equipped to compete in the marketplace, and elderly women with meager retirement benefits from poorly paid jobs. Yet nationally and locally, programs targeting boys received much more support than those targeting girls. I was inspired by Helen's Dallas Women's Foundation. Surely we could follow her example to create a public charity to support nonprofits across the state.

To launch the endowment, we would concentrate on collecting major gifts. We wouldn't even announce our existence until we had a million dollars pledged or donated. Controversy swirled around whether we should offer a seat on the board to every major donor ($50,000 or more). We agreed that those wealthy donors on our board would be at least joined by an equal number from traditionally un-derrepresented groups. But to avoid being diverted by political argu-ments, we also agreed that we wouldn't diversify until we'd met our financial goal.

Then came the meeting that transformed my life. As we were sit-ting around our planning table, Josie Heath, a local civic leader, said, "Swanee, others will gauge their gifts by yours, so you need to set the standard with a quarter of a million dollars." I thought I would fall out of my chair. I had a middle-class income and lived in a middle-class neighborhood. I drove a Chrysler and wore inexpensive clothes with jewelry from craft fairs. My ranch was in a beautiful setting but wasn't posh. I didn't throw catered parties. Hunt Alternatives Fund had no endowment, and we gave small grants. Why on earth did Josie think I had that kind of money?

But then why shouldn't she? The *Forbes* annual list of America's four hundred wealthiest individuals credited my family with hundreds of millions. Of course they were counting the value of our family-owned business, and those funds should never leave the company. Or should they? The more I thought about Josie's request, the more I wondered if it was *I* who wasn't thinking straight. Others on the *Forbes* list did important philanthropic work. Why didn't the Hunt sisters? That mo-ment was a turning point. It was *my* perception that was warped, not my friend's. Agreeing to the pledge, I eventually paid it several times over. I was the first woman irrevocably changed by the Women's Foun-dation.

With credibility as the largest donor, I became an aggressive recruiter. For six months Dottie and I crisscrossed Colorado (which was in a serious recession), beating the bushes for support. I became a frequent guest at the governor's mansion, with backdoor entree. The First Lady and I had lunch with every wealthy woman we could ferret out, asking each for at least $50,000 over five years. Charles was eager to contribute to my success by introducing me to the wealthiest among his Colorado Springs Symphony circle. His stalwart Republican friends told me, "I'll join, because it's not part of the women's movement." Dottie knew the Democrats, including a large contingent from liberal Boulder. They'd say, "Sign me up. I've been a feminist all my life."

This was my introduction to people who rotated seasonally among four houses. But wealth didn't necessarily imply financial generosity. Women would send their alma maters $500, while their husbands donated $5,000 without blinking an eye. I listened for the gasp to determine if I'd asked for enough. Most of my prospects said no, and a long string of no's wasn't easy to hear without becoming exasperated. (One day I peevishly asked my guest at least to give as much as she'd spent on the designer suit she was wearing.) But one in eight said yes, and a yes went a long way.

We planned our public announcement for Dottie's last week in the governor's mansion, but our fundraising was so successful that we kept increasing our goal. The night before our press conference, I hosted a black-tie dinner for the board. We were $70,000 short of $2 million. As my guests arrived, I stopped a few of them on the porch and asked them to increase their pledges beyond the small fortune they'd already committed.

Engaged in doorway solicitation, I managed to burn the buffalo stroganoff I was about to serve. Undaunted, I added more seasoning and tried to cover by announcing that my guests might notice a gamy taste. Everyone who took a second helping I secretly blessed. Burned buffalo or not, the evening marked a grand success. When time came for a toast, I raised my glass, announcing that we had $2 million.

Soon before that evening, a group of prominent and articulate women of color had gathered in my living room to protest bitterly their exclusion from our early efforts. I'd worked closely with several of them through Hunt Alternatives Fund. "We expected it from others, Swanee, but not from you," one scolded.

I countered that we'd focused only on the big fundraising . . . of course we were going to invite them in when it came to grant making . . . surely they could understand the timing issue. . . . As I heard my own words, I was no more convinced than they. Eventually there was nothing to do but admit that we'd insulted them the way women had been insulted throughout history. We immediately added black, Hispanic, Native American, and Asian board members, who emerged as leaders.

Although trying to see people rather than skin tones, I certainly wasn't colorblind. For all my talk about reaching out to those on the margins, I thought of racial minorities as victims who needed my help. Like most privileged whites, I'd never been a member of an organization, or even a committee, chaired by a Native American or Asian. Apart from the refugees Mark and I had resettled, no black person had ever spent the night in my home. I'd never been invited for dinner with a Hispanic family. Now I was in a mixed group—planning, arguing, and traveling.

After we launched the foundation, I flew to the annual meeting of the National Network of Women's Funds with Katherine Archuleta, the savvy aide to Mayor Peña and one of the women of color who had confronted me in my living room. Her style and comportment were much more sophisticated than mine, even as she carried her infant daughter, a curly brunette, brown-skinned like her mother. Walking down the airplane aisle, I smiled at Donald Sutherland, sitting in first class, who looked dashing in a dramatic gray cape. After Katherine and I found our seats in coach, I went up front to say how much I enjoyed his movies.

"I noticed you when you boarded," he smiled. "Was that your nanny with your little girl?" I went back to coach and laughed as I told Katherine the story. She didn't find it nearly as funny. I had a lot to learn.

My next lesson was some hours later in Atlanta, at the meeting of the dozens of women's foundations whose members had gathered to share their experiences. Though our board was multiracial, our contingent to this meeting happened not to meet the diversity criterion. Furthermore, we were looked on with not only envy but also distrust when we described our fundraising methods and success. The criticism began. We were élitist. We didn't value diversity.

"Diversity?" I countered, standing up during a plenary session. "I'd like a show of hands of how many of your boards have at least 40 percent directors who voted for Ronald Reagan." Not one hand went up. But being right didn't mean I was going to win a popularity contest. In fact, I continued to lose points.

In a small group, we were discussing political positioning. "Our state is a real mix of liberal and conservative, and our funding comes from both communities," I explained. "So at this point we're focusing on themes that cut across political lines, like economic empowerment. That means, for example, we're not going to be marching in the streets for gay rights." It seemed an obvious statement to me. But an hour later, the lesbian caucus held an emergency meeting.

When we gathered the next morning, the chairs were in a large circle. Two women stood in the middle. "Given the insensitive statement made yesterday, we feel we must respond." Hearing me inhale sharply, Katherine stretched her arm across my lap, like a mother protecting a toddler as she slams on the car brakes. "If you say one word I'm going to have to slap you," she muttered through the side of her mouth.

The speaker continued, "We share responsibility for creating an environment where such a statement could be made. As lesbians we've made ourselves invisible, so now we'll let you see who we are." About a third of the large circle stood. I thought of that revival service in Dallas when the evangelist asked the saved to be seated and then pray for the unsaved, still standing. That was horrible. This was beautiful. I admired my friends who'd stood up and felt wretched about the gap between us.

I was in the distressing position of being an outspoken advocate for gay rights, but perceived in this setting as a bigot. In the hours that followed, as always, private conversations were different from public stances. A founder of the San Francisco Women's Foundation confided to me that even in a community where gay rights demonstrations were commonplace, they did no overt lesbian funding for the first several years of their existence. I thought back to the women's suffrage movement one hundred years earlier, which was almost derailed by a split over whether to combine efforts to abolish slavery with the campaign for women's voting rights. Moral purity versus getting the job done. The bar was high—too high for me, I was finding.

The controversy took its toll. My sister Helen, the primary force behind the network, found a board member of the Dallas Women's Foundation crying in the bathroom. "In the south, we're concerned about whether our purses match our shoes," she said. "Our city council debates whether shelters for battered women are anti-family. I just shouldn't have come. I don't belong here." My wise sister responded, "Now you know how lesbians feel most of the time."

As the Women's Foundation grew, I grew. Speaking at civic clubs or low-income housing projects, I found my voice. Chairing committees, I saw my ideas become policy and grew accustomed to having others look to me. And working to better the lives of hundreds of thousands felt like an answer to my early religious calling. But I was reluctant to take center stage, determined that the Women's Foundation must not become Swanee Hunt's Foundation. After all, I'd managed for thirty-five years without a formal leadership position.

In its fourth year, I decided to face my fear of power, agreeing to rotate into the presidency. Being in the company of women I trusted helped me feel safe enough to assume a role out front. On our board retreat soon before I was to assume the presidency, I told my friends about a dream I'd just had: I was shoveling piles of manure in my basement, while my mother looked on disapprovingly. As I talked about the nightmare, I broke down, saying, "I really don't want this job." It was a cathartic moment for me, and a confusing one for everyone else. Beneath the calm and cheer, their high-energy, organized leader was a complicated tangle.

Open vulnerability often creates soul mates, especially among women. My self-disclosure was made as we went around the group, each of us relaying a challenge in her life. In the safety of that space, one woman put her hands over her face as she described having been raped. Another cried as she talked about her father's advances. True to statistics, though still shocking, one in every four described some sexual abuse. Many of us had known each other a dozen years but were oblivious to these dark and thus all-the-more-powerful secrets.

Over the next year, it was up to me to maintain the sense of intimacy while we went about our business of raising money and giving grants. At the first board meeting I chaired, I made up an exercise. I brought twenty-five different flowers, handing one to every board member as we stood in a circle. Each introduced herself by saying whatever was on her mind, then put her flower in the vase in the center. At the end, there would be a gorgeous bouquet, every blossom different.

The hour unfolded as planned until we got to a Latina who ran a clinic for migrant workers. She turned to the woman next to her: "I've been staring at your fancy alligator high heels, wondering how many months of birth control pills they'd buy for some worker. And furthermore, I don't particularly like rich women." This could be a long year, I thought.

In fact it was a very long year, filled with philosophical battles among board members. We almost never reached full agreement, but some debates were particularly bitter. After a heated discussion, we decided with a 13–12 vote not to take out a newspaper ad supporting abortion rights in the reheated battle over *Roe v. Wade*. I had argued that we shouldn't, since I'd personally assured our conservative donors that we were centrist. "Join NOW, join NARAL, join any organization you want to support abortion rights. I'm a member too," I said. "But that's not what *this* organization is about." After the vote, my most vocal opponent met me at the coffee table in the back. Our feelings were frayed, but we knew we were in this for the long haul. We put down our cups and embraced.

As I presided over one close vote after another, I waited for the inevitable moment when the financial bottom lines of our board members would become the philosophical fault lines of the foundation. That day never came. To my amazement, several wealthy women voted against incentives to attract big donors. They were countered by women raised in housing projects who insisted that the foundation was about money, and our policies needed to reflect that reality—politically correct or not.

Inside the organization, to my fault I was constantly biting off more ideas than we could chew. Often my high-pressured style was rough on all concerned, a dynamic that a brave co-founder, Marjorie Seawell, pointed out to me in an eternal hour of honest assessment. But occasionally my expansive thinking paid off. Planning a trip to Chicago, I asked another co-founder, Merle Chambers, if I could go see her mother to plead for a large gift. Charles was once again at my side as we drove up and down the street, thinking that the house at the address Merle gave me was too unpretentious to match my mission. But when I finally rang the doorbell, Mrs. Chambers appeared, smiling.

Over lunch I shouted to our hostess, who was nearly deaf, that she might donate $1 million as a surprise gift during her daughter Merle's upcoming presidency. "Why do you think I have that kind of money?" I imagined her echoing my earlier response. Instead, she nodded yes, and added, "Have I told you about my trip to China?"

On our way home, I reviewed the conversation with Charles: "The good news is she said yes; the bad news is I don't think she heard me," She had. I felt high as a kite and emboldened. I was learning that some of our pain as women is self-inflicted as we trivialize ourselves, fail to develop personal and professional gravitas, or capitulate with small gestures like giving up our places behind the steering wheels of our cars when we are out with men. Across the years, news articles about "the family of H. L. Hunt" had described the successes of my brother and the shenanigans of my half-brothers, rarely mentioning the existence of sisters. But the Women's Foundation was the one place where, *because* I was female, I could grow and thrive.

The foundation itself would grow and thrive, building an endowment surpassing $10 million, while spreading more millions to women across the state. We had conceived and given birth to a new model. Its success felt like my success and spurred me on to think bigger and bolder.

The King Was in the Counting House

As a girl, when people asked me about my future, I drew a blank. With no role models, I didn't imagine myself past twenty-one. But I pledged to do better for my own children. And so one of my lowest parenting moments was when I asked Lillian, then three, what she'd like to be when she grew up. She thought for a few seconds, and then replied, "A nurse."

"That's wonderful, Lil, because you're so sensitive and nurturing." I paused. "You know, you'd also make a good doctor."

"No, Mommy," she corrected. "Boys are doctors, and girls are nurses." That day we switched to a female pediatrician.

I couldn't believe that this had happened in *my* family, an environment with very little TV time. The gender stereotypes must have been airborne. From that point on, I became more fully aware of the messages that Lillian, and later Teddy, picked up. And I decided to add my own. In my bedtime stories, princesses rescued princes in distress. The seven dwarfs came home from the mines each day and found the heroine studying her law books; all eight made dinner then took turns cleaning up. Never, ever, was Snow White left with the dishes.

I could identify with Ms. White, torn between wanting to be taken care of and independence. For every woman, the script is different. In my case, coming into my own as a woman included coming to terms with money. I'd moved past the chagrin I felt when "Hunts" were used as the symbol for "sin" in my seminary classroom. When, as we sat on the porch swing, my neighbor Jeanie volunteered completely out of the blue that my wealth never, ever crossed her mind, I only smiled at the innocent illogic.

Less benign was the orthopedic surgeon who sat on a stool in front of me, manipulating my leg, with its torn ligament. Holding my injured limb in his hands, he asked if I would buy some new equipment for the hospital. He named the price, which was huge. I said I didn't have that sort of money. "I've read about your family. You could do it if you wanted to," he retorted, as he bent my leg. I took my knee and went home, having been manipulated enough.

I didn't know the concepts or vocabulary of money talk, partly because my parents never imagined their daughters as anything other than wives and mothers in Dallas. Until well into our thirties, June, Helen, and I had little exposure to finance or business. Ray was the only one of my mother's children integrated into the company. We were typical of the families of wealth described by Robert Coles in his book *The Privileged*: money was simply not discussed at home.

In a sense, we sisters could afford that lapse. Ray had arranged a comfortable income for us, and our lifestyles weren't flashy. None of us drove fancy cars or wore designer clothes. Over time, however, we three came to realize the importance of understanding our finances, and that became a problem as we reckoned with the ghost of Dad, the concern of Mother, and the reticence of our brother.

Helen and I shared great frustration over our parents' expectations. As a result, neither of us was willing to stay in Dallas. Helen had created an independent life in New York, knee-deep in work with nonprofits in East Harlem, while encouraging the replication of women's foundations across the country. When we teamed up in our philanthropy, she was often my inspiration in demanding social justice. But she was also a visionary, promoting a new paradigm of women helping women.

June had also struck out on her own, leaving her staff position at First Baptist and creating her own ministry. She'd transformed her conflict with Dad and defense of Mother into help for people troubled on many counts but especially those abused as children or wives. Speaking and singing for groups around the country, she offered a biblically based cure for social ills. Her radio programs, "Hope for the Heart" and "Hope in the Night," were a great success on Christian airwaves. Some far-right stations thought she was delving into matters better left alone. My sister wasn't dissuaded. While quick to describe herself as fallible, she took a tough stand on holding people (mostly men) accountable for the pain they inflicted in violent domestic situations. In later years I introduced her, tongue in cheek, to the founder of *Ms.* magazine as "the Gloria Steinem of the Religious Right." June and Gloria each looked at me incredulously before we all broke into a laugh.

Ray, while involved in many civic endeavors, had taken a different path from his sisters. After working summers in the oil fields and at the office, majoring in economics and business, and assuming positions of greater and greater responsibility at Hunt Oil Company, he was clearly destined for a career within the family enterprise. Except for Hassie, all of Dad's publicly recognized sons and sons-in-law worked at the company, but Dad maintained that Ray was the smartest of them all.

Our father was so attached to his youngest son that when Ray married in his early twenties, Dad wanted him to live next door and be available at any time. Ray and Nancy Ann acquiesced for a year, but even after they moved across town they never had the freedom that Mark and I enjoyed. Once we married, my visits to Mt. Vernon were very much that: visits. But for Ray, Dad was a constant. Even in college my brother never lived outside Dallas, and he rarely traveled except for business. As Dad's health declined, he assumed the burden of patriarch on behalf of Mom and her children, growing into that responsibility at an amazingly early age as he shouldered the weight of not only the business but also family management.

By most standards, he fulfilled his role superbly. At Dad's death, my brother formally picked up the reins, although he had already put in more than a decade at the company. With vibrant leadership, he restructured the business, created a successful real estate development arm, cultivated strong ties with (mostly Republican) politicians, and inspired confidence among lenders. As I pursued my interests outside Texas, Ray was guiding the company through points of peril; rebuilding Hunt Oil into a robust enterprise many times the size it was when he took over. In the process he was widely admired as a civic giant and—that *Time* magazine I picked up in Belgrade had it right—a remarkably nice guy.

Given the differences in our lives, when we four siblings got together at dinners before the quarterly meetings at the company, the dynamics were striking. I realize now that at those dinners Ray was meeting with the majority of his stockholders (words I never heard), but at the time I was only aware that he was carving out precious hours away from his wife and children to devote to his sisters. I was also aware that we three, uneducated in business and particularly the oil and gas industry, did a huge amount of listening as he talked animatedly about the ins and outs of the company. Every day our brother was fighting for us on the dangerous free-market battleground, determined to stay not only competitive but also ahead of the pack. His anecdotes were informative as well as fascinating. But it was striking to me that he never asked us about our work.

After several evenings devolved into multi-hour monologues, I suggested to Helen and June that we stake out some ground, as it were, by asking each other questions that would help Ray enter *our* worlds. The dynamic changed, but only slightly. Mostly my brother waited silently, smiling, until it was his turn to talk again. Still, he once assured us, "You've had a much greater influence on me than you can imagine."

"Ah, Ray, I bet every night, as your head hits the pillow, you think how grateful you are for us!" I poked, as we all laughed.

For a brief time, we sisters tried to bridge between our worlds and the company. Helen and I were collaborating with business leaders who had extensive corporate philanthropy programs. We asked Ray whether Hunt Oil might develop a philanthropic profile. Although he gave personally, Ray asserted that robust corporate charitable giving would send employees the wrong message: that the company had more money than it needed. In the same way, he brushed aside June's suggestion that we have a pastoral counselor for our employees. From his polite but firm refusal to consider the proposition, it was clear that we weren't just singing from different pages. We weren't even holding the same hymnbook.

Ray called his leadership a "benign dictatorship," a mode, granted, typical of a CEO of a privately held company. And as the years went by, I became the troublemaking (and ungrateful) dissident in my brother's eyes.

He had good reason to be concerned. During one Dallas visit, I decided to test the patriarchy. Ray had been elected president of the Dallas Petroleum Club, where deals were made and careers advanced —and where only men were admitted as members. I invited a vice-president of Hunt Oil to lunch, insisting on making the reservation myself. When the elevator opened, we faced a tall, middle-aged black man in a red coat, who smiled graciously and pointed to the "Ladies' Dining Room" on our left. I'd recently been leading a women's assertiveness training group. So I smiled back, pointed to the main dining room on our right, and informed the maitre d', "Our table is reserved in there. It's under 'Swanee Hunt.'"

The maitre d' was flustered. He hadn't realized "Swanee" was a woman. "We have a lovely table by the window for you in *here*," he stammered, pointing to the left.

"But my reservation is in *there*," I insisted.

"You've made your point, Swanee. Let's go," the vice-president whispered, with a halfhearted laugh and a tug in his voice.

"No, I'm sure I have a table reserved in the main dining room," I was firm.

A pause. "You can sit in there, Ma'am," the maitre d' said quietly, "but it will cost me my job." We left and had sandwiches delivered to the vice-president's office. In that moment, I realized how much I had in common with a black man in Dallas, also, in the 1970s, barred from main dining rooms.

Failing at civil disobedience, I tried to create empathy for us sisters by asking Ray to hypothesize: If he'd been born female with exactly the same talents, intellect, and personality, how did he imagine his life would be? "I hope I'd be doing exactly what Nancy is," was his response. I was amazed. Nancy Ann, well educated, talented, and very smart, had opted for being a stay-at-home mom with five children.

There was nothing I'd ever seen in Ray to indicate he personally would make that choice over business leadership. The only explanation I could come up with was his gendered view of social roles. Thus we three sisters, with multiple advanced degrees and running our own operations, were radically different from the Hunt Oil CEO's concept of the ideal woman. Every senior position at the company was held by a man. Perhaps it was by chance; more likely, culture: a woman's place was a far cry from the corner office.

The reminders were frequent. I rankled when Ray sent us three sisters a business letter, copied to the two vice-presidents, which began, "Dear Girls." Although aware that my umbrage might seem petty, I enlisted Helen and June to send him, and his two vice-presidents, a cheery reply. "Dear Boys," began our offer to help out the company any time. That was the last time we were "the girls"—at least in our presence.

When I step back, it's clear that women weren't relegated to being appendages of husbands simply because Ray or his company leaders were out of touch. We were all in some ways products of time and locale. When June, Helen, and I were invited to tour our Fort Worth Hyatt, elegantly renovated under Ray's leadership, we were shown luxury suites, each named for a leader in Fort Worth history. All white men, Helen noted, inquiring whether some women hadn't figured prominently in the city's past. The project managers—all white men— dismissed our inquiry. Their researcher hadn't turned up any women.

I hired my own researcher, my childhood friend Carol Edgar, who discovered that a hundred years ago, women had started a school for immigrants and a children's hospital, alongside the men's slaughterhouses and oil companies. So, we asked, couldn't the fountain in the lobby be named in the foremothers' honor? The low point of this saga is that when our efforts were stonewalled, we sisters folded. But our failure was instructive. Fort Worth's female pioneers hadn't mattered to historians. The present-day wishes of the female majority owners of this hotel hadn't even been humored by our own employees. That lesson sank in deep.

Thirty years had passed since my father created four equal trusts for Ray, June, Helen, and me, thinking that they would hold assets from the Kuwaiti oil concession for which he was angling. But the deal fell through, and the trusts remained empty. After Dad's death, Ray untangled my father's three families at a financial level, then reorganized the company so that the four trusts held equal shares of the common stock (the growth of the company), while Mom was given preferred stock.

Meanwhile society was evolving, with women demanding to be taken more seriously. I read the story of my struggle in Gloria Steinem's article "The Trouble with Rich Women," which conjectured that we privileged females had low self-images because we had no control over our families' assets.

After years of suggesting then requesting that Ray allow distributions from the company, we sisters organized into a cohesive force. It was a classic struggle. As CEO, he wanted the business to grow as large as possible and as rapidly as possible; that meant reinvesting the profits. The company was Ray's life work. By contrast, we three stockholders wanted the company to distribute a dividend so that we could maximize *our* life work.

I could see Ray's side. We'd let him become our family provider, a role in which he excelled. Now he felt unappreciated for the care he'd provided his sisters. There was also a philosophical gulf between us: at the same time Hunt Alternatives was making grants to level the playing field for minorities, Ray declared his adamant rejection of "affirmative action." Company hiring, he said, would be based on merit only —except for gays. Anyone known to be homosexual would be fired. How, I wondered, could my brother feel good about money leaving the company for Helen and me, knowing that we might turn around and fund an initiative pushing for racial quotas or same-sex rights?

Negotiations took several extraordinarily difficult years, with mixed results. My income increased enormously, but only after we sisters agreed to give part of our equity to Ray and forgo any role in company governance, present or future. From my perspective, Ray's demands were egregious, but the deal was the best we could do without a legal battle. We simply weren't willing to put our mother through any more headlines. That's when I realized the power of Mother's love, as it was returned to her by children who were determined, come hell or high water, to protect her.

In the course of the negotiations, Helen, June, and I grew closer. I also gained a more realistic view of my brother. He and I would learn over the years to compartmentalize our resentment, ac-cen-tuating the positive, as Mother would want. Still, one of the greatest regrets of my life was the damage to my relationship with him, even as my relationship with the world strengthened, since I now had resources to back my values.

Few gains in life are made without a price. Bottom line, we sisters had stormed the counting house and emerged—battered, but also blessed.

Philanthropic but Flawed

With a dramatically higher income, I maintained my practice of giving away half. As a result, my leverage in the community grew significantly. So did my sense of responsibility. To the Denver community I was a new civic leader, capable of stepping up to a microphone with aplomb and engaging an audience. And I was a valuable board member, helping to found or stabilize a dozen organizations. I began to receive many more requests for my time and talent than I could handle But whatever outer successes others applauded, I was always wrestling inner demons. Was I living up to the responsibility that came with privilege?

In meetings with Lauren Casteel, executive director of Hunt Alternatives Fund, she would hand me a request from a tall pile of grant proposals—for example, job-training for women in a public housing project, a simple enough consideration. But the proposal fragmented as I examined it with different eyes: as a funder, influential and competent to provide remedy; as a social activist, redistributing my ample income; but also as a civic leader concerned about my own career. In addition, I brought my personal history into my giving: I was a child from the segregated South, a teenager who'd committed her life to missionary service, and a young woman discounted by men in my family. Most important, as I considered why our society needed a job training program at all, I was the daughter of a single mother of four children, who could have found herself turned out on the street in a heartbeat.

Try as I might to create a unified persona, certain aspects seemed not to fit with other parts. I smiled, recognizing myself when I looked at cubist paintings on the walls of portrait galleries—hardly flattering, but an honest portrayal of the irregularity in every one of us. Given that complexity, philanthropy was a worrisome enterprise. The conversation with my ethics professor at Iliff about how money can corrupt frequently crossed my mind. I resented wealthy people who weren't philanthropic, and I wished others could see the difference between simple charity and strategic change-making. Admirable motives ensure neither success nor virtue. In other words, I slipped easily into self-righteousness. Maybe I, convinced of the need to reshape society, was reenacting the overreaching zeal that my father had directed toward saving the Republic USA.

Although we expected from the start that some of our ventures would go under, a few of my failures with Hunt Alternatives were nothing short of stunning. A yearlong effort to help community leaders design criteria and strategy for distributing the contraceptive Norplant to poor women resulted in a shouting match with Lauren. "You're targeting black women so they won't have babies. That's *genocide*." I was horrified by her accusation. But that moral question turned out to be moot. The implant's future was destroyed by lawsuits over difficulties in extracting the small tubes from women's arms. Our expensive initiative led nowhere.

In addition to outright failures, my personal and professional lives were peppered with contradictions: for all the leftist flavor of many of our grantees (one child wrote a note thanking us for supporting "communisty"—instead of "community"—programs), sometimes a conservative twist shocked my colleagues. For example, I argued against higher welfare payments in favor of job training and child care for single moms. At one event exposing the injustice of federal cuts, I asked a man on a panel how his bad back justified his being on the dole for years when one of our grantees was helping severely cerebral palsied persons find jobs.

Sometimes my life didn't fit my funding. No one could tell me that the embryo I miscarried was less a child than my later two, yet I gave money to organizations protecting women's choice to abort. While my children enjoyed the benefits of private schooling, we supported a dozen efforts in the public school system. When we wanted to help the new superintendent build trust with the minority community, he arrived late at our meeting because of a demonstration outside his building organized by one of our grantees. I balked at spending tens of thousands to make our historic landmark office handicapped-accessible, but I was happy to give the same amount to an organization whose members chained their wheelchairs to municipal buildings, demanding equal rights.

There were straight-out disappointments too. One day Lauren came in with a great idea. We could invite to our board meeting a reformed gang leader who would talk about his work with one of our grantees. As he spoke, I sat at the long, elegant table, thinking with self-satisfaction about how inclusive we were, and how we were bridging divides. How I could have been the mother of that young man, could have stayed up nights sick with worry, and could now be so proud. Later, I learned that he'd returned to crime and had been sentenced to seventy-four years in the penitentiary. My first reaction was to kick myself, as if I'd been duped. But that was a shallow reaction. The young man was making choices, good or bad, for a hundred reasons, just as I was. Still, it was a bitter pill when I thought about how we'd invested in him dollars that I had disrupted our Dallas family to gain.

Despite these letdowns, I never lost faith in alternative approaches. After all, conventional wisdom wasn't getting to the roots of problems either. We needed fresh interventions at multiple key points: in the first five years of a child's life, for a teen mother just after she gave birth, between dads and daughters, around community rituals. . . .

All those concerns would have been enough, but I was determined to make this a family foundation. Henry became an active junior board member in his late teen years. I was elated to discover that he shared my views on social justice. But he had more than an intellectual commitment. I watched his eyes blaze when he heard accounts of raw discrimination. And rather than resentful, I felt gratified when he probed and prodded to be sure we were as effective as we might be in our work.

But in the earliest years, before Charles changed his views, I found myself at odds with my husband who had joined the Republican Party as a result of his year as a White House Fellow, inspired by President Ford and discouraged by President Carter. He was never a Reagan supporter, but still, I asked myself, could I stay married to someone who didn't share my political views about the cleavage between the rich and poor? One afternoon, as we drove down from the ranch to a dinner party in Denver, our disagreement came to a head. "I think you should be supporting the arts for art's sake," Charles proposed, "because music, dance, sculpture are fundamental to a healthy society."

"Are you kidding? There will always be rich people to fund the opera, because they want to show off their jewels and furs. But Charles, the gap between rich and poor has steadily widened. We have to focus on bridging that chasm." He was steaming and I was shouting by the time we pulled up to our friends' home. Although we may not have used the raw words, I essentially accused my new husband of having no empathy for those who suffer. And he was countering that I was an ideologue.

Our argument went on for hours as we remained parked in front of the brightly lit house. We never went in for the party, but we emerged that evening with a new foundation program: "arts as a vehicle for social change." Over the next five years we helped minority-run arts organizations, put artists inside schools and prisons, created joint marketing among arts nonprofits, helped buy buildings for theaters and exhibit halls in low-income areas, and hired development professionals. We also invited hundreds of our friends to performances of soul music or drama in neighborhoods they'd otherwise not venture into.

My lowest moment with the Hunt Alternatives Fund came when after more than a decade of combined work, Helen decided to split off and form her own foundation. Helen's second husband was her former professor, Harville Hendrix, who became a best-selling author on marriage. She was in the midst of creating her own space in her relationship with an older man in a high-profile position. That identity struggle carried over into our relationship. She couldn't become all that she might be, she worried, if we stayed together. Distraught, I clung to her, arguing that she was every bit as accomplished as I. We were a team, and stronger for it. But no words of mine could change her reality. One more time, I felt I had pushed my partner away with my combination of confidence and drive. And I didn't know what to do about it.

Helen named her new foundation the Sister Fund. I cried when she said sweetly that the name was to honor our relationship. But she was also making a statement of solidarity with her grantees: women of color. I admired that decision. It had been decades since Helen and I had turned for help to the black women who'd taken care of Mt. Vernon, day in and day out. In Denver one of our grantees was an inter-generational health program that called itself Sistah-Girls Coming Full Circle. Helen and I were coming full circle as well.

Growing up, we never visited any Mt. Vernon staff in *their* homes, nor did we talk about *their* children. It didn't dawn on me that "the maids" had lives of their own. But when I went into Denver's black neighborhoods, I flashed back to myself as a tow-headed child, follow-ing Celestine around the house with her dust rag as she crooned reli-gious tunes. So what about my caretakers, in their starched pink uni-forms and white aprons? Did anyone really care about their financial pressures? Or the violence in their neighborhoods? Or whether they or their children could pursue their dreams? Now, in my Denver site visits, I was seeing those women from the other side, as they tried to balance their work and home responsibilities.

On one of our visits, an African American minister told how a five-year-old child had come to his church, crying hysterically. The boy had locked himself out of the house and was frantic to get back in. The minister was disquieted that such a youngster would be left alone in a dangerous neighborhood, known for easy drugs and rampant crime. He tried to coax the boy into staying at the church, offering him apple juice and coloring books until his mother returned. But instead of calming down, as minutes went by the child became more hysterical and eventually confessed, through his sobs, that his two-year-old baby sister was inside, assigned to his care.

That scene occurred a stone's throw from my comfortable house, two cars, three televisions, and five silver candelabra. I struggled with how to integrate it all: accidents of birth and every hour that follows, moral compromises that marble the purest moments, external critics out-shouted by internal voices of condemnation. The silent, structural bias in our everyday lives, I realized, was as damaging as blatant dis-crimination.

Filament, Filament, Filament

Meeting with hundreds of grassroots activists, I learned the ins and outs of helping at an individual level. But federal government funding for social programs had plummeted, leading states and municipalities to slice the resource pie into thinner and thinner pieces. I wondered if instead we should be figuring out how to make a larger pie. That would mean inducing more wealthy people to become private funders.

Even that idea was laced with controversy. Some social justice advocates argued that donors who wrote large checks to organizations shouldn't be allowed to hold board positions, since they already wielded too much power in the world. I understood the argument, but regarding money as a stain rather than an opportunity left wealthy activists like me with a poor choice: either not to get involved with organizations that we funded, or to join boards and then refuse to support those organizations financially.

After chewing on this conundrum, I concluded that wealth was neither good nor bad, but neutral. The heart, on the other hand, was generous or greedy, just or power grabbing. Before long I would test out that notion in the highest-stakes game on earth, presidential politics. But for now, my sphere was city and state.

Governor Romer asked if Hunt Alternatives would pay to send a delegation of Colorado officials to a national "policy academy." Over eighteen months, expert faculty would work with officials from a dozen states to develop ideas for families in need. Sponsored by the Ford Foundation, ARCO, and the federal government, the initiative epitomized the new "public-private partnership" model of the times.

Our foundation specialized in small grants for grassroots groups. Comparing the governor's request to the Black Arts Festival or elderly home visitation, I was disinclined. The project seemed too bureaucratic, and not juicy. On the other hand, maybe there was some entrepreneurial fruit to be plucked. We agreed to put up $30,000 for travel expenses if I could be a member of the delegation. I'd be the only nongovernmental participant, but after more graduate study than any one person ought to do, and a decade of organizing and activism, I could hold my own.

Crassly put, I bought a place on the delegation. More graciously, the state received more than a check. The gain was mutual. As we reviewed cases of individual kids in trouble and debated how the government programs might or could not help, a new world opened to me. I gained an inside view of the public system, not only the organizational chart and job descriptions, but also the never-committed-to-paper institutional jealousies and generosities. That experience helped me to envision systemic reforms in the decades following. And having grown up in a household where "bureaucrat" was a slur, I felt surprised and inspired by saintly government employees who woke every morning puzzling about ways to make society function better.

In turn, I brought more than dollars and opinions; donors like me had private-sector savvy and fat rolodexes. But I also had a fresh view, and as an outsider with little to lose, I could be totally honest. "I'm speaking as a divorced woman, so this may seem hypocritical. But if we care so much about children, and we know single parenthood correlates with poverty, why don't we figure out how to promote marriage and reduce divorce?" I asked. My teammates were stunned, but they let me stir the pot.

At the macro level, our Colorado team was one of the most successful of the dozen, pushing through legislative reforms that created a new department and merged others, to streamline and strengthen family services. But apart from that grant, most of my philanthropic time was spent tromping around neighborhoods. By contrast, some of our wealthy friends were reluctant to be around those who needed their money. I passed on to them Jessica's wisdom: "Of course people will use you. That's fine. Just don't let them abuse you."

Abuse, after all, could go either way. Grant makers could harm grant seekers, who needed to leave meetings at Hunt Alternatives Fund with their self-respect intact. When people apologize as they ask me for money, I remind them, "It's just an accident of birth that I'm on one side of the table and you're on the other." They're doing me a favor. The more choices I have, the sharper my giving can be.

After half a dozen years as a philanthropist, my image took on a sheen. I became a sought-after honoree of groups who raised money through an annual lunch or dinner. My friends could afford their expensive tickets, so I found myself on the short list of desirables. The symbiosis was clear but unspoken: my ego got plumped; their coffers did too. Only once did I look the gift horse in the mouth, as Granny would have said. With all my work on women's empowerment, how could I possibly accept a "Frontiersman" award? The organizers discussed my objection, and I gratefully accepted the "Frontier" award, albeit a statue of a raccoon-hatted, bearded fellow peering out across the fruited plain.

For every act of generosity, there's secondary gain. My life has been much more fulfilled than that of friends who glide from one vacation into another. As they amuse themselves on an Alpine slope or African safari, they miss out on the greatest joy—knowing that they've made a solid difference in the lives of others. That connection to the real world runs in two directions. My work has served up a feast of soul-nourishing moments, as when a teenage mother of three introduced me as the speaker at her graduation from a G.E.D. program. She was the only member of her family with a degree, and despite living in a crummy neighborhood, without money, models, or miracles, she'd bucked the odds. As she thanked me for helping her go to college, I felt her smile radiating through me from head to toe. No Caribbean cruise could match that warmth.

But philanthropy is also Pandora's box. Having lifted the lid, I often felt overwhelmed by the needs coming at me. One morning, when Charles asked his predictable breakfast pleasantry, "Do you have a good day ahead?" I barked back, "Hardly. We're going to cut 100 proposals to 50—and we've already eliminated the babies with AIDS." But what kind of person would I be if I decided, because the need was so great, not to help at all?

During a sixteen-year period our foundation would make grants to over four hundred organizations. A few times, as I worked with exhausted activists or beleaguered bureaucrats, I felt unappreciated, distrusted, or even maligned. But overall I emerged with experiences of giving—resources and self—that endowed meaning to the white hairs beginning to frame the network of creases on my face. They were experiences worthy of Walt Whitman's "noiseless, patient spider," launching forth "filament, filament, filament out of itself, ever unreeling them, ever tirelessly speeding them." Until, after the last check was written and the last thank-you accepted, a web remained, connecting me to points I never would have imagined.

Passing the Torch

An integral part of my life in Denver was my deepening relationship with our children. I loved giving them tasks to help them develop their reasoning and their values. Driving down the street, or snuggled in bed, we talked about historic heroes. I knew I'd hit my mark one day when four-year-old Teddy was in tears because his sister ended up with a larger piece of cookie.

"It's not fair!" he wept, loudly.

"Teddy, life isn't fair," I explained, perfunctorily.

"But Martin Luther King changed that!" he howled, even louder.

For the kids to have or do something out of the ordinary, I often required three independent good reasons. ("I don't need a nap because: One, I slept a lot last night. Two, I made my bed and a nap would crumple it up. Three, You just called me 'Teddy Bear,' and Teddy bears do not *ever* close their eyes.") And even though they were caught up in their own worlds, I frequently asked them to expound on moral questions beyond their years; so I suppose it was partly my own doing that my children molded me—pushing, pulling, and punching.

Still, I found meaning both in my kids and beyond them. My family included the community's children, and I responded to their needs, sometimes at a cost to my own three. I guess I never reconciled that tension between parenting and career, although critics on both sides offered plenty of advice: "When your child wants you, your child needs you. Other work can wait." Or, equally vociferously: "Don't let your children control your life. It's not good for you or them." Instead, I settled on what many would consider a worst third alternative: inconsistency.

In our big, rambling house, I had the luxury of live-in child care, so I could leave them to play at home in loving hands or take my kids with me whenever I and they wanted. For example, Helen and I were notorious for bringing our infants on site visits. We rationalized that the sound of our babies breastfeeding in contented oblivion would put nervous potential grantees at ease. Of course as the children got older, school filled in. But like millions, maybe billions of mothers, I never could shake the guilt of sometimes letting my work preempt my kids.

Occasionally dividing my time between my kids and the world's kids made sense. Sometimes it seemed preposterous. I was asked to introduce Governor Dick Lamm, Dottie's husband, when he addressed Colorado's monthly foundation lunch group. Before he rose to lay out his agenda for the state, he launched our getting-to-know-you conversation. "What's the last book you read?" he queried, pushing aside his chop suey.

"I just finished two," I responded. "Reinhold Niebuhr's *The Nature and Destiny of Man*"—he nodded approvingly—"and *The Little Engine That Could*." The governor didn't crack a smile. We became friends anyway.

But generally I'm glad I decided to blend my life with my children and my work. That's partly because our kids have been not just a distraction from my career but a boon as well, helping me to keep perspective. Above my desk I have kept a quote from Anne Frank's diary, "Nobody ever became poor by giving." But it took little Teddy to remind me, his voice filled with concern, "Mommy, maybe you shouldn't give away so much, because *we* might need it sometime."

"If we do, Teddikins, let's hope others will help us," I answered.

I didn't know whether the message sank in until a year later, when Teddy suggested that we give away *all* our money to poor people. I told him we gave away a lot already. "But *all*. We should give away *all*."

"How would we buy groceries?" I asked.

"Well, we'd be poor. But that's okay. Every now and then there should be a change. People who have a lot should become poor, and people who are poor should have money."

All three children would be my teachers as well as students in the public and personal aspects of philanthropy for years to come. Henry sure took his turn making me squirm. But more often it was Lillian who would crack my carefully constructed unreality. One summer day, stopping at a red light, I noticed a bearded man in a down jacket pushing a grocery cart. I turned to my kindergartener, pleased to have a teachable moment for inculcating social awareness. "Lillian, do you know why that man is pushing a cart?" I asked.

"Yes, Mommy," she piped back, "He doesn't have a home." I felt satisfied with both of us until Lillian continued, "But let's bring him home with *us*. He can have the guestroom. Can't we? Pleeease."

I mumbled some less-than-convincing pabulum about how there are other ways to help. But Lillian's incessant pleading was like a drill, boring through the obvious, down, down to the unexpected. I realized I was assuaging my guilt about being privileged by spouting moral platitudes. But for Lillian, morality required action.

That traffic intersection lay in the shadow of a skyscraper where my high-powered estate lawyer had his office. Don Hopkins, my long-time advisor and confidant, often mused that families who share businesses tend to split; those who share philanthropy become closer. He and I met over the years to think about what Warren Buffett and other wealthy businessmen were saying about the dangers of huge inheritances and their plans to leave money to a foundation, with just enough to their children for education and a relatively modest financial base. Hearing that trillions were being handed down, mostly to people with little preparation to handle their fortune, I was thinking about the difference between passing on my social values and simply letting my wealth flow to unknown generations.

I had so many questions about children and wealth. Could I impress upon our three my passion for philanthropy? I could fashion a laboratory at the foundation, but they also needed to develop as individuals, not just take on my interests. Being on the board might give them a voice or make them feel like echoes. Yet if they pushed for their own interests, the focus of the foundation might split, making it less effective.

But apart from the effect on the Fund, what would be the effect on them as people if they were involved in my philanthropy? They might resent not having their own grantmaking accounts. But too much power too soon might also warp a sense of self. Dealing with large sums could skew their sense of proportion, making their own individual giving seem inconsequential.

And sharing philanthropy could be wearing on relationships. The kids would undoubtedly experience the same embarrassments vis-à-vis friends and strangers as I had. But within the family itself, I knew I would be creating problems. When Helen and I started the fund, we successfully bridged the distance between New York and Denver; but even between close sisters, a joint board meeting was a stretch. My children had strikingly different temperaments. I didn't want them to experience the tension I'd had with Helen. And the angst over money related to my brother? I had to spare them.

In short, passing the philanthropic torch was dangerous. Egos could get scorched. So Charles and I asked wealthy friends for advice. One described his family's problems with second- and third-generation "warring entities" vying for control and funding for pet projects. By contrast, another friend, whose family was known worldwide for generations of philanthropy, recounted how teenage members were brought to the family business center to spend a day and then taken to meet grant recipients, to awaken their own philanthropic interests. He called it the "how to spend it" division of their "how to make it" office.

My work had developed completely outside my parents' orb. Mother, as generous as she was, had no organized giving program. And although we'd seen our father's anticommunist campaign up close, Helen and I smarted over Dad's belief that charitable giving was part of a communist plot. We wished that he had taught us philanthropy instead. So, trusting that the advantage would outweigh our concerns, we set a policy of inviting our children, at around the age of sixteen, to foundation board meetings as "junior board members." They accompanied us on site visits and learned to articulate their opinions at meetings.

Of course as Charles and I searched for the line between constructive advice and meddling, I wondered what I'd do if my kids turned their backs on philanthropy, much as I'd left my parents' conservative politics and religious fundamentalism. I'd have to wait a long time to find out. Meanwhile, each year before Christmas, I helped Lillian and Teddy thin out their toys, knowing that when Teddy gave up his tricycle or Lillian handed over her doll and carriage to children at a homeless shelter, they learned more than they could have learned from a hundred of my sermonettes. I also asked our kids to put aside some of their allowance, to tithe, really, for those less fortunate. And I matched their contributions: Henry's to organize farm workers, Lillian's to a children's hospital, and Teddy's to save the ozone layer.

But my bar was set high. As so many times before, Helen was my standard. Her children worked in shelters and prisons with grantees in East Harlem. By contrast, though Henry excelled in sports, in friendships that would last for decades, and (occasionally) in studies, his lack of interest in community service as a young man frustrated me. When I complained about this, Lauren, who'd been on site visits for the fund with him, told me to relax. She reminded me that when he was still in college, he was often the best-prepared around the table. He went through the board book meticulously and held his own in elevated debates. Helen's wise daughter Kathryn reminded me, "The observed is changed by the observation. You'll never see who your children are without you." In fact, his dad and I learned later that Henry was a volunteer leader of a "grief group" for a local hospice. Still, all was not sweetness and light. Family rough patches carried over into board meetings, and chairing a meeting at which a brooding adolescent sat with his back turned as far as possible was no fun. But he would indeed be a model for Lillian and Teddy coming along behind him.

Of course the kids were watching Charles as well. They saw how as treasurer of Hunt Alternatives Fund he added financial rigor to our board, even though he didn't always feel the same urgency I did to right social wrongs. Then, after Helen and I divided our foundations, we added community representatives to our boards. Those members had their own relationships with our children; they could help me back off and not pressure the kids too much.

All these matters I discussed at length with my attorney, Don. But he was also extremely helpful to me when I took hours, bless him, to ponder the larger questions: Beyond money, what should, or would, I leave my children? Of course a portion of my genetic makeup. A serious dose of various hang-ups. Some habits. Traditions. Mannerisms. Turns of phrase. But no legacy would be more important than their being able to slice through social strata like geological layers, into the molten core where character, personality, and experiences alloy with values. In the process Henry, Lillian, and Teddy would cause me plenty of grief. And ultimately I'd have to allow my charitable efforts to be exposed to the critical standards of a fresh, idealistic generation, who would jab my conscience with one version after another of: "But *why* can't he stay in the guest room?"

Perspective

My foundation work wasn't done in isolation. Every day—no, every hour—I was trying to live an integrated life. But finding the exact right balance was always impossible. And I found that with greater responsibility, as mother, graduate student, wife, reformer, daughter, political activist, and philanthropist, the role that suffered most was that of friend.

I've never had trouble being close to others, and friendship (more with women but also a few intrepid men) has been a source of strength, comfort, and wisdom throughout my life. I frequently get through tough situations by calling a friend for advice, or even imagining what she or he would say if I *had* called. Charles kids me that I have more "close friends" than most people have acquaintances. But that's not because I'm casual in my calculation; it's because we're tenacious. Two of my dearest, Jan Fox and Carol Edgar, stretch across forty-five years.

Knowing I'd be enriched by a chunk of time away from distractions, I carved out a week to go whitewater rafting through the Grand Canyon with seven women colleagues who became an ongoing group of confidantes. Marjorie, Fern, Lori, Judi, Lila, Katherine, Lauren, and I have been a legendary support group, the best example of sisterhood that I can imagine. But in my thirties, such experiences were few and far between. Mostly I responded to friends in need: a neighbor during her miscarriage, another fleeing in her nightgown during a marital crisis.

Jessica was not only my colleague at Karis but also my closest friend in Denver. She didn't want to impose, but she found a way to remind me that she was still around. One spring day, as I drove out of the parking lot at Iliff onto busy University Boulevard, I burst out laughing. She'd rented advertising space on the back of a bench at the bus stop and had it painted with "Happy Birthday, Swanee."

She was looking after me, even as I was looking after her. I was concerned about Jessica's health when she developed diabetes and an uncharacteristically round waistline—so concerned that she agreed to report to me every mile she walked. But my life was so hectic that when she went into the hospital for a coronary bypass, I missed a message from her husband to my office and didn't know the surgery was happening or that she'd asked me to come. When I got word and raced to the hospital, I wasn't in time to squeeze her hand and laugh at her nervous pre-surgery jokes. I could only wait with her family, and then try to console them when the doctors came from the operating room to say she had died on the table.

Her husband and daughters, who knew how much I loved her, allowed me to sit alone with her body. I stroked her shapely fingers, admiring her painted nails, wondering at how quickly her hand was turning cold. This was my chance to say all the things I would have said had I arrived two hours sooner—about how strong she was, about how much she'd taught me. But now there was more: about how bad I felt that I hadn't made more time for her, about how much I would miss her.

At her funeral we told funny stories, just as she would have done. I played the piano, in an irreverent moment departing from *Ave Maria* to launch into her favorite Irish bar songs as her friends passed her coffin. I knew she wouldn't want me to feel guilty. Yet I couldn't escape the terrible truth that in her last days, and in her final hour, I failed her.

How could I have let her down? I asked myself. How, when I was trying so hard to live the right kind of life? As I mourned my friend, I mourned myself. Yes, I was busy. My work had meaning. I had loving family and friends. But every day I raced from Charles, Henry, Lillian, or Teddy, foundation staff or board meetings, and speeches. I knew Jessica could forgive me. Still, in all the running, I'd lost my balance. I needed to step back. Or maybe forward. Or maybe up.

In the kitchen one afternoon, I watched out the back window as Lillian and Teddy played in the sandbox, and sorted the mail. I found a flyer announcing an Outward Bound women's trek in Nepal. It was an Outward Bound ropes course that had given me the confidence to make it through my divorce, and I'd entrusted to them the mental health reform group in the rapids. But I'd never signed up for one of their adventures, designed to stretch the mind while challenging the body.

When Charles came home that evening, I exclaimed over the meatloaf, "I'm going trekking in Nepal!"

He shook his head. "Better thee than me."

For months I worked out on stair machines at the gym, since I'd heard that the Nepalese mountain sides were terraced. Finally, I felt nervously ready to tackle the trails.

In Katmandu, I met up with the six women in my "patrol" for the weeklong journey in the Ganesh Himal, near the Tibetan border. We ranged in age from our twenties to our fifties. I begged Susan, our leader, to describe in detail the course. She insisted, in true Outward Bound style, that I could just be confident that I'd make it. When I pressed again for the routing, saying I'd like to look at the map, she said we'd be following uncharted trails up and down, then up again and down again. Small comfort.

The trip's challenge was more than physical. It was also a minute-by-minute exposure to the other side of the world. Every day was a series of astonishing sights. One day we were in a jungle, with monkeys playing in the trees; another, we were on the wide-open mountainside, with women wrapped in bright red cloth, cutting, twisting, tying, and threshing long golden stalks of grain. We passed by twelve-foot-high poinsettias, rhododendron, and bougainvilleas, listening to bird calls exotic to my ears. We stepped gingerly by woman-eating nettles on our way to exquisite hanging moss, waterfalls, and rocky stream crossings. And when we chanced upon a festival to honor crows, as well as another to awaken Vishnu, the god of preservation, we wore garlands of blossoms made into necklaces.

After moving through one mountain village, our group went on to our camping spot in a nearby rice paddy. But I hung back to spend time with a shy young girl. On her family's mud porch, I held her on my lap, playing with her toes as I talked to her, and sang songs. Lillian or Teddy would have been grinning and squealing, but she hardly responded, and I left feeling that we hadn't really connected.

At six the next morning, when I unzipped my tent, pulled back the flap, and looked out, I was face to face with the girl, who was crouched outside in the cold. Wrapped in a blue-and-red woven blanket, she had a decorative crescent on her forehead. She stared at me expectantly, as if we were midway through a conversation. I guess we were. The annual per capita income in Nepal was less than I would spend on one night at an upscale hotel. How, my conscience was asking her . . . how could I extend the care I felt for my own family to her, this young girl, growing up in a country where one child in five dies? Even if she'd had the words, she wouldn't have had an answer. So one more morning I packed up, ate some hot cereal, and moved on, without a sense of grounding.

My energy was high, and for several days I led the group, one time getting so far ahead that I feared I was lost as I waited an hour for the rest to catch up. But as strong as I was, I missed Charles terribly. I had my own ways of keeping him near, wearing a "Symphony Run" T-shirt with a screen-print of him conducting. Still, as the days wore on, I became more and more thirsty for my family. Passing through more villages, I started pulling out my journal, which had a picture of Teddy and Lillian (holding a white pet rabbit) in Charles's lap. Henry was leaning over us all "Mero padular," I explained.

The villagers showered my family with grins, and one in return invited me to look inside her home. Like all the others, it was one room, with a leaf-covered roof and dirt floor. A few aluminum plates and cups were all I saw inside. I made myself part of that village scene, sitting awhile with an old woman who was spinning coarse white yarn, and watching a man weaving reeds into a mat. Chickens, goats, water buffalo, and pigs roamed freely or were tied in the middle of the front yard. The youngest children were naked or bare-bottomed beneath their shirts.

With each day, the villages were more remote. We were far away from a tourist trekking route, and the people we found had never seen strangers like us. Still, they greeted us with "Namaste," saluting the god within us as they held their palmed hands to their bowed heads. My friend Jill developed a bad knee and had to take a lower route out. At the steepest sections she was carried by a porter in a large basket on his back, secured by a wide band across his forehead.

We were several days' walk from the nearest clinic when we stepped off the path to make way for four men running, carrying a loaded stretcher with a large black umbrella attached. Knowing how steep the journey was, I doubted that the patient would ever see the clinic in Gorkha. That same day I held in my arms an eighteen-month-old boy, limp with fever as he tried to fight off a raging infection. A large patch of his scalp was oozing pus, and we could see the swelling beneath; but when his mother begged us for help, we could only administer iodine and bandages. Penicillin might have saved his life. I wondered how a parent would decide when to take a sick child to the doctor. By the time the several-day-long trip seemed warranted, wouldn't it be too late?

Near the Tibetan border each of us went off for a solo afternoon. I sat in a sheltered spot just below a snowfield, trying to capture in verse the wisdom of time and space away from my workaday grind. As I put down my journal, I knocked over the famously indestructible Nikon camera lens at my side. It started rolling, then bounced from boulder to boulder, finally disappearing over a ledge. I looked down into the smoky blue folds of mountain and cloud and smiled, enjoying the freedom of a setting where nature was so clearly in control—and I was not.

I had one more piece of equipment—a Walkman, with small speakers that I pulled out in the evenings so that we could dance away our last ounce of strength by the light of the moon. In one village, I put the earphones on a wizened woman, who mimicked Christopher Parkening's guitar playing Bach. Her grin gave me a lift. I needed it, since our trail had gains of up to five thousand feet in a day, with sheer drops in between. To distract me during the steepest climbs. I played over and over the gorgeously emotive Mahler Adagietto from his Fifth Symphony. Each time I heard it I saw Charles's eyes as he gazed up at me during a concert when we first met—at risk of losing his concentration, he later confessed.

The night before our final ascent, I didn't sleep. I had developed a respiratory infection and lay in my tent, at fourteen thousand feet, miserable. The next morning I put on my parka and began slogging up the final thousand feet up a glacier field, slipping, sliding, and sinking into eighteen inches of snow. Hour after hour I labored, dropping further back from my group until I lost sight of it. My whole body was trembling. My strength was spent.

The rest had made it to camp on the other side of the pass. But Susan had stayed back with me. "The sun is going to set soon. We're running out of time."

"I know. I'm moving as fast as I can."

"Let me carry your pack. This is no time to be a hero." I burst into tears, partly for not being up to the task, partly out of exhaustion, but partly in gratitude for a gesture that reached into my solitary struggle. That was all I needed. I made it to the top, pack and all. The expansive vista cleared my head, as did the realization of my physical strength. But I was steeled also by the reminder of my infinitesimally small place in an enormous world, and my ever-so-real limitations. Around me were white flags planted in rock cairns. They were inscribed with prayers carried by the breeze, believers said, up to God. The same God who received the prayers of Franny's votive candles, I was sure.

But just what should my prayer be? I was haunted by the girl waiting wide-eyed outside my tent, and the expressionless face of the child with the infection. I didn't have a prayer flag to carry my thoughts to heaven, just my actions every day.

Strength, insight, and prayers. I had no idea just how much I would need all three over the next few years.

You must do the things you think you cannot do.
— *Eleanor Roosevelt*

CHAPTER 4

Politics, Prestige, and Peril

Victory Redefined

Nepal had widened my outlook. Standing near the top of the world, I'd seen powerful beauty and enormous need. That trek inspired me. No goal seemed out of range. The role of the "dutiful woman" that I'd imagined to be my fate in Dallas had all but disappeared as I ratcheted up my aspirations. In one sphere after another, I began taking on challenges I wouldn't have considered a decade earlier.

Denver, gateway to the Rockies, breeds adventurers. Our urbane friends cross-country ski to each other's mountain cabins and scale the peaks of the Continental Divide. Dinner conversations are as likely to cover a slalom race as a political coup. At one such table in January 1989, I sat beside Jack Klapper—a pain specialist, fittingly—who described his recent marathons. "Someday, I'd love to try one," I confided.

"I've got just the race: Venice. October," he replied casually. "It's flat and sea level."

"You're on," I said impulsively, shaking his hand. After all, I had ten months to get in shape. I began training the next day. Charles had taken to asking me, "How's my little chickadee?" But it was a joke; we both laughed at the thought that I would ever be of chickadee proportions. Still wearing a size 14, I could jog a very slow two miles.

My marathon inspiration was Ellen Hart, a world-class runner. We'd met years earlier at yet another ballroom benefit dinner I'd organized to raise money for Denver's mentally ill. Mayor Federico Peña agreed to give the welcome. I'd considered asking the mayor to be my dinner date, since we were both single, but according to rumor, I was too late. Indeed, at the head table I sat next to Ellen, the mayor's new girlfriend, whom he'd met at a race. She and I were blond, friendly, and decidedly casual when it came to fashion. But I was chunky, whereas Ellen was remarkably lean—not an ounce of fat—just as a runner ought to be, I noted with envy.

Ellen and I had immediately found a link in our admiration of Robert Coles, the Pulitzer Prize–winning child psychologist and ethicist. She'd taken his courses at Harvard. I was in the throes of my doctoral dissertation, examining the way he crossed lines imposed by society and zeroed in on the person behind the labels.

As we talked, I realized that Ellen was accomplished and smart. But although her eyes sparkled, I sensed a harbored fragility. Since I was applying Coles's approach to actual people, I asked if she was willing to let me interview her. She readily agreed. My intuition was right: Over hours of conversation, Ellen led me into a netherworld of brilliance burdened by bulimia. That secret was her demon, day and night eroding her sense of self, threatening her health, and, she later concluded, preventing her from building the muscle mass she needed to reach the top of her field. She would later go public to help others, and a TV documentary would be made about her battle with an eating disorder.

In the course of the hours of discussion, we became great friends, so I was thrilled that despite her own problems, Ellen was at my side, emotionally and physically, as I trained for the marathon. For hours we circled the lake at City Park, my friend talking fluidly as I panted at her side. I felt like a lumbering elephant next to her gazelle-like gait, jogging as fast as I could at a pace that was a stroll for her. Ellen told me I could bank on my inner strength. "Train to thirteen miles," she coached. "You're so stubborn, you can depend on willpower to carry you the second half of the race."

Over the coming months, I ran only twice a week. The first run was four miles, and the second increased week after week till I reached thirteen. Other days I cross-trained: lifting weights, swimming, stationary biking, and hiking. My progress wasn't steady. One day I started cramping in my gut at mile seven and had to stop. That night I lay in bed obsessing: "Charles, what if this happens the day of the race?"

"Don't worry."

"But what if it does?" I persisted.

"Go to sleep, Love," he said. "Old Chinese saying: Mornings are wiser than evenings."

For all my fear, as a marathon wannabe I enjoyed being part of a new élite. At parties, friends and strangers eagerly offered advice. Over hors d'oeuvres and margaritas, Mayor Peña recounted a failed marathon when he started too fast and his body gave out. I would have to be extremely disciplined, he warned.

Not everyone thought I could succeed. The father of aerobics, Ken Cooper, a family friend, told me I'd never make it. My internist Rick Abrams tried to break the news kindly: "It takes a certain body type, Swanee, to run that distance." Rick knew me well; his doubt made me all the more determined. Dr. Klapper, who first encouraged me, cautioned that my training mileage was inadequate. Most marathoners run forty to sixty miles a week, he insisted. But my neighbor, Fred Lewis, was even less gentle, "Remember what happened to the original Greek marathoner? He dropped dead at the end."

Ten months later and only twelve pounds lighter, time was up. Although I still had rolls of flesh at my waist, I stopped training two weeks before the race, hoping to trick my body into a "rebound" effect. My friends gave me a surprise send-off, with a Colorado T-Shirt (size medium: too small), shorts (also too small), and a tiny booklet with greetings from various celebrities and family: twenty-six pages, one for each mile, to read as I ran. Not exactly serious running gear, but great inspiration.

Charles and I flew to Venice the day before the race. I was extraordinarily nervous, wondering if my body could really pull this off. For encouragement, Charles rode with me on the bus taking runners to Stra, a town twenty-five miles outside Venice. We made jokes about how distinctly different I looked compared to the sinewy bodies around me. At the starting line, thousands queued up according to how fast we'd be running. I took a place near the back and glanced around nervously.

There were very few women. Unlike popular races in the United States, this marathon was serious business.

At last the gun sounded. Up front, runners sprinted off. Back where I was, a shuffling began. Finally the crowd around me lurched forward. Having trained at eleven-minute miles, my plan was a slow jog until near the end. Then if I felt like speeding up, I could. Soon after we took off, I checked my watch. I was running far too fast. As Federico had warned, adrenaline had given me an extra push that could leave me depleted before the race was over. I forced myself to slow down.

The run itself was glorious. I read my mother's cheerful message in the booklet at mile 1, Lillian's encouragement at 2, Governor Romer's at 3, Fern's at 4. This was a group effort, I realized. With each mile, I dropped further to the rear, setting my pace by my watch rather than by the racers who kept passing me. I picked up running pals, all men, and conversed in Italian, French, and German, figuring as long as I had enough blood reaching my brain to let me think in another language, I'd be okay. "Forza!" people lining the streets of the towns called as we passed.

Approaching mile 10, I recognized Charles up ahead, in his classic khaki trench coat. He had spied me and was waving both arms in a wide arc. When I reached him, he was grinning ear to ear. I jogged in place for a few moments. "How's my dear wife?" he asked earnestly.

"It feels like I just started!" I told him excitedly, as he rubbed a cramp out of my left shoulder. Ah, the wonders of endorphins.

My dependable husband appeared again at the twentieth mile. By then I was so far back from the crowd that he'd been waiting for more than an hour. Two separate buses had come by to pick up lame and wounded stragglers lying or limping alongside the road. Charles had boarded each, searched anxiously for me, and then disembarked, even more concerned than before. He later told me that he feared I might have collapsed and not been found.

While my husband was becoming more and more apprehensive, I was sauntering along on my own terms, undismayed. This was my race. Mine alone. I knew if I stopped, I'd have a hard time starting again, so walking or resting wasn't an option. The only breaks I allowed myself were the two minutes with my husband, and a moment of privacy behind a railroad car.

On the endless causeway leading toward the island city, headwinds were so strong I felt as if I were running in place. But worse was the assault to my pride as an official vehicle passed me, gathering up the race mileage markers. "Wait for me!" I called to uncomprehending workers as they collected the signs.

For a while I was alone. The grumpy Parisian businessman I'd been chatting with had dropped out around mile 22. Wanting company, I gave an extra push and caught up to a cheerful Bavarian pharmacist for the last mile. We were now in Venice proper and running on cobblestone and across small bridges arching over the canals. After five hours on flat land, my calf muscles couldn't adjust to the new angle. I hobbled over each bridge and then resumed my exhausted jog, until I came around the last corner in front of Santa Maria della Saluta.

There were still some faithful few in the bleachers at the finish line. Suddenly Charles was at my side. "You did it!" he cried. As I leaned into his arms, I sensed that he was the second-happiest person in all of Venice. Someone wrapped my sweaty body in a wind guard of plastic sheeting. I looked at the official clock: 5 hours and 13 minutes. We made our way ever so gingerly across the river to our hotel. My muscles were groaning, but I was glowing inside.

From our room, I called two-year-old Teddy back in Denver. "I finished the race!" I said.

"Did you win, Mommy?"

I paused. "Yes, Sweetie!" I answered, honestly.

Gentlefolk

I couldn't really convey to Charles the flood of satisfaction that I felt from the marathon. Perhaps he understood anyway, after all the symphony opening nights he'd prepared for, worried about, and pulled off. In a sense they were his marathons, and he had stacks of tapes, posters, and programs that were his mantel full of medals.

But apart from the pressure of performances, Charles and I met at a deeper level around the power of music. Granted, music was a profession for him and a pastime for me. But it was critically important to us both. It was the way he articulated his passion. And it was yet another form I used to express my life message that "we are all in this together," as Carole King would sing.

There are inner compartments of the psyche, as real as if they were physical. They seem separated, even protected, from other cognitive functions. Education theory talks of "multiple intelligences," distinct forms of perception. That fits my experience. It's as if, far away from linear thinking, music shares the address of emotions, faith, ideals, and spirit—in a place where they insist on being more than chemicals and impulses coursing through spongy gray matter.

I've drawn power from those compartments. Why did Nadja playing Bruch's violin concerto always move me to tears? When I was pushing harder than I possibly could to make it over the Himalayan pass, why did my strength surge with the strings of the Adagietto from Mahler's Fifth Symphony? Each lyrical experience skipped over the noise from other parts of my life, connecting to the musical experience before it.

Searching for my voice, all my life I have discovered it in melody and harmony. The music I've created on my own, or shared with Charles, is to me intensely beautiful, intensely stark, intensely joyful, intensely sweet, intensely pained—distillations of human emotions. Intensity has never scared me. Conflict I could endure. I could understand hatred. Love I cherished. The only thing unforgivable was apathy, and there was nothing apathetic about music in my life.

Music was a link, a way to connect to people around me. Every year for more than a decade I hosted Colorado-flavored Christmas caroling parties. From the bustling kitchen came the wassail, cornbread, and buffalo chili, which always created a stir. As a personal touch, we paused and acknowledged our gratitude to "Ernie" or "Ralph," or whichever beast was simmering in the stew. Then we pushed back the furniture and scattered pillows on the floor for our guests, a mix of gentiles and Jews, who sang out as if they truly believed Jesus was right then tucked away in a manger.

I collected my favorite carols and bound them in our own book. A few friends snickered at my lyric rewrites, but "God Rest Ye Merry Gentle*folk*" was more in keeping with my values. Some guests were assigned solos as they entered the house. Lillian and Teddy charmed us all with "The Littlest Angel." I pounded away at the piano. Friends pulled out oboe, violin, or guitar. Under considerable duress, Charles even dusted off his cello and let me accompany him for carol duets I'd arranged.

The idea was contagious. Hearing about our Christmas fêtes, David and Diana Rockefeller Jr., whom I'd met while forming Hunt Alternatives Fund, hosted a similar talent show. David belted out Broadway tunes. I led Southern Baptist hymns for Northerners who, truth be told, had a hard time singing with gusto about sinners plunged beneath a fountain filled with blood drawn from Emmanuel's veins. David dubbed the occasion a "Swarée," in my honor. Back in Dallas, we would have called it a "highfalutin hootenanny."

I'd learned that in unfamiliar and intimidating settings like that one, I could always enter singing. When David invited Charles and me to crew on a two-week Alaskan sail, I was out of my league, yanking on sheets in the high waters. But in the evening, on a damp piece of paper with a dull pencil, I composed a three-part round for our hearty crew. Sailor or singer, I had a place.

I dipped my toe into New York City society the same way, organizing music for a fundraiser supporting reproductive rights. In the apartment of Ace Greenberg, CEO of Bear Stearns, David sang new words to "Old Man River," with my robust piano accompaniment. Warren Buffett bellowed a modified "Battle Hymn of the Republic," and his wife Susie, a fiery torch singer, crooned a Norplant-inspired "I've Got You under My Skin." Helen and I provided back-up vocals, swaying with hand motions worthy of the Supremes.

It was all so natural for me. More and more, I was appreciating that June had insisted that I sing alto or tenor with her at church. No matter what the life situation, I'd find a way to harmonize.

Ever since I was a girl, I've written songs commemorating births, loves, deaths, anniversaries. But I'd never thought of myself as a serious musician until a dozen years after my last piano lesson. To fill lonely weekends during my separation from Mark, I went to the ranch, where I composed an hour-long cantata, a religious song cycle organized according to the classical theme of Jesus's last words on the cross—seven passages found in the gospels of Matthew, Mark, and Luke. The words conveyed despair, forgiveness, resignation, and hope.

For corresponding texts I pored over books by Elie Wiesel, as well as poems by William Blake, Theodore Roethke, and Anna Akhmatova.

Wiesel endured Nazi concentration camps. Blake had been an impoverished misfit in industrial London. Roethke was repeatedly hospitalized with mental illness. And Akhmatova's son was cruelly held hostage by the Soviets for eighteen years, to prevent her from writing.

For balance, I added two poems of my own, which brought in a different image of God. The motherhood of God, the theme of one my published articles, had become increasingly important to me. Taking seriously the biblical assertion that God is spirit, I could hardly sit through church services filled with liturgies and hymns that made God exclusively "He." I now realize another reason why I was so adamant. The cantata had been prompted by the pain of my failed relationship with Mark. If I couldn't rely on the man I'd married, why should I attribute my newfound strength to one more father figure? The God I turned to for strength during those years was loving, understanding, and nurturing—sadly, not my image of a father.

Composing the cantata was an eerie experience, more intuitive than intellectual. I'd never studied music theory, much less composition. But years of singing in choirs had tuned my musical ear. It sounds like a New Age tale, but sitting at the old cherry upright piano at the ranch, I propped the words of a poem on the music holder above the keyboard, stared at them, and waited, my hands on the keys and a pencil between my teeth. It seemed as if a muse was directing my fingers as they searched out the melody that transported the words into music. I urgently scribbled the notes onto staff paper. Then the next weekend I filled out parts around the bare melody for choir, piano, viola, harp, cello, percussion, four adult soloists, and a boy soprano. After a year of weekend composing, *The Witness Cantata* was performed. The audience response was enthusiastic. I'd found yet another voice.

Charles's and my first date was only a few months after that performance. Some months into our relationship, I summoned my courage to play the tape for him. He listened somewhat impatiently before diplomatically suggesting that I move on to compose an Easter sequel and leave my beloved composition to history. He was the pro. I was the impostor. I wiped away a few tears of disappointment, took the tape out of the player, and put it away, embarrassed.

It's much easier to see looking back how we pass on to our life partners the best and the worst of what we've known in our own families. When Charles was in high school, a music teacher befriended him.

Even though Charles had repeatedly been the principal cellist in the Vermont youth orchestra, his teacher encouraged him to put aside his instrument and try his hand at conducting. Soon he was told that he could conduct a movement from a complex Mahler symphony for the school concert, an amazing compliment. Charles assessed the needs of the piece and compared them to the abilities of the school orchestra. He then rewrote some parts to fit his schoolmates.

After the concert, someone approached his father. "Professor Ansbacher, I'm sure you're proud of your son tonight!"

"Why should I be proud?" the professor asked.

"Well, young Charles is so talented!"

"Mozart was talented. My son is no Mozart."

Twenty-five years later, my husband didn't mean to quash my music making; marrying a serious musician created an enormous obstacle for me as an occasional composer. Realistically, he and I were coming at this from very different places. I'd written the cantata as a personal expression of grief and redemption. For decades Charles's passion had been expressed by stepping up on a podium, trying to deliver a perfect performance of a masterpiece by Mozart or Beethoven. Every year he listened to a score of aspiring composers, and that's how he listened to my tape. He didn't take into himself the pain I'd expressed in a mournful soprano solo, or the hope that resounded in a final Amen chorus.

The result was that my magnum opus sat on a shelf for several years —until one day when, training on a stair machine at the gym, I mentioned to Ellen something about my music. "Do you play the piano?" she asked. I looked at her, puzzled, wondering if she was kidding. She wasn't. What did it mean that such a close friend had never glimpsed this part of me? Tears came to my eyes—the tears of a musician who'd abandoned her music.

Since being with Charles, rather than expand artistically, I'd shut down. Charles had a doctorate and had spent years in conservatories, so my crooning "Moon River" in the shower was painful to his ear. After he moved in, I responded to his scowls by no longer singing around the house. I put my guitar, dulcimer, recorder, and harp away and, apart from Christmas, rarely played the piano, ceding the musical sphere to my new husband. But over the years that my music stayed hidden, my professional and physical accomplishments made me more confident. In that moment with Ellen, the compartment in which my music was locked sprang open. I called the symphony choir director, Duain Wolfe, who shared my southern religious tradition. Duain came over to the house and listened to the piece, at one point with tears. We agreed to meet periodically, so he could advise me on revisions.

Around this time, I met a talented music maker who brought over his computer and synthesizer, to show me the latest software for composing. A click with his mouse, and notes appeared on the screen. He clicked again and they all moved on the staves, transposed into a different key. I was way behind the curve, just learning Word Perfect on my PC. After his first sentence I was lost, but I spent the next several minutes, while he was droning on, unaware of my internal dialogue:

"This is nuts. I can't possibly do this."

"But I climbed to fifteen thousand feet."

"But I have no idea what his words mean. I'm already lost."

"But I've run twenty-six miles and given birth twice without anesthesia."

"Great," I said, aloud. "Order the equipment and teach me how to use it."

I created a small studio in our basement, where I worked most evenings once the children were asleep. After each compositional breakthrough I'd call Charles to come listen. He was a tough critic, and it was hard not to be defensive. But sometimes his help was essential, such as when he informed me that a line I'd written for the cello sounded fine on the synthesizer, but that the real instrument didn't have those notes. We were back on our first date, when I didn't recognize an oboe. But my self-assurance grew as I resolved cacophony into flowing, full-bodied harmony. And as he observed Duain's enthusiasm, Charles began to appreciate that what I'd composed had some merit.

Duain arranged for the second performance of the cantata, which he conducted at the large Montview Presbyterian Church. The evening of the performance, my dear friend Dick Bunch brought me six dozen flowers. And that's how I felt: in full bloom. The chorus was magnificent. The five soloists superb. I had chill bumps as I sat in the front row, wondering, "Did I really write this?"

The piece was wonderfully received. Mother had flown up in the company plane, with June and family friends, including Hannah and Lee Roy Till, my chapel choir director from First Baptist, whose daughter, Jenni, sang the soprano part. Helen was in Dallas visiting but didn't come along. Knowing that her decision would hurt, she explained, "When you're big, I feel small." I wished I could wave a magic wand and help her appreciate how gifted she was, without being judged against her little sister.

Every family has imbalances, real or imagined. Often they decrease with time. Sometimes they grow. My family was no different. My brother, sisters, and I pursued life as if goaded by internal furies, and we compared ourselves, as most siblings do. That wasn't our parents' fault; each of us was raised with criticisms, love, exasperation, and encouragement. And it wasn't the fault of culture. We nodded off to the same nursery rhymes, memorized the same Bible verses, and played tag with similar friends. But although Helen and I took turns feeling, or being, in each other's shadow, the love between us existed in perpetual sun.

Objectively there was no reason for Helen to feel eclipsed. She was toasted and fêted as often as I. The Gloria Award she received from the Ms. Foundation reflected a particular poetic justice, since leaders of that group had tried to dissuade her from starting the New York Women's Foundation. But Helen stood firm, and in her mid-forties she was inducted into the National Women's Hall of Fame for groundbreaking work promoting women's philanthropy nationwide. Fewer than two hundred women in American history had been so honored. I was immensely proud.

Mother flew up for the ceremony in Seneca Falls, New York. Helen wondered how Mom would fare, since she once described the women's movement as "worse than drugs." But just as our mother had found something ebullient to say about my music (which, thinking back on my *Fantasie Impromptu* fiasco during college, probably left her cold), in New York Mom gravitated to the life-sized bronze sculptures of Susan B. Anthony, Elizabeth Cady Stanton, and other pioneer feminists. One more time ac-cent-uating the positive, she pointed to their wide-brimmed bonnets, tied beneath their chins. These were her mother's contemporaries, with rural roots. "Boy, Howdy . . . now I see why you admire these ladies!" Mom's voice was almost breathless. "Oh . . . those bonnets!"

With the Himalayan trek, Venice marathon, and cantata performance, I'd broken through expectations, mine and others'. Why not
continue? Borders aren't neutral. They can be helpful, delineating
"personal space" or creating tidy expectation. But they can be harm-
ful, convincing people that they can go so far and then must stop.
That's why I promised myself that every year I'd attempt something I
didn't think I could do. It was a shocking, uncomfortable, and exhila-
rating notion, linked not to any particular goal but rather a determination not to confine myself to operating inside the lines. I was very
much my father's daughter as I vowed to live the rest of my life pushing past limits.

That resolve was enabled in part by my changed financial circumstances, but more by my inner sense of myself, which was crystallizing.
In 1992 my annual seemingly impossible feat was throwing my hat
into the political ring. A new chapter in my life had been launched in
July the year before, as I sat nestled on a sofa, leaning against Charles,
with Teddy asleep on my lap. We were watching the only part of the
Democratic convention I'd made time for: the acceptance speech of
the party's presidential nominee, Bill Clinton, governor of Arkansas.
We'd tuned in partly out of interest, but more out of curiosity. Alle-
gations of his affair with Gennifer Flowers had taken the edge off my
optimism about Clinton's candidacy. As Helen said, he was "damaged
goods" and a sad reminder that the Democrats were once again squan-
dering an opportunity to take the White House.

But as I listened, I was drawn back to an afternoon three months
earlier, when I'd met the candidate in a friend's living room in Denver.
I had been sitting on a chair with my leg propped up, recovering from
knee surgery. Governor Clinton sat down beside me and we began to
talk—about my work, about his meeting my brother Ray years ago (he
said he remembered how nice Ray was), and about my political diver-
gence from all my family except Helen. Soon after, he fielded questions. I was impressed with his grasp of issues from housing to the arts
and left behind a check five times larger than the admission price to
the event.

On the TV, Clinton was speaking with passion about jobs, education, health care, justice—causes I'd spent the last fifteen years addressing. If the speech had been my own, I wouldn't have changed a word. I asked myself: What knight in shining armor am I waiting for, to sweep me up into political action? A few days later, Peter Decker, a former speechwriter for Bobby Kennedy, mentioned to me that if he could, he'd be working full time on the campaign. "I didn't know grown-ups did that," I said. The more I thought about it, the more intriguing the idea became.

The Republican National Convention pushed me over the edge. In the wake of riots in Los Angeles, speakers demanded a religious war to take back the cities. Hillary Clinton was called "unnatural" for balancing career and family responsibilities. Referring to her having written, some twenty years earlier, that the rights of children are often ignored by courts and that at one time in history women, like slaves, had no protections, Pat Buchanan accused her of saying that twelve-year-olds should be able to sue their parents and of equating marriage with slavery. As a woman, I took personal exception to the anti-Hillary harangues, but I also worried about the jeering and screaming of the crowds as right-wing speakers spewed hatred against gays. "It was probably better in the original German," I remarked dryly to Charles.

Soon I received a phone call from Merle Chambers, co-founder of the Women's Foundation, who'd been raving about Clinton at a cocktail party. "You should talk with Swanee," Charles had told her. The two of us began to dream. We decided to scope out the situation and do something big, although we didn't know yet what it would be. I called the Democratic National Committee. Like a fly to honey, a DNC staff fundraiser flew to Colorado. I suppose she'd received word that we knew what we were doing out on the frontier. Building on our experience organizing the Women's Foundation, Merle and I told her we would put together an issues-oriented women's symposium featuring Hillary and Tipper Gore, along with other experts. We vowed not to shy away from policy debate and social criticism. Now was our chance to impress on the future president, the future vice president, and the party that women were an untapped fount of ideas and resources.

The meeting took place at the Malo Mansion, my turn-of-the-century office. During a lull in the planning, Merle pulled me aside. "Okay, Swanee, we need to say what we're going to do personally," she said in her gruff voice.

I took a deep breath and then declared, "I'll have to sell some stock, but I'll put up $100,000." That was twenty times more than I'd ever given in a political campaign.

Merle was not impressed. "My Mama is doing a hundred, and I'm doing two-fifty. I think you should match me."

My heart was pounding. But within five minutes, as Merle and I talked, I realized that no other use of those dollars would go further to promote social justice. With the stroke of a pen, any president of the United States could have an impact that people like me spent decades trying to accomplish. Once I wrote the check, I figured, I'd pretend I'd never had the money.

When we rejoined the group in the conference room, it was to say that we were launching our effort with $600,000. We would create a public policy symposium called "A Million Dollar Day with Hillary and Tipper," an unheard of feat without the candidates themselves as a draw. An event by women, for women, and about women. Within a few days, Hillary called to thank me for my "gift to Bill."

"That wasn't for him," I explained. "That was for you." Long silence. She said she especially appreciated my gesture, since she was "spending a lot of time these days in foxholes." Then she asked if I wanted to join her, her husband, and the Gores on the campaign bus tour.

I laughed and said, "Sure, and I'll bring along my five-year old." Another pause, until Hillary realized I was kidding. It wasn't until months later that I discovered she was serious. I was so naïve, not understanding the power of the purse. I didn't think of myself as being in the inner circle of political power.

The perception was surely otherwise, since Charles and I did fly to Nashville for our first big donors' meeting at the labyrinthine Opryland. I was once more enormously impressed with the affable DNC chair, Ron Brown, whom I'd met some months earlier at the Colorado governor's mansion. "How you doin', Honey?" he said, as he gave me a bear hug in the hall. Ron and I were tied in so many ways. He'd been a protégé of Whitney Young, at the Urban League, and Lauren Casteel, the executive director of Hunt Alternatives Fund, was Whitney's daughter. Added to that, as DNC head Ron was the successor of Bob Strauss, father of my fourth-grade best friend Susie. These men were alike in many ways: a ready laugh, great memory for names, and outrageously affable.

The highlight of the weekend was a rally. Six thousand people filled the hall, with another thousand turned away. From our perch high in a corner, I was struck with the impossibility of security as Clinton worked his way into the hall, shaking every hand that he could reach. I identified with Tipper. There was no way she could be on that stage, with that music playing, and not dance. As Gore introduced Clinton, he recalled Mahatma Gandhi: "We must become the change we seek." He described following Clinton during a campaign stop as the governor embraced a woman holding a child with AIDS. I was wiping my cheeks when Senator Gore finished.

Hard-Working Women

Back in Colorado, Hillary came through on a campaign swing. Merle and I met her in a closed airport cafeteria. Hillary was friendly but got right down to business, planning the policy symposium. We ran through themes, speakers, and format, agreeing that we'd include women from a range of economic backgrounds. She was clearly used to making decisions—a big-picture thinker who understood how to manage details. I told her she could bring Chelsea to spend the symposium day with Lillian, but she said she was keeping her daughter out of the limelight. I recognized the theme: mothering and mission.

Just then, a woman with a mop and bucket walked by. Hillary sprang to her feet, extended her hand, and asked the woman her name. "My husband will need your vote," she said, looking the startled cleaning woman straight in the eye. Every American, it seemed, was on Hillary's schedule, not only those planning fundraisers.

Being around Hillary pushed me to think through my own focus and resolve. As she was being publicly dragged through the mud, I was struck by the personal price she was paying for the chance to influence public policy. Why did she do it? I'd been with the Clintons enough to be convinced that they were devoted to ideals that permeated their waking hours and, I imagined, their dreams. But for that commitment they'd been sneeringly labeled "ambitious." I wondered why we, as a society, wouldn't insist on ambitious leaders.

Ambition implies energy, determination, and commitment, traits that are fundamentally neutral, assuming value only when linked with good or bad goals. It's a curse when it motivates a malicious boss and it's a blessing when it inspires a beneficent one. Of course, most leaders are sure they're among the beneficent. That's why enlightened leadership is open to critique from others.

Clinton was famous for asking the opinions of a wide range of people who disagreed, wanting to hear all sides before he made a decision. I took some comfort in that thought as I plunged into his campaign, hoping that criticism from my conservative family would leave me stronger. Still, my political decision sent shock waves through the Hunt clan, since Ray was a co-chair of President Bush's reelection campaign. My brother quoted Voltaire, "I may disagree with what you have to say, but I shall defend, to the death, your right to say it." That being said, my using income from the company to oppose his candidate probably added insult to injury.

As in any family, my brother, sisters, and I were actors in each other's scripts. Consciously or not, we reenacted variations of certain plots until they became second nature. At night, troubled dreams told me that our sibling saga was being played out on a national stage. But when I worried about that dynamic, I remembered the emotional distance already between Ray and me. Sadly, I had little to lose. And just maybe, I told myself, in this political work I'd confront old demons that might not be about Ray at all. Perhaps my brother was simply, as so many times before, a surrogate father. I resolved to win not only the external political campaign but also an internal psychological battle. Only then could I declare independence.

A few weeks later, I flew to Little Rock, not so far in distance or tone from Idabel. At a dinner for supporters, I was seated next to Hillary. She wanted to hear about my mental health reform work, the council on affordable housing that I chaired, and my legislative advocacy on behalf of impoverished children. After we talked for awhile, I turned to the retired judge on my left, asking him about this now famous couple whom I'd known for a few months, and whom he'd known for years. The judge raved about their talents. "Who is smarter?" I asked, pointedly.

He paused and then answered, "*He* is brilliant. But, I have to admit . . ." With a nod of his head toward Hillary, he cast his vote. "*She* is a genius."

Governor Clinton seemed extraordinarily tired but, amazingly, recalled our conversation in Denver six months earlier. As we walked out of the museum, I turned to him for a final goodbye. Despite all I had to offer, I felt like a groupie as I seized the man's hand.

The next day included a fascinating tour of campaign headquarters—semi-organized chaos, with hundreds of young people working nonstop. The site was a former newspaper building, with sections designated "Hillaryland" and "The War Room." The air was charged with humming voices, constantly ringing phones, and strong coffee. Carnations brightened someone's corner. Dozens of desks were cluttered with papers and topped with feet. Signs proclaimed, "It's the Economy, Stupid!" and "Saddam Hussein still has a job—Do you?" I was drawn to the buzz and bustle.

Some days later, Clinton spoke in Denver at Civic Center Park. From our VIP seating on stage, I heard an aide tell Governor Romer as he walked out with the candidate that the crowd was estimated at twelve thousand. At the podium, Romer announced fifteen thousand. The next day the press pushed it up to twenty thousand. Clinton's speech was fabulous. I was brimming over. As he worked the crowd, the city attorney and I pulled back the chairs on stage and danced to the blaring soul music. I greeted Governor Clinton as he left, saying we were making good progress on the upcoming Million Dollar Day. Once again, as I vied for his attention, I felt pushy and small.

That evening Merle and I gathered at the governor's mansion for a dinner with Clinton. A local attorney, renowned as a Democratic kingmaker, had promised to raise $350,000 for the event. He was out of sorts, blaming his difficulty in reaching his goal on the fundraising that Merle and I were doing. Since we were over our goal, she and I had the pleasure of telling him he could claim credit back in Washington for a few of the donors we'd solicited. After all, we said, in the largest sense we shared the same purpose. In return, he publicly thanked "two lovely ladies" who'd been so helpful.

The next morning, at breakfast, I asked Lillian the difference between "two lovely ladies" and "two hard-working women." "Lovely ladies spend their time putting on makeup," Lillian replied.

"Right on, Honey," I said.

Colorado wasn't targeted by the Democrats until Merle and I started planning our symposium. Suddenly, because of our and others' organizing, it seemed possible that the state might go for a Democratic presidential candidate for the first time in three decades. I knew the state pretty well, having worked in several cities and towns organizing the Women's Foundation, so I felt confident when I was asked to join a small strategy group. I argued against spending resources to take on Ross Perot, the third-party candidate from Dallas. "Clinton mustn't make him a martyr. Coloradoans won't take lightly to our insulting a self-made rugged individualist," I intoned.

To my great surprise, the campaign seemed on a winning trajectory. One of my Grand Canyon friends, Judi Wagner, called me at the ranch to urge that I consider becoming part of a Clinton administration. That thought had never crossed my mind. I turned once more to Charles, my confidant and mentor, to talk over the notion. Charles and I walked up the old stage road. It was late September, and the aspen leaves were a dazzling gold against the azure sky. On the side of a steep hill, we sat down on a log and gazed out at the limitless high expanse of South Park, spread before us like a pale green blanket.

"I think you should do it," my husband said. As we talked over possibilities, he became more and more enthusiastically supportive, remembering his year as a White House Fellow in the nerve center of the world.

"Are you sure?" I said, chewing on some tall grass blades.

"Yes, I'm sure," he answered firmly. He stood up first, then turned and pulled me up. It dawned on me that my husband had more faith in me than I had in myself. The more I thought about it, the more I realized how all my life I'd been building toward this moment. Dad's political work. Mom's religious values. Once convinced, I flipped into my buffalo roundup mentality. For clarity, I developed a concept paper on what my role in the administration might be: managing a synapse between the federal government and the philanthropic community. I could make use of my networking skills, foundation experience, and political connections.

Wise friends like David Rockefeller Jr., Fern Portnoy, Vinny McGee, and Pat Schroeder (our congresswoman) each had admonitions. But Pat spoke most vehemently against my being in Washington: "You'll never see your children. If you leave your desk before 9 p.m., you'll come in the next morning and find someone else in your chair. And unless you're one of the top three priorities of the president, you'll be competing with sharp-elbowed twenty-two-year olds, lining up for photo ops in the Rose Garden." Telling me about various humanitarian organizations headquartered in Rome, she urged me to pursue the embassy in Italy where, she said, I'd be "king of the roost." A most unfortunate expression, given her and my feminist inclinations.

I'd studied Italian in college and traveled there often, so I could imagine life in la bella Italia. But ambassador? My first reaction was that I was unversed in foreign policy. But as the idea germinated over the following weeks, I became more and more intrigued at the thought of learning a whole new field in my forties. I was committed to public service. And some lessons from Colorado, in politics and social reform, could be applied internationally. Further, I was ready for a leadership challenge and didn't want to run for office. Maybe an ambassadorship would be ideal.

Somewhat like when I was training for the marathon, a string of experts warned me I was overreaching. A senator with whom I consulted brushed aside the idea as highly improbable. I had to decide whether to let myself be talked out of the possibility, or believe in myself more than he believed in me. I'd learned a lot since the days when I was too timid to chair the Mental Health Commission. Now I pushed forward.

A mutual friend put me in touch with a former ambassador to Italy, who could give me a sense of the job. That led to a horrific phone conversation, with the former diplomat offended that I should consider myself ambassadorial material. "Those jobs should go to people who've spent their lives in the trenches, earning the right. Of course there are those who've raised millions in this campaign. It's too bad, but they'll get something." Then he added the clincher: "Besides, I haven't decided what *I* want." I later heard that he desperately wanted to be ambassador to the United Nations or go back to Italy. I wished I'd known that before I called.

Our theme, "Serious Women, Serious Issues, Serious Money," raised eyebrows at campaign headquarters in Little Rock. Women had participated in social events in the past, but a full-day public policy symposium exclusively for women was new. To solicit the final $400,000, I'd cleared my calendar of work with Hunt Alternatives and flown around the country to meet with potential donors. My fundraising in Dallas resulted in hard feelings on Ray's part, who considered my effort there a personal affront. After he vented his frustration, I offered not to plow those fields out of deference to him. My capitulation didn't sit well with me, though. The same act that springs cheerfully out of generosity feels terrible when it's appeasement. Bitterness is bred as the giver begrudges the gift, and the receiver resents the giver. When we placated the kingmaker back in Denver, that was easy, because Merle and I held the trump cards—or, literally, the checks. But with the radical imbalance of power in my relationship with my brother, I felt I lost a piece of myself as I gave in to his demand that I not raise money in Dallas.

Eli Segal, heading the campaign, personally called me a few days earlier asking that we drop the words "serious money." Some at the campaign were concerned it would sound crass, others said élitist, to link women and big money. But from our years with the Women's Foundation, we'd learned the importance of making exactly that connection. Eli (one of the kindest men on earth) let himself be persuaded.

Subplots aside, the day of the symposium arrived. Merle called me at home.

"Now Swanee, no offense, but remember: serious issues, serious clothes." Instead of my usual flowing ensembles of purples and pinks, I dutifully put on a black-and-white plaid suit I'd bought in a rare moment of insecurity. I was the only woman that day dressed like a man. Merle wore a smashing, bright yellow designer outfit. She consoled me that I could pass for a female accountant.

Marjorie Seawell, another (well-dressed) friend from the Women's Foundation, had assembled thought-provoking political and policy experts to discuss the economy, health care, reproductive rights, and foreign affairs. She had also handled invitations so that the crowd was a blend, racially and socio-economically.

Hillary arrived for a small lunch before her speech. As she went with me table to table, shaking every hand, I stood behind her, whispering information about each person. She incorporated my tidbits into warm personal greetings. An hour later, when she addressed the symposium, I was amazed at her polish. Not one glance at notes. Not one "uh" or "you know." Every word counted, as she laid out her husband's agenda for his presidency, weaving in a visit she'd made that morning to a neonatal hospital ward.

The room was packed. The speakers were excellent. The event flowed smoothly. We pulled it off, with style—our style. "You'd think for a million dollars you could have gotten the candidate," the kingmaker goaded.

I slapped my forehead and replied, with more than a dash of sarcasm, "Darn. I knew we were forgetting something. We didn't invite him."

More Serious Issues

As satisfying as the symposium was, throughout Clinton's campaign I felt torn. I was already conflicted as I curtailed my civic work for political activity. But if I jumped in fully and claimed a place among the politicos, what about my children? Staying on the inside track could be life-consuming. I had to resist the frenzy that would suck my spirit dry.

One day I was invited to a private meeting with Senator Gore during his layover en route to Aspen. Time was tight, but I picked up Lillian at school, planning to drop her off quickly at our house before heading to the airport. When she objected I turned the wheel, pulled into our garage, and went inside to lie with her across her bed. For an hour we planned how she might redecorate her room.

In those days before ubiquitous cell phones, I didn't know how to contact the group meeting Gore. But the candidate, I imagined, couldn't care less. Surely I could create other opportunities for face time with him. I didn't give the decision another thought until I saw the kingmaker that night at a dinner. "Where were you?" he asked with a frown. "We waited for you at the airport but finally went ahead." Turns out only four had been invited to meet with Gore. Only one hadn't shown up. I'd felt like such a good mom in the moment. But that night in my dreams I tried to live the day differently.

Who mattered? What mattered? As I was rubbing shoulders with political Pooh Bahs, I could feel myself being pulled into an orb of headline names. To counter the seduction of the famous and influential, I needed grounding. I needed a solid home base.

A family is its own being, and a thin-skinned one at that. The dynamics are remarkably tender, as at any point in time egos are developing unevenly, comparisons abound, feelings get buried or trampled. Family-building efforts may pay off, be ignored, or backfire. Creating a home is not for the faint of heart.

Charles and I were working hard to blend our families. I was careful to have frequent chunks of individual time with each of our three kids, to maintain strong dyads, so that we would be more than five people milling aimlessly in and out of each other's lives. We created rituals, such as holding hands before meals, with each person saying what he or she was grateful for. I kept a separate journal for all three children and put together exotic trips with scrapbooks for each so that they would have a shared history.

Henry had grown up to be a winsome young man—fit, smart, and levelheaded. We drove down to Colorado College for his lacrosse games (he was a terrific goalie), and he came up to Denver to introduce his girlfriends to us or to attend events where his father or I was in the limelight. Inviting a young adult son to come clap along with an adoring crowd may feel right at the moment, but it takes its toll. In addition, the strong voice that I was developing professionally sometimes dominated the airwaves at home so that only the boldest could chime in. Our older son was becoming his own person in spite of those challenges. He still wasn't completely at ease with me, but there was a healthy respect and genuine love between us.

Sixteen years younger than Henry, Teddy had a chipper, easy personality. He was cuddly, sweet, and affectionate. But he was also what my mother called "all boy," picking up sticks and stabbing bushes looking for Ninja turtles as we walked to preschool. To my horror, he also reveled in sadistic verse: "Oh me, Oh my, stick a knife in your eye." But he had a strong musical sensitivity. At two and a half, Teddy sat through Charles's concerts, afterward enthusiastically demonstrating with his hands the violins, triangle, cymbals, and drums. "Mommy! Do you hear? The cellos just came in!" he cried out when listening to a tape of songs for toddlers. That passion translated into his ability, like his sister's, to sit enraptured through a three-hour opera long before he was old enough to read the libretto.

Before I had children, I imagined that my relationship with each would be the same. It was an ignorant assumption. Each child is a unique puzzle of needs and gifts, proclivities and limitations. We may wish we could treat each the same, but ironically that simplicity would be unfair and unequal. One child is soothed by a smile, a hug, and a nod, while another requires every ounce and more that we have to give. The difference isn't bad kids or bad parents. It's a function of the "fruit-basket turnover" that lands one child in a family with a certain pair called mother and father. Coming to grips with that random reality was one of the most difficult adjustments I faced over the next decade.

My relationship with my daughter was qualitatively and quantitatively different from that with the two boys. She was living between two households as Mark and I shared custody. If it was difficult for us as parents, it was agonizing for her.

Lillian was a wise old soul trapped in a child's body. At two, she was described by teachers as "contemplative." At three, "serious." At four, "a little philosopher." That same year, for a private school admissions director, she drew her self-portrait: a large, round head with legs. In developmental terms, the director explained, she wasn't ready for school. But she needed someplace that would challenge her, so I found a school for gifted children. At five, Lillian tested as having the attention and memory of an eight-year-old.

Educators we consulted said the good news and bad news was that she would be able to finish high school before she was a teenager. We needed to think through options. More important to me, her intelligence was matched by her depth. Duain Wolfe, who also directed the Colorado Children's Chorale, told me, "She sings from someplace inside her. You can't teach a child that."

I didn't want her to go off to college before she was emotionally ready, so instead I helped her pursue nonacademic passions. The complexity of opera—story, acting, and music—fit the complexity of her thinking. Given her love of opera, she was thrilled to have a walk-on part for an Opera Colorado production of *Otello*. Lillian carried off the role with poise, although my jaw dropped when I saw her singing along with the chorus in Italian instead of sticking with her silent part in the tableau on stage.

There were heavenly moments raising Lillian, when I felt as if she was an angel, dropped into my life as a source of warmth and wisdom. One day at ranch camp, with other girls mostly older than she, I created a competition to see who could find the most litter as we hiked. Bad idea. The game quickly devolved into a nasty grabbing scene as two or three tried to get the same scrap. I separated the girls and told them to go off by themselves and think through what had happened. Ten minutes later, we sat down in a circle to reflect on lessons learned.

The first said, "We shouldn't litter."

Another added, "We shouldn't get crazy over winning the prize."

"We shouldn't be mean," the third contributed.

After each, I nodded. Then I turned to Lillian. She looked at me, then at the other girls, and offered a little sermon: "There are lots of ways of winning. And when you do something that's good, like picking up trash, then you're a winner. Even if you don't get the prize that you're trying for, you know that you're doing what God wants, and that's a prize."

It didn't take long for me to realize that my little girl was considerably smarter than I was. She was also the only person in the family who really understood when I was trapped in a thicket of sadness, or delighting in the goodness of life.

But there were formidable moments raising Lillian. Her childhood tantrums were frequent and uncontrolled. She'd pull every book off her shelves and throw them across the rug. One evening, rather than lock her in her room, I dragged the sofa in front of my bedroom door to keep her out. I was determined to "extinguish" her behavior, as psychologists would say, by ignoring it. I telephoned Charles in Colorado Springs.

"Just checking in," I said as a book slammed against my door.

"How was your concerto rehearsal tonight?" THUD.

"Oh, Lil's just having some trouble getting to sleep." BAM. THUMP.

No lesson was learned that evening, except that neither my daughter nor I had a clue what to do. Setting limits was like waving a red flag in her face. When I said she couldn't come to dinner until her room was straightened, she upped the ante by refusing to eat. When I added that she couldn't watch TV, she said she didn't care to anyway. Finally, I dished out an ultimatum. "It's 7. Get your room picked up by 7:10. I'm taking every item you leave out, and I don't know when you'll see them again."

She not only didn't put her things away; she emptied her drawers and shelves onto the floor. Later, she looked at the boxes of clothes and toys and implored, "Mommy, please don't throw them away. Give them to the poor."

Having come from a disrupted family, I felt terribly guilty about her unhappiness. One night as she fought sleep, she was sobbing, saying she wished I was still married to her dad. "I'm so, so sorry." I was crying too. "I wanted you to have a wonderful, happy home. I didn't mean to give you a divided family."

She looked up at me, with a fragile half-smile of forgiveness. "Isn't it God's fault, since He's the one who makes babies be born?"

"You're not anyone's fault, Sweetheart," I said through my tears. "You're a gift." But such questions were never far away. My daughter wrestled, as I had, with the reconciliation of divine power, perfect love, and painful reality. What could a preschooler understand? I thought of reciting to her the sermons I'd heard, explaining how there was an active, perfect will of God that could create heaven on earth, and a passive, permissive will that lets us humans make a hell of it. But I'd given up on that convoluted theology years before. I wouldn't, couldn't, ascribe my daughter's disappointment to God.

But Lillian persisted, in her tiny voice, "If God loves us and can stop bad things from happening, why doesn't He stop those bad things?" The pat answers I'd heard at five, fifteen, and thirty-five wouldn't do.

"Lillian, that's the question called 'theodicy.' Even the wisest people in the world don't know the answer." Many times ahead, we would long for those elusive answers. We would wish for some divine plan, some redemptive purpose that would justify what she had to experience.

When she was six, I heard Lillian screaming and I ran into her room. She was standing on her chair—actually Hassie's chair from Mt. Vernon—trying to get away from snakes that she saw crawling around her. I lay down with her until she fell asleep, then called the psychiatrist with whom I'd organized the mothers' group at Karis. Apologizing for the late hour, I described with a quivering voice what I'd just witnessed.

"We call them night terrors," he said. "You don't need to worry. It's common. Put her baby brother in her bedroom. She'll be okay." Only long after did I learn that Lillian had also been hearing voices and seeing flames at home and at school. I didn't know how to draw a line between her spectacular imagination, which her teachers reveled in, and what seemed to be psychotic hallucinations. Even in preschool, she could tell stories that went on for half an hour. Her imagery was so vivid, I could imagine how it might be hard for her to sort truth from fiction.

She also had finely tuned intuition. I've always been hesitant to believe in the paranormal, but I had no explanation for the many times my daughter seems to take complicated thoughts straight from my mind. For example, during a symphony, as I noticed a musical treatment I could use in my cantata for a piece called "Mary Magdalene," Lillian leaned over and whispered, with no context at all, "Mommy, did Mary Magdalene have very long hair?" Those times were a signal to me of our closeness. But my earlier experience with extrasensory perception had been with Hassie, so naturally I wondered about links between ESP, psychosis, and a wondrous imagination.

Even if they were simple imagination, her fantasies often didn't breed delight. Lillian was preoccupied with death and separation. Before she could write, the stories she told her teachers were laced with tragedy: a child killed in a mineshaft as he went down to take lunch to his brother; twins who buried their father before their family vacation, then couldn't save their mother from a terminal illness that she contracted on the trip. . . . Her first poem, at seven, was entitled "Why Are You So Sad?" A couple of years later, a school writing specialist told me, "I've been teaching twenty years. This is the most talented child I've ever had. We writing teachers pray we'll have one student like her in our career." But when the teacher submitted a story by Lillian to a children's magazine, it was rejected as "too dark."

Like all children, Lillian had delightfully effusive moments. She announced that when she was a mommy she was going to have sixty-five boys and sixty-six girls, because she liked girls better. But instead of the confidence that should have accompanied her intelligence, she told a preschool tester that she didn't know colors, because she had only recently learned burgundy, so she was sure there must be some she didn't know. She was afraid of going down a playground slide, and she peeked fearfully out her window as other children rode their bikes up and down the street.

As close as a mother and child may be, there is no guarantee, or even likelihood, that as one changes, the other will evolve in the same direction. Despite the best of intentions, rather than grow more alike the two may become more distinct, until they have to strain to understand each other. What an irony, that as I was feeling more at home in the world, more sure of my competence, I was raising a daughter who was feeling more and more unsafe. Until she was seven, she woke repeatedly through the night, needing to be comforted. Often in the morning I'd find her on the floor by my bed. She told me that at her father's she slept outside his bedroom door.

I was having troubled dreams myself—about being a bad mother. But I was beginning to understand: I didn't have a problem child. I had a child with a problem. So I took Lillian to a "talking doctor." After months, the psychologist produced a report, describing my daughter's therapy with dolls. I felt like a knife was cutting through my heart, hearing how she play-acted herself in the role of a mother—abandoning her doll, having no time for her, telling her she was bad and unlovable. I listened to psychological jargon, about how Lillian had internalized me as neglectful and had uncontrollable fear associated with my leaving her, even for an hour.

The doctor hadn't told me anything I didn't already know. I needed to understand the cause. Most children move between two households without sustained trauma, and Lillian had always been in the care of loving adults. I'd arranged my life so that I drove her to school each morning, went to my office and worked like the devil, then picked her up and brought her home. I'd resigned from national boards because they required travel, and almost all local ones that met outside her school hours. Yet she remained terrified that I would abandon her, and that fear fed her fury. Why?

A few years later, a psychiatrist counseled that Lillian might have bipolar disorder. The condition, formerly called manic-depressive illness, usually showed up as extreme irritability in young children. Selfishly, I felt encouraged to think that I might not be the only reason for my daughter's problems. But we didn't follow up with that doctor; Mark wanted us to manage the situation ourselves, since we were both trained professionals. In fact, he had concluded that I was provoking our daughter's problems, since she was always obedient, even cherubic, at his home. If in my home she was angry and falling apart, he reasoned, it was because of me. I didn't know why there should be such a contrast.

Life with Lillian had become a theme woven through every part of my life. I couldn't separate questions about my mothering from my outside work. My daughter was a chunk of my heart, now living outside my body. My political activities and humanitarian advocacy were also an integral part of who I was, a manifestation of creativity and passion that came from my core. If I gave them up, I wouldn't be me.

Triumph

Election eve, 1992. Colorado had a beautiful snow. That didn't bode well for Democrats, whose turnout tends to drop with the temperature. Returning from a long day at my foundation office, I started calling friends from my rolodex to "leaflet" door-to-door; I had twenty signed up by the time I reached the C's.

The air was snappy, and so were our spirits as Lillian and I headed out. I grinned, watching my daughter, bundled up and so earnest with a stack of fliers under her arm. That made me think of my last political door-to-door walk: thirty-two years earlier with Susie Strauss, pounding Kennedy signs into the thick green grass of Dallas. We were ten, my daughter's age.

Our whole family was excited as we went to sleep. Clinton would be flying through several cities on an all-night campaign swing, stopping in Denver at 5:00 a.m. before heading on to Little Rock. At 3:00 a.m. I heard Teddy's sweet voice: "Is it time to go see Bill?" There was no getting him back to sleep, so I plopped him into a bubble bath for an hour to keep him quiet.

Soon Charles, Lillian, Teddy, and I made our way to a United Airlines hanger, where we waited onstage with the Peñas, Wirths, Romers, and other political friends, enduring an ear-splitting rock band assigned to keep the crowd of well-wishers awake. At long last the gigantic doors of the hanger parted, revealing the plane and the candidate, looking for all the world as if he were walking on a heavenly shaft of light. It was a Cecil B. DeMille moment, accompanied by the strains of a gospel choir. Emotions were at fever pitch as we shook hands with the candidate couple.

A few hours later, Charles and I were at the airline ticket counter. Chuckling, Senator Wirth made a big show of sharing his upgrade coupons with us penny pinchers, so we could join him, Merle, and other friends in business class as we made the pilgrimage to Little Rock.

The scene at Governor Clinton's home base was approaching hysteria. Outside our hotel was a large outdoor platform, where excited campaign workers swarmed. Inside, we blended in with the crowd assembled in a darkened conference room before a giant television screen. Election night news showed Bill and Chelsea jogging in the rainy dusk.

As the election results began to come in state by state, the scene was euphoric. Outside, Clinton's acceptance speech was delivered before a cheering crowd that spanned the world, but for me it was a personal victory. Little Rock was crammed with people whose past and future were colliding in that moment, and I was one of them. I stayed inside feeling strangely pensive, sensing the changes that this victory could portend.

The morning after the governor's triumph, Charles and I ambled the statehouse grounds, which were still littered with debris from the festivities the night before. A dozen satellite dishes looked like overgrown moonflowers. Making our way to the campaign headquarters, we passed Tipper as she piled her children into a limousine. I called out and waved. She recognized me and waved back, but once again I felt like a star-struck intruder. At the headquarters Clinton's strategist James Carville, asleep in his desk chair, opened one eye to acknowledge us. Judging from the smiles as our guide introduced us around, I was more integral to the scene than I'd imagined. Still, I couldn't relish my notoriety, assuming that it had everything to do with my campaign contribution and little to do with my values or my work.

I called Lauren at my office, asking her once more to shoulder the load, and adding breezily that I'd be staying over. She laughed at the understatement. At dinner I was seated beside Al Gore. I wasn't sure how to address him. "Mr. Vice-President Elect"? "Senator"? I settled on, "How about you can call me Swanee if I can call you Al?" He smiled and agreed, but we had a hard time striking up a meaningful conversation.

I excused myself and went over to Alida Rockefeller Messinger, a cousin of our friend David Rockefeller. "Trade places with me," I begged. "You're both environmentalists. You'd get much more out of sitting with him."

"That wouldn't be proper," she insisted. Proper or improper just wouldn't occur to me. But I returned to my seat. Gore obviously had extensive banquet speaker experience, I realized as I watched him wolf down his food, however politely. At the podium he made self-deprecating jokes, bringing the house down with a comment that he was so stiff he was going to have his next physical done by the Forest Service.

A few months later, at another big donor evening put together by the DNC, the vice president entered the restaurant and began pressing the flesh. Since Little Rock, I'd read his book *Earth in the Balance*, a remarkable interweaving of the mental, physical, and spiritual dimensions of the environmental crisis. The book was a principled call to action, positing that American ingenuity could help us to stabilize population growth, spread social justice, boost education levels, create green technologies, and negotiate treaties to bring us back from the brink. I reminded him that at dinner in Little Rock we hadn't had much to say to each other. Now that I'd read his book, the next time together would be different. He thanked me warmly and added, "But I thought our dinner conversation was great."

I guess it's all relative, I mused to myself. This poor guy, and brilliant policy wonk, had to spend untold hours in surface conversations. I'd imagined that he found them tedious. Too many years of immersion in philosophy and theology had left me impatient at social niceties and political chatter. Having organized my share of conferences and seminars, I understood that the meaty deliberations were often behind the scenes, while the actual event was just gravy. I wondered how much gravy thoughtful people like the Clintons and Gores could stomach.

Christmas week, I packed up the kids and flew down to Dallas. As always, Mother and her driver met us at the gate, all smiles and hugs. I especially appreciated her coming, since she had a pattern of staying up all night and sleeping during the day. Her staff had handled the holiday preparations, which over the decades had assumed rhythmic predictability. The nine-foot Christmas tree with presents spilling out into the living room. A motorized Santa waving his mittened hand as he rotated. Life-size Raggedy Ann and Andy dolls sliding down the polished banister. It was a magical setting. But more than the things all around, I loved seeing Lillian curled up in Granny Ruth's bed, sharing the secrets of the season.

Holidays with Mother were larger than life. Over time she'd filled closets, the attic, and basement with gifts she intended to give. A warehouse held her overflow. Only later would I recognize that her gift buying had a compulsive aspect. Presents that she selected throughout the year often didn't strike her as quite right for Christmas, so she sent out her staff to buy even more for her children and grandchildren.

Charles was back in Denver, planning to come the next day. When I called to say goodnight, I was surprised to find him lingering in his office at 11 p.m., wrapped up in a discussion about Peña Investments. He was a founding investor in the firm that Federico had created when he stepped down from being mayor. Our friend had promised his investors that he would stay with the company and not return to political life. But as he passed through the Albuquerque airport during the holidays, he was paged by Warren Christopher, who was advising Clinton on the new cabinet composition. Peña hadn't considered such a position and was taken off guard when Christopher asked him if he would like to be secretary of transportation. If so, his appointment would be announced the next day in Little Rock.

We'd stayed close to Ellen and Federico since they'd married and through the births of their two daughters. From hours of conversation during my marathon training and dissertation research, I predicted that she would welcome leaving the "make-money world" of her husband's investment company to return to the "lose-money world" of public service. In the wee hours, Charles and I set up a conference call with the Peñas. We talked about Federico's promise to his investors. I urged him to take the cabinet post, saying that he could do more for the causes and people he wanted to help. Federico made his decision at about 2 a.m., but Ellen said she wouldn't go with him to the announcement because one of the girls was sick. "You should be there," I insisted. "I'll join you to help with the kids."

A few hours later I'd packed a briefcase, left my own brood with Mom, and was landing in Little Rock on a plane that also brought a disheveled Mickey Kantor, a long-time colleague of Hillary's who'd taken the red-eye from California. He had been called in the middle of the night, as cabinet selection dominoes fell in rapid order. Bill Richardson, a Hispanic congressman from New Mexico who had been in line for secretary of interior, was opposed by environmentalists, who pushed for Governor Bruce Babbitt of Arizona. But Clinton wanted his cabinet to "look like America," so he needed a Latino.

Federico had developed Denver's new airport; if he took Transportation, Babbitt could take Interior. But that left open Babbitt's intended position, U.S. trade representative. So Mickey was pulled in. The frantic shuffle was orchestrated in a whirlwind twenty-four hours by Christopher, a respected diplomat and attorney who'd reportedly insisted that he would accept no position, but at the president's request became secretary of state. Such was the topsy-turviness of setting up an administration for the most powerful country in the world.

As the newly nominated cabinet officers met for a hurried moment at the governor's mansion in Arkansas, I found Ellen trying to corral her two young daughters. We all filed in for a crowded press briefing. One of her girls fell apart, so I whisked her up and paced in the cold alley, with her buttoned under my coat until she stopped screaming. We went back into the press conference, where Bruce, Mickey, and Federico were about to be introduced. The second daughter was asleep in Ellen's arms. George Stephanopoulos, the dapper young aide to the president-elect, was standing against the wall. He motioned to ask if the chair next to Ellen, in front of me, was free. I gestured for him to take it. He scooted in and sat down. A dismayed look spread across his face as he reached around and pulled pink Silly Putty off his trouser seat.

I'd reminded Federico to thank Ellen in his remarks. But once he got started at the microphone he was on a roll, thanking not only his wife but also the man who'd flown him in, the pilot's son, who'd come along, "and my friend Swanee Hunt." Not even the good deed of baby-sitting goes unpunished. A columnist in Denver commented on the former mayor's new position, wrongly linking my campaign contribution to his appointment: "It's amazing what $250,000 will buy."

Back in Dallas that same day, I reentered the Christmas scene at Mt. Vernon. Helen and Harville were there, as usual, with their Leah and Hunter, interspersed in age between Lillian and Teddy. The four kids created and performed plays for family reunions. "Aunt Swanee" directed, helped make costumes, and enlarged parts to fit egos. That Christmas we skated right up to the edge of good taste, casting a new puppy as baby Jesus.

From one drama to another. My head was spinning. I told Helen excitedly that Hillary had looked over my biographical material. The Clintons definitely wanted me to be part of the administration. I said

I'd love to help out with the pre-inaugural transition in Washington, especially since Charles had already been enlisted to help design an arts plan. Hillary had pointed me toward Melanne Verveer, heading up her Washington office. The president-elect was committed to having women in leadership roles throughout government. Melanne and I agreed that I would analyze our foreign policy sector for places where the appointment of women could be particularly beneficial.

Space was limited, and Hillary was in Little Rock. Still, I was amazed to find that I was assigned to her private office in the D.C. transition headquarters. I interviewed dozens of people with experience in agencies and departments related to international affairs and compiled their recommendations in a policy paper for the First Lady's staff. Melanne mentioned to me that as I was thinking through these larger issues, I should keep in mind a position in which I might be interested. Her aside hit home. As I began to seriously consider my options, I constantly turned to Charles for encouragement and counsel.

On New Year's Eve I wrote a letter to Clinton, asking, as Congresswoman Schroeder had suggested, to be appointed ambassador to Italy. Before turning it in, I showed it to Bill Coleman, secretary of transportation under President Ford and Charles's mentor from his White House Fellow days. A Republican civil rights veteran, he was one of my strongest allies. I'm sure he meant to bolster me when he concluded, "You should be ambassador to Italy even if you didn't have money." High praise inside the Beltway, but my real-world heart sank.

A kind campaign worker, Keith Henderson, was a self-appointed mole in the bowels of White House personnel. He took on my appointment as a cause, following up on rumors, casually inquiring in hallway meetings, calling with advice, dropping off notes to my friends in Hillary's office. But despite his best efforts, it was an excruciatingly long wait.

Dangling in the Wind

Clinton's inauguration, on January 20, 1993, heralded a hopeful future. I sat in the huge crowd in front of our nation's capitol, bundled up with my husband and children, trembling not only from the cold but also from the sense of possibility. The incoming president was talking about how "this new world has already enriched the lives of millions of Americans who are able to compete." But, he said, this was also a time "when most people are working harder for less; when others cannot work at all; when the cost of health care devastates families and threatens to bankrupt many of our enterprises, great and small; when fear of crime robs law-abiding citizens of their freedom; and when millions of poor children cannot even imagine the lives we are calling them to lead."

These were the words I'd been waiting for. Words of inspiring and intelligent compassion. But the president had another message about the political sphere into which I was stepping:

> This beautiful capital, like every capital since the dawn of civilization, is often a place of intrigue and calculation. Powerful people maneuver for position and worry endlessly about who is in and who is out, who is up and who is down, forgetting those people whose toil and sweat sends us here and pays our way. Americans deserve better. . . . Let us resolve to reform our politics, so that power and privilege no longer shout down the voice of the people. Let us put aside personal advantage so that we can feel the pain and see the promise of America.

This was *my* inauguration. The *Denver Post* ran a two-page spread of photographs I'd taken of the historic events. With filial devotion, Henry put together a framed collage of clippings, to celebrate the occasion. He understood how I was stirred by Clinton's admonition that "in serving, we recognize a simple but powerful truth: we need each other. And we must care for one another." But no one in my life knew how to deal with the dog-eat-dog world I was about to enter. Even the president of the United States, as it turned out, wouldn't have the power to tame the beasts inside the Beltway.

Back in Colorado, I tried to resume my normal crush of activities. But in February 1993 I received a call from my friend Anne Bartley, yet another Rockefeller cousin who, like Alida, had given generously to our women's symposium. She was an assistant to Melanne, who'd become the First Lady's deputy chief of staff. Anne said that Hillary would like to "sponsor" me for the ambassadorial appointment, a rare distinction. (Contrary to press scuttlebutt, when it came to White House appointments, Hillary wasn't calling the shots. Her staff quipped that if she were, decisions would be made much faster.)

Anne said that Hillary couldn't also sponsor Charles, who was being considered for the National Council on the Arts. She said we needed to choose. I said I would get back to her. As soon as I hung up the phone, I called Charles and told him I'd received some news; he said he'd come over to my office right way.

I asked my assistant to hold my calls and closed the door. Sitting at my table, I waited, with my chin in my palm, staring at the etched French doors but not seeing the traffic outside. What should I do? Well, what would my mother do? Wrong question. What would *we* do? With trepidation, I wondered if Charles would opt for his career over mine. And even if he chose mine, would he later regret it?

My stomach clenched when I heard his step in the hallway. I stood and turned to greet him as he entered. He had an apprehensive look on his face. "It's not bad; just a tough decision," I said.

As soon as Anne's question left my lips, Charles took me in his arms and said, "Oh, Love, there's no question. I've been a star already. It's your turn."

I made about ten trips to Washington over the next months, each time renewing contacts on the Hill and moving freely between the Old Executive Office Building and the West Wing. Several illustrious older Beltway personalities with whom I met were amazed to discover, "You're that little girl who sang with your sister at Mt. Vernon!"

I always dropped in on Eli Segal, who'd moved from heading the presidential campaign to creating AmeriCorps, Clinton's national service initiative and Segal's passion and legacy. (From his funeral in 2006 I carried away the words: "Love doesn't die. People do. So when all that's left of me is love, give me away.") Eli was the second person sponsoring me for the appointment. I felt embarrassed by my bald self-promotion when I gave him a résumé, with a long list of initiatives I'd chaired and organizations I'd started. But he was dear, and kissed me on the cheek, assuring me, "My friendship will outlast any ambassadorial post."

With ample but astute advice from Charles about the way Washington works, I'd launched a carefully sequenced crusade, with a chart of key decision makers and a strategy to reach every one. Yet when Keith overheard a comment in a bar that "Swanee Hunt is really campaigning for a post," I felt mortified. The truth is, D.C. is filled with people angling for one position or another. But I had a tackle box with more bait than most. My actions were clearly incongruous with my long-time defense of equal opportunity. Beneath the veneer of polish and poise, I found the whole enterprise humiliating. Still, I'd been told repeatedly that a campaign was necessary. A dozen famous names were circulating for every appointment. Catty speculation was that White House personnel choices were often made according to whoever was last out of the Oval Office before the moment of decision.

Occasionally, I merged mothering into the campaign. I brought Lillian to a Saturday afternoon meeting in the West Wing with a former fundraiser who'd joined the White House staff. He was warm and funny with her, suggesting that I leave the room while they discussed her mother's future. He also acknowledged that the longer indecision stretched, the more the press reported rumors, and the more people's lives were entangled. He would call the president's closest aide, Bruce Lindsey, and find out what was happening, so I "wouldn't be left hanging in the air, twisting."

But he ended the conversation by asking if I didn't want an exit mechanism, so that I could save face if the appointment didn't pan out. I found that offer bizarre. This wasn't an ego matter. It was a decision that others and I were making about a job.

On the positive side, I received a call from Keith telling me to "brush up on my Italian." Delighted, I began working with a tutor several times a week. But with all the uncertainty, I was wound tight, so Charles and I decided to do the unthinkable—a weekend at a tennis resort. I went out on the courts, determined, I laughed, "to spend my nerves on my serves." The next morning, we settled in for a long, quiet breakfast. We looked for all the world like middle-agers in a TV ad from the 1960s for Post Toasties cereal, but our conversations were anything but common as we analyzed the Beltway buzz. Between sips of grapefruit juice, I thumbed through index cards: "Governo, bambini, senato. . . ." Charles had brought a *New York Times* to the table. His eyes widened. Then he passed me the paper. On page three was an article listing, one after another, the notables we'd repeatedly heard were on their way to specific posts. At the end, it named me the top contender for Germany. Discombobulated, we gave up on our retreat, threw our things into our bags, and got on the next plane to Denver, where we could stay in closer touch with the news-making world.

Mentors

Soon after, I was invited to Washington for a meeting of big Democratic donors, with presentations on two issues of great concern to the president (and to me): health care and welfare reform. I felt bold, parking myself next to Pamela Harriman, English-born and a veritable institution in Democratic politics for twenty years. She was, after all, in a class by herself, with an early White House announcement of her nomination as ambassador to France. Pamela and I passed each other notes with strikingly undiplomatic remarks about various speakers (a pastime I'd learned from Helen to liven up tedious Dallas meetings). Penetrating her aura of distinction, I simply liked her.

The next morning, I had an energized bounce in my step as I walked up the sidewalk to the White House, pretending that this could be an everyday occurrence. The guard checked me in, and I tried to look nonchalant as I climbed the enormously wide stairs of the East Wing, to the room where a hundred of us had been invited for breakfast. Pamela presented the president with a huge pair of shears, tied with a red ribbon. She'd bought them long ago at an English antique shop and announced that she'd "been waiting for a Democrat to get to the White House, to cut through the red tape!" I watched with amusement as he thanked her, warmly but politely, first as "Mrs. Harriman," then as "Pamela." This woman made even presidents unsure of themselves.

Clinton went on to praise Pamela as the godmother of the Democratic Party, crediting her with helping usher in his new life. And speaking of . . . He then recounted how a few days earlier, when being ushered through a hall between the living quarters and the Oval Office, he'd found himself surrounded by a group coming to meet with Hillary for her health care initiative. His White House escort was flustered. "Oh, Mr. President, I'm sorry. I'll be sure you never get mixed up with people again."

"It's okay," he responded. "I used to be one of them." We all laughed heartily, except Pamela, who smiled benevolently on the president as if he were her protégé. Elegance and regal manner set her apart. In her presence, I felt like a bumpkin.

Despite that insecurity, I asked to visit Mrs. Harriman a few weeks later. I walked up to her red-brick house in Georgetown, exquisitely aware that I would be entering the abode of a legend. In those rooms she'd entertained the party's political élite, identifying talent and backing her candidates with high-visibility fundraisers. A butler formally greeted me and showed me into a room to wait. Instead, I wandered through the downstairs, admiring Van Gogh's irises, a canvas by Cézanne, a Matisse. I finally settled myself on a loveseat, slipping off my shoes and tucking my feet underneath me. For a few minutes, I took in the peace of her enclosed porch, overlooking descending gardens behind the house—a welcome oasis amid the madness of Washington.

I heard the door open and close, and Pamela Harriman entered, blue eyes shining warmly even at the end of a grueling day. She was perfectly coiffed, and wearing a form-fitting suit. Style was a statement, even in her mid-seventies.

We were a study in contrast. I didn't need to be like her, but I knew this was a woman from whom I could learn a lot. She apologized for her lateness, saying that State Department briefings had been nonstop. We compared impressions about trends in European politics. I talked about growing up with Dad and my determination to make the most of who I was and what I had. After all, she was sure making the most of her life. Pamela was heading off to become what President Jacques Chirac would later describe as "the best American ambassador to France since Thomas Jefferson." I asked her advice. "Italy is chaos," she counseled. "I wouldn't want to go there."

Pamela's insights helped ease my disappointment when I learned that my posting had become increasingly complicated. The Sons of Italy, Italian emigrants to America and their descendents, were unhappy that neither Geraldine Ferraro nor Mario Cuomo, veteran politicians, had received an appointment. The advocacy group insisted that the embassy in Rome should go to an Italian-American. "This is a really important constituency," Bruce Lindsey explained when I met with him to talk over my future. "So we've found a foreign service officer with an Italian mother to fill the post."

I screwed up my courage. "If you'd like, Bruce, I'll organize the women of America," I said provocatively.

"Swanee . . . please don't. *Please* don't," he begged. I didn't respond.

Bruce's space was a snug spot next to the Oval Office. His desk was crowded, no, overwhelmed, piled high with résumés, each a life in limbo. As we parleyed, a tall stack fell onto the floor—an amazingly accurate metaphor for what I was experiencing.

Bruce asked me for a second choice. Charles had coached that offering options would scuttle my chances, and I was determined not to fold, as I had fifteen years earlier when advocating for the women of Ft. Worth history. "There is no second choice," I insisted. Bruce leaned over and scrutinized my face. I stared back.

"Could we have a grown-up conversation?" he petitioned. He rattled off a litany of disappointed insiders, including the fabulously talented DNC chair Ron Brown, who'd been given Commerce instead of State. I looked at Bruce unmoved. "Al Gore didn't get *his* first choice either," he pressed, referring to the vice president's long-standing aspiration for the top post in 1988. That, I found convincing.

Back in play, in the course of several weeks, my name was leaping like a flea from one list to another. When I heard that the First Lady suggested me for chief of protocol, I cautioned Melanne that formality was hardly my forte. One day I was told I could go to Spain if I made up my mind within twenty-four hours. But Spain was outside the current European political maelstrom; and besides, I didn't know a word of Spanish, so that seemed silly. The next call was to choose between Portugal, Switzerland, and Austria. What was this? A bunch of guys in a basement, spinning a globe and playing point and propose?

Now my *head* was spinning. I called up Bob Strauss, the fondly remembered father of my childhood friend Susie. On nightly news over the years, I'd watched with pride as Mr. Strauss negotiated President Carter's Middle East triumph at Camp David, chaired the Democratic National Committee, and represented George Bush as ambassador to Moscow immediately after communism's collapse. Happily, he hadn't forgotten me. At his law firm, Ambassador Strauss embraced me with familiar Texas warmth, chatting as he escorted me past a gallery of photographs that chronicled his decades as a global power broker.

I told him about the choices I was facing. He urged Vienna. "It's the hub of change. Much better for you than Rome." The collapse of European communism had put Vienna in the middle of one of the most fragile regions of the world. Convinced, I called the White House to say I wanted to serve as the U.S. ambassador to Austria.

My carefully construed rationale was lost on one White House official who, confusing his kangaroos and Lippizaners, soon after relayed excitedly to me that I was indeed "the leading contender for Australia." Pamela, meanwhile, was faring better. Pleased that she invited me to her May swearing-in at the State Department, I entered the lobby and stared at the row of flags I'd seen as backdrop to a hundred TV news programs. A group from the Italy desk was waiting for me, with expectant smiles. As they eagerly chatted me up, I realized that they thought I was the next emissary to Rome. "You seem like nice guys, but sadly I'm not going to be working with you," I told them. Still, the attention was flattering.

Upstairs, several hundred stalwarts of the Democratic Party had gathered in the elegant Ben Franklin Room, lit with eight large crystal chandeliers ringed by thirty-two maroon columns with gilded tops. Vice President Gore officiated. Pamela's son, Winston Churchill Jr., stood beside her. "You must all come visit me," she said to the crowd. There was a stir. "Well, not all at once," she laughed.

Following the ceremony, Ambassador Harriman greeted friends for an hour. I waited until the end, in awe of her stamina. Pamela was her diplomatic best, composed and in control. She took me aside and whispered, "What do you hear?"

"That I'm probably going to Austria."

"Mah . . . velous!" she exclaimed in her deep contralto drawl. "You'll be close to Paris!"

I continued to receive word that the recommendation to send me to Austria was "on the President's desk." But day after day passed. Then week after week. In June, Melanne comforted, "If it's any consolation, everyone's being treated this shabbily."

She assured me of Hillary's continued support. That same day, the *New York Times* ran a front-page article about empty U.S. ambassadorships, resulting in embassies run by deputies. I was mentioned as a "Democratic fundraiser from Denver" whom the president purportedly wanted in a position. The piece was followed by an editorial the next day bemoaning the constipated process.

A few days later, a White House official contacted me to say that the president had signed off on Austria. He himself would call in about a week. I was sworn to silence because the official was still notifying candidates who, he said, would be quite disappointed.

It seems that silence travels quickly. My office in Denver received an invitation to breakfast in New York from the new U.S. ambassador to the United Nations, whom I knew mostly by reputation. Elated, I accepted the invitation to what I assumed was a broad networking event. For the umpteenth time, I asked Charles to take care of Teddy, requested that Mark keep Lillian, left Lauren to manage the foundation, and flew to the East Coast. The next morning, I took an elevator up the Waldorf Astoria tower to Madeleine Albright's apartment. I rang the doorbell and then, noting the quiet hall, worried that I was mistaken about the date. Or maybe the time.

The butler opened the door. Glancing quickly inside, I saw a long, elegant dining table, with two settings at one end. Before I could ask him if I'd come on the wrong day, my host, a short woman wearing a dramatic brooch and a big smile, met me in the foyer. Still puzzled, I shook her hand. "Let me show you the art collection!" she said, for all the world as if she expected me.

After a quick tour of her living room, we sat down for a tête-à-tête. We talked about our careers, the new administration, Russia, our marriages, issues before the UN Security Council, and the riddle of mothering. All the while, I wondered why I was there. Until the end of the hour, that is, when Ambassador Albright concluded, "You know, it can be lonely for women in high-level roles. Feel free to call me any time."

For years I'd made speeches about mentoring younger women. But only once in a blue moon had anyone sought me out like this. Maybe it was a sign of just how far Madeleine thought I would go, or how far I needed to stretch. Whatever the reason, I vowed to do the same as Madeleine, to help nurture the next crop of women rising up in this male-dominated field. It wasn't an easy task we all had before us: creating a new model of ambassador and a new career path for women at the same time.

June 10. Keith left a cryptic message at my office. "It's done. Be sure Swanee's reachable this afternoon. *He* will be calling." I waited on pins and needles, but the phone didn't ring. Unfazed, I broke the good news to my family. Ray was pleased. He'd made supportive calls to Republican contacts on the Hill. When flowers arrived from Helen, our imaginative house manager asked if I was pregnant. In a way, I suppose.

On June 12, a State Department official called to begin the administrative process. "I guess it really is going to happen," I said to Charles, who gave me a huge hug. Still no call.

The next week, another message from Keith. "This is it! Stay by the phone." I canceled my doctor's appointment, not wanting to be talking with the president of the United States while I was on the examination table. By now I'd learned the meaning of "Clinton time" and wasn't so disappointed when the call didn't come.

Wheels were in motion. Hunt Oil prepared a document for the media describing our family, but ignoring my father's children by Frania Tye Lee. I reinstated them as siblings. I handed over all responsibility for the fund to Lauren, kissed Charles and the kids, and flew to Washington for weeks of meetings, organized by Debbie Cavin, the marvelous Austrian desk officer. One was with the State Department's officer in charge of "equal opportunity." I encouraged him to send "diverse" people to our embassy. "I've never had anyone say that," he replied with surprise. That worried me a bit.

I also had an appointment with Hattie Babbitt, like Hillary an attorney and former state First Lady (of Arizona), who'd spoken at our Serious Issues symposium. She was moving into her beautiful office as ambassador to the Organization of American States. "Bruce and I can see each other's windows," she laughed, pointing to the Department of Interior, which her husband was now heading.

She hugged me and then led me in so we could talk. Hanging on the back of her door was the family dry cleaning. I asked Hattie how the move was affecting their two boys. "It's not easy for kids," she warned. "Take your pets."

Although the State Department was well into the clearance and briefing process, the call from the Oval Office still hadn't come. Instead, the First Couple invited Charles and me to dinner on June 22. This would be the moment, I was sure, that the president would finally ask me to serve as his ambassador. Without Merle to remind me to wear serious clothes, I stretched the meaning of "business attire" and donned flowing white silk pants with an oriental tunic top. The summer night air was heavy as Charles and I walked the half-hour from our hotel to the White House. Strolling across the spacious green lawn, past the guards, I knew I'd arrived. As we made our way through the house, we passed the room set up for dinner. I paused to glance at a chart. I would be seated on the president's right. That was it. He would, no doubt, ask me that night.

Other guests had assembled for drinks on the Truman Balcony, overlooking the South Lawn. Charles reconnected with the opera star Kathleen Battle, who'd been his student in a strings class at the Cincinnati Conservatory. I made a point of introducing myself to those who looked especially nervous. Eventually our hosts appeared. Perhaps I was projecting, but I imagined they'd been checking Chelsea's homework in a private kitchen in their living quarters.

The president and First Lady led us on a tour of the upstairs rooms, pointing out paintings and furniture they'd selected from museums and vaults. I split off from the group and wandered over to the president's private desk. *The Bridges of Madison County* lay there. Soon, another guest walked over to look at the bookshelves. "Hi. I'm Swanee Hunt," I stuck out my hand.

"Amy Tan."

"What do you do?"

"I'm a writer."

My cheeks burned; I'd just seen the movie version of her *Joy Luck Club*. In fact, everyone in the room was a famous name. When I remarked to Hillary about the fascinating collection of people assembled, she nodded, pensively. "It's amazing. Everyone we invite shows up." Seemed we were both having trouble coming to grips.

A military ensemble was playing gorgeous romantic music in the foyer as we made our way down for dinner. Charles stopped suddenly to chat with one of the violinists, with whom he had performed in a quartet. Every element of our lives was changing.

I took my place next to President Clinton at one of four round tables and joined a lively conversation about the day's happenings.

The president had just named Ruth Bader Ginsburg to the Supreme Court. He described the process with considerable relish, giving credit to Marty Ginsburg's tireless campaign for his wife's appointment. (I took heart, given how miserable I felt about six months of promoting myself.) That subject was a perfect lead for the president to turn to his right and, in a low voice, ask me to be his ambassador.

Instead, someone raised the current gossip: that he had a long-lost half-brother. I was the one whispering, "I know what that's like."

He looked puzzled for a moment, then said, "Ah, yes, I remember." Still, he didn't segue into the question of the evening.

The mood hit a lull, so deciding to that add a little pickup, I recounted for the entire table the story I'd heard on TV while dressing. Reporters had had a heyday with news that a hair stylist named Christophe had been called to Air Force One while it sat on the tarmac in LA; and worse, that he'd been paid $200 to cut the hair of our populist president. That haircut story had set the president on his ear, and Democratic insiders worried about his image in hometown America.

"Christophe gave the perfect comeback," I declared, with relief. "He said, 'I don't know how anyone could look at the president and First Lady and accuse them of spending too much on their appearance!'" Dead silence.

Thinking my tablemates hadn't understood, I stupidly repeated the story. I was the only person who thought that Cristophe's insult was a political godsend. Clinton said nothing. I looked across for support from Liz Claiborne, who stared at me stone-faced—which made sense, once I stopped to think. Stopping to think is something I should probably learn to do before I become a diplomat, I thought sheepishly.

As the main course ended, the president rose and led a toast celebrating Senator Dianne Feinstein's turning sixty. The entire entourage joined in "Happy Birthday." Now I could add to my résumé that I'd sung with Kathleen Battle. He'd better hurry up and ask, I thought, as dessert arrived along with the Air Force Strolling Strings, who threaded between tables, filling the air with themes from *Phantom of the Opera*. "Savor these rich moments," I said to the president, "when every sense is satiated."

He nodded. Now it was his turn to speak to me. I waited. His eyes met Hillary's across the room. Suddenly they both stood. "Let's all move to the next room for coffee," he said. What on earth was he thinking? How was he going to ask me with all those other people standing around?

Indeed, guests who hadn't been sitting next to him for two hours now flocked around the president. Frustrated that the easy opportunity had passed, I approached Hillary. I told her I was already receiving briefings on Austria from the State Department, but the president had never asked me to serve. Just now at dinner he'd forgotten again. What did she advise?

Hillary looked across the room at her husband, shook her head, and laughed softly, "Poor thing. He probably thinks he's already asked you. You can't imagine what a whirlwind we're in. Go talk to Skip, over there."

I approached the president's aide and explained my situation.

"So, you've been Clintoned?" he said with dry humor.

I suggested that he whisper a reminder in the president's ear.

"He really hates when we mix in business on an evening like this," Skip replied.

It seemed I'd have to take matters into my own hands. I walked over and popped the question: "Uh, Mr. President," I smiled feebly, staring up at him and feeling very short. "I mean . . . Do you . . . ? I mean . . . Isn't there something you'd like to ask me?"

The president looked at me puzzled, then answered with uncertainty, "Uh, yes. But I was told there's a clearance we're waiting for."

"Ah hah. Well, they told me you'd be calling a couple of weeks ago, so I was just checking."

He apologized for the miscommunication, and we each mumbled something to ease the embarrassment. "I'll talk with you next week," he said.

The call never came, and eventually I stopped waiting. If it was okay with him to send an unasked emissary to Vienna, it was okay with me.

Taking on the Unknown

My father would have been proud of me, I think. Despite my bravado as I insisted on the Italy post, he would have said that Austria was best for me. Of course my German was stronger than my Italian, but that wasn't the point. The Red Menace, my father's obsession, had faded. The America of *Life Line*, long defined in opposition to its tyrannical enemy, was totally unprepared for that political development and in the throes of an identity crisis. So was Austria, which had been a neutral force between the two superpowers: the United States and the USSR. Now neutrality itself was under attack. Neutral between what? some asked. The question struck at the core of Austria's role in the region. With the meltdown of the Iron Curtain, Vienna no longer made sense as a listening post to penetrate bastions of communism.

But more than Dad, Mother was on my mind as I thought about whether to leave the States. For the second time in my life, I'd be spending four years a continent away from her. But unlike when I escaped to Heidelberg in my twenties, now I regretted the distance. She was seventy-six—an old seventy-six—and hadn't been in good health for decades. My leaving, and with two of her grandchildren, seemed downright unkind.

That loss would cut both ways. I'd come to appreciate that Mother was as generous with her time as with her prayers. Sometimes she went to a hospital to see an employee who had a child in danger; but she ended up staying the whole day, going from one room to another, to another, visiting strangers who the nurses said were alone. When a Hunt Oil employee, or employee's family member, died, she attended the funeral then stayed with the family for hours. And as soon as she got the call that the house of our cleaning lady burned down, she went over, only stopping at a nearby 7-Eleven for something that might be useful to the family. Looking around the convenience store, she told the clerk, "Just give me two of everything, please."

Even truth bent to her bounteousness. "If it's not worth exaggerating, it's not worth telling," she proclaimed. Every friend she had was the dearest, every child she encountered the most precious. Each grandchild had the distinction of being the sweetest. It wasn't hard to understand why Helen's and my children stayed for weeks or months at Mt. Vernon, and why the family gathered religiously around her at holidays.

I particularly remember Easter Sunday of 1993, several months before we moved to Vienna. We were staying at Mt. Vernon, and when the last car of other family reunion faithful had pulled out, I took

Mother up to her bedroom. It was only six in the evening, but she was spent, so I helped her into bed. She lay under the covers, still in her colorful silk dress. This was Mom as few saw her.

Soon her reading glasses lay loosely in her limp hand near her chin. The radio played softly: Christian pop tunes. Her room had a muted glow, the pink satin on the walls creating an elegant softness, graced by romantic oil paintings and porcelains. An oval sepia Madonna watched over her bed. A dozen piles—bulk purchase orders for World Trade Mart, and dull green stenographer notebooks—cluttered the room. She'd been raiding the basement again, bringing up memorabilia on late-night forays into those nether reaches. Just outside her door, the hallway walls were crowded with dozens of family pictures: a framing and hanging project I'd undertaken a few summers before. The floors were covered with custom-made oriental rugs. A grand bookcase was crammed with a dozen Bibles and volumes she'd never read but whose covers held special appeal.

Mother's lined face, so peaceful, unaware of me or the rest of the world. I turned off her lamp and left the door to her lit bathroom ajar so she wouldn't be disoriented, and then pondered whether to wake her to take the half-dozen pills that three doctors had prescribed. No, I would let her rest. I took the glasses and propped her hand over an embroidered pillow that read, "The older the violin, the sweeter the music."

Mother's short-term memory loss created occasional chaos; but that day she'd remembered it was Sunday and had been in tears because her children weren't going back downtown to church for the evening service. When I reminded her that her cup was at least half full, she nodded and replied, "Why should I be talking about you? If I could be up all afternoon, I could have gone to church tonight too."

That was the denial in which my mother lived, seemingly forgetting that I'd tried to escort her to church that very morning. Her hair was a mess, but that didn't stop her. "I'll just go, even though I look like Wild Willy," she'd laughed. But we didn't even make it down the stairs; she was coughing and tired just from the hour of getting dressed. Later, I'd watched her with her grand- and great-grandchildren as they hunted eggs and played chase across the lawn. She was amazingly beautiful, loving, pleasant. No sign of the immobilizing weariness of the morning.

Mother was always ashamed of her poor health. "I'm gonna do better; you just wait and see," she apologized again and again. But looking at her asleep in her Easter dress, I saw the ravages of the angst that had marked her life. I'd played a part in her distress, and I remembered with regret how years earlier I'd walked in and found her kneeling with my baby picture on the bed, crying as she prayed for me to return to the fold of the faithful. But as Mom aged, her expectations had lightened. She stopped trying to make me into her image of a lady. Of course I'd matured; I was more secure and could let her be disappointed in me without becoming angry in return. Although she always wished I would come back to live in Dallas, my sense was that we emerged with a loving relationship precisely because I didn't.

I wondered what a move to Vienna would mean to my marriage. My husband had already relocated for me. In Denver he'd not had an easy time putting together life as an independent arts entrepreneur; still he'd racked up an impressive list of accomplishments. In addition to chairing the Colorado Commission on the Arts and Humanities, he'd overseen the opening of a high-tech theater, created a plan to integrate arts into the new airport, and organized weeks of festivities for the opening of that mammoth public project. After five years of reestablishing himself, he would once again be uprooted on my account. Charles's base in German would help as he created meaningful work in Vienna, an artistic capital of the world. Still, I imagined how resentful I would be, in his shoes. Instead, he rose repeatedly above his own self-interest.

I had few worries about how the move to Vienna would affect our boys. Teddy was the easiest child imaginable, blooming wherever he was planted. All he needed to know was that he would get to sleep over on the plane to Europe. "Yes, Honey, really sleep over! Overnight!"

Henry was grown and ready for independence. More important, he'd found the love of his life at college, Karma, who was his match in intelligence and kindness. But Henry and I were calibrated differently, and I frequently rubbed him the wrong way. I figured that he might appreciate more distance from me, as I had wanted more space from Mother when I was his age.

In contrast, I was dogged by concern that ten-year-old Lillian would suffer with the move. I asked a close friend to remind me, if I called to say my daughter was having a hard time in Austria, that she'd been having a hard time in Denver too. I also quietly nurtured the hope that a new setting might beget new strength.

I tried to engage Lillian in activities to boost her confidence. Setting out from the ranch one day, the two of us rode horseback on the Colorado Trail to the Lost Park Campground, twenty miles out. We were saddle-sore by dusk and switched steeds, so that new spots would hit the horse. The ride out took eight weary hours. The ride back the next day was only four, since our horses smelled the barn and ran most of the way. I hoped that our wilderness adventure would impart to Lillian some of the pioneer passion that fueled me. We were left with a great memory, but the two-day marathon ride was not enough to help her withstand the terrible pressure she was now under.

Just before the election, I'd met with Mark to let him know I might join the Clinton administration. I wanted to be completely open, so that we would have time to work out a mutually agreeable arrangement for our daughter. He refused to tolerate altering our co-parenting schedule. I said I wasn't talking about changing our 50–50 division, only the schedule, and his rigidity far exceeded the adjustment I was proposing.

I loved Mark for being an attentive and steadfast father to Lillian. He'd provided her with the paternal care I'd longed for as a child. She considered him her best friend. So it seemed callous to repay that goodness by moving his daughter across an ocean. But Mark, whose wisdom I usually respected, was adamant that he wouldn't work with me to find a compromise. He wrote impassioned letters to my mother, begging her to intervene. Then, with unprecedented poor judgment, he brought his case to Lillian herself, saying that he would take me to court to stop me from moving her.

I implored Mark to keep the discussion between us only, not our daughter. He said that was impossible because it involved her. Soon I heard vitriolic accusations about my selfishness and conceit coming from our daughter's mouth, with her father's vocabulary. Over the months I weighed whether to forgo my aspirations because of his resistance. But I knew I would resent not only him but also Lillian if I let his anger keep me from joining the new administration.

Trying to let Mark gradually adjust to the idea of our move had backfired. Instead of being more comfortable with the move, Lillian was an emotional wreck. I found a mediator, who convinced Mark that no judge would give him what he wanted, which was for Lillian to have only a two-week annual visit with me in Europe. We settled on her having six months in each location, but the process exhumed Mark's harsh negativity toward me that had rarely been so actively expressed in our marriage or even our divorce.

Apart from Lillian, the most emotionally difficult aspect of taking the post was leaving my nonprofit pursuits. I decided to maintain the Hunt Alternatives Fund in Denver, but I knew my personal involvement would be extremely limited. While I welcomed a fresh challenge, I was bothered by the thought that I was turning my back on the troubled inner city and the people with whom I'd worked since 1977.

But I wasn't really jumping track. There were lessons intrinsic to domestic policy that I would apply to foreign policy, lessons such as the rights of minorities, the principles of consensus building, and the importance of grassroots leadership. Central and Eastern Europe were politically unstable in part because of the same problems that plagued Denver: unemployment, environmental degradation, and discrimination against women. My new job overseas would be an outgrowth of my Colorado work, not a departure. My values and those of President Clinton were 99 percent congruent. I told myself I would be representing those values in Vienna, just as I had in Denver.

I had one more fear as I met with former ambassadors and State Department personnel: that I might lose myself behind the diplomatic persona. I'd generally tried to live a transparent life, warts and all. A friend in my twenties said that when I walked down a sidewalk, half the flowers perked up and half drooped over. Said another way, the same openness that some found refreshing, others found jarring. What if the careful ways of a diplomat required me to close up, until my spirit withered? Finding the right settings in which to speak openly, finding the right people with whom to laugh uproariously or cry freely, would be vital. Literally.

My stress generated a dream in which I left Lillian as a toddler on the sidewalk on rough Colfax Avenue. True, my intentions were good. I'd gone into a store to buy her a gift. But when I came out, she was gone.

Becoming more and more frantic as I searched, I was finally unable to bear the panic and woke myself up.

The dream wasn't just about the vulnerability of my daughter or compromises in my mothering. It was also about my psyche; my inner child was in danger. I went to see Chuck Lobitz, the same counselor who'd helped Charles and me with the Myers Briggs test. We took stock of a whole series of life experiences: shaking up the Dallas patriarchy, losing myself in relationships but finding myself on the other side, exploring alternatives to social problems. I recited my journeys into other cultures. How I'd introduced feminine imagery of God into my cantata. And finally, I visualized the Nepal trek, the Venice marathon, the Alaskan sail, and those crazy buffalo roundups.

As I talked with Chuck, I brightened. Ambassadorships weren't designed for people like me: a woman, with young children, irrepressibly personal, iconoclastic. But who said they shouldn't be? Maybe the problem wasn't that women needed to change to fit the jobs. Maybe the jobs could change. That thought was a defining moment for me, a second-guessing of assumptions, an impudent questioning of the way things have always been. I would no longer rely on a job description written according to someone else's wishes or worldview. From then on I would be the author, with all the blessing or burden that the role demanded.

Rather than try to fit into the feminine equivalent of a diplomat's pinstriped suit, I decided to refashion the job. I began to visualize myself as a pioneer in a long skirt, my children tucked into the deep folds, with a tall rifle at my side. I was willing to forge paths into this new frontier, paths that others could follow. Transforming my worst fears into a vision based on strengths, I was ready to take on the unknown.

Money Matters

Questions of wealth and identity haunted me more than ever. Jesus had warned that the love of money was the root of all evil. But money could also leverage life-saving changes. I'd paid a high price back in Dallas to have an income that would allow me to make significant contributions to the Women's Foundation, Hunt Alternatives Fund, and the Democratic National Committee. To be indelicate, money bought a seat at the table. People returned my phone calls. They came to our parties and meetings. But money also shielded me from honest criticism. My soul had a certain swagger. I could buy my way out of many uncomfortable situations. I was, in a moral sense, poorer for my power.

Inside the Beltway, not unlike other settings, my wealth was a mixed blessing. Politicos cared about their ideas . . . and my money. I, on the other hand, cared about their ideas and my *values*. The negotiation between political operatives and funders often occurred at the level of innuendo. Various glad-handers described me as "a good friend of the president" before he and I had spent fifteen minutes together. "Friendship" clearly had a price tag. The compliment lost its meaning.

Given these subtle dishonesties, as I was being considered for an ambassadorship money was always on my mind—but only because I knew it was on the minds of others. Outsiders usually view wealth as an answer to problems, not a problem itself. So it would surprise most people to know how frequently I felt embarrassed. When told by an aide that Eli Segal was contacting White House personnel to pave the way for me, I was immensely grateful. But when I asked what message Eli had left at the White House, I heard: "He said you'd given a quarter of a million dollars to the campaign, and you want to be an ambassador." I started to call Eli to protest but realized there was no point. He was my friend and was only naming reality. My friend Vinny had warned that this would be my image in Washington. And why shouldn't it be? Still, it was hard to feel confident in my abilities when I was introduced with a contribution invoice pasted on my forehead.

I needed tougher skin in D.C., where I would never be able to estimate my value apart from my checkbook. I understood the pressures, having been on the other side of the table, raising millions for various causes from rich people, whom we called "targets." But I wasn't prepared for one meeting with a White House official, while I was waiting to hear about a diplomatic post.

"I've got a problem and you can help me out," he explained. "The National Park Service is upset that the lawn of the Mall will have to be re-sod after the upcoming gay pride march. Be a friend and cover the $150,000."

I ducked the question the first time.

"It would really help me out," he made another run.

I said I didn't think it was an appropriate solicitation while I was under consideration for an appointment. But what I really wanted to say was "Hell, no."

In a political system in which candidates spend an obscene portion of their time dialing for dollars, money is always a factor, spoken or unspoken. When I told Congresswoman Schroeder that I couldn't ask for an embassy just because I'd made a large contribution to the Clinton campaign, she told me to "just get over it." I would later learn she was right—that an occasional wealthy ambassador was necessary for the upkeep of the fancier embassy residences like those in Rome or Vienna. In fact, political appointees were often private-sector executives who spent hundreds of thousands of private dollars refurbishing or entertaining for the U.S. government.

But no rationalization, even when borne out by fact, could soften my feeling mortified when Common Cause sent out a newsletter singling me out as a flagrant example of money wielding influence. I'd long supported the organization, which combats political corruption; in fact, a former employee of Common Cause had staffed my fundraising effort for our Million Dollar Day. Reading the organization's account of how I'd bought an embassy, I felt as if I'd been mugged.

Why didn't the critics acknowledge that my domestic policymaking experience would stand me in good stead? I had proven management skills, knew how to organize initiatives, and was experienced in long-term strategic thinking. I had political contacts that would make me an excellent conduit between the U.S. and Austrian governments. But then I imagine all wealthy persons have ways of rationalizing their extraordinary privileges. My self-righteous reaction was shallow. Sometimes truth hurts.

Hillary was one of the few people in D.C. who I felt could understand me. She and I had lived along parallel tracks: from early years of church youth gatherings (hers were Methodist, like Granny's); past the Republican Convention in San Francisco in 1964 (we were both Goldwater Girls); to concerns for the most vulnerable in society (she'd worked for the Children's Defense Fund, a grantee of Hunt Alternatives). Although we hadn't known each other along the way, our paths had ended up at the same place: Democratic politics. That's why I was so much interested in her life as it was unfolding.

The adjustments she had to make were trivial and major. "We found out the chefs were disappointed when we asked to have a jar of peanut butter and a box of cereal in our upstairs kitchen," she told me. Later in Vienna, I would think of her remark often, understanding better the challenge of being hostess of America's White House when stripped of the privacy that others take for granted. In fact, one of her oldest friends told me that because the First Lady's life was so pressured, for the two to see each other she had to come from New York and ride for ten minutes in Hillary's car between speaking engagements.

But sitting by her father's deathbed a few months into the presidency, Hillary had time for reflection. During those dark days, she had to fly to Texas for a major address. Her right hand, Melanne, shook her head with admiration as she told me how Hillary jotted down a few notes on the plane, then delivered a complex treatise on the value base of political action. She articulated the concept in a cover interview for the *New York Times Magazine* entitled "The Politics of Meaning."

"That story was very, very important," I told her, "although I'm not surprised that few in the Washington press corps appreciated it." In fact, the piece was derided by Beltway cynics, who had little patience for pondering the impetus behind policy and practice. But that was a level on which Hillary and I connected. Alone for a few moments, we could speak theological shorthand, ruminating on the figures whose lives and works we had studied. Hillary is a woman of extraordinary intellect, contradiction, self-understanding, and practiced contemplation, who was able to put even the inflated presidential scene into a larger context.

We shared raucous moments as well. I took a couple of days off from my diplomatic training to fly with the first family to Denver to meet Pope John Paul II. The plane was filled with notables, some with hidden musical talent. Congresswoman Schroeder, Secretary of Health and Human Services Donna Shalala, and I penned a song, which Bruce Lindsey printed out for us in the plane's computer center. Our trio traveled—at least as far as the Air Force One conference room, where we sang to the First Lady, who looked up from reams of paper scattered across the long table. She grinned through all three irreverent verses, each ending with a chorus to the rousing tune of "Oh, Susannah."

"When the man from Hope gets together with the Pope, You had better check the weather 'cause you're on a box of soap."

Inspired by our song, we faced torrential rains at the Denver airport, where we gathered for the ceremony between the president and the pope. They stood on the stage under giant white umbrellas. I sat in the audience, on the ground by Hillary's chair, to get the angle I wanted with my camera. She looked down and, with a concerned smile, opened her gray raincoat to cover my head.

The day was fraught with difficulties. When the president spoke into the mike, there was no sound. He tried again, then looked down at Hillary. "Should I go on?" he mouthed.

"Yes," she mouthed back. He began to speak, and the PA system kicked in.

I was taking mental notes. Instead of being an appendage, Hillary was clearly a solid half of this couple. Her presence in the administration was making headlines as well. There had been much ado about this First Lady's taking an active role in the West Wing, where policies are formulated. But contrary to press accusations that made her out to be a dragon, a high-level domestic policy maker told me that her personal warmth kept them all going. In a dozen small ways every day, her thoughtfulness lifted people out of obsession over the obstacles they faced.

I got a hint of the source of her strength one day when she was away. Her assistant gave me the First Lady's office in the West Wing, as I waited an hour for a meeting with someone else. Sitting at her desk, I looked straight into a portrait of Eleanor Roosevelt. Hillary's shelves held several books on the life of one of the most active, and criticized, first ladies in American history. Searching for a pen I opened her drawer. There was notepaper with a photocopied newspaper headline: "First Lady Not to Stay Caged In." I imagined her staff had laughed when they presented the stationery to her, but the struggle that it suggested was no joke. Like so many women who have taken stands against social ills, Hillary was considered fair game. She'd put herself in the field and could be hunted and hounded at will.

Using a different metaphor, Mike Keefe, cartoonist for the *Denver*

Post, sent me his caricature of HRC standing on the Truman Balcony, her hair sticking out wildly. The caption: Hillary Lightning Rodham Clinton.

Rocky Goodbye

Even as—or perhaps because—Hillary was being pummeled, I wished that I could be a recognized member of the Clinton team. I was a racehorse pawing the ground, wanting my confirmation to move forward. Outside the Beltway, friends from my First Baptist, Hockaday, and Denver worlds called to let me know that the FBI was canvassing my life. It was unnerving, hearing that my history was passing in front of someone's eyes, someone looking for dirt. But odd as it was, at least I was sharing my experience with my friends.

I was living in a time warp. Months before my name was announced by the White House, I was assigned an office at the State Department, where I met with Central and Eastern European experts. I was painfully aware of my ignorance, and before heading out to post did everything I could to learn from those who'd gone before. I paid calls on a dozen Democratic and Republican former ambassadors. Lillian and I went to California to visit Shirley Temple Black, who'd served as chief of protocol, ambassador to Ghana, and ambassador to Czechoslovakia. After holding her dog and petting her Oscar, we settled into a lengthy question-and-answer session. Except for her hair, which was strangely uncurly, she seemed quite normal. If she can do it I can do it, I thought, forgetting that the woman hosting me had starred in twenty movies by the time she was six.

Even after the official White House announcement, the Senate had the prerogative to disapprove my nomination. I'd been warned not to seem presumptuous by saying in public that I was going to Austria. The Austrian ambassador to the United States, however, was anxious to meet me. I refused to go to his office but agreed to his residence. Upon arrival, he asked me to sign his guest book. I demurred, not wanting to leave a trail. As we sat in his small garden, having breakfast, the ambassador described his political quandaries, including his great hope that I could arrange White House visits for Austria's highest officials. I was a novice, listening carefully to this pro, trying to pick up vocabulary as well as concepts. I was also trying to be myself in a situation that didn't feel at all natural.

A waiter came in and refilled my coffee cup. Looking down, I noticed an unusual bulge at my left elbow. My shoulder pad had migrated twelve inches into my sleeve. The right side soon followed suit, as it were. Within the next five minutes, I managed to reach up both narrow wrist openings, remove each shoulder pad, and stow them in my purse—all without interrupting the flow of the conversation. Either my host didn't notice, and I really did have the makings of a diplomat, or else he *did* notice, and *he* was the perfect diplomat.

Midsummer, the State Department provided new appointees and their spouses with a two-week ambassadors' seminar, the topics ranging from emergency evacuation procedures to elementary espionage. Charles didn't appreciate the session for him and my colleagues' wives on the niceties of china—unfortunately the plates, not the country. Meanwhile, the ambassadors-in-waiting flew to Fort Bragg, North Carolina, for a testosterone-charged demonstration. Behind glass, we watched a simulation, with soldiers in camouflage kicking in a door and spraying a room with live ammo. Sharpshooters demonstrated their fine art, then offered us a turn with a rifle. They were surprised by my marksmanship—a holdover, oddly enough, from Texas church camp.

At "charm school" I sat next to Richard Holbrooke, reputed to have the grace of a German Panzer, which was appropriate since he was heading to Bonn to head the U.S. embassy. Like naughty children, Dick and I traded irreverent notes.

Former Vice President Walter Mondale, slated for Japan, didn't make it to the sessions, but his wife, "Joan of Arts," whom Charles had assisted as a White House Fellow almost sixteen years earlier, did. I found some comfort hearing Mondale quoted as saying that waiting months for his nomination was one of his toughest experiences since running for president.

It was fall before the White House announced my appointment. That day, Hillary was speaking to a group of women on the importance of health care reform. Following our lead in Colorado, the DNC had formed a group of high-end women donors. I was invited into a small holding room with about two dozen others to greet the First Lady before she spoke. Her advance team arrived and broke up our conversations, then placed us in a circle. After we'd stood like obedient schoolchildren for half an hour, I stepped into the circle and led introductions, to make use of the time. When Hillary finally arrived she walked around the circle, shaking hands. Then we filed into the ballroom, which was packed with women who saw in her a fulfillment of their private dreams, a validation of their own struggles.

At the podium, Hillary laid out her philosophy of government's duty to promote economic justice, including the stories from people she'd encountered in endless hearings across the country. When the mistress of ceremonies mentioned my nomination, I felt enormously proud to be part of the First Lady's team.

My name eventually moved to the Senate for approval. The first hurdle was the Foreign Relations Committee. Debbie Cavin and other Foreign Service officers had drilled me on European and Austrian political affairs. But I remembered my humiliation when I failed the oral exams for my doctorate, and I was nervous.

The day was crisp and the changing foliage magnificent as Charles walked with me up the Capitol lawn. As so often before, he knew just how to put me at ease. Taking my arm firmly, he imitated Senator Jesse Helms's drawl: "Way-ell, Mizzez Hunt," he said, stretching each word. "Whatcha wanna say 'bout that big contr'bution you gave the Dem'crats?"

I was still grinning when we entered the Senate office building. After embracing some friends who'd come to offer moral support, I sat down with three other nominees, all men, at the long table I'd seen so many times on C-SPAN. Several senators sat opposite me, in a raised semicircle. Senator Joe Biden chaired the meeting. He apologized for being late, saying he'd been with President Alija Izetbegovic, who had escaped from besieged Sarajevo to beg for American intervention in the ongoing genocide. Little did I imagine how intertwined my world would become with the beleaguered Bosnian's.

The committee members threw me a few softballs, asking about Austria's role in a changing Europe. As I headed home to Denver, I felt a huge relief plus disappointment, after all my preparation. The committee passed my name to the full Senate, where final approval of all political nominees was held up several weeks by one senator, angry with Secretary of State Warren Christopher over an unrelated matter. These were relatively easy weeks, filled with German and macroeconomics lessons, punctuated by friends hosting farewell events, and more family time than ever.

At last the Senate voted. It was time to pack up and move. Leaving Denver was brutal. It's a mystery, how a place can be alive. How instead of shelter to a family, a house becomes a member of the family. The wallpaper, stained-glass, furniture, rugs—each keeps a secret. As I walked through our home one last time, memories crowded noisily into my mind.

I thought of how, just as a tour bus had pulled up in front of Mt. Vernon, people new to Denver had listened to guides standing in front of our home, giving some impersonal account about Charles and me. But hundreds, maybe thousands, had crossed our threshold for political fundraisers with high-profile speakers or foundation events celebrating community saints. Every nook and cranny held years of memories, seven with Mark and nine with Charles. I thought back to how I'd asked Charles, when he moved to Denver, to be home for breakfast and dinner at least the four days a week I had Lillian. That rule paid off as our kitchen became the heart of our home.

I ran my hands over the double sink that I'd pointedly insisted on so that we would share the cleanup. I thought using dirty dishes as political fodder was my own invention. Not so. After responsibilities and income had accumulated and I hired a housekeeper two days a week, eighteen-year-old Henry sullenly asked if I was too good to clean up after myself.

"I've washed my share of dishes, and paying Amber to do housework gives her a job," I countered. "Besides," I pulled out the big moral guns, "having her lets me reform the care system for the homeless and hungry." Of course that altercation had nothing to do with dishes, jobs, or my worthy endeavors. Just jabs. But even as I sulked, I appreciated that our son was inclined to rail against my collusion with injustice.

That last walk-through meant that I'd never again hear each family member's signature step on the wooden floors. I remembered how my old dog's toenails made a clicking sound that we could hear all the way upstairs. As Dostoyevsky's mind went, so did parts of his instinctual patterns: instead of circling before lying down, he went round and round and round, forgetting what to do next. Charles would hear the clicking, get out of bed, and go downstairs to lay him down so he could rest.

And then there was the Saturday morning when I interviewed potential executive directors for the Governor's Coordinating Council on Housing and the Homeless. Twice in one hour, Teddy padded barefoot into the kitchen where we were sitting, grinned at Mommy, and peed on the floor. Twice I grabbed a dish towel and kept the interview moving.

As my professional portfolio became more polished, kitchen productions suffered. Culinary consistency hadn't been our goal, nor, therefore, our end. Charles didn't have Mark's bread-baking prowess, and I had other fish to fry. On the other hand, I must feel some remorse for my neglect; otherwise I wouldn't remember with crystal clarity the moment when, as I was preparing for my Senate confirmation, the family gathered for a dinner of red Jell-O, white sandwich bread, and pea salad. Charles looked down, then up at me, his eyebrows arched, and remarked, "Would you say this is an all-time low?" I burst out laughing. "I'd say so." Then we all joined hands to bless the Jell-O.

Despite our efforts, all was not smooth as my career choice rippled across others' lives. Tensions were inevitable. Jumping into the fray, I organized a meeting with Chuck Lobitz, our occasional sounding board. I told him that Charles, Lillian, and Teddy might vent their resentment about leaving and their fears about our new living situation. Henry might reflect on his sense of loss because of our moving away.

Instead, as we sat in a circle, the children let me know that my failings as a mother and as a person were the problem. Every strength comes with a price. What I thought of as directness they described as onslaught. In my work, I set a goal, organized my resources, summoned my courage, and pushed past obstacles; but they knew that. You can't run a family like you run a project, was the message.

As the second hour wore on, the barrage continued. At dinner, if I talked about what I'd done that day, I had made them feel insignificant. If I suggested that we plan ahead for a vacation, then I was controlling. If I left drudgework for others so that I could devote myself to my family, then I was spoiled.

As the arrows found their mark, I resisted thinking of Saint Sebastien, tied to the post. I looked across the room at Charles, hoping for relief. But he was busy adding more horribles to the quiver. That therapy session was far more painful than the Senate Foreign Relations Committee. But at least I'd managed to unite our blended family around a common enemy: Me.

The day of my public swearing-in, I stood on the same stage as Pamela had, in the Ben Franklin Room. Before me stood friends from the Rocky Mountains and every other peak and valley of my life. Mother was there with two planeloads of well-wishers from Oklahoma and Texas. The company vice-president I'd embarrassed at the Petroleum Club was beaming. Various father figures had convened, creating unlikely alliances: this may have been the last time the Kennedy confidant Clark Clifford stood near the nonagenarian Senator Strom Thurmond, who had confessed amorous intentions toward me when he was in his sixties and I was a teenager.

Helen and Harville came. June was there, with her friends. A second private jet came from Hunt Oil, but my brother wasn't on it. One employee said that Ray didn't want to steal my limelight. During the festivities June composed a hilarious poem about our giving up buffalo to go to Vienna, with lots of jabs at my dubious supposed diplomatic skills. Little Teddy sang an adorable "Do, Re, Mi," and eleven-year-old Lillian enchanted us with "Edelweiss." Henry and his girl-friend Karma comported themselves with grown-up grace. But who could know what was going on in our children's heads? I had a heart-rending glimpse from a few lines of Lillian's poem, which she called "Swearing In":

> Those I live with
> But do not recognize
> Join me in body
> But not in spirit.
> Joyful bells mock me
> Because I do not ring in answer.

A day later, uncharacteristically nervous, I sat with Helen in a waiting area at Kennedy Airport. Charles had stepped away to give us some privacy. My sister had come to be with me for our one-hour layover, en route to Vienna.

I needed her more than ever. "You know, Helen, I generally have a high regard for my abilities. But I don't really know if I can do this job that I'm about to take on."

She stared into my eyes and squeezed my hand.

The many moods of Lillian

Charles and Teddy: bonding time

Blended families—more art than science

Mother holds the Bible, Al Gore swears me in

Senate hearing: All that prep for softballs

Viennese caricature:
comic relief

How do you like being a queen?

With Henry—two heads are better than one

Ray plays Santa to his three sisters—again

My portrait of Elly and Viktor Frankl: in loco parentis

Sculpture from remnants of Ron Brown's plane

Arguing with
the president

Teddy entertains Plácido Domingo

Jamming with Hillary and Val in Salzburg

Vital Voices: A meltdown-in-the-making photograph

Nichts, Gott sei dank. [Nothing, thank God.]
—Helene van Damm, former U.S. ambassador, when asked
by Viennese friends, "What's new?"

CHAPTER 5

Queen for a Day

Continental Drift

My favorite circus act as a child was the man who rushed around keeping an impossible number of plates spinning on tall, thin poles. In late 1993, I began my own four-year performance on the world stage. The pace was dizzying. Much more intense than anything I'd experienced before. It would require every bit of training, energy, wisdom, and pluck that I had—and then some.

I was beset with quandaries: Would I forfeit family life to the role of diplomat? Could I manage a staff of five hundred? Would I stay connected to people and values that grounded me? And how on earth would I keep all those plates spinning?

Each ambassador's job was to tend the relationship between the United States and his or her "host country." Beyond that, the diplomat's work was mostly defined by individual interests. My immediate predecessors specialized in business exchanges and the arts. At the time I arrived, the entire region of Central and Eastern Europe was hurting, so ignoring borders, I took on that hurt with a passion.

The optimism of victorious cold warriors was dimming as postcommunist economies crashed in the early 1990s. Eastern European countries and the former Soviet states were reeling, trying to find their footing in an open market. Millions of people were newly destitute, and social service systems had disintegrated. Capitalizing on this instability, organized crime was exploding around the world with a commodity more profitable than drugs: women from collapsed economies who signed up for jobs in the West, only to find themselves in the clutches of pimps or imprisoned in brothels. Even more ominous, cartels of wealthy criminals were trying to procure nuclear material to sell to terrorists.

One state, Yugoslavia, had descended into a bloody war. Four of its six republics had declared independence. European powers had tried, and failed, to stop the atrocities that were making headlines. Slobodan Milosevic was attempting to expand his power by driving non-Serbs out of multiethnic Yugoslavia. Foreign ministers alternated between pleading for greater American involvement and resenting that only our engagement could halt the murderous rampage. The Pentagon wanted to stay out of the conflict, which had already cost the Yugoslavs 100,000 lives. But experts at the State Department insisted to me that the United States should have stopped Milosevic at the beginning, and we still should intervene. I wanted to understand why we hadn't.

I hoped I could be of help, but my hope was laced with trepidation: I was not sure I could master the substance of international affairs. The evening news was peppered with pictures of the new administration's appointees being grilled by angry members of Congress. Seasoned political figures, more experienced—and careful—than I, found themselves subjects of investigations that consumed months or years. My expertise was domestic, not foreign, policy.

In truth, I was arriving well equipped for this job. I'd assimilated a huge amount of information about Central Europe. I felt confident that I could think on my feet, and I was at ease on stage. But the responsibility of representing the president of the United States was a heavy one, and throughout the long flight over to Vienna, Charles listened tolerantly as I rehearsed the remarks that I hoped would set the tone for my four years. He held my hand for hours. He seemed as excited as I, but without my fear. Given my husband's experience in Washington and his often critical nature, his confidence in me boosted my courage.

My first challenge came minutes after the plane touched down on the tarmac of Vienna's airport. Charles and I were greeted by several members of my new staff and a score of Austrian journalists. Then we were whisked inside the VIP area, where my introductory press conference would be held. "Are you ready?" asked the embassy press attaché.

"Ready," I answered, taking a deep breath.

"I'll let them in," he said. I walked over to shake the hand of each entering reporter, cameraman, and technician. My embassy colleague looked puzzled, but it seemed to me the gracious thing to do. Afterwards a reporter was overheard commenting, "*Sie ist ein Mensch.*" I was a "real person." Or as Dad and Mom would have said, "just plain folks."

Turns out plain folks sometimes need elaborate sympathy. I delivered my few lines nervously, at the microphone: "When I last saw President Clinton, he said to me, 'Keep your ear to the ground, Swanee. There's a lot happening in Central America.'"

Central America? President Clinton was no fool. He knew his continents. I didn't even hear my mistake but noticed a rustling in the corner as our embassy press officers sprang into action. Just a quick huddle to strategize before they fanned out across the room, approaching reporters individually to secure promises that each would do the German "voiceover" without the slip, or would expunge it in print. My bloom was already off the rose, and we hadn't even left the airport.

We drove on to our new home, just outside the walls of the enormous Schönbrunn Palace, summer home to the Hapsburg monarchs. The residence was built in 1933 by a Jewish coal mogul, who subsequently fled the Nazis. Third Reich officers used the residence for their own purposes. In 1945 the estate lay within the Russian zone, when Vienna (and all of Austria) was divided and occupied by Allied powers, who remained for ten years.

As we walked through the boxy Bauhaus residence, I recalled how I felt as a seven-year-old, moving into Mt. Vernon. This time I wouldn't get lost. Instead of an overwhelmed mother, Charles, ever so competent, was at my side. The butler announced lunch, and we sat down in the airy dining room. Three courses later, when we went upstairs, we were amazed to find that our bags had been unpacked, our clothes organized on shelves.

I wandered through the house, trying to imagine how I would make it feel like a home for Teddy and Lillian. They were back in Denver, finishing their semester of school, Lillian with Mark, Teddy with a nanny.

I missed them already—Teddy's infectious laughter, Lillian's relentless inquisitiveness. I longed for Christmas, when they, with Henry, would be around our table together.

That evening, the whirlwind continued. We were honored guests at the ball marking the birthday of the U.S. Marine Corps. This was the annual highlight for our contingent of twenty-one young men and one woman who provided security for the U.S. embassy, in buildings spread across the city. A sea of faces watched as I took my seat at the elevated head table. On my right was a mountain climber, who began describing her Himalayan trek. I responded enthusiastically with tales of Nepal. We were well into our conversation when an embarrassed gunnery sergeant approached me from behind and prodded: "Ma'am, I believe they're waiting for you to begin."

Surprised, I looked out on a roomful of expectant guests. As I lifted my fork, hundreds of forks immediately followed my lead. I had a lot to learn.

The next morning, Charles and I decided to have some couple time. We meandered through our lush gardens and out the driveway—with three armed, plainclothes Austrian guards following a few steps behind. Carved heads above windows smiled down upon us beneficently, and cherubs hung garlands around entryways. Fine art-deco designs had been plastered and painted, just for the pleasure of onlookers like us. Peering into café windows, we saw old women with boiled wool hats perked up with pheasant feathers. Many must have been widowed during the Second World War. Watching them sip their thick coffee in clear glass mugs, I thought about what they'd lived through—fathers, husbands, and sons killed, homes reduced to rubble. I imagined them as beautiful young women, hiding from notoriously aggressive Soviet soldiers.

We continued into the Schönbrunn gardens, past a street corner, where we stopped in our tracks, seeing my portrait in caricature covering the entire front page of the most popular newspaper. I was wearing a mortarboard (education was a high Austrian value) and draped in Austrian and American flags, which I was stitching together. I wish I'd been so appropriately clad that morning. While the rest of Vienna was sporting traditional Sunday strolling costumes—tweed jackets, gray skirts or trousers, and chunky brown walking shoes—I was dressed in

Colorado casual. People stared at my colorful T-shirt, yellow socks, and bright yellow high-tops. I felt like the stereotypical ugly American tourist.

I was starting to realize that I'd traded my privacy for a public persona. It was hard to believe, but my arrival had been the top story of the weekend. Since Vienna was the birthplace of protocol, everyday Austrian consciousness included the goings-on of diplomats strolling imperial parquet halls, bearing messages from their governments. So most of Austria had watched me descend the stairs of the plane and heard (the expurgated version of) my airport speech.

I'd grown up in a fishbowl, so being stared at didn't unsettle me. Still, I wasn't prepared for the scene at the *Drogerie* the next morning, when I asked my embassy-assigned driver, Horst, to pull over on the way to the office. As I studied the shelves to see what feminine hygiene items were available, a commotion ensued. The owner had been hurriedly called to the store by his clerk. "Your Excellency, what an honor!" he gushed, even bowing slightly. "Here, let me hold your things! I'll ring them up myself!"

Handing them over, I blushed. From that day on our house staff bought my toiletries.

Whenever I try to describe my four years in Vienna, I find myself slipping into a rapid-fire pace. For better and worse, that's how it came my way, and that's how I lived it. The rushed stride made it seem as if I'd spent my first forty-three years lolling through life. On the phone with Dick Lamm, the former governor of Colorado, he commiserated: "I know exactly what you mean. It's like trying to get a sip of water from a fire hydrant."

Not only did I have to learn how to relate to the Austrian public, I was still on stage when I went to my office: One sneeze from the ambassador and the whole embassy caught pneumonia. Accustomed to an honest and free-flowing exchange with my staff at Hunt Alternatives, I found that hypersensitivity oppressive.

I'd been told that I'd be astounded by the competence of Foreign Service professionals, and I appreciated those dedicated public servants who worked for pay far below what they could earn in the corporate sector. But despite their individual high standards, the collective bureaucracy was often inert, smothering ideas, initiative, and vitality. Besides that, these were people I hadn't hired, and some didn't share my vision. I couldn't really blame them. I'd dropped out of nowhere, promoting an agenda they hadn't created.

I found some embassy practices nothing but absurd. Upon my arrival, I discovered that the monthly "large staff meeting" included only the American half of our employees, who rotated every three years. Their expertise ranged worldwide, but they often lacked savvy specific to Austria. It made no sense to exclude our Austrian employees, many of whom had doctorates, knew the local players intimately, and had worked for the embassy more than twenty years. We opened up the group for all.

But only Americans, about sixteen of them, attended the weekly "country team meeting" in a room like a bank vault, secure from technological espionage. They were from fourteen parts of government including Treasury, Defense, Agriculture, Transportation, Immigration, the FBI, and other intelligence agencies. Within my first few weeks, I was immersed in discussions of the possible expansion of NATO and the European Union, but it was holiday season, so my protocol office was planning a celebration, which I was told should include employees and spouses.

"How do you handle gay partners in your invitations?" I asked the country team. My new colleagues looked at me blankly. Finally one spoke. "There are no gay people at the embassy."

On my left was a woman I knew was in a long-term, same-sex relationship. "This must not be a safe place to be out," I responded.

In fact, homosexuals had been dubbed a security risk because they could be blackmailed. The argument was circular, of course. No stigma, no blackmail. All I had to do was raise the question and we revised our rules of etiquette. I began more than ever to ponder the opportunity that accompanied my authority.

I was not only responsible for dealings between the United States and Austria, but also was expected to represent the American position on current events worldwide. My staff prepared me for scenes such as the one that enveloped my lecture at the University of Innsbruck, where I faced an energetic student demonstration toward Cuba. A parade of twenty protestors, led by one dressed as Uncle Sam, interrupted my speech. They were chanting loudly and holding signs damning our unenlightened policy toward Cuba. I shook my head. "I won't argue with you on *that* one," I said.

I could not conform to the description of a diplomat as "an honest man sent abroad to lie for his country." As difficult as it was to speak compellingly about issues to which I was committed, it was more challenging to maintain some semblance of integrity when I disagreed with a policy I represented. I was, after all, never a private citizen on Austrian soil. I was the United States of America. Determined to not lie, sometimes all I could do was stay silent, lest I reveal what I was really thinking.

The stakes were high. I asked for my political briefings each day to be in German and, in an unusual move, led by Austrian staff so that we Americans wouldn't pass around bad grammar. I was a step ahead, given my years in Heidelberg. But there my vocabulary had been built around train stations, meals, and theaters rather than bombers, boycotts, and mass graves. With *hoch* professionalism, our Austrian staff members were patient when I stumbled into a tangle of German syntax.

Once I crossed the psychological line of freely admitting that my experience was in domestic policy, I could enlist help from an extraordinary array of experts. Whether the problem was Syria or Sudan, someone from our spy-riddled community had served there. They'd worked in secrecy, tracking nefarious operatives, but now they could finally talk openly about something they knew. I, in turn, emerged with a hearty education in foreign policy—as well as intelligence gathering.

Our front office set a standard admired or resented throughout the embassy, depending on how willing other departments were to adapt to our fast pace. I spread myself exquisitely thin, often attempting to be in three places at once. By the end of the day, I felt like a cow with a weary udder. I trusted my talented executive secretary, Susan Ray, to slide the right briefing papers into my hands as I walked out the door and to tell me what was happening in the world, since I couldn't get through my mail, much less a news magazine.

For the first time in my life, how I looked really mattered. I was photographed constantly. It was unsettling to realize that if I had a bad hair day, I reflected a disheveled United States of America. I'd never spent much time with hairdressers. Now I went every week, bringing my work with me, balancing a computer on my legs. I was always on the run but still had to worry about my weight. As a successful professional, I could feel poised as I delivered an animated speech. But the next hour I could be utterly disheartened, at home in a yoga plow position with my generous, loose stomach plopped onto my face, almost smothering me.

In general, I tried to behave more decorously than ever in my life. Except once. I was seated on the front row of a stage at a fancy and formal occasion, next to an Austrian official who hadn't publicly acknowledged his Parkinson's disease. As TV cameras moved in close, the official's head, legs, and arms began twitching.

Looking to my right and left, I pondered what to do. I decided that his movements were obvious in part because everyone else on the stage was sitting up straight and perfectly still. I kept wishing that I could reach over and hold his legs down, or put my arms around his shoulders to stop the jerking. That I couldn't do, but at least I could join him. For the next twenty minutes, I scratched my forehead, tapped my feet, crossed and uncrossed my legs, shifted in my chair, folded and unfolded my arms.

Goodnight Moon

Beneath the cosmetic, my professional life was full to overflowing as the Clinton administration staked out a role in the new unified Europe. Old friendships were on temporary hold. Personal pleasures I could forgo. Sleep I would do without. But my children . . . they wouldn't be children long. Every day I served in Vienna, I was not only ambassador, or boss, but also mom. They had arrived as planned and were settling in. But the adjustment for Teddy and Lillian was enormous. Phone calls from or about them during my day felt like fire alarms going off, reminding me that I wasn't at their side.

Teddy's and Lillian's needs didn't fit the neat, tight schedule I was handed each morning. Instead, I listened for their voices through a barrage of Balkan bomb blasts, insipid questions from grinning celebrity seekers, shouts of protestors on the embassy doorstep, or cheers from an audience applauding an American orchestra. Like hundreds of millions of parents, I never had the sense that I was doing enough for my children as I juggled job and family.

I thought about my mother at Mt. Vernon, how she gave up tucking us in at bedtime. My job was every bit as demanding as her husband was. So I stubbornly insisted on slipping upstairs to crawl into bed for a story with Teddy or to check how Lillian was faring. Nothing was as convenient as the truth when I leveled with the guest of honor on my right, saying I'd be back after I said goodnight to our children. Whomever I asked to fill in and sit in my chair those few minutes would be grateful for the opportunity for face time with the honoree. I just had to be sure the butler checked in on me. Nodding off for the night midway through *Goodnight Moon* would be hard to explain to the chancellor waiting downstairs.

The kids were welcome in my office. Teddy's "cootie catcher" had a permanent place on my giant desk, and my drawers were filled with his paperclip chains. During the foreign minister's ski trip, I was the only diplomat who brought children; I clutched Lillian between my legs in an Olympic bobsled and sang songs on the bus with Teddy on my lap. Teddy and Lillian—once more, the only children—joined me for performances at some of the world's finest opera houses. And I occasionally lured them to dinners, such as with the Omani ambassador, who promised that they could eat in the Middle Eastern style, with their fingers. But there were limits: when I invited a visiting Treasury official to move our appointment to the infirmary, where I was checking out Teddy's possible chickenpox, he prudently deferred our meeting.

I talked openly about parenting challenges, in part because I appreciated when others did the same. Louis Freeh, director of the FBI, told me about a Friday evening call from the national security advisor, Tony Lake, asking him to meet at the White House the next morning at 10:00. Hearing the topic, which he figured could be dealt with on Monday, Freeh declined.

"What's the problem, Louis?" Lake asked.

"My son has a basketball game, and I'm the timekeeper."

A long pause ensued. Then a halting "All right, Louis."

"All right, Tony."

As we talked, Freeh backtracked. "Maybe I shouldn't be telling that story."

"Just the opposite," I insisted. "We moms need you dads to tell those tales—and often."

Like any family, ours had rough patches. But I adored our children.

Henry called frequently to keep in touch across the miles. Teddy and Lillian were a constant source of joy and interest, although also exhaustion. I tried my best to keep our nest intact, but a high-ranking role for me was no boon to our family life, and in later years I would hear plenty about how the kids longed for a "normal" home, an echo of my feelings from Mt. Vernon years. I didn't expect Teddy and Lillian to understand what it meant for me to carve out hours from my diplomatic agenda to hear who had hurt their feelings, to work on homework, or to meet with teachers.

But what I gave I got back, if not in gratitude then in diversion from what could have been an all-consuming job. Our children were an antidote to all the glory streaming my way. To them, my official title of "Ambassador Extraordinary and Plenipotentiary" was nothing more than a string of long words.

I was not only an ambassador-mother but also an ambassador-wife. My husband is an organizer. He's a can-do, push-past-the-obstacles kind of guy. I once asked him if in thirty years he'd ever missed attending a concert because it was sold out. "Never," he admitted. He always found a way in. That same attitude astounded me at airports; when people behind the counter said there was no room on a plane, he went to the gate and waited until the last person had boarded, then asked the flight attendant to please look around the aircraft and see if, after all, there wasn't one empty seat. Sometimes he was lucky—if luck is part chance and part attitude.

In Austria, that can-do spirit was directed toward creating a festival in honor of Leonard Bernstein, America's twentieth-century genius and a favorite in Vienna's music world. As much as he was a conductor, Charles was an arts impresario who had put together grand public occasions. Looking for his own niche separate from mine, he set about planning a series of performances, exhibitions, and lectures, all centered around the man whose televised Young People's Concerts had inspired him to enter the world of classical music. With the program designed, he began having meetings to secure the funding. But America's foundations and corporate philanthropies weren't mirrored in Austria's socialist society. Instead, Charles found that he needed government support if the project was to take off.

One evening, after Teddy and Lillian were in bed, I sat with my husband in the library of the residence. We seemed so small in that space, sinking into the red print sofa, surrounded by Remington paintings and bronzes, and even a buffalo head from our ranch. Every nook contained a vestige of adventure and power.

"I don't think it's going to work," Charles said simply. "The minister of culture I met with today said he would support the festival, but I'd have to get the support of two other ministries."

It didn't take a policy genius to recognize that we had run into a conflict of interest. What would happen if I needed to press for a change in Austrian policy, confronting a minister who was funding my husband's project? "I'm so, so sorry, Charles," I said, squeezing his hand.

He took off his glasses to look at me, close up. Then his freckled face broke into a slight smile. "Well, Love," he said, "In a way, you're my greatest success now."

There are different theories about leadership. Some stress vision, charisma, the ability to set a course and have others follow. But my years as an ambassador taught me about a less obvious element: having a partner willing to sacrifice, to lay aside his own ambitions, his own ego, to allow me to be the most I could be.

I'd hoped that Vienna would be as fulfilling for Charles as it was for me. But we couldn't pull that off. I wasn't able to create an environment in which my life partner could be challenged and fulfilled. And the obstacles to Charles's finding significant work in Vienna weren't only external. Soon after we arrived, my cultural attaché objected vehemently when I asked Charles, given his career in public art, to represent me at the opening of an exhibition. I realized I'd have to push hard for him to have any sort of meaningful embassy-related role. That's when he pulled out his baton and developed his own work apart from mine.

Charles was eventually conducting throughout Eastern Europe, but getting started was tough sledding. He good-humoredly described himself as a "trailing spouse," which was in fact how much of Austria saw him. I had a very different take, as I occasionally took the opportunity to follow my husband from one fascinating country to another. I knew how commanding he could be, so I was delighted when a news magazine asked to do a profile of him. But the spread came out with the title, "The Man Next to Swanee."

It was such a disservice to the person who'd helped me come of age vis-à-vis my Dallas world, learn the ropes of Washington, and strategize my agenda as an ambassador. I tried in numerous ways to let him know I remembered and let others know that I was only half of a team. But the power of my position and the lack of a formal role for the ambassador's husband foiled me.

I was in a bind. The more successful I was as an ambassador, the more attention I received. And that attention disgusted my family. If Teddy or Lillian were present, I tried to ignore pomp and praise directed toward me. But as I did, I risked hurting people who'd planned long in advance how to make the arrival of the American ambassador an event that I, and they, would never forget.

Charles stayed away from the embassy, where he said I was a queen bee surrounded by workers awaiting my command. Indeed, before we came to Vienna, he confided one fear: that I would become imperious. I reminded him how years before, when I began effusively talking about the enthusiasm of his audience, he stopped me short. With no bitterness, he said, "They'll forget tonight before the stage lights are cool."

As a gift to myself, and a gift to our marriage, I had a crystal paperweight for my embassy desk engraved "Queen for a Day," with the date of my swearing-in.

Diplomatic Dance

Every ambassador begins a posting with the presentation of credentials to the president of the host country. In Austria that ceremony included a review of troops in the courtyard of the Hofburg Palace, formerly the Hapsburg winter residence. An army band, replete with a large, pony-drawn drum, played as the Austrian president's chief of protocol escorted me up red-carpeted stairs, passing honor guards with noses pointed toward the ceiling. At the top of the stairway I peered through a telescoping series of rooms, with tall, gilded doors flung open to welcome me.

Hapsburg emperors ruled most of the western world at one time or another, and these chambers incubated ideas that shaped history. At the very end was the bedroom of Maria Theresa; it was her daughter, by the way, whose "Let them eat cake" ignited the French Revolution. Processing through opulent rooms where Marie Antoinette had romped, I could understand how she'd have no concept of a breadless citizenry.

The empress's bedroom was now the office of the president. As I approached the tall former diplomat, I wracked my brain for the careful choreography of handshakes and handing-over of papers that had been drilled into me only half an hour earlier. It was as if the instructions had fled in panic. I did remember, though, wise words from *The King and I*: "Make believe you're brave, and the trick will take you far. You may be as brave as you make believe you are." Newspaper front pages the next morning showed President Klestil's head slightly bent, while I held my head erect.

Such formality wasn't natural for me. Hailing from the friendly southern and western regions of the United States, I found Viennese manners stiff, almost feudal in rank-consciousness. Neighbors of thirty years might still address each other as "Herr" and "Frau," either both comfortable with the distance or each waiting all-too-patiently for the other to suggest plunging into the intimacy of first names. Society was oriented around knowing one's place and staying in it.

I wondered if I could fit in, or if I wanted to. One day, while I was out for a run, I reminded myself that Bill Clinton was known for his own informality. He had appointed me as I was, not as I might be. In fact, I consciously tried to match the pitch of the Clintons. Unlike Foreign Service officers whose careers traversed administrations, I considered myself an extension of the president's and First Lady's values, political goals, and inclusive style. I remembered the thrill of my first visit to the White House. We could pass on that pleasure to others — and we did, hosting more than a hundred events a year in our residence, mostly working breakfasts or dinners with guest speakers such as David Rockefeller Jr., Madeleine Albright, and George Soros.

My official work kindled my intellect and exercised my gumption but didn't fill me. And while mothering had delicious sweetheart moments, it was depleting. One day at the office, when I told Susan that my creative well was drying up, she introduced me to Valerie Gillen, her vivacious partner, who sang in a barbershop quartet. Val pulled together professional American singers who performed on Viennese stages. The twenty or so gathered a dozen blessed Sundays a year in our music room. As lady of the house, I had second soprano privileges. We sang for hundreds at our backyard Fourth of July bash, entertained at holiday parties with Father Christmas (a.k.a. Charles, cloaked in a burgundy velvet robe), and crooned "Home on the Range" at the Naturhistorisches Museum for the opening of a U.S. National Parks exhibit. Blending in was a respite in my leadership-laden life. I felt preciously relieved to meld in with a chorus, where most mistakes were forgivable.

Like most political appointees to "plum positions," I substantially supplemented our budget for entertaining and refurbishing. By contrast, some U.S. ambassadors serving in the former Soviet Union were living without heat and washing their clothes in bathtubs. I cringed when the wife of a diplomat who served successively in three Central Asian countries commented, "Vienna? Oh, yes. The department gave you our $3,000 entertainment fund."

"Why was that?" I asked.

"We didn't have a house," she answered dryly.

Whether we entertained or were guests of others, my position afforded Charles and me access to almost anyone we cared to meet. With my unabashed appreciation for father figures, I gravitated to elderly men like the kindly Cardinal Koenig, a hallowed name in overwhelmingly Catholic Austria. When Charles and I were invited by President Klestil to the New Year's Concert of the Vienna Philharmonic, purportedly with a worldwide listening audience of one billion people, I was seated between our host and the cardinal. I knew he had been appointed by the great reformer Pope John XXIII, but times had changed, even behind the walls of Vatican City.

As we waited for the concert to start, I asked, "Do you like your job?" The cardinal was sure he'd misheard. When I repeated my question he stammered, and then a smile spread across his face. "Never mind. You've answered," I told him.

My new friend was frank in return at a lunch when I asked about the insufferably pious man on my left. "More Catholic than the Pope," he whispered with a smile. Moments with the cardinal made me think of holding Franny's rosaries under my bedcovers. As I had in Dallas, I would need such solace in Vienna.

I was searching for a community, for friends. That need couldn't be met by the Austrians or the more than one hundred ambassadors posted to Vienna. Newly arrived diplomats were obliged by protocol to pay me a "courtesy call." But the term conjured up my mother's imploring me as a girl to "act like a lady," by which she had in mind southern women on a veranda, wearing one white glove, holding the other, and sipping lemonade. Not my style, although my diplomatic visitors were accomplished in such finesse. In our half-hour, they greeted me in the name of their government but kept hidden what was on their minds and transacted no business. As years passed, to liven up these stepping-stones of diplomacy, I began to interject personal questions. Most of my colleagues readily opened up with stories about their frustrations or failures. Maybe they were hungry for a real connection too.

As in all of life, in the diplomatic sphere stereotypes often got in the way. I once joined the Canadian and Mexican ambassadors to address a university group on the subject of the North American Free Trade Agreement. The poster advertising the lecture featured a tall, uniformed Canadian Mounty, an imposing Uncle Sam, and a pint-sized figure with a huge sombrero hiding his face. I felt as if I were back in Texas as I protested to the organizer the demeaning portrayal of Mexicans.

Maybe I earned a point or two—which I spent again by missing the hundred or so annual "national day" events, each country's equivalent to our Fourth of July. A seasoned embassy officer suggested that if I didn't want to go to all, I could accept just the NATO countries' invitations. I said I wouldn't show up for France but then stand up Algeria. Rather than make a political statement by being selective, I attended none, sending my deputy and flowers.

When our protocol antennae picked up rumblings about my absence from the cocktail circuit, we threw an old-fashioned Valentine's party for the diplomatic corps, with the butler's two children as winged cherubs, wrapped only in loincloths, standing in our entryway with plastic bows and arrows. Economic woes and political pressures were left at the door. The Czech ambassador brought his violin, the Finn played the piano, and I plucked my harp while seventy diplomats sang at the top of their lungs as if love—and not Realpolitik—made the world go 'round.

Of course some moments were less romantic. The ambassador of a close ally of the United States made my skin crawl when he told me, in a clipped voice, "I don't see why one of our boys should risk his life in Bosnia. Those Balkan people made their bed. Let them lie in it."

I asked if Americans should have assumed the same posture toward

Britain in 1944. He didn't answer. Some months later, he sent out a black-rimmed card announcing the death of his dog.

There were other times when diplomacy shed its decorum in favor of festivity. Each year when the president of Austria held a New Year's reception for the diplomatic corps, we lined up respectfully in the order in which we'd presented our credentials and waited until government luminaries inched around the circle to shake our hands. Tuxedos and women's formal black suits were interspersed with national costumes: robed torsos, hatted heads, and decorated chests. I felt as if I'd been plopped down in the middle of a costume party. Drawn to a striking military attaché in resplendent blue and red, replete with sword and boot spurs, I laughed, "I'm in love with you and don't even know your name."

More innocently, the ambassador waiting next to me in the circle was a tall, handsome former head of Jordanian Airlines. As we waited, I raised my hands, offering to straighten his crooked tie. Cameras flashed, and our picture appeared in papers across the Middle East. (He told me later that he had to explain himself to his foreign ministry!) In the course of becoming a hot item, we chatted about the upcoming visit of King Hussein and Queen Noor. I said, offhandedly, I'd like to meet them. Within hours our office received a call fixing the time and place.

On the way to our office a few days later, Horst and I were delivering the kids to school. "What's on for you?" I asked.

"Math test," Lillian grumbled.

"Spelling quiz," Teddy chirped.

"I'm going to meet a king and queen," I threw out. Their interest was at least piqued, so together we made our way to the Imperial Hotel, former Hapsburg guesthouse. I was dressed in a properly ambassadorial suit. Teddy was in red sweats. Lillian was wearing a T-shirt with a large portrait of Snow White's sidekick, Grumpy, his hands folded in disgust. I insisted that Lil tuck in her shirt. She pushed it into her pants awkwardly as we made our way up the graceful staircase, which guests of the monarchy had descended a century earlier. As we processed, I muttered threats to Teddy: "You even mention your strep infection and you're dead."

We were shown into an exquisite waiting room for a soft drink and then finally taken past a dozen protocol and security aides to the parlor of Their Majesties' suite. On a table was a large silver tray, loaded with fruit. "Have a strawberry if you want," I told the kids. Both declined. Speaking in hushed voices, we continued to wait.

Eventually the tall door opened, and in walked a man with a cropped beard, followed by his willowy, strikingly handsome wife. After a cheerful greeting, we all sat down—we three on a sofa, with the monarchs on either end. Lillian was next to Queen Noor, and I was on the king's right, with Teddy beside me. King Hussein, perhaps the most gracious man I've ever met, went over to the table, picked up the fruit tray, and held it before us. *Now* Teddy took a giant strawberry, which he proceeded to suck on throughout the hour.

Our conversation ranged from Middle East policy to Washington politics. Queen Noor, American-born, questioned me about the Women's Foundation of Colorado. I kept talking, with my eyes on her, as I felt Teddy take my right hand and deposit the mushy remains of his strawberry. No napkin was within reach as the mix of warm juice and saliva spread across my palm and between my fingers. As we stood to bid farewell I discreetly dropped the strawberry pulp in the flowers on the table.

As a conclusion to our meeting, I assured King Hussein that Americans felt a profound appreciation for his contribution to the Middle East peace process. Tears came to his eyes. This had been the core of his life's work, he said. I was moved by the simple goodness of his vision. "You're what Americans call a 'real prince,'" I said spontaneously. Then seeing the king's tilted head and puzzled look, I paused. "Oh, I guess you're one of the few people in the world for whom that's not a compliment."

His Majesty smiled indulgently. He extended his hand to shake mine —red ooze and all. Someone opened the door and we all filed out into the hallway. Half a dozen photographers were waiting—bunched up, some standing, some kneeling, snapping away. I have a picture of us all on my shelf today. A tall blond beauty with voluminous hair, wearing a hot pink silk blouse and elegant striped suit. A good-looking man with a gray mustache and enchanting smile, his kingly high forehead framing dark eyebrows. I'm in a rather staid brown suit and hat. Lillian's white T-shirt explodes with the dwarf's huge, bulbous brown nose and "G-R-U-M-P-Y" in three-inch block letters across her chest.

And Teddy, strep and all, has his hands casually stuffed in the pockets of his loose sweatpants like a cherubic ruffian.

As the five of us stood in a row, smiling at the cameras, Her Majesty whispered to me, "How do you like being an ambassador?" It was much the same question I'd put to the cardinal.

"How do you like being a queen?" I returned. We agreed to take up those topics someday in a different setting.

We were living in a wonderland, creating our new life from a storybook. The few evenings we didn't spend with our kids, or in professional obligations, Charles and I walked the city . . . past the Mozart Café, a notorious spy rendezvous . . . down a cobblestone alley with small restaurant tables for hungry wanderers . . . beside enormous fountains and copper-colored kiosks advertising concerts and exhibitions. Graffitied walls were almost nonexistent in this island of European civility. But we also passed a sign marking where thousands had been transported to Nazi camps. That was Vienna too.

The tree-lined Ringstrasse, once an open swath protecting the city from invasion, had become a boulevard when changes in military tactics made it obsolete. "The Ring" boasted several of the great performing halls and museums of the world. The Austrian government's cultural spending was larger than its federal defense budget. In fact, my meetings with the Austrian chair of the Joint Chiefs of Staff began with a critique of the newest production at the State Opera.

Vienna itself, with one million people, has an art budget several times the federal support for arts across the entire United States. The city is a bastion of historical greatness created under imperial aegis by the likes of Mozart, Beethoven, and Mahler; when neon lights were used in a State Opera production, critics declared a "scandal." Nonetheless, Vienna's overwhelmingly traditional style was enlivened by splashes from Klimt's unruly turn-of-the-century Secessionist art movement, a beautiful and bizarre city incinerator designed by the colorist Hundertwasser, and funky exhibits at the Museum of Applied Art.

Mother said that when I was a toddler, the first song I crooned was "The Tennessee Waltz," so I felt quite at home when I discovered that the blood of the Viennese pulses in 3/4 time: *Eins, zwo, drei / eins, zwo, drei*. Late winter ushered in ball season; that's when I understood why

I'd been warned, "When you arrive in Vienna, set your watch forward eight hours, and your heart back a hundred years." Until I actually stepped onto the ballroom parquet, though, I couldn't fully appreciate the power of the past in the former imperial capital. Hundreds of balls were held, generally on Thursday nights, until the wee hours. On Fridays many people didn't show up for work. But employers didn't dare confront a tradition so revered, where ages and social classes mixed in a swirl of music and movement.

I made it to a couple of balls each year. After a day preoccupied with concerns of ethnic nationalism, free-market reforms, and nuclear proliferation, I was happy to surrender to the dizziness. The music was regal and full. So were my gowns. I had three—as I assured a radio interviewer after a news story complained that I'd worn the same dress to the same ball two years in a row. But apart from the trivia, I deepened political relationships while twirling to the strains of Strauss. One minute I might be arm in arm with the federal chancellor (the prime minister); the next, waltzing with the mayor or jitterbugging with the defense minister. Here, being a female ambassador to a male-dominated body politic was a distinct advantage.

Sophia's Bell

The balls in Austria were fanciful; meanwhile in the adjacent former Yugoslavia reality was worse than dire. The conditions that led to violent conflict developed after the death of Marshall Tito, a charismatic communist who led the Yugoslav Partisans resisting the Nazis. At the end of the Second World War, Tito became the head of Yugoslavia, composed of six republics (Serbia, Montenegro, Slovenia, Bosnia, Croatia, and Macedonia) and two semiautonomous areas (Kosovo and Vojvodina). For decades, Tito suppressed ethnic differences. Intermarriage among groups was common. People of different ethnicities were scattered throughout each republic. And most citizens identified themselves as "Yugoslav" rather than by a subgroup.

Internationally, Tito became a leader among the so-called non-aligned countries, which remained neutral in the Cold War. To reward him for refusing to be a Soviet puppet, the United States doled out financial aid for Yugoslavia, supporting the economy and, early on with the Soviet Union, helping Tito to build a powerful military. His death in 1980 left a dangerous political vacuum.

Soviet-based communism across the region imploded a decade later, and America no longer desired to buttress Yugoslavia as an independent regime in Eastern Europe. As support from Washington dropped dramatically, the Yugoslav economy suffered. With war-mongering speeches and a vicious media campaign, Slobodan Milosevic moved incrementally into the political space left by Tito. Granted, Marshall Tito had exerted brutal control in his early years, but Milosevic fanned the embers of ethnic conflict, which was the antithesis of Tito's policy. In the late 1980s Milosevic intensified political repression against non-Serbs.

The break-up of Yugoslavia was so politically complicated that few in the outside general public could follow it. "Greater Serbia" madness sparked ethnic nationalism in Bosnia, Croatia, Slovenia, and Macedonia, each of which declared independence from Yugoslavia in 1991–92. That left Milosevic presiding over a "rump" state, comprising only the republics of Serbia and Montenegro.

Rather than being the largest ethnic group within a united Yugoslavia, now Serbs were a minority in each of the four newly independent states. Milosevic seized an opportunity to infuse them with fear. He used his control of the media to spread ethnic terror and hatred, and converted the Yugoslav army into a Serb-only force. In concert with ruthless paramilitary bands, the army unleashed a campaign of ethnic cleansing that eventually drove millions of non-Serbs from their homes. The onslaught was dramatic and barbaric at a level almost incomprehensible in sophisticated Europe—until one remembered Germany in the 1930s. Horrible devastation was first reported as Serbs attacked Croatia in August 1991. We arrived in Vienna while the fighting was still raging in Bosnia. Although it had subsided in Croatia, a large portion of the population had been displaced from their homes and the majority of the new country was under the control of the Serbs.

In April 2004 Charles and I were invited by Peter Galbraith, the first U.S. ambassador to Croatia, for dinner in Zagreb, a four-hour drive south from Vienna. Peter and I were the same age. He had been a brilliant staffer for the Senate Foreign Relations Committee and had an extraordinary depth in international affairs. In his toast he noted that three of us in the room lived in the shadow of fathers of gigantic proportion: on my right sat the son of President Tudjman, and Peter's father was the celebrated economist John Kenneth Galbraith.

Susan Hovenac, Peter's capable public affairs officer, had put together a meeting earlier in the day with some thirty women leaders. To add imprimatur, the American flag was set in the yard where we gathered, while I described various American women's initiatives as models for this new democracy. The women stayed for hours, telling me, in turn, their stories.

One described how she'd moved to Chicago years earlier with her teenaged son. She was a costume designer, and their lives were settled and secure. She found American life gratifying, although she always wondered, when she looked at milk cartons showing the faces of missing children, how a parent could endure such calamity. When the Serbs invaded Croatia, her son insisted on returning to his homeland to fight. At first she heard from him regularly. Then the letters stopped. She flew back and went from office to office, seeking information about her son. Officials shut the doors in her face, she said. So she took her search to the people, going from town to town, village to village.

Eventually she found someone who'd seen her child lying dead in a field. Now, she told me, all the sleepless nights, the gnawing fear, the tears of rage were being transformed. "I'm not a victim any more. I'm acting," she declared, and described the organization she'd created to help others find missing sons, husbands, and fathers.

Such conversations stayed with me as Charles and I drove with Ambassador Galbraith to Karlovac, near the front line. Rubble spilled out of the schoolhouse, and a blue children-crossing sign had been used for target practice. As I roamed with my camera, Peter warned me to stay on the sidewalk. The week before, his embassy driver had lost a foot to a landmine.

Back in Zagreb, we drove past a bustling market, where country folk, pretending that a war wasn't going on, sold homemade lace, fresh eggs, boisterous flowers, and round, golden loaves of bread. But down the street was the Center for Women War Victims, where volunteers helped women driven from their homes, many of them repeatedly raped. The organizer greeted me with a bouquet. "I should be bringing flowers to you," I said. Then I paused, and smiled as I accepted the flowers. As fleeting as it was, that was an important moment, as I reminded myself that the act of giving builds a sense of self—a sense of being graced enough to have gifts to share. For givers who are themselves in desperate straits, giving is more than a transaction. It can be a transformation.

One final impression stayed with me from that first of many trips to Croatia. An artist told us how, while sketching a destroyed church, he'd met a villager named Sophia. She was old, and her role in her community was simple. Each day at noon, she hobbled to the church and pulled on the long, thick ropes that rang the large bell in the steeple. When Serb military thugs came through with their tanks they followed their usual pattern, shooting up every non-Serb home and then blowing the steeple off the Catholic Church. The heavy bell now lay on the ground, surrounded by splintered wood. Still, every day at noon Sophia was in the churchyard, bent over, her gnarled, wrinkled hands clasping the clapper as she swung her arms, ringing the bell.

No one was more persevering than Bill Clinton, who was determined to use his position to bring about a more stable and just world. Impassioned about domestic issues, he had to learn foreign policy at lightning speed. Like him, I found this new arena riveting. I was one hundred percent in agreement with Clinton's abhorrence of American hegemony; we had to find the right balance of exerting leadership without bullying. The balance was different in every country, and within borders different among various constituencies.

Part of my job as ambassador was to figure out in which situations the United States should be a dominating presence, pushing human rights, good governance, and economic partnerships. When, on the other hand, should we not get entangled, not intervene? When the American ambassadors appointed to Europe were called to Brussels for a State Department conference, I realized there how my view from Vienna would sometimes be at odds with those of another ambassador or strategists at State. I would have to figure out when to stand my ground and when to give in.

Speaking broadly about the administration's priorities, Strobe Talbott, deputy secretary of state, noted that concerns for one country trumped all others. I finished his sentence in my mind, knowing how hundreds of thousands were fleeing atrocities in the Balkans.

". . . and that's Russia," Strobe concluded. I sat back. How could our views be so different? Strobe had been a journalist in the Soviet Union. Moscow was his backyard. I couldn't assume that others would be as distressed as I about stopping the war that was ripping apart Austria's southern neighbor.

After overrunning most of Croatia, in April 1992 the Serbs had laid siege to Sarajevo, a modern European city of nearly half a million, which had hosted the winter Olympics in 1984. With high-rise housing and offices, the Bosnian capital was without electricity or running water for months at a time. Shelling was relentless. The civilian death toll was climbing every day. Bosnia was able to pull together only a poorly equipped, ragtag semblance of an army.

The deployment of American ground troops was ruled out because of resistance from the Pentagon, although some in Washington advocated using air power against the Serbs. But our European allies were concerned that bombing might endanger their own ground troops, committed as UN forces to protect relief deliveries. And the Russians, who considered the Serbs their cousins in the Orthodox faith, opposed American intervention.

In fact, I'd flown to the ambassadors' meeting in Brussels directly from Washington, where I was with President Clinton in the Oval Office immediately after he hung up the phone with President Yeltsin. Yes, the two agreed, Milosevic was out of control in his push for power. Yes, he needed to be stopped. But the Russian leader had ended the conversation abruptly with Clinton: "No bombs." Click.

That scene was fresh on my mind as I sat listening to my diplomatic colleagues. At one point the assistant secretary of state for Europe was interrupted during his presentation to take a call from Washington. After ten minutes he returned to the podium. "We're starting air strikes in Bosnia," he said, with noticeable energy in his voice. My pulse quickened. The intervention was finally beginning.

"Did anyone tell the Russians?" a voice boomed out from the back of the room. It was Tom Pickering, one of State's most celebrated figures, then serving as ambassador in Moscow. I wasn't privy to subsequent discussions in the Oval Office weighing the risks of American casualties against the lives of Balkan innocents. I didn't hear cabinet members who feared international entanglements arguing with those who felt a humanitarian imperative not to stand by watching the slaughter. I only know—and deeply regret—that it took two more years for the air strikes to start.

Looking for the Light

A few days after the meeting in Brussels, I received a request from Washington to host negotiations between two warring Balkan factions: the Croats and the Bosniaks. War creates heroes, but villains too. With about one-third of Croatia seized by the Serbs, the Croat general and president Franjo Tudjman plotted with Milosevic, his enemy, to conquer and divide up Bosnia, which was situated between their states. As Milosevic had incited Bosnian Serbs, Tudjman encouraged Bosnian Croats to seize areas where they could claim to be a majority. Now Bosniaks (Bosnian Muslims) were battling off Croat aggressors from their north and west, as well as Serb aggressors from their east. The secular Muslims, descendants of Slavs who had converted to Islam during the Ottoman reign, were targeted in a genocide that left some 200,000 dead and more than two million, half the Bosnian population, displaced. The United States aimed to persuade the Croats to reverse their aggressive position toward Bosnia and instead ally with the Bosniaks to push back the Serbs.

A seasoned negotiator, Chuck Redman, was dispatched from Washington to Vienna; and negotiation teams from the war areas made their way, however they could, into calm and immaculate Austria. Chuck based himself in my office as he shuttled back and forth between a dozen Croats in my private embassy dining room and the Bosnian delegation in our administrative conference room down the hall. The war-weary men were making little progress, so Chuck and I decided to bring them together in a relaxed setting to ease tensions. I called our chef at the residence: prepare dinner for fifty.

This was the only time since the start of the negotiations when the two sides would be in the same room. Trust building among traumatized people requires minute attention to detail. Anticipating the scene, I realized that traditional large tables could be a prescription for hostile boredom. In my training in Denver as a therapist I'd learned the psychological impact of seating arrangements, so a week earlier I'd had tables made that were a meter in diameter, around which six guests could crowd. I asked our butler to bring out those tables. He called back to let me know that he was setting up large tables instead because we didn't have tablecloths yet and the stores had closed.

"Use our bed sheets," I said. Hearing the incredulity in his voice, I hastened home. Two butlers, two chefs, and three chambermaids stood, mouths agape, as I spread a sheet on the French wool rug, turned a table upside down on the sheet, knelt on the floor, and started cutting a giant circle. When they stopped tittering, the chambermaids assumed scissors duty.

To break the tense mood for the evening, I'd found a harpist to come in. As my guests began to arrive, I had to send a butler over to stop her from playing "Send in the Clowns." The exhausted men were holding their orange juice or wine, standing stiffly and not wanting to look at, much less speak to, each other. I was exuding every bit of charm I could muster, but their distrust and anger were prevailing.

Suddenly, my six-year old Teddy came charging down the stairs, joyfully jumped into my arms, and wrapped his legs around my waist. He kissed me on the cheeks and clasped his hands behind my neck, which pulled his nightshirt up. I felt his bare bottom, exposed.

I continued to greet my war-weary guests, who now were smiling at Teddy, holding onto me like a monkey. As much as I loved having him in my arms, my guests seemed to enjoy him even more.

The evening was thrust into motion, but still subdued. At least until Teddy padded over to the piano and began regaling us all with the theme from "The Pink Panther." His fingers flew, and his grin was packaged in an innocence that gifted our guests with the goodness of life.

Soon he was joined at the keyboard by the Bosnian foreign minister (killed a year later when his helicopter was shot down by Serbs). That drew us all into the music room for what became a home concert of Bosnian folksongs, jokes, and laughter. The Croats knew the same songs and joined in lustily. The men, so stuck in their ethnic identities, were now like kids as they posed for pictures together in front of a life-sized painted pageant of Native American women on our library wall.

Years later, a UN employee in Geneva relayed to me a remarkably accurate description of that gathering, now ensconced in diplomatic lore. For me, it was simply the way I felt most comfortable doing business—with considerable help from my cheery little son.

Another set of negotiations was needed to put final touches on the agreement. The negotiating teams asked that they be held in Vienna because, they said, the ambience of our embassy was conducive to reconciliation. I hosted another dinner where I offered this toast:

I believe that in the mix of who we are, good and bad,
there is the light of God in every person.
Sometimes that light shines so bright that it dazzles young children,
and makes grown-ups weep.
It lights up dark memories hidden in a thousand-year-old corner,
or shows the way along a treacherous path.
Sometimes that light is so dim as to be imperceptible,
almost drowned by heavy drops of sweat, blood, or tears.
Then, just when you least expect it,
the light reappears.
I also believe there is, within each of us, a capacity for darkness
that we do not willingly recognize.
It casts a greed-shaped shadow over our best moments.
It grows silently like a fungus in our cleanest sheets.
The darkness denies life to hope
but allows seeds of doubt and suspicion to sprout
into violence and cruelty.
May we in this room, working here together,
have the wisdom to look for the light in ourselves
and in the person sitting next to us and across from us.
May we not be surprised when we recognize the darkness
in ourselves and in each other, but simply nod in understanding,
then keep peering through the darkness until the light, at last, reappears.

My words, too heavy for another occasion, hit home for people who were living a nightmare. After arduous give and take, the negotiations were complete, providing the first hopeful turn in the war. Croats and Bosniaks joined in a tenuous military alliance and began to regain territory that had been seized by the Serbs.

Two months later, on July 4, 1994, a break in the fighting allowed my first visit to Bosnia. The American Embassy to Bosnia had been sharing our embassy facilities in Vienna for over a year, with diplomats staying in Sarajevo only for short periods. Now, despite the continued siege,

Washington was moving the embassy onto Bosnian soil. I'd wangled permission to fly down for the official opening.

For months I'd wanted to go, but the undersecretary of state for management had refused. The last thing he needed was the kidnapping or death of an ambassador to complicate an already impossible situation. Even that day was considered too unsafe for me to stay overnight.

I had to take a commercial flight north to Frankfurt, spend the night on the Rhein-Main U.S. Air Force base, and retrace my path by flying south, strapped in with fifty thousand pounds of flour on a thirty-year-old military cargo plane. As we descended I sat in the cockpit, listening through a headset and peering into the dense white clouds. The thick German intonation of air traffic controllers during takeoff had been replaced by an unfamiliar Slavic accent. Voices from the hidden city below seemed like spirits rising from the valleys.

After we broke through the cloud cover, the first sign of life was children playing soccer beneath our flight path. But the innocence evaporated as soon as we landed, when I was told to put on a flak jacket and run from the loading ramp of the plane toward a pile of sandbags, from where I was whisked into an American-made armored sedan. Our route was alongside the suburb of Dobrinja, where a year earlier two shells had exploded among players and spectators at a soccer match, killing at least eleven and wounding one hundred. Even a game of soccer could be deadly.

All around were vestiges of the twenty-seven-month siege: buses turned on their sides as barricades, buildings with gaping holes, hand-painted signs that warned "SNIPER DANGER," and endless rows of window openings covered with plastic stamped with the ubiquitous blue UN seal. As I looked at the sky through wreckage of someone's former kitchen, I noticed red geraniums blooming defiantly on the window ledge of pock-marked façades. Our bulletproof car sped along empty streets, pulling up to the new embassy, a relic of Tito's administration being prepared for American occupancy. The building was freshly painted but without furnishings.

I joined Vic Jackovich, the American ambassador, as he greeted a mix of Bosnian political and military leaders and representatives of the UN, NATO, and the international media. We were three hundred well-wishers gathered on the lawn to share in a moment of hope. When the beleaguered Bosnian president, Alija Izetbegovic, arrived, we walked onto the stage. I stared into the crowd. "The man on the roof with the rifle is one of ours," Ambassador Jackovich said out of the side of his mouth.

I'd asked for a text from the State Department to read, but what I received just before I left was so tepid that I considered it an affront to people who'd suffered so much. Standing behind the flag-draped podium, I decided not to deliver those words. Instead, I reminded myself that I was the president's representative, so I should feel confident speaking on his behalf. I brought the Sarajevans greetings from President Clinton that described how our country too was built on principles of tolerance—on people celebrating differences rather than fearing them. That's why we could understand their struggle. The crowd applauded enthusiastically.

It was the most stirring Fourth of July in my life, taking stock of the founding of another country struggling to honor its diversity. Even in the middle of a war, the ambassador had managed to arrange for hamburgers, hot dogs, and a military color guard. I watched as the Stars and Stripes were slowly raised above the embassy for the first time, with loudspeakers broadcasting a tinny rendition of our national anthem. The flag hung limply as it crawled up the pole, finally catching a breeze and unfurling as the anthem declared "the home of the brave." I'd never felt prouder to be an American. But I wondered what most Americans knew about bravery, compared to the people gathered on the lawn.

I was coming from the capital of an erstwhile superpower, the Hapsburg Empire, once the political and cultural home base of Bosnia. And I was bringing greetings from the current superpower. So my presence that day packed a double meaning. Soon afterward, the fighting resumed and the city was once again closed to me. But I'd left a piece of myself there, among the ruins.

The scenes of destruction and courage in Sarajevo resonated with other times I've felt compelled to action: Hassie's paranoia, hopelessness in the inner city, dying children in Nepal. I have friends who refuse to visit places of extreme poverty because they find beggars and scenes of abject want so disturbing. But the way I see it, trying to protect our luxury, our vast pleasure, from being diminished by witnessing others' privation—that is the ultimate self-indulgence. I've not lived the virtue of giving all I have to help the poor, but I've sometimes put myself in earshot of their cries. As Sarajevans were terrorized over the next year, I lay in my comfortable bed in Vienna with a tormented conscience.

Tough and Tender

Everywhere I turned, I found people in need. I went to Vienna believing that if I were an attentive mom, my kids could have a stable life. But as the months unfolded, I discovered that although I was able to help thousands of refugees and reach out to millions of Austrians, I couldn't ensure the well-being of my own children.

My parenting style was casual—out of synch with rigid Viennese society and my diplomatic job. I constantly wrestled with the demands of the three worlds. Twice when my scheduler overbooked me, squeezing out a parental obligation, I lost control in a tearful rage, shouting at my trusted and stunned aide, "How could you do that?" as if she'd murdered my child. My over-the-top reaction had little to do with my aide's culpability or any real damage to my kids. The roar came from an instinctual place.

I poured every ounce of ingenuity I had into creating a warm home for our children. To make our fifteen-thousand-square-foot residence less imposing for them (and the child in me), we covered our walls with friendly portraits—I called it "people art"—and spread our living spaces throughout the building. Charles and I picked out paintings to borrow from museums and private collections through the State Department's "Art in Embassies" program. Vance Kirkland's ethereal *Adam and Eve* loomed over Teddy as he played SimCity for hours on the computer in the downstairs office, puzzling over whether to spend his budget on new streets or housing. Dinner was in the formal dining room illuminated by the torch of Peter Max's colorful *Statues of Liberty*.

Occasionally we had a family evening of Monopoly, a celebration of capitalistic avarice too close to home for me to enjoy unreservedly.

"Your turn, Miss Lil," said Charles, as I held the video camera.

"C.A., take the camera," I said, "so I can disprove the notion that I never played games."

"And here is the ambassador," Charles intoned, in a serious voice.

"Marvel Gardens!" Teddy screamed.

"Damn it," snapped Lil.

"Hallelujah!" yelled Teddy. Meanwhile, from the wall, Mary Cassatt's *Girl in a Green Bonnet* watched over us, to make sure we went directly to jail and didn't pass Go.

I was reliving Mt. Vernon, where my sister Helen and I sat on red-carpeted stairs, peering through banisters, as we listened to the clink and chatter of guests below. Having learned then to maneuver the split between public and private spaces, I made sure that our kids knew they were always welcome at our events. No matter how formal our entertaining, Teddy frequently appeared in pajamas to crawl into Charles's lap or pull up a chair next to mine.

Occasionally the kids added sparks to conversations, such as when Lillian challenged Supreme Court Justice Ruth Bader Ginsburg on Balkan policy. "So what if we didn't intervene in Argentina?" my thirteen-year-old pounded. "Two wrongs don't make a right!" I didn't say a word, but I was proud.

But then there was Teddy's query to the vice president of Bosnia, "Why don't you just give up? You're getting creamed by the Serbs." Oh, Lord.

For one particularly elegant dinner, Teddy decided to promote some social conscience among the muckety-mucks. I helped him make the sign—"The children in Bosnia are hungry. Will you help?"—and set it next to a basket, primed with a five-Schilling note. Next to the basket was a plate with "made by Teddy" origami hats, fish, and purses.

The display was at the top of our entry stairwell. Chancellor Vranitzky was the first to leave that evening. He insisted that I not escort him out but stay with our other guests. I heard the sound of him walking down to the front door, then footsteps coming back up the stairs. Glancing around the corner, I saw that the chancellor had returned to drop a large bill in the basket. Teddy raised 2,000 Schillings, about $200, from our dinner guests for refugee children who would have been amazed to know the source of the fresh fruit smuggled in for them the next month.

Not every scene was so sweet. Our kids had trouble fitting in at the American International School. On the first day both were in tears, and while other ambassadors were no doubt following every detail of Clinton's European visit, I spent the evening finding the area of a rectangle, looking through a book on snakes, wiping chocolate ice cream off my bed, and scratching my daughter's back while I tried to absorb one measly page of a newspaper. Teddy's first-grade teacher wanted to hold him back in math because he didn't pay attention to minus and plus signs. And by the way, she complained, he was slow with cutting and pasting. With a not-so-nice push in my voice, I told the veteran pedagogue that it was fine with this mother if my child never mastered the scissors.

The tension from our move and my position was taking its toll on us all. Teddy confided that he wasn't happy in Austria. "I'm used to having sparks at my feet, but now I'm standing on a burning log," he explained in an earnest voice. So for second grade we moved him to public school, within walking distance of the residence. Each morning he blithely headed out like a small, ruddy-cheeked Hummel figurine, with his rucksack on his back, to the armed guards at the end of our driveway . . . along the chain link fence topped with barbed wire . . . past the policeman stationed in front of the residence . . . and beyond the extra guard, with a semiautomatic weapon, assigned to our corner at rush hour.

Teddy didn't speak a word of German. Lillian and Henry protested our decision to put him through the linguistic ordeal. I reminded them that our little son had been sailing through life. "Time for some grist," I declared philosophically. The teacher told us at Christmas that he was a pleasure; unlike the other boys, he was quiet. By spring, of course, he was chattering away, in perfect Viennese dialect.

His Austrian school placement was by and large positive. Still I cringed for him when at the outdoor talent show, the principal pointed out to all the students and parents: "This is a very important day, because the American ambassador has demonstrated her admirable interest in her child by being with us." As the crowd applauded politely, I looked at Teddy, intently digging a hole in the grass with a stick. Maybe he hadn't heard her opening remarks? No such luck.

Likewise for Lillian . . . at the American International School, which was significantly supported by the U.S. government, and where the U.S. ambassador was a big deal. The publicity that made me effective made life terribly difficult for my daughter, who repeatedly begged to have a private tutor. Lil was subjected to rumors that started long before her arrival. She sobbed after a classmate wrote in her yearbook, "Hi there, Rich Babe." Her intellectual gifts created more barriers. Some students gossiped that I'd paid to have her placed in classes two years ahead. At the end of the school year, one mother said to me, "I think the kids are finally giving Lillian a chance now." I'm sure that was supposed to reassure me, but the words cut straight through my heart.

Lillian had fought the move to Vienna for all she was worth. She could find nothing right about the city, and she was furious at me for disrupting—she would say destroying—her life. Heaping isolation on top of unhappiness, I'd torn her from her best friend and confidant, her father. After six stormy months, it was time for her to go back to live with Mark, as we had agreed. I kept myself together as we packed, then went to the airport. But Charles held me as I cried inconsolably after the door to the plane closed.

Two months later I received a call that turned me inside out. In Denver, Lillian had taken an overdose of over-the-counter sleeping pills. After her stomach was pumped, she was admitted to a mental hospital. I left Teddy with Charles and took the next plane home. Mother came up from Dallas. Henry and Karma were at the hospital every day. After some time for observation, the psychiatrist confirmed the hunch of the previous therapist: manic-depressive illness, an often lethal mood disorder.

The doctor told us that her problem was an inherited brain chemistry that made her swing from one emotional extreme to another, hence "bipolar." After years of trying to understand Lillian's almost constant inner turmoil, I felt a tumble of emotions: yearning to spare her this ordeal; relief that we had a diagnosis; reassurance to have medication; guilt over whether I'd damaged my child; and profound gratitude that she was alive.

The psychiatrist explained that in children, depression often appears as irritability rather than sadness. Now her often miserable mood made sense. As Lillian got older, he said, she would probably show a manic side as well. And typically for people with this illness, mornings were tough, but she could stay up late into the night, like her grandmother. That was a dangerous pattern: missing sleep altogether could trigger a mood swing, and the doctors said that Lillian was high risk for suicide if she didn't take her medication, or even if she did, if symptoms "broke through." With anguish, I faced the fact I might not have the power to keep my daughter alive. Every day would be a gift.

From that point on, I lived life concurrently in two distinct spheres. More than ever, thoughts of my family were interwoven into my work. Each day I spent hours on transatlantic calls. Like all public figures, I had to tuck my grief into a deep compartment and keep going: presiding over a meeting, making a speech, managing staff. But in the car with Horst, between ministerial calls and radio tapings, I dropped my guard. In the quiet, unasked tears would stream down my cheeks. Dear Horst would say nothing—just look at me through his rearview mirror and then reach down and hand me back a box of tissues.

Being with Teddy was enormously important for me during these months. In my most worried hours, his smile crept onto my face before I knew it. I relished our evenings, snuggled up together in our pajamas, with mountains of pillows piled up around, as he practiced his reading, chatted to me about his day, or did arithmetic gymnastics in his head. But he missed his sister.

Weeks after her admittance, Lillian left the hospital—for good, we thought—to return to Mark's house. One afternoon I was in the midst of a painful chore, firing a member of my embassy team, when I was interrupted by a call from an undersecretary of state dealing with a terrorist situation. Excusing myself, I went down the hall to a secure phone, in a secluded booth. When I emerged, Susan was waiting, her forehead wrinkled into a worried look. "Not now," I said impatiently, as she tried to hand me a note.

"Stop. Read it."

My sensitive, creative, graceful daughter was on her way to the emergency room after another suicide attempt. Lillian, whose imagination was dazzling, had become fixated on heaven. She would take 240 over-the-counter painkillers, trying to ease a hurt beyond the reach of my love.

I walked back through the tall doors into my office, sat down, and tried to maintain my composure as I finished the termination session with my distraught employee. When he left I looked around at the flags, photographs, and memorabilia surrounding me: vestiges of power on every wall and shelf. Those symbols could not touch my vulnerability. I walked over to my desk and curled up in the space underneath, waiting there for the ache to subside.

For the next several months, Lillian recovered in Denver in a hospital and then a residential program. It was wrenching not to be at my daughter's side, caring for her. But when I told her that I was considering resigning as ambassador to attend to her full time, she rejected the idea out of hand. My daughter understood how much I'd always thrived on impossible challenges and a full-tilt schedule. As her therapist quipped, "Lillian, you may be mentally ill, but your mother's *crazy*."

Despite Lillian's saying that I should keep my position, I continued to feel torn. Through daily phone calls to her and the people caring for her, I tried to close the distance between us. Separation from Lillian was by far my heaviest worry, pulling at me in a way that nothing else could. But there were other strains too. Those years in Vienna yielded the most intense stress of my life. At times I felt consumed by the personal and professional demands, and I was barely able to stumble through the hours. Charles was often away. I was without my closest friends. And so I relished the replenishment I found in visits to the countryside.

Friendly political and religious leaders arranged lunches overlooking a glacial lake in Tyrol, or an evening in a milkmaid's alpine cottage, where we sang along with harmonicas, guitars, and impossibly long alphorns. They took me on a carriage ride through the vineyards of Burgenland, where laborers along the road handed up to us clusters of ripe grapes. Near the Hungarian border I was presented with barbed wire twisted into an "S" and an "H," a remnant of the Iron Curtain that had cut across the fields spread before us. My anticommunist father would have loved to be at my side, climbing up into a watchtower. A few years before there would have been armed border guards in those towers, to shoot escapees. That day, I spotted only cranes, herons, gulls, and starlings.

In the province of Styria, between university speeches and press interviews, I stopped in at a bilingual school serving a Croat community and sang with the children, a guitar in my lap as we sat together on the floor. The next day I visited a home for severely disabled people. The residents, I was told, had been rehearsing a dance performance —just for me. I didn't know what to expect as I looked in the room and saw a dozen people in their chairs, many slumped over. Someone pushed a cassette player button and the performers' feet started shuffling to the music, ever so slightly, between the legs of their chairs. With a secret rhythm all their own, they added an occasional wave of the hand or nod of the head. We clapped appreciatively; it felt good to be on the clapping end for a change. As I said goodbye, I realized that I felt more comfortable with those dancers than I did at a diplomatic ball.

As Horst sped us back to Vienna, I put aside my stack of papers. Looking out my window at the pastoral countryside, I felt indulgent to take a minute and calmly cry. It wasn't pity. I was simply grateful for a connection that didn't involve status or public persona, a connection that reached below the cerebral, into a quieter chamber.

One other province, Salzburg, was already well known to Americans from *The Sound of Music*. It was a beautiful three-hour drive from our residence, and we went often for cultural events, although the Salzburg Festival no longer featured the likes of the Von Trapp family. Single tickets sold for several hundred dollars as throngs of wealthy Germans filled hotels and restaurants. Offstage there was political import to my visits. When for a decade after the Second World War Austria had four occupying powers, Salzburg was the hub of the American section. As the fiftieth anniversary of the war's end approached, I heard stories from elderly townspeople who had prayed that American forces would reach them first from the west, before the Russians coming from the east.

Austrians were conflicted about their role in the war, to say the least. They were victims of a harsh German occupation, but as the Nazi hunter Simon Wiesenthal pointed out, a disproportionate number of Austrians were among the most brutal guards in the concentration camps. Famous photographs show Salzburgers waving enthusiastically as German troops entered their town. But Hitler's bloodless invasion of Austria occurred just before a local referendum on German-Austrian unification, which polls said he would lose. Photographs also show an enthusiastic welcome to the Americans seven years later.

Such psychological and historical complexities and contradictions were always on my mind as I represented the United States in anniversaries of victories, defeats, liberation, or occupation—depending on one's point of view. The walls of Catholic churches had marble slabs engraved with the names of the war dead, a dozen with the same last name in one small village.

Should I expect townspeople to look back with appreciation on American forces, whose bombs inflicted such damage on their families and communities? I was thankful that their attitude was more strongly colored by the postwar years, when the United States, by all accounts, did a magnificent job of reaching out to Austrians through the Marshall Plan, helping them rebuild from the ashes. In Salzburg, where horse-drawn carriages clopped along cobblestone streets, memories were long. During every visit strangers stopped me to express, with great emotion, their gratitude for American help after the war.

Although warmed by their thanks, my mind was on another war, one in which the United States wasn't intervening. At St. Martin's, a quiet hamlet in the hills overlooking a brook-fed valley, I was invited to the country home of a saintly man who made deliveries into the Balkans for Catholic charities. While we sat in the little house on log furniture rough-carved with faces, a local choir gathered outside, dressed in traditional lederhosen and dirndls. The group sang one song after another, allowing my spunky protocol assistant and me to join in. An accordion eventually appeared, and we danced a polka on the lawn.

It was a sunny, happy scene, the mood broken only when our host, over homemade cheese, thick smoked bacon, and fresh dark bread, described the hardship he'd recently witnessed in Sarajevo. He had a refugee's carving for me. A simple woman holding her child and a handkerchief with their few possessions. Now, strangely, the carving would belong to a woman with overabundant belongings.

Pamela Harriman was my mirror as well as my mentor. I often saw in her what I was and what I could be. Since meeting the grande dame of the Democratic Party in her Georgetown home, I realized what a treasure she was to the administration. Career diplomats could claim great skills in analysis and writing. Many were able negotiators. But few approached Ambassador Harriman's ability to make mush of hostile people in high places. Technocrats were trained to make no mistakes, and for career Foreign Service officers risk taking was discouraged. But risk was basic to Pamela's nature. Her ability to lean into another's space and create intimate relationships translated into skills that made her a diplomatic star.

I remember one meeting in Europe with other ambassadors. I entered the nearly empty room and sat down in the front row. Then, concerned about appearing too eager, I self-consciously moved to the second. I was relieved when Pamela came in and sat next to me, as if she'd validated my choice. During the meeting she protested the proposed closing of our consulate in Lyon, rattling off statistics about American business needs. She seemed so self-assured—in contrast to me.

In the car, riding back and forth to the meeting, she spread before me a historical feast with accounts not only dramatic but gutsy. I loved her description of life in a bomb shelter with Winston Churchill, her former father-in-law. "I got along with him much better than with his son," she added matter-of-factly.

Though she turned down my idea that we American women ambassadors in Europe might combine forces in some way (women helping women wasn't on her radar screen), I wanted to hear more stories, so I suggested that we take a walk. I wore running shoes. She wore heels. But she had no trouble keeping up.

I was still finding my balance in Vienna when Richard Holbrooke, now ambassador to Germany, invited me to join Pamela for a visit to Bonn. I found myself unexpectedly sitting with them in front of mikes at a press conference about European-American trade. Dick and Pamela opened with talking points prepared by their staffs. I winged it, introducing myself as "the junior partner of Holbrooke, Harriman, and Hunt," hoping that my commerce ad-lib wouldn't come across as diplo-babble.

That evening, Ambassador Holbrooke and I sat across from Pamela at dinner. Dick warmly toasted the guest of honor, whom he'd known since he was in his twenties and working for her husband, "the Governor." I noted how what Holbrooke achieved with muscle, Harriman accomplished with grace. But often the masculine version was admired, the feminine version devalued. A book was coming out describing Pamela's past romances, including her multiyear relationship with Governor Averell Harriman of New York before they married. Ambassador Harriman, in her early seventies (four years younger than my mother), was worried about what President Clinton would think of his emissary, now derided as the courtesan of the century. Granted, she'd used every arrow in her quiver. But in Pamela I saw an archetypal woman—at the same time nurturing and narcissistic, cerebral and seductive, industrious and enticing. Mixing talents and tactics, we women can slather on a lilt and a laugh, whether we want to be taken care of or achieve positions of responsibility. Perhaps womanly wiles are not a betrayal of feminist ideals; maybe girlish charm is the human species' variation of a man's puffing out his chest and raising his voice.

That thought reappeared when I stayed with Pamela in Paris. One day I went up to her third-floor apartment. She was wearing a pantsuit as we curled up in elegant chairs, our conversation moving between Beltway headlines and comparisons of our new lives. An American publisher was arriving soon to see her. "I should put on a skirt," she sighed. "There's a man coming."

Our next time together was on my turf. After long discussions on European politics, we posed like schoolgirls in the grand doorway of our embassy. But when I tried to take Pamela's picture from a lower step so as to include the embassy seal above her head, she stopped me: "It's not becoming to have the camera below." So that's how it is, I thought, weighing the tradeoff between embassy seal and flattering face.

Back at my residence, we were two women thirty years apart but connected at an intuitive level. As I sat with Pamela on her bed she began to weep, and I realized that despite all the people in her life, she was lonely. She told me about the lawsuit being brought by her husband's heirs, who accused her and other trustees of irresponsible investments. Those legal proceedings had cast a shadow over what could have been the triumphant years of her life.

I understood. I'd had few if any businesswomen as role models; like Pamela, my mother had been excluded from financial discussions. Dozens of times I'd agreed to "just sign here" at Hunt Oil Company, before I had the chutzpah to hire my own counsel. True, investments made with my money had been successful, but what documents might some day surface, confirming my consent in matters I'd never examined? I kept those questions to myself as I massaged Pamela's shoulders.

"I wasn't taught to think for myself," she was saying. "What did I know? I just did what I was told. Averell set it all up and said the other trustees would take care of everything." She paused and looked at me, her voice pleading for understanding: "I wasn't raised like you."

If only Pamela had known what it took to gain some say over my business affairs. But having the gumption to question authority was a progressive lesson. I continued to learn in Vienna not to believe everything I was told—including by "our side." For example, at State Department briefings before coming to Austria I'd been repeatedly assured that the most intense political issue—which had wracked relations between Austria and the United States for six years before my arrival—was over. Not even close.

As UN secretary-general from 1972 to 1981, Kurt Waldheim was one of the most successful public figures Austria had produced since the humiliating dissolution of the Hapsburg Empire fifty-three years earlier. After the high-profile UN position, as Waldheim was running for president of his country in 1986, his "brown past" was discovered. A story in the *New York Post* bearing a three-inch headline denounced him as a "Nazi Butcher." As the piece circulated around Austria, many Austrians perceived it as provocation by the American superpower and interference in their domestic affairs. They resented what they considered distortions by outsiders who accused Waldheim of war crimes, as opposed to being a soldier carrying out normal tasks of war. His role as a young lieutenant, most of his countrymen insisted, was no deeper than that of men across Europe who weren't singled out.

Rather than being hurt by the controversy, Waldheim came from behind to win the presidency. But Austrians found themselves in an international quagmire. In 1978 the U.S. Congress had barred entry into the United States to anyone who had "assisted or otherwise participated in persecution." Even if he was far down the chain of command, Kurt Waldheim had been part of an operation that led to the deportation of Balkan people to Nazi concentration camps.

From 1986 to 1992 the only European country that would receive the president of Austria was the Vatican. As people occupying a meager remnant of a great empire, most Austrians felt that this was an unwarranted international slap, especially since Europe was riddled with Holocaust perpetrators and collaborators. For many Austrians of conscience, it wasn't what Waldheim did during the war that marked him. It was his *Unfähigkeit zu trauern*, his inability to mourn, that was unforgivable. Like most Austrians of his generation, especially men,

Waldheim showed little emotion. A repentant spirit could have made him a leader among Austrians coming to grips with their country's Nazi past. But Waldheim, ever the consummate public official, provided no cathartic moment. Instead he argued that apologies were appropriate if you stepped on someone's foot, but not for genocide. The logic didn't really hold; but more important was that he turned to logic at all. Waldheim failed to offer a convincing, heartfelt statement about living with a tortured conscience after having been part of a death machine.

In 1994 the former secretary-general hoped to attend the fiftieth anniversary of the founding of the United Nations. I was sure he would be turned away at passport control, even though that would be a violation of the arrangement between the United Nations and the United States, its host government. To avoid a stand-off, I met with the foreign minister and chancellor separately, stressing that Waldheim wouldn't be issued a visa. Overturning a longtime prohibition, I met too with Waldheim, who protested for the thousandth time that he was being unfairly treated. Whatever the case, I said, he wouldn't be at the UN. But Waldheim insisted that he was "hoping for a miracle." "Don't hope," I countered. His wife, Sissy, began to cry.

A few days later the UN acted. Word hit the streets that the former secretary-general would not be invited. A TV interviewer tried repeatedly to get the elderly statesman to rail against the United States, as everyone expected, but he refused to do so. I regarded that as one of my quieter diplomatic victories.

The impact of the Waldheim affair reached far beyond him as a person. The decade-old strain had precluded a meeting between a U.S. president and an Austrian head of government or head of state. (The United States is one of the few countries where one person holds both positions.) My success as an ambassador, at least in the eyes of the Austrian political leadership, rested on my finesse in getting a meeting with President Clinton for their president and their chancellor. Arranging such meetings was much easier for diplomats who were political appointees, because we had White House connections that career officers could only dream of. In 1994 I began writing direct letters to the president, which was much more effective than going through labyrinthine State Department channels.

The natural person for Clinton to meet with would have been President Klestil, since he now had replaced Waldheim. But Klestil's wife had just left him, protesting a romantic relationship he was having with a staff member. Given rumors about President Clinton's personal life, we decided that it wasn't the best time for the two of them to get together. We could all draw the cartoons. I focused instead on arranging a meeting with Chancellor Vranitzky, whom President Clinton had liked when they met years before at a gathering for up-and-coming political leaders.

We planned Washington meetings with the Federal Reserve chairman, treasury secretary, Speaker of the House, and others, culminating with the Oval Office. In Vienna, as we finished going over the itinerary, I asked the chancellor if I should come on the plane with him. He looked puzzled at my naïveté, and then explained that no, I should be at the gate to greet him. (I didn't tell him that I'd managed to do both during President Clinton's visit to Denver by rushing down the back steps of Air Force One and then slipping into the welcoming group on the tarmac.)

On April 20, 1994, while the chancellor was speaking at the National Press Club, I was meeting with National Security Council staff, who told me that the president had been dissuaded by the Pentagon from taking a strong stand on Bosnia. It was almost time for the chancellor's meeting with the president. Although I was already at the White House, I jumped in a cab in time to intercept Vranitzky as he walked out of his speech. Although he had indicated no particular passion for the affairs of Bosnia, I figured that he owed me for this trip, so I made one request: stress to the president that the United States must lead in stopping the conflict in Bosnia.

A few minutes later I stood with our dapper secretary of state, Warren Christopher, the national security advisor, Tony Lake, and several other officials who stood very tall and straight in front of the president's Oval Office desk as the chancellor waited to be shown in. President Clinton's tie, covered with drawings of children's faces in bold primary colors, matched the red and yellow tulips waving at us through the window. Vice President Gore entered as we were speaking, put his arm around my waist, and kissed me hello. I briefed the president on Vranitzky's recent speech at Hebrew University in Israel, in which he'd talked about Austria's "collective responsibility" for the Second World War. As Clinton listened, he flipped through index cards prepared by his National Security Council staff. "What about Waldheim?" he asked, looking up from his reading glasses.

"He won't come up," I said, as if I knew. "But do mention Syrian President Assad. Vranitzky has an entrée there."

The chancellor and his entourage were escorted in and took their seats. I quietly asked Secretary Christopher where I should sit.

"They'll pull up some chairs behind," he said, indicating that I wasn't in the inner circle. But President Clinton motioned for me to sit on his left on the striped sofa, next to the secretary. I hesitated.

"Where should I sit?" I whispered to Christopher again, not wanting to make a mistake.

"The *Man* said for you to sit here," he answered. Perhaps I imagined his irritation. For comic relief, a giant horsefly buzzed around the head of the secretary. Neither he nor the fly seemed to mind.

The press was ushered in for the frenetic photo op. A network White House correspondent, whom I'd met socially, called out, "Hi, Swanee!" I savored her familiarity in that formal setting. Beyond the flashing cameras, I noticed a bronze Remington cowboy balanced precariously on his rearing horse. He seemed more real than some of the people in the room. We were a semicircle of high-level officials and foreign policy experts recording every jot and tittle of the conversation of two large men in suits, posing in uncomfortable chairs covered with gold silk, not knowing what to do with their legs. How much more effective the meeting could have been with beer, blue jeans, and a soft, roomy couch.

Vranitzky's first words were to note that this was Hitler's birthday. A bizarre beginning, I thought, until he made the connection to thank the United States for intervening five decades earlier in "a European problem." Clinton responded with a comment about Bosnia, at which point the chancellor delivered the message I'd hoped for, stressing the importance of American leadership to unite the Europeans. Sympathetic to its Serb Orthodox cousins, Russia loomed as a huge presence; and Austria, now facing west, was still looking over her shoulder at the big bear.

The president asked about the new NATO program "Partnership for Peace," created after the collapse of the Warsaw pact and the USSR to allow the militaries of formerly communist countries to work with NATO and learn how militaries functioned in democratic countries.

The chancellor said that I'd talked with him about it; he left the door open for participation—a big step, given Austrian neutrality. The president closed by saying that he knew Vranitzky had a good relationship with Assad, which might be important for the future of Middle East peace. Leaders of two sovereign nations were delivering talking points that I had proposed to each. The thought seemed almost absurd.

It was almost time to go, and I sensed the conversation winding down. Not knowing how many rules of protocol I might be breaking, I spoke up, noting how helpful the Austrians had been in recent Balkan negotiations in Vienna. President Clinton nodded and made a remark to that effect. That contribution from me, generally unremarkable in substance, was nonetheless a conscious act. As the only woman among a dozen men I was determined not to sit through a meeting without opening my mouth like a bump on a log. Not even in the Oval Office.

As I left, the president gave me a kiss on the cheek. This meeting—a mammoth effort to arrange—represented one twenty-fifth of one day in his presidency. At the same time, it was a milestone in Austrian-American relations, recovering from the strain of Waldheim.

The triangle of Vienna, Washington, and Dallas overlay an ugly part of my past. I couldn't right the wrong of my father's anti-Semitism, but through a score of relationships and actions, I could try in a small way to balance his prejudice.

Dad was a product of rural turn-of-the-century America, without formal education, inheriting the bias of his context. His feelings about individual Jews weren't unusually virulent; he might well have appreciated Charles as a person, as Mother did. But in a broad sweep, he, like other ardent right-wingers, linked Jewish America with his nemesis, the communists.

I'm not sure if he realized that the affluent Hockaday School had a disproportionate number of Jews compared to the population of Dallas. But if he'd known that Susie Strauss, daughter of Robert Strauss, was my best friend in fourth grade, he would have been rigidly opposed, and there might well have been hell to pay. As it was, that illicit friendship joined a very long list of topics not to be discussed. My relationship with my father was so empty that I just lumped this prejudice in with other distasteful aspects of his eccentricity.

Mother didn't share my father's anti-Semitism. Long after Dad's death, she recalled a sweet memory: how she'd received a call from Susie's father, delivered in his thick, unhurried drawl: "Missus Hunt, this is Bob Strauss. I hear Mr. Hunt's away. You may know that Dad's Day is comin' up at Hockaday, and I'll be there with Susie. I was wonderin' if you'd like me to step in with Swanee." Mom gratefully agreed, and for that one day, my dad was Jewish.

I'd not known that story until I told Mother I'd run into Mr. Strauss in Washington. I smiled when it dawned on me then that he was living out Jesus's injunction to love our enemies, even those who persecute us. My work in the Balkans had made me think long and hard about how, if "the enemy" is understood as a human being on the opposing side rather than an incarnation of evil, reconciliation is possible. Humanizing the enemy, we preserve not only the dignity of the other but also ourselves.

Earthy, outrageous Bob Strauss epitomized that dignity. By the mid-1990s he was up to his thick eyebrows in trade deals with Russia. I knew he'd be pleased to see that I'd taken his advice and gone to Vienna, and that as ambassador I too was trying to support the transition of Eastern Europe from communism to democracy. So I was delighted to find myself seated next to him at a private dinner hosted by friends in Washington in honor of Chancellor Vranitzky's receiving the Fulbright Prize for International Understanding. Around the table were some ten movers and shakers, including the chair of the Joint Chiefs of Staff, John Shalikashvili, a key decision maker regarding Bosnia. I was briefed, poised, and dressed for my diplomatic best.

After the usual Beltway dinner conversation about the breaking news of the day, I stood and held up my wine glass. Proposing a toast to two inspiring great men, I referred to Vranitzky's historic address to the Israeli Knesset, in which he acknowledged and apologized for Austrian complicity in the Nazi movement. "Hear, hear," the other guests chimed in.

Then I turned to Strauss, on my left, and put my hand on his shoulder. I said we'd known each other in the sixties. He'd spent the intervening years becoming one of Washington's key political figures. I'd spent the intervening years growing up. I recounted how I'd called him out of the blue, seeking advice about my political appointment, and how he'd led me up to the edge of the Iron Curtain and encouraged me to look across. But I ended with Mother's story of Mr. Strauss's kindness to a young girl on Dad's Day. The other guests joined me, toasting a generous soul.

No way could Bob let me have the final word. In his Texas-sized voice, he boomed, "Well, I have something to say, Mr. Chancellor." He chewed his words like warm taffy. "Thinking back on when I first knew little Swanee, I'm probably the only one around this table who ever said to Her Excellency, 'Pull your skirt down, Honey; I can see your panties.'"

Losing Touch

Charles was asked to lead a ballet performance at the Vienna State Opera, by any account a world-class cultural venue. Such an engagement represented the pinnacle of a select few conductors' careers. This was the podium of Richard Strauss, Gustav Mahler, and Leonard Bernstein. Nureyev danced there, Plácido sang there. And now Charles would conduct there.

I've never seen my husband so nervous. A colleague who'd performed there frequently told him about the "little pink pills" he always took, but my husband didn't want to experiment. Instead he relied on deep breaths and remembered his friend's advice: "The main thing is to stay out of the orchestra's way." The players were so confident that many performances were staged without rehearsal. Charles was able to negotiate having *one*, but certainly not several, which was customary with any other orchestra.

At last the evening came: Schumann's Symphony no. 2, with choreography. From my perch in a box, I took pictures into the pit without a flash, my camera hidden under a shawl and resting on the red velvet rail (a trick I would use later in the Taliban's Afghanistan, driving through Kabul).

I, in turn, imagined myself captured by Degas, painting his impression of an audience in the loges; what nobility, I wondered, had peered down on performers past. I walked down the wide staircase to mingle with the crowd. They were pleased.

Charles was relieved. Still, he couldn't fall asleep until after 2 a.m. By sunrise he was out of the house, traveling twenty-four hours via

Frankfurt to Duschanbe, Tajikistan, a neglected region of the former Soviet Union now plagued by a low-intensity civil war.

Duschanbe was so poor that there were no postcards. An eternal flame honoring victims of the Second World War had long since burned out. The economy had dropped by half since the implosion of the Soviet Union five years earlier. Calendars on the walls were long outdated. Building cranes had rusted in place at construction sites.

It was March, and the rehearsal room was frigid. Some of the players wore coats and even gloves. Charles conducted in his bulky ski parka as they practiced Gershwin's *Rhapsody in Blue*. Normally, of course, the conductor would be compensated, and handsomely. But when he asked, Charles learned that the players were paid only five dollars a performance—and even at that rate hadn't been remunerated in months. He refused to accept a fee, and at the end of the concert handed out a five-dollar bill to each musician, from his own wallet. Much more than the money, of course, they appreciated the gesture. "Maestro," one said to him, "If you'll come back next year, I'll stay in the orchestra."

I asked Charles, when he returned and I pulled the story out of him, "Which concert meant more to you—venerable Vienna or down-on-its-luck Duschanbe?"

He thought a moment. "Well, I was only a blip on the Vienna screen, but in Duschanbe, I made a difference."

The stretch from Vienna to Duschanbe was no greater than the stretch from Vienna to Dallas. We constantly faced an impossible integration of our disparate worlds. Not that my family didn't try. I appreciated it greatly when Helen, June, and Ray came by Vienna as part of their other travels. It gave them some understanding of this hugely formative experience for their younger sister.

But Mother came each year for a week. That meant a lot to me. As the child who'd wandered farthest from home, I was anxious for my mother's validation and wanted her to see inside my new life. And she won the hearts of my colleagues—a match for well-mannered Austrians with her thick southern charm.

For one visit, June came along. It took considerable effort for my sister to make the trip, given her responsibilities with her radio broadcast ministry. Since its inception in 1986, "Hope for the Heart" had won important awards from the National Religious Broadcasters and spread to hundreds of stations. It was, as self-described, "a worldwide ministry with a two-fold mission: providing Bible-based counsel to renew minds, heal hearts and bring hope to the hurting, while empowering Christians to disciple others." Within that sphere, June was a star.

After a day of discovering Vienna, June set up her equipment in our guest quarters to tape her program. My sister had never married, and she poured attention onto my children, who loved being with her. Sitting in the makeshift studio, Teddy, seven, was listening excitedly through Aunt June's oversized headphones. Suddenly one of our many family pets, a Great Pyrenees, lumbered into the room, ignoring Mother, as she tugged at the huge dog's harness.

"And what would your mother do if your room wasn't tidy?" June was asking a caller, as our own mother tried to get her giant granddog to sit at her feet.

"Isabella. Down, Isabella. Down," Mom whispered. But Isabella knew she outweighed the other end of the leash and pretended to be deaf.

"So your mother was majoring on the minors," June was concluding to her caller. This was family at its best—chaos, cute, and comfort, rolled into one.

The next evening, Mom sat in the front row as I delivered a speech in German on the relationship of Clinton's economic plan to the European Monetary Union. Later, around the dining-room table, she was in rare form, throwing her head back, laughing, as Teddy danced through the room, singing and twirling, and having a rip-roaring good time as a magician's assistant to Aunt June. Bedtime was approaching, so to calm my rambunctious son I asked him to rattle off some German to Granny Ruth. But he just roared louder as Mom tried to make up a logical response to a language she didn't know. "Teddy, you know, Granny Ruth is *so proud* of you. I just can't believe it."

"OK, G.R.," I said. "I'm going to tape you here at the dinner table." I positioned the camera.

Mom turned to June and Teddy, as if she hadn't heard me. "*Children, Children,*" she began with her usual call to attention. "I wish you had been with me today. This is honest to goodness. It's not that I'm prejudiced. It's just a fact." Her hands moved in graceful, small sweeps as she described the scene: "Swanee walked up on stage after a *wonderful* introduction." She paused. "Although it was in German, of course, so

I couldn't understand it," she giggled. "Then Swanee started. She was speaking *German*. And she was smooth as velvet, for forty-five minutes. And she was talkin' all the time. She wasn't just playin' around. And every now and then I looked back over my shoulder. *Every eye* was centered on her. And most of the audience was *men*! I was as proud as a peacock."

"Cut! OK," I said. "One more time. Take six."

Over the next several days, Mom watched as I opened a cultural exhibit by an American painter and listened as I interpreted the current mood of the U.S. Congress to a political gathering. "You're brilliant! Brilliant!" she gushed. She spent time in my office, where pollsters, military officers, business owners, and environmental activists filed through in half-hour intervals. "You don't miss a trick!" she applauded. She stood beside me stoically as I greeted hundreds of guests to discuss the political morass in Ukraine or celebrate a famous conductor. She saw me huddle with embassy staff about an impending trade war and the Slovak political crisis, and waited patiently when I was called to the telephone at home to confer with Washington about a global mafia threat.

"Angel, I'm so proud of you—I mean '*grateful*,'" she declared. Then she added, *sotto voce*, "I don't like the word 'proud,'" caught between a mother's delight and a heart humble before God.

The day she was to leave, she pronounced, in her singsong cadence, "If ah don't go ah can't come back!" As we approached the airport, Mom and I were in the back seat of the car. I thanked her for coming. With stars in her eyes, she said she "wouldn't have missed it for all the tea in China." Then she tilted her head toward mine and added, a bit apologetically, "But tell me, Honey, exactly what do you do?"

Mom was the most effusively kind and caring person I've ever met. I can say with full appreciation that I never doubted my mother's love, and I don't want to take away from such charmed moments. But—and I think this is a common experience—I often felt unknown by her. She, like anyone, could love only what she could understand. Sometimes, instead of the comfort of being accepted for who I really was, I had the sense that to her I was a precious memory or a fantasized ideal.

Still, no love is perfect. Old relationships are tainted by lesser moments and misunderstandings; but new relationships lack the scratching and digging of time, and thus the depth and complexity. Whatever our limitations, I never doubted that my relationship with my mother had plenty of complexity.

Even in the simplest sense, staying connected to folks back home was also a huge challenge, logistically and emotionally. When we returned for a stateside visit, Mom hosted a reception for Charles and me at Mt. Vernon. At her request, we stood in a reception line as scores of friends from my past and her present filed by. They hugged us warmly and wished us well. Hardly anyone had a clue about what an ambassador did, or about political developments in Europe, for that matter.

Some of Mother's friends generously tried to ask questions, like "Do you two speak Austrian?" I found myself pulling back, not trying to bridge the gulf between us; with so little shared understanding, it was hard to launch into a discussion of enlarging the changing alliances inside Europe or the failure of the National Security Council to galvanize a multilateral response to the Balkan crisis. Even at family reunions, I was amazed at how Charles and I were rarely asked about our new world. I hated feeling as if I was losing my roots. But even more, I regretted the arrogance that was seeping in. I feared I was drifting into a sphere of know-it-alls, losing touch with everyday Americans.

I couldn't blame them. After all, American media carried very few stories from our part of the world. From Vienna, I tried to maintain a tie back home by writing a monthly column, "Ambassador's Journal," for the *Rocky Mountain News* in Denver and sending the articles to our closest friends. But press clippings couldn't take the place of shared experience.

Politisch/Persönlich

Despite the limitations, I had become even more involved with "public diplomacy," the State Department's term for patriotic media forays. After my success with the Denver paper, I decided to go for another bone. One of my predecessors, Henry Grunwald, had headed *Time* magazine, so I had a reason to gather media pros for dinner when he visited.

"I'm sitting between an angel and a devil!" I exclaimed undiplomatically to the saintly Catholic cardinal and the crusty publisher of the daily *Neue Kronen Zeitung*.

That newspaper reached two million people in a population just short of eight million, making it the most widely read paper per capita of any in Europe. But it was a tabloid, with stories short and sensational. As a staunch defender of Waldheim, "the *Krone*" had developed a markedly anti-American tilt. According to my public affairs shop, even American sports victories lost to editorial bias. I particularly detested how topless women flaunted their wares daily in the vicinity of page four.

In our dinner conversation, I mentioned that I was writing a monthly column in Colorado, then allowed a pregnant pause. A week later I was meeting with the chief editor, who asked me for a weekly two-hundred-word column. The title would be "Politisch/Persönlich." I laid out two conditions: Not a word could be deleted or changed without my express permission, and my column would not run on the same page or opposite any bare-breasted women. I didn't want my readers distracted.

Staking my new space won praise and raised eyebrows. I had traded off some respectability for voice. The foreign minister, president, and cardinal declared the column a coup and gave their unequivocal approval. My public affairs officer, a kind but make-no-waves fellow, was opposed, preferring to keep the paper at arms' length and hope for the best. Back in Washington, the State Department was divided about my assertive move; the usual media mode there was damage control.

The Austrian Jewish community was likewise mixed. Some expressed relief that there was a different voice coming through such a powerful megaphone. But I was concerned by the opinions of several thoughtful Jewish friends who commented that the *Krone* was "a bad address," given its support for Waldheim. I decided to meet the issue head on. In an early column, I reported that I'd received criticism from people whom I greatly respected, and then laid out three reasons why I would continue to write for the paper. First, I could reach a huge number of people with my message. Second, I'd been criticized in this very paper and thought that I deserved equal time. And third, there were things about the paper that I agreed with, was neutral toward, or found abhorrent. This would give me a chance to express my opinion. To his credit, the editor ran the piece without changing a comma. I found out only months later that the publisher was furious.

I wrote about a broad range of topics—from the chemical weapons treaty to how we raise girls. As months rolled by and I became a regular feature to Austrians munching their morning *Kaffe und Semmel*, cab drivers began to call me by name, and I received sweet postcards from couples in alpine villages, asking me to come visit. Still, some controversy lingered, especially with outsiders who didn't understand the diplomatic importance of the column.

A rabbi affiliated with the American Jewish Committee in New York was in Vienna on Good Friday. He read the column announcing that my *Witness Cantata* would be performed at the historic church of the Hofburg Palace. The date was also the anniversary of the accidental American bombing of the Vienna State Opera, where civilians had gathered for protection from air attacks by the Allies. In the first paragraph of the article, I made reference to the suffering of Austrians during the war. In a later paragraph I described the cantata as dealing with the suffering of Christ, using texts by the writers Akhmatova, Roethke, and Wiesel, among others.

The rabbi was incensed. He wrote to the State Department that I'd compared the suffering of Austrians to the Holocaust. I had not. Genocide is clearly a different magnitude of evil from accidental civilian casualties. But when the State Department did not respond, the rabbi sent the same letter to a columnist at the *Washington Post*, who published the accusation.

I decided not to engage but to let the storm blow over. Then *Newsweek* (owned by the *Post*) picked up the story. Elie Wiesel, whom I regarded as a personal hero, sent me the magazine piece with a simple handwritten note: "Dear Ambassador, did you really do this?" I sat with his fax in front of me and put my elbows on my desk and my face in my hands, wondering how I'd stumbled into this pool of quicksand.

The story had now bounced to Denver and was spreading. As always, I turned to Charles for counsel. He advised me at that point to meet fire with fire. So I went through my database and selected about a hundred mostly Jewish opinion shapers (from Justice Ruth Bader Ginsburg to the Wall Street investor Ace Greenberg) and sent each a detailed description of what had actually occurred. The presses stopped.

Beneath the surface, however, the story simmered. Without meaning to, I'd stirred the pot. On my mailing list was a new acquaintance, the producer of "Good Morning America." He sniffed a story and went after it. I'd already been booked to say a few words for the show's broadcast from the Belvedere Palace in Vienna. Cameras were set up, makeup applied, microphones attached. I was wearing big Texas hair and a shocking pink suit, ready to face an audience of twenty million. As we walked onto the set, the local producer confided that instead of the innocuous questions about Austrian-American relations I'd been advised of, the anchor, Willow Bay, would ask about my comparing the Austrians' suffering to the Holocaust. Bait and switch.

"Recently, you caused a little bit of a controversy, at least in the press back in our country. . . . *Newsweek* reported that you had written a column for what they called a 'far-right daily' and suggested that you compared the suffering of Holocaust victims to the suffering of Austrians."

"I could never ever do such a thing. I don't believe it and would never do it. That was a gross misunderstanding. But what's interesting is the role of an ambassador in terms of reaching out to the people of Austria using public diplomacy by writing this column for the most-read newspaper throughout Austria, with a readership of 2.7 million." There. I'd turned the conversation.

But Willow would not be dissuaded. "According to *Newsweek*, this was a diplomatic nosedive, and yet you say it was a coup; I'm not sure I understand why."

"Well, there've been no ruffles in Austria. I have very close ties to the Jewish community here, and no one has been offended by what I said."

Three ironies enriched the situation. The first was a private conversation I had with Elie Wiesel ten years earlier, in which he said his life purpose was "to requite the messianic moment in every person I meet." Given a piece he had just written for *Time* magazine blasting American tolerance of Serbian atrocities, he and I were united in a "messianic moment," even while we were being pitched as adversaries. The second irony was that the *Newsweek* reporter's purported call to the embassy for a comment from me (no record of his attempt exists) was on the very day I was in the States receiving an award from the Anti-Defamation League, a watchdog group combating anti-Semitism. The third irony was that the cantata performance in ques-

tion was dedicated to, and attended by, my mentor Viktor Frankl—
famed chronicler of the Holocaust.

Never Again

Dr. Frankl was a sharp and witty year-shy-of-ninety when he and his
kindhearted wife accepted my invitation to lunch. After the bell rang
and the butler opened the heavy copper door, I stood at the top of our
stairs, a bit confused. The diminutive man walking toward me wasn't
at all the giant I'd expected.

My eminent guest had wispy white hair and wore large glasses with
thin metal rims, and his face sparkled with a cheery smile. I greeted
him and his wife, Elly, with a handshake, saying that as a college freshman I'd been moved by *Man's Search for Meaning*, recounting his three
years in the camps. His writing had shaped me, giving me courage to
shape my own life. Twenty-five years later, I told the illustrious author
and teacher, I still remembered his book.

"Do you remember it in your mind, or your heart?" he asked, touching his forehead and then his chest.

"In my heart."

"That's good," he nodded. The book, he told me, had been published in twenty-one languages, with over nine million copies sold.
Over ninety speaking tours in the United States had prepared him
for my American openness. In their town apartment crowded with
manuscripts and books, in their pleasant country place just outside of
town, or around my dinner table, the Frankls talked with me for hours
about their lives and mine, Bosnia, our families, the future of psychotherapy, and Viennese current affairs. I had a picture of Viktor above
my desk. He and Elly treated me like a daughter, with the warmth
that flows easiest when there's need. I loved them back. In addition,
I valued Viktor's counsel, and he was more than gracious with his
time.

On one visit, Henry and Karma came with me to the Frankls' apartment. In a corner was an oxygen tank. Our host was almost blind,
yet he seemed lively as he showed us around. I'd brought along my
friendly video camera, which Henry held. Viktor talked with us about
the paintings and drawings of himself hung against the pattern of

gold fleur-de-lis wallpaper. Nearby were two drawings by the Austrian artist Egon Schiele, which Viktor had purchased long ago for $10. We laughed to think what they would fetch today. Then we settled into the mustard gold chairs, to taste the *Apfelstrudel* that Elly had prepared. "Sometimes I'm so tired, because to be married to Viktor Frankl, it's not easy," Elly said. "He's bombarded. We receive twenty-four pieces of mail each day. I read to him five hours a day."

I took Elly's hand in mine as we sat on the sofa, wondering if I dared be the twenty-fifth request for her husband's attention. "Henry has become a youth counselor. Can you give him some words of wisdom?" I asked.

"Wisdom?" he laughed. "I'm not a wise old man, just a senile man!"

We laughed and chatted, until it was time to go. As we left, Dr. Frankl sketched a caricature of himself on the front page of his book, which he gave to Karma. I didn't want to leave without letting him know how important he was to me, but my words came out clumsily, "Charles's father is a famous psychologist in the U.S. Since my father-in-law isn't here, you can be my surrogate."

"And *you* are the *original*," he drolly replied, as he shook my hand goodbye.

In more serious conversations, we talked broadly about how the United States, as the lone superpower, was searching for meaning. For seventy years we Westerners had known exactly who the enemy was. Whether in Korea or Cuba, the Soviet Union or Vietnam, Nicaragua or Angola, the lines were clearly drawn and we knew which side we were on. Wars against communism—hot and cold—had been the focal point of not only our foreign but also our domestic policy, with a significant part of our industrial sector oriented against the threat. In the 1950s our entire education system had pushed math and science so that we could beat our enemy in the race to space, and our religious institutions had targeted "Godless communism." The fall of the Berlin Wall, heralded as a hopeful Jericho, was also a precursor to global unrest.

Dr. Frankl listened as I puzzled over my part in Clinton's reshaping of America's identity from communism's foe to humanity's friend. More than challenged, I felt anxious about whether I, so new to foreign policy making, could meet the historical moment.

"Who cares?" he finally asked, stopping me in my tracks. I studied his face, carved with age, hardship, and concern. Then I laughed, realizing that he was asking two questions: Why is it so important? and Whom in your past are you trying to please?

It was a liberating moment, but a heavy one. His questions pulled me back to the porch of Mt. Vernon, when I'd put my foot down, perhaps literally, and refused to serenade my father. That self-assurance had been difficult to maintain through adolescence. Then as a young adult, I'd vacillated widely between seeking to serve others and needing to be taken care of. Enough. Now, instead of trying to impress the vast unknown and unknowable, I needed to figure out who really cared, whom I wanted to have care, and whose caring I couldn't care about.

Over the next years, Viktor and Elly made time for my anguish: Should I resign in public protest over the lack of action by Washington to quench the raging Balkan conflagration? What did we learn from the Second World War, I asked my confidants, when we waited so long to oppose the persecution of Jews? How many suffered and perished while people like me sat at our big desks, shuffling papers? Would intervention in the Balkans lead us into a deadly quagmire like Vietnam?

Dr. Frankl's counsel helped me focus, as he warned that exacting lessons from history could become an obsession. In moral crises, he said, we look forward or backward but often fail to look within. He didn't accept my assertion that I needed an objective way to determine the right foreign policy. There's never a simple right policy, he insisted. In fact, sometimes the right choice is only 55 percent right. That's when choosing requires real courage, since we must act, even while staring at the 45 percent that's wrong.

That fundamental construct, a gift from a great existentialist, was one of the most important lessons of my life. I've carried it ever since like a precious jewel, tucked away in my mind.

I had friends in Germany and Austria who were of fighting age during the Second World War. Often I'd wondered how I would have met the pressures of the period: whether I would have acted heroically and lost my life, or focused on protecting my family and myself. I tried to hold these thoughts as I encountered a history of evil that defied comprehension. Some postulated that the Germans and Austrians were uniquely capable of virulent anti-Semitism. Yet Frankl, who had not only thought about but also lived through atrocities, had a different view. Asked why he'd stayed in Austria after what the Viennese had done, he answered, "Which Viennese do you mean? The woman living next door who risked her life hiding Jews? The man down the street who brought us part of his rations?"

Viktor came to dinner on May 4, 1995, when I hosted another spry octogenarian, Richard Seibel. A front-line fighter, he commanded troops whose tanks had been rolling across the hills of central Austria when he discovered seven hundred corpses among eighteen thousand emaciated prisoners in the concentration camp of Mauthausen. He was totally unprepared for what faced him. In spite of his heroic efforts to set up an instant city to manage the crisis, another thirteen hundred died. "People treat me as if I'm a hero," he said, matter-of-factly, "but I was only doing my job."

One of the prisoners at Mauthausen was a young architect named Simon, who had been working in Prague when Hitler invaded. Weighing only a hundred pounds and badly injured from a beating, he remembered being carried into the room to meet his liberator.

Soon after his rescue, the architect realized the importance of recording the hell in which so many had perished. He and helpers sent out 200,000 questionnaires to former prisoners. Within three months they had thousands of documents bearing witness to crimes that otherwise might have been forgotten. That was the beginning of Simon Wiesenthal's world-renowned work tracking Nazi perpetrators.

The morning after our dinner, Horst drove me down the highway from Vienna toward Salzburg, past peaceful, onion-domed churches. After we turned onto a small country road, he mounted two American flags on the hood of the car. They flapped frenetically along the final kilometers to Mauthausen. Over 120,000 people—mostly Hungarian Jews, gypsies, handicapped Austrians, homosexuals, and political dissidents—perished there. As I peered over a steep ledge into the quarry where they were literally worked to death, I imagined them surrounding me.

The time came for us diplomats to line up alphabetically to lay wreaths in memory of the dead. United States: *Vereinigten Staaten*. I was in the back of the line. For an hour we inched forward toward the memorial plaza, through a throng of thirty thousand survivors and families of the living and dead who had come from all over the world to remember. Although I was flanked by a marine honor guard, people broke through the side restraints to touch me. "Thank you, America." "*Merci, États-Unis.*" "*Dankeschön.*" "*Grazie.*" And, of course, "*Shalom.*" When I reached the center and bent over to lay the wreath, applause and cheering built in a dramatic crescendo.

Colonel Seibel took the microphone to describe the horror he had stumbled across. Wiesenthal sat beside me in a crowded row. Tensions were high and a skirmish ensued in front, as a group of Americans claimed that they, not the colonel, had first discovered the camp. I hastily left my seat just behind the chancellor, and went up to the protesters, put my arms around their shoulders, and escorted them out. After I returned to my place, I heard behind me another elderly camp survivor, extremely upset that communist youth were using the occasion to demonstrate. Thinking of my pastoral care training, I felt I could calm him, so I stepped up on the bench and moved back to sit beside him, speaking softly to his agitation.

I was steeped in stories that sun-bathed day—stories of inhumanity, of courage, of pain, of kindness. But there was a story no one retold. That was the story of policy makers who coexisted with the evil, unable or unwilling to end the horror, who had let Hitler light a torch of twisted sadism that set flame to a whole culture. I pictured them at big mahogany desks, running their offices, as panic crept across the land. And I wondered, with contempt, how could they carry on as if nothing were happening, as the very structure of European society imploded. We, on the other hand, would never forget. Never again. Never again. The words were intoned throughout the day.

Back in Vienna, on *my* big mahogany desk, was a pile of urgent messages from the field, with titles that could have been written fifty years earlier. They warned of encroaching tanks surrounding tens of thousands of refugees, who huddled together for protection promised by lightly armed UN troops assigned to Bosnian towns like Zepa, Gorazde, and Srebrenica.

On July 12, 1995, I wrote in my journal,

the overrun of Srebrenica, the first of the eastern enclaves to fall. The UN has played out this tragic script line by line . . . I have never taken so little pleasure in saying 'I told you so.' Seeing this travesty evolve up close has been the most dramatic civics lesson I may ever have. The scenes from the fall of Srebrenica are horrible—the males have been separated from the women and children and are being screened by their Serb captors as 'possible war criminals.' That means, in plain language, execution. The refugees are being herded along the road like cattle, the infirm in wheelbarrows. Children are being born by the side of the road.

I received reports through State Department channels, confirmed later by eyewitnesses, intelligence sources, and the gruesome excavation of mass graves, that up to ten thousand unarmed boys and men were slaughtered in the few days that followed. The Bosnian Serb soldiers expelled thirty thousand women, children, and elderly from Srebrenica, by bus or on foot. They ended up fifty miles northeast in Tuzla, which remained under control of the Bosnian government. The refugees spent weeks crammed into tents on the tarmac of the airfield, waiting for their boys and men, who would never appear.

One evening during our family dinner, the butler came in to say that Queen Noor was calling from Amman. Could I help her figure out how a Jordanian cargo plane might deliver medicines and blankets to Bosnia? I tracked down the phone numbers of the UN high commissioner for refugees, whom I connected to her palace so that the deliveries could be made.

I'll never forget the push in Her Majesty's voice as she insisted that she couldn't sit back and watch the refugees on CNN. "If we don't act, we are guilty too," she said. But the truth is I hadn't done everything that I could have. And so I was guilty too. And I had to live with that guilt.

Family Afloat

Morning and night, I thought about those families torn apart forever. That self-reproach, on top of the weight of my work, was too much. I needed a break, some respite. And we also needed someplace for our own family to reconnect.

I looked for a setting where we could have quiet, undistracted time with Lillian, who had finally joined us in Vienna after months in hospitals. A week in Greece, I imagined, would be wonderfully restorative. And so our family embarked on what turned out to be our most challenging—and unifying—trip, on a boat with all five of us, plus Karma.

Just before we left, Lillian spent the night pacing and rubbing her hands incessantly. I had training in mental health; I should have recognized the signs.

Before I continue, I must step outside my role as autobiographer, to remind my reader that my family has had the chance to edit everything I've written before here. Lillian's story is essential to my own. But it is so personal to her that recounting it could seem like a terrible violation of her privacy. Yet she hasn't flinched from her decision almost a decade ago to be frank about her experience, with the hope that she can help others. Lillian has asked me to add that her openness is partly in response to the tendency of many to be closed, as if mental illness comes packaged with shame. Her second request was that if I tell her story, I try to tell it in its fullness. And so I shall.

Our journey began in Athens, with an overnight at the U.S. ambassador's residence there. I was due downstairs to attend a dinner honoring the prime minister, along with Sargent Shriver. Instead, as I was dressing I noticed Lillian sitting motionless, staring intently at a corner of the ceiling. Soon she began talking to spirits unseen by the rest of us. She was calm and comforted by their presence. I felt quietly grateful to her apparitions for their benign form, even as my heart sank.

I abandoned the dinner and began phoning halfway around the world to find help for my daughter. Lil's psychiatrist in Denver was dismayed but not surprised, since, he told me, 40 percent of bipolar patients experience psychosis. "You've got to get it stopped; think of a train picking up speed. And remember, she's seeing what she's seeing, she's hearing what she's hearing. Don't try to tell her she's not. It's completely real to her."

It was the middle of the night, one of the longest of my life. At some point the phone rang. An emergency call from the State Department. As Karma and Teddy watched over Lillian, I learned that my office had been implicated in a security violation that could require a congressional hearing. "Fine," I said. There was nothing I could do that night. For now, my daughter was standing at a precipice, looking over the edge. Nothing else mattered.

Karma and I took turns staying up all night, helping Lil to interpret what she was seeing and hearing, and waiting beside her when she finally dozed off. For the most part, her visions were innocuous. My deceased father and Mark's late grandmother were among those guests only she could greet. But their implicit message was dangerous—proof to her of the afterlife that so often beckoned her.

When day broke, Lillian was delighted by tiny angels on the lawn and terrified by sharks in the ambassador's swimming pool. It took another twenty-four eternal hours to find a doctor in Athens to prescribe anti-psychotics. I waited outside the door as the American psychiatrist spent over an hour with my daughter. When he emerged, he said to me simply, "She will be a spectacular adult, if she makes it. I wish I could be her doctor. Good luck to you."

We would have to start the medications very gradually, he said, and it would be several days before they took effect. So Charles and I decided to take the family on to Rhodes, where we boarded a small boat for a five-day passage back to Athens. I figured it was probably going to be a rough ride wherever we were—hotel, hospital, or home. Better to stay with our plan and make the passage together.

Our family of six was confined to the cramped quarters of a boat day after day, taking care of Lillian. The winds were against us the whole week, so we motored across choppy water fourteen hours at a stretch. The drugs made Lillian physically unbalanced and lethargic, but she managed to sit with Teddy and me on the bow for hours. We three were like Broadway wannabes, belting out "You'll Never Walk Alone" at the top of our lungs.

But behind the bravado, I was counting the hours, wondering when the meds would kick in. Near sunset one day, the crisis peaked. Suddenly Lil's expression turned wild. A host of demons, led by Lucifer, were hovering in the air. She cowered against the rail of the boat. Karma and I quickly clutched her arms, to keep her from trying to escape overboard. I began to sing hymns with her to drive the demons away. Teddy's eyes were wide with worry for his sister. "Come sit next to her," I urged him.

Our seven-year-old put one little hand in Lil's and began patting her on the shoulder with the other. "It's going to be all right, Lillian," he soothed. With a quivering voice, she began to sing "Amazing Grace."

We all joined in. Eventually the demons gave up and went elsewhere to work their torment.

Back in Vienna the meds began to work, and the psychosis cleared. But the side effects were terrible. At times Lil slept sixteen hours and still felt like a zombie when she woke up. Her feet were so swollen that she couldn't fit into her shoes, and she moved slowly, with a shuffle. For months her hands had a constant tremor. She wore reading glasses because of her blurred vision, although she couldn't concentrate enough to stay with a book.

It was hard for me to tell how much Teddy was taking in. Sometimes he talked to me about his concern for his sister. But when he didn't, I was reluctant to bring it up. My guess is that she was almost always on his mind.

Even watching her try to eat dinner, her hands trembling uncontrollably, was wrenching. One evening, as she kept dropping the food from her fork, I stared at Charles across the table. "Do you see what I see?" my eyes asked. "Of course I do," he answered.

We didn't know what to do. We were just guessing. Over and over, I reached back to lessons gleaned from my experience with two brilliant people: my half-brother Hassie, who was consistently disabled, and Donna at Karis, who could be fine at breakfast and psychotic at supper. I kept telling myself that a person can never become an illness. Donna and Hassie were still alive and just as truly "themselves" as before their illnesses. Who else, after all, could they be? As I watched and waited at my daughter's side, I knew that like them, she was sick, but not gone.

Charles was unable to help when he was away conducting. Late-night transatlantic conversations with old friends like Carol, Fern, or Lauren helped me maintain some balance as I tried to take care of Lillian and keep the rest of my life going. Talking casually about how things were going with my friends' children kept me from becoming completely absorbed in our own family's trials.

Colleagues in Washington were wonderfully supportive. Dick Holbrooke, now assistant secretary of state for Europe, listened with empathy but advised me to resign to devote myself to my sick child. I weighed his words carefully but ultimately disagreed. Spending all my time focused on Lillian's illness wasn't the answer.

One evening I lay in bed alone, confronting the reality that my daughter was disabled. As Lillian's illness had grown more complicated, her statistical chances of surviving had plummeted. Yet I couldn't surrender her. Somewhere inside me I was cradling the promise of that bundle of pink I'd held in my arms a dozen years earlier. What terrible force had visited my child, with her Gerber-perfect face beaming up at me, eliciting every ounce of joy in my being? Minutes, then hours passed. Slowly my thinking and feeling began to shift.

I thought of the women from Srebrenica, whose lives had turned out so tragically different from what they imagined, from how it was supposed to be. But why was life *supposed* to be any particular way? I admired their fortitude. And in the same way, I admired my daughter's willingness to face another day. But that was, after all, the most we could count on—another day. Why did I ever think Lillian—or anyone—was entitled to a particular future? Nowhere was it written, much less promised. My dreams were only that: wishful imagination.

We would live life as it unfolded. If that meant hospitals, it meant hospitals. If it meant home care, it meant home care. If it meant . . . but I didn't want to go there. Instead I pictured myself sitting at Kennedy Airport with Helen, not knowing if I would be able to pull off the ambassador job. Well, I had, and somehow we would pull through this as well. We'd all get up in the morning and deal with whatever a day brought. And the day after that, we'd do the same.

My secrets cry aloud,
I have no need for tongue.
My heart keeps open house,
My doors are widely swung.
An epic of the eyes
My love, with no disguise.
— Theodore Roethke

CHAPTER 6

Call Me Swanee

Goddess of Many Arms

December 1994. My secretary Susan interrupted my meeting. "It's the White House." I did a quick mental scan of politics in Washington and Vienna but could think of no pressing issue. Puzzled, I picked up the phone.

"Swanee, this is Hillary. I hear Lillian's having a hard time, and I want you to know I'm thinking about you."

I stared at a signed picture above my desk, which the First Lady had sent over the morning of my swearing-in. Radiant smile. Bright blue suit. Pink roses. More than anyone, she was my role model. While my charge was to represent her husband in Austria, in my heart I felt like an extension of Hillary. We were both reaching wide for change, while holding dear ones close.

I told Hillary how my life was: How in the mornings, before heading into the office, I pulled my overmedicated daughter out of bed, propping her up as she walked to our car. How she slept with her head on my shoulder in the backseat as we rode to her tutor's. How I jumped into my day, which was waiting like a racecar with engines revving. And in the evenings, how I ached as I watched her, manic, dance with her shadow on the wall, or found her cowering in a bathtub, clothed, with a towel over her head to hide from demons.

With the full onset of my daughter's illness, I grasped for the first time Dad's intense concern about Hassie, his almost oppressive optimism and endless preoccupation. Lillian could be so depressed that she would sit in bed crying for hours. On those days I moved my work home to be with her. Other times I brought her to my office, covered her with an afghan, and pulled my chair up to the sofa where she lay sedated. With one hand I held a phone, planning a reception for a visiting author or vigorously insisting on immediate aid for refugees. With the other hand, I stroked her head.

After agonizing through weeks of her depression, we'd all feel relief when Lillian's mood would swing toward mania. But what might begin as a welcome smile radiating from her whole being would turn into giggles, then raucous antics and sleepless nights. She described mania as a ride on an out-of-control roller coaster. I'd find her gazing at her hands in wonder, marveling at them as masterpieces. She was sure she'd ascended into a higher state of mind where, as she put it, "nothing is quite clear, yet everything seems perfectly obvious."

As is typical of mania, she was obsessed with religious asceticism. This was far beyond my own upbringing, and there was nothing in our environment to trigger her fixation. But she begged me, and I refused, to strip her room so she could sleep on a bare mattress on the floor.

One evening, drawn by the quiet down the hall, I walked into her bathroom. "Oh, Lillian!"

"What is it, Mother?"

"Your hair. Lillian, Darling, what have you done?" Long, strawberry blond tresses lay in piles at her feet. I took a razor out of her hand. She was about to complete the job by shaving her head.

Given her psychosis and mood swings, with school out of the question, I worried about how my daughter could piece together a peer group. Her closest friends in Vienna were employees of the embassy, and occasionally their children, whose friendship included sharing cigarettes. Lillian's nicotine addiction at thirteen felt like one more failure on my part, and I tried everything: exhorting, bribing, restricting—until she ran away. After we found her, Henry, who'd been critical of my inability to stop his sister from smoking, came around. "I guess we'll be grateful if she lives long enough for lung cancer," he said, darkly but tenderly.

As my daughter moved into puberty, her mood shifts occurred more often, with dramatic swings sometimes inside twenty-four hours. The doctors warned that this "rapid cycling" was more difficult to treat. They added one medication on top of another and then another, trying to find the right "cocktail." Eventually Lillian was taking twenty-four pills a day. One side effect was weight gain: about eighty pounds. With silent despondency, almost every day she nudged the marker to the right on our tall scales. The clinicians were accustomed to this side effect; but for a girl finding her way through adolescence, it was hard, really hard. Yet whatever her size, she always maintained exquisite grace in her movement and a stylish elegance in her dress.

Raising children is one of the most difficult jobs around. It's hard enough to understand, love, or forgive a child chosen and nurtured from infancy. It's much more difficult to accept the quirks of a daughter gained through marriage. From Charles's and my first date, we'd been stretched into a tired triangle, with Charles and Lillian each feeling displaced by the other. I was put out at Lillian for her barbs toward my new husband. But I felt humbled when, years later, my daughter said she was trying to defend me in those first years of marriage. It infuriated her to see me crying after my frequent arguments with Charles—even though I'd picked the fights.

With perfect hindsight, it's clear how Lillian's stubborn rejection of her new stepfather and stepbrother was exacerbated by her mood disorder. Still, her refusals to accept their affection exacted a precious toll. Charles and Henry were judgmental, toward her for her crankiness and toward me for flawed mothering. But as her illness became more apparent, their feelings softened.

Teddy never expressed anything but adoration for his sister. When he was about eight, and Lillian left Vienna to spend some weeks with Mark, I was relieved. She had been taking out her misery on her little brother, mercilessly, and I worried about how that might injure his self-esteem.

"Are you kinda glad your sister's away for awhile?"

"Oh, no, Mom." He looked at me, and his eyes brimmed with tears. "I miss her horribly."

As for me, my awareness was split every moment, with part of me riveted on my daughter, even when she was hospitalized months at a time. More than ever I wondered if I could manage her illness, be a good enough wife, stay in touch with Henry, give Teddy adequate attention, and fulfill the needs of my job. I felt like a Hindu goddess with multiple arms, a different responsibility tugging on each.

The stress penetrated my safest relationship, with Charles. In my journal I wrote, "At this pace, I'm spinning like a whirling dervish. Query for Charles: How do you hug a whirling dervish?" In contrast to the beaming ambassador others saw, with him I was slamming doors and shouting names when I felt deserted or misunderstood.

I confided to my friend Merle, visiting from Denver, that our relationship had roughened. "You don't have time to get divorced," she replied dryly.

We did have time, though, for a "save the marriage stroll" in the Schönbrunn gardens. Walking briskly along the tree-lined paths, Charles listened patiently as I groused about my difficulties with parenting while he was away conducting for a week, unaware of the burden that his absence created. With admirable candor, Charles admitted that he didn't carry the family responsibility as I did.

But as my complaints grew shriller, he insisted that he had his own troubles to deal with. Once he had been the person surrounded by crowds; bouquets of roses bore his name, not mine. "I'm used to lifting my baton and having seventy players respond," he reminded me. "But the other day I was literally shoved by a photographer wanting 'a better angle on the ambassador.'"

I thought of how my husband took control of an orchestra, pulling the musicians into a tempo, coaxing them into a mood. I was feeling somewhat sympathetic as he went on, "It's not easy being married to an ambassador." Then he couldn't resist adding, "And a radical feminist."

I stopped walking, turned, and looked up into his face. "First, Charles, a radical feminist wouldn't be married." Then a cheap shot: "And second, not to *you*."

I wasn't the only person tilting and pivoting, trying to balance it all. Hillary was such an inspiration to me, I accepted almost every invitation to be with her. When asked to introduce her at an economic conference, I planned a trip back to Denver. Three thousand people had come to the lunch, hosted by the Women's Foundation.

I took my seat on the dais, and applauded with the crowd as she came onto the stage. A woman standing below handed her a note before she sat down next to me. She glanced at the paper, and then continued her conversation with me and the foundation president.

In my introduction, I compared her to Eleanor Roosevelt, another First Lady whom people loved and hated. I quoted Roosevelt's story about agreeing to do an advertisement for margarine. Americans were split: some horrified and some pleased. Horrified that she had disgraced herself . . . and pleased that she had disgraced herself.

The crowd laughed, but when Hillary began to speak, she was all business. Then, for the umpteenth time, I was impressed as she wove into her remarks a passage from the note expressing thanks for the Family Leave Act, which had allowed the writer of the note to stay by her dying husband without losing her job. Hillary had mastered the challenge of integrating her own ideas with the experiences of others, and in doing so, moving an audience from policy to practice.

On the plane returning to Washington, I found the First Lady asleep, her shoes off and her feet up. Her hair was in a ponytail on top of her head as if she were fifteen. Her hand was over her face. That day I'd heard her called a "femi-Nazi" on a radio talk show. But I'd seen a decent woman who was wearing herself out to bring a bit of hope to some Americans left out of The Dream.

While Hillary slept I spoke to Melanne Verveer, by now her chief of staff. I wanted to talk with her boss about Bosnia. She said she'd see, and I went back to my seat. Later, as we were getting off the plane at Andrews Air Force Base, Melanne whispered, "Now's your chance."

Melanne motioned for me to slip into the back of the limousine heading to the White House. As the car pulled off the tarmac, the First Lady and I settled back into the leather seat. It had been a long day, and we both welcomed some time for a quiet, thoughtful talk. Hillary wanted to hear about Lillian. She winced as I described a recent night back in Vienna. Lillian had called on the intercom by my bed, and when I answered, cried out, "You're alive!" I'd run to her room, where she told me, sobbing, that a tall, thin blue woman had grabbed the back of her neck with icy fingers, telling her I was dead.

"That's so horrible," Hillary said. "Poor dear." We talked on, until I switched the focus. I knew Hillary was going through her own tough times, watching her heroic effort on health care reform go down the tubes. "You and the president birthed this administration with enormous expectations. How do you deal with the setbacks?"

I expected some rancor, or at least frustration. But her answer was philosophical. "This is a transformational time for our society. It's not about me. Something's happening in the consciousness of the American people, the way they see their own lives and how they view women. Tremendous insecurity and anger out there gets directed at me."

"But I have a question for you," she continued. I was seasoned to political "asks," and possibilities dashed through my mind. "What can we do to heal our country, to cut through the hate language, to unite citizens, not behind a political party, but around constructive values?" Her concern was the well-being of the country. Not the Clinton legacy. Not her career. Not partisan politics or polls.

I said something obvious about the power of media and religious institutions. But as I looked beyond my friend, into the dark window, my mind was on the people in the former Yugoslavia, who were enduring horrors that very night. So I asked my own question: What could America do for Bosnia, beginning with military intervention to stop the genocide?

I suppose my query was as difficult as hers. To anyone looking in, we might have seemed like girlfriends chatting. But we were each trying to grapple with huge problems created by forces far beyond us. That churning inside, the sense of constant struggle, was what we had in common, and we knew it.

It was midnight. She'd be getting up with the dawn to work on her book. "Meanwhile, my brother's visiting, and I'm hardly seeing him. I'm holed up in a little room writing. It's such slow going."

It was strange to think of the First Lady of the United States of America under the eaves of the White House, laboring to put her thoughts on paper. When I later heard that *It Takes a Village* surely had to be the work of a ghostwriter, I thought of Hillary's weary face as she described her days and nights pent up in the attic.

Watching the media attacks on Hillary was alarming, since as a public person I was also potential prey. I'd been showered with my predecessors' publicized triumphs and better-publicized foibles, so I knew that a successful diplomatic tenure was not a foregone conclusion. Happily, my relationship with the Austrian press seemed almost charmed.

When the first reporter came for an interview, he kissed my hand and stammered, not sure how to address me. Viennese are strictly formal and tightly attached to titles; but as Ambassador, Excellency, Doctor, Frau, and Mrs., I had more than were manageable.

"Just call me 'Swanee,'" I offered. His eyes widened, and then he grinned. The next morning, "Call Me 'Swanee'" was the headline of his article, in big, bold type.

Big and bold I remained. In addition to my weekly column, I crafted op-eds and delivered a weekly radio commentary. The press favorably reviewed my cantata and regional exhibits of my photographs. I worked with state television on four documentaries, the first a profile of my pre-Austria life and work in Colorado, two highlighting work in Bosnia and throughout Eastern Europe, and the last titled "Swanee Hunt's America." This flood of media coverage brought me into millions of Austrian homes while I was in my own, with our kids. I knew this strategy to amplify my efforts while preserving family time had paid off when one magazine headlined a lengthy profile, "The Most Spirited Ambassador Ever."

I needed the journalists for my work, and they needed me for theirs. But over the years, several of my warmest friendships were with reporters. They asked me questions, and I asked *them* questions. I knew their spouses and kids, and knew that we were all able to dance at my raucous birthday parties. Those relationships became critically important when I had to do damage control in touchy political situations. In particular, an incident of the CIA's "housekeeping" created a mess for me.

In the early 1950s, under cover of postwar confusion, the United States buried seventy-nine caches of weapons and other supplies in Austria. That scheme to equip hundreds of partisans in the event of a Soviet invasion included high-level Austrians who would have been needed to implement the operation. The involvement of those officials was a clear violation of Austrian neutrality. Every school kid understood that neutrality was the reason why only ten years after the war, Austria, unlike Germany, had wriggled out from under Soviet occupation of part of the country. The concept was core to Austria's postwar identity and reaffirmed in various treaties and laws.

Now for the housekeeping: the United States had never officially informed the Austrian government of the caches. But, I was told, someone moving to a new office within the CIA had just rediscovered files with maps and decades of notations that someone should tell the Austrians. "Why didn't the agency deal with this before?" I asked our station chief.

"I guess we were waiting for someone like you," he hedged. I rolled my eyes.

When I said I would immediately inform the president, chancellor, and foreign minister, the station chief asked me to wait until Congress, adjourned for the holidays, was notified. Fearing a leak, I gathered our key embassy officers to create a contingency plan. I sent it to the State Department with a note stating, essentially, if we don't hear from you, here's what we'll do. Most Foreign Service officers are unschooled in the notion of framing a story, so negative accounts often flourish unabated. Instead of taking direct action, they're taught to "ask for guidance" from the bureaucracy, where there is almost always someone up the decision ladder who says "no." I couldn't and didn't live by the ladder.

Sure enough, four weeks later, in the middle of the night, a phone call from the White House National Security Council woke me.

"Bad news," the caller said sympathetically. Congress had been briefed without my being advised by the CIA or State Department. As I predicted, the intelligence committee almost immediately sprang a leak. In a few hours the *Boston Globe* would declare, "Hidden U.S. Arms Stir Diplomatic Concerns" and "Caches Strain Ties with Austria." The headlines were pure fabrication; the Austrians didn't even know about the caches as the paper went to press, nor had the *Globe* contacted my office. I hung up the phone, woke my aides, and asked them to meet me at 8 a.m.

It was Saturday. We had sparse staff, not much time—and a lot to do. This flap would involve the Austrian justice, interior, and defense ministries. We tracked down the Austrian president in the provinces, an opposition leader traveling in Germany and another in the hospital, and the chancellor on his massage table. In five meetings, I broke the story to the editors of the largest Austrian newspapers.

The timing was terrible. The Russians were hypersensitive, having just lost their sphere of influence in Eastern Europe. And the Austrian-Russian relationship was strained because Austria was contemplating bending its neutrality by sending troops to Bosnia to stop the Serbs, whom the Russians treated as cousins. In essence, the United States had exposed its cards just as its partner, Austria, was in the middle of a diplomatic finesse.

By mid-morning I was sitting in the angry chancellor's gilded office. A similar cache incident had caused an Italian government to topple. Further, this deception made the United States appear hypocritical, he scowled, when it blamed President Waldheim for concealing information about his wartime past. True enough. But at a more practical level, I was disquieted by the thought that our explosives might be buried under a playground.

By 2 p.m. Austrian time, the hour when the papers in Boston were proclaiming the diplomatic strain, the defense minister and other officials were sitting around my dining room table, strategizing, of all things, a coordinated media plan. My Austrian colleagues urged me to apologize on TV for America's forty-year lapse of candor. At 5 p.m. I was at the station, staring into a camera and speaking directly to the public in German. It was rather wonderful, voicing an apology to little Austria from the world's lone superpower.

Press interest skyrocketed, but story after story presented the United States as the protector of Austria. Ironically, I received a message from Holbrooke's deputy emphatically instructing me to say nothing to the media. Fortunately his message was misrouted and arrived days after the dust had settled. By then the State Department spokesman had publicly supported our handling of the situation. In a reversal of the standard process, we'd even sent "talking points" back to D.C. for the spokesman's briefings. Over the next weeks, local and international investigative reporters delved into the story of the caches. But we had set the tone.

Concerned that weekend treasure hunters could blow themselves up—the *Globe* suggested that the caches might include gold to finance the resisters' cause—the interior minister and I staged a handing-over of CIA information. A score of international TV and radio commentators watched me give him an envelope (empty: the real box was huge) and say a few words thanking everyone for their understanding. To discourage an accident, I tossed out, "Sorry, guys, no gold."

Were I to be buried in Austria, those words would be on my tombstone. Every paper used them as a headline, in English, and they were later named "quote of the year" by one. The story twisted and turned, involving the possible complicity of former Nazis, a disappeared file and internal investigation, and top-secret satellite photography. After the last caches were unearthed, the Austrian military created an exhibit of rifles, grenades, and explosives, widely publicized with black-and-yellow posters declaring, "Sorry, Guys, No Gold."

My renown extended to Austria's border with Italy, we were amused to learn. A guard examining the diplomatic passports of Debbie and Guyle Cavin, from our embassy, grinned broadly and without asking another word, exclaimed, "Schweinehund!" Guyle turned to Debbie and said, "I think that guard just called me a piggy dog." Not so. What had sounded like "Schweinehund" was "Swanee Hunt" in southern Alpine dialect.

But fame—or notoriety—sometimes worked against me. I looked forward to the second President's New Year's Reception as an opportunity to compare political information with other diplomats. Ambassadors were advised, as before, to wear formal attire or traditional garb. I quipped that I might wear blue jeans as our national costume. Laughing, the other women diplomats and I conspired to at least wear brightly colored suits to break up the monotony of black. As it turned out, only I stayed true to plan. When we formed our semicircle, my assigned place fell dead center, and there I stood, in fire-engine red. The next day the newspaper captioned the group picture "The Lady in Red." In Vienna, etiquette rules! The following year my protocol chief conveyed, with embarrassment, that the Austrian president's office had called her to emphasize the appropriateness of black.

I couldn't believe I had to pay such attention to what I would wear, instead of how we should conduct foreign policy. It felt like a throwback to pre-feminist times. I'd long railed against news articles about women political figures (no pun intended) that led with a line about the senator's mauve suit or the director's teal scarf. So I was vexed when, at the black-tie dinner of the American Chamber of Commerce, I suddenly realized that my flattering blue chiffon was too frilly for my speech on the American response to EU currency integration. I felt flowingly effete, holding my skirt as I walked up the steps onto the stage.

I stood at the lectern, but before my first word was out I saw that on my right a tall American flag was blocking a portion of the audience. So I took matters into my own hands. Frock or not, I tossed my long scarf over my shoulder, bent down to clutch the pole, and dragged the flag back a few meters. The guests let out a gasp, then they burst into applause.

Unabated, I went over to the Austrian flag on my left, but six men had jumped up to do the job. Good help is hard to find. As long as they were there, I asked them to also move the flowers in front so that people seated below could see. That gesture was more than redecorating, of course. The crowd got the message that we were making things happen. This was function over form.

That evening my text on economic policy had been drafted by an embassy officer. It was fine. Boring but fine. Afterward, I asked my political counselor what she thought. "Not bad. But you're so good spontaneously. Why did you read?" she asked. I held myself back from retorting that she'd been my advisor, plus had written the speech.

From that evening, when it came to style I was my own counselor, remembering the Southern Baptist revivalists who had moved me as a young person. Whether the topic was defense spending or structural unemployment, I learned to travel between stories and policy, songs and policy, and jokes and policy, mapping the flow between head and heart. An audience needs to be thinking, yes, but also laughing and crying. Or they can be stunned and silent. But not bored.

One decidedly un-boring strategy, which also helped me integrate my worlds, was to bring our children to some public events. News photographers made sure that we could fill scrapbooks with Lillian chatting up the likes of Jimmy Carter, Mikhail Gorbachev, or Steven Spielberg; Teddy showing his magic tricks to Shirley MacLaine or the NATO commander George Joulwan. It was hard for me to stay soulful under pressure, but having our two youngest nearby helped.

Of course having a kid along adds an element of surprise. At the Austrian Stock Exchange, as I promoted commemorative coins to help fund our Olympic team, Teddy was on stage with me behind a skirted table. When he was unexpectedly called on to draw names from a tumbler, he hopped up and performed his assignment with great aplomb —and no shoes. The crowd tittered, and once again, cameras flashed. It was a stunning departure from Austrian norms to have children at formal occasions; even so, years later a former government minister laughed as she regaled a Viennese audience about our signing an air space treaty, with Teddy crawling around under the table.

I'm sure not everyone was laughing, and there were raised eyebrows from time to time; but having the courage to establish my own style, constantly integrating the personal and the public, was essential to my years in Vienna. The power of that mix became clear to me at an economic conference at which I described American fiscal policy. In my remarks, I first established my legitimacy by telling my audience what they already knew regarding the global economy. But I added that they couldn't understand Clinton's fiscal choices unless they understood his desire to help our inner cities. One in four children in the United States was living in poverty. President Clinton had grown up among them and had vowed not to forget them, I told the audience. Every foreign policy decision he made was against the backdrop of that domestic reality. I closed with a story, based on the children with whom I'd worked.

The finance professionals didn't move a muscle as they listened to a word picture of little Joey and twenty-two-year-old Shannon, who was trying to be a good mother despite having no role models. Things were so bad that she began prostituting herself to support her child and her drug habit. The parole officer had told her he would take Joey away, so she'd spent $40 on a child development text at a university bookstore, hoping that it would help. Only problem was, she couldn't read.

Not knowing if the audience would stay with me, I'd been watching their faces carefully. Even in this assembly of accountants, men and women did not disguise their tears, and a long line formed afterward, with people wanting to thank me personally. They knew it was highly unusual for a diplomat to talk frankly about imperfections of his or her country. More important than bouquets or standing ovations was when a man told me, "Ihre Wörte hatten Herz." "Your words had heart."

Just Managing

Lonely. I'd been cautioned before going overseas that an ambassador's life could be lonely. And even though every day I laid eyes on hundreds of people, I often longed for the comfort of close friends. I thought my life was busy in Denver, but Vienna was twice the pace. When friends came for several days from Texas, Colorado, or New York, the best I could do was invite them to fold into some of my already scheduled activities. I was devoting almost every nonprofessional minute to my children, with only a few moments a day for Charles. Friends back home were hardly on the radar screen.

It wasn't appropriate for me to be completely uninhibited with Austrian officials, and Charles warned that personal closeness with my own staff would breed jealousies. I agreed, but I was just as certain that I wouldn't survive without genuine friendships. Talking about adversity couldn't be reserved for speeches.

So when Lillian's condition deteriorated, I invited four other embassy mothers to a Turkish café down the street for a lunchtime escape —trailed, albeit, by two Austrian security agents. Sitting in a booth in a dark corner, we passed our stories around the table.

The first mother, a CIA operative, described her high school daughter's distance and sullenness. I'd gladly trade problems with her, I thought.

After ten minutes of sympathy and hummus, a political officer began. Her middle-school daughter was plenty smart but lagging in math because of a learning disability. I'm sure she's frustrated, but this is no great shakes, I said to myself: wait till they hear what I'm going through.

The next mother, an economist, explained that she was worried sick about her two young children. They were in the custody of a violent father in the States, because a divorce judge had ruled that Skopje, her previous post, was an unstable environment for kids. As I watched her fight back tears, I imagined her standing before a judge who was a product of Cold War prejudices. How could she ever sleep? I realized with renewed appreciation the confidence I had in Mark's fathering of Lillian, as different as we were.

Four of us turned to an immigration officer whom I'd admired for her plainspoken kindness. As though reporting on her work that day, she told us that her daughter had just gone to prison for killing her abusive husband. I put down my fork; the baklava could wait. Her three-year-old grandson had been put in foster care. I stared a long time into my demitasse, as if counting the grounds on the bottom.

The security guards were pacing outside, but I refused to rush as I told the other mothers how Lillian had become dangerously impulsive. One night on the Autobahn, she begged Charles to stop the car. "There's a rest area up ahead," he said.

"*Now!*" she shouted, trying to save herself from a compulsion to jump out of the moving vehicle. He pulled over, and I walked with her for a few minutes on the side of the highway, in the headlights, my arm around her shoulder. Returning to the car, I put her in the middle of the back seat, fastened her seat belt, and rode the final hour with my arm stretched across her lap.

We were holding on for dear life. I don't remember the advice of the other mothers, but they gave me something more enduring, a sense that I wasn't alone. In that one hour, instead of seeing my situation as extreme, I'd moved squarely into the middle of moms trying to manage.

I had learned the value of such group bonding from my studies in psychology and pastoral care. But no course had prepared me for the thorny conundrums of management. As the dollar dropped, sending our budget into a tailspin, Congressional cuts to the State Department required me to downsize my staff. My good-natured driver Horst, bless him, was assigned a desk in the front office. Whenever he and I weren't on the road he opened mail and sent faxes—retooling, I laughed, just as he was reaching retirement age. But other cost-saving decisions were tougher. We had two full-time car mechanics, and no fleet. They'd been kept on because they'd worked for the embassy for decades. Should I think more about the American taxpayer or the Austrians on payroll? Further, most of our employees were terrific, but some who'd lost their edge hadn't been asked to move on, in part because firing someone in a socialist society was so complex and because the Americans, who would oversee the process, were constantly rotating.

I hadn't yet seen the social science research showing that when men and women act decisively in tough situations, men are respected and women disliked, but I knew it intuitively. Outside the embassy Ambassador Hunt was a resounding success, but inside the embassy I wondered: Was I too soft because I was a woman or too tough as I compensated for inexperience? Did it hurt or help that I asked employees how their kids were doing in school? Maybe I didn't seem ambassadorial to those who'd worked in six other embassies led by men in dark suits.

It was outrageous that until 1971, a female Foreign Service officer had to leave her job if she married, and the great majority of women were still assigned to administrative or consular positions outside the political or economic "cones," from which most ambassadors were drawn. Some women had filed a class-action suit against the State Department, settled only in 1996, mandating an end to sex discrimination. Good for them, I thought. But a few who weren't up to the job had been promoted. Should I point this out, to show that I wasn't biased? Of course incompetent men had been promoted for decades. I decided to keep my critique to myself.

The overwhelming authority of the ambassador discouraged honest communication. My opinion could propel or destroy a career. State employed some of the most talented people I'd ever met. Good human beings. Dedicated public servants. But the bureaucracy suffered from a promotion system based more on the reviewer's writing ability than the employee's job performance. Walking on water was an assumed skill. "He only walks? Doesn't run . . . or at least skip?" There was no way to indicate extraordinary performance, since everyone had to be exceptionally talented and wonderfully heroic.

When I told the assistant secretary I was going to send in candid evaluations, Holbrooke advised me not to burst the balloon. Our employees would be compared not with each other at the embassy but with Foreign Service officers worldwide. It was unfair for me to be frank unless all ambassadors were.

I absolved my conscience a bit each year with a memo to the secretary of state saying that I'd just signed my name to a pile of papers riddled with inaccuracies . . . and because the personnel system was so dysfunctional there was no way for him to know whom I was lying about . . . and would he please fix the system? That rant produced no remedy. On my watch, several people already in over their heads were promoted, and some of our stars were passed over. One person I dismissed for incompetence was moved—then immediately advanced. He won.

Some career Foreign Service officers, I'd been warned, resent and even disdain political appointees, who haven't come up through the system yet receive plum positions. I conscientiously worked at overcoming that divide. But the truth is that despite my efforts to connect, my employees hardly knew me and didn't completely trust me. Come to find out, I couldn't completely trust them. After several years, I was stunned to learn that someone was trying to sink my career when a reporter from the *Washington Post* called Holbrooke's office to confirm a list of my supposed transgressions. His aide called me in Vienna. Had I really taken personal vacations at embassy expense?

The accusations were wrong, but twists rather than fabrications from whole cloth. Yes, I'd traveled to organize meetings with women leaders in places where Charles was conducting, but I'd always paid my own way. Where the hell was this coming from? Hearing the list of my travels, I realized that the anonymous source was an insider with access to administrative information.

I called the reporter, who accepted my denial. "Sounds like a disgruntled employee. I'm not going to run this. If I did, we'd be inundated with 'leaks' from embassies all over the world." I felt relieved but flattened.

Given whistleblower protections, the inspector general's office cautioned me to do nothing to ferret out the source. Reluctantly, I tried to expunge the accuser from my mind, but couldn't stop wondering. When I addressed our staff meetings, was he there smiling and applauding? Or was it a she? From day one, there were those nasty things said behind my back—by her? Was this the price of making personnel cuts? After all I'd done to be kind and fair. Or maybe . . .

However I tried to rationalize the experience, I noticed less of a lift as I jogged up the marble steps to my office each morning. I was angry, without the satisfaction of knowing toward whom. Before I could sink into too much self-righteous pity, I had a letter from an anonymous administrative assistant in D.C. Susan, feeling protective, held onto it for several weeks before slipping it into a pile of material for me to review away from the office. I came across the unsigned letter as I sat with coffee over breakfast, working my way through a tall stack of mail. My stomach tightened as I read the words excoriating me for my rudeness toward her as I'd waited for an appointment with her boss. I felt horrible, especially because there was no one to call to apologize. By then I had no recollection of the incident, only a reminder that grand values are lived out in small actions.

I preferred, of course, to selectively remember starring in other interactions. There was the time I was waiting for a State Department official to finish up a phone call. His secretary was out, so I sat down at her desk to work at my laptop. A very considerable man walked up, shoved some very considerable papers in my face, and barked, "These are important."

"I'll be sure he gets them right away," I said with a smart nod, as the not-so-gentle man turned on his heels.

"That was terrific, Ambassador," a junior officer observed in disbelief.

Then and many other times, I tried to reach behind the pomp and the promise, the successes and shows, to touch the underside of my position. That meant not only keeping myself grounded but also making time to be a presence for others as they felt their way through dark times.

One day, after hours of searching, we found a relatively new embassy arrival in a drunken stupor. He was brought to the infirmary before being permanently sent home. I told our doctor that I wanted to see the employee before he left. The doctor, a devout man whose evangelical concern stopped short of alcoholics, said that a meeting would be worthless. I responded that I wouldn't feel right about having a staff member leave defeated, with no closure.

"Ambassador, I know his type. I'm advising you *against* seeing him."

"Thank you. I'll be over within the next half hour."

By the time I got there, the doctor had left his offices. This was my first, and last, time to meet the thin, young man. He was alone in a small room, staring out the window, chain-smoking. I shook his hand and sat down on the bed. My words were slow and deliberate. "I've been trying to imagine how this feels for you. I bet you arrived in Austria wanting to do a good job. And I guess you're wondering what went wrong."

He looked at me surprised. "Why did you come see me?"

"I came to say goodbye. To say thanks for the good work you've done and wish you well. The things that have gone wrong don't cancel out what went right. Remember that."

He stared at me a long time, drew on his cigarette, and said, "I really like you."

"Thanks," I replied.

Then he added, "I don't know why other people don't."

For all I tried to concentrate on officialdom, life—and death—kept interrupting. With five hundred embassy families, we had many hard times. Two deaths from cancer, a child with leukemia, a suspected rape, an unsuccessful wait for a liver transplant, the brutal murder of a sister triggering Vietnam flashbacks, marriage breakups, a beating in a bar, two plane crashes.

I was particularly haunted by the disaster that cost the life of Commerce Secretary Ron Brown, along with a beloved member of our embassy, Steve Kaminski. Steve frequently came bouncing into our front office with gifts—roses for Valentine's Day, Christmas ornaments from a Slovakian market . . . A peace agreement had been signed in the Balkans, and as the regional representative of the Commerce Department, Steve was traveling with Secretary Brown on the fateful trade mission to demonstrate that economic development in the region was a sensible idea.

Ron called just before the trip, saying that he wanted to visit me in Vienna after he left Dubrovnik, the Dalmatian Coast town where Enron would sign a deal to build a power plant in war-damaged Croatia. "No Ron, buddy, you can't visit me, because I'll be in Washington with *you*. You're on the host committee for my cantata performance to benefit the Children's Defense Fund."

"Oh, of course! Now I remember. I'll check my flights to be sure to make it home in time."

I was already in D.C. for rehearsals when my deputy called from Vienna to say that Ron's plane had gone missing. Hour after hour, as I sat in a pew, coaching the musicians, my mind was constantly moving between my safe Washington space and the ragged Croatian coast. I kept calling the embassy for the latest word. Pacing and preoccupied, I imagined the plane, with Ron and Steve on board. I was determined to somehow lean forward into the tale, as if by sheer force of will I could reverse the unfolding tragedy.

Word finally came. In a savage storm, the plane had crashed into the top of a mountain just shy of the airport. That night I lay in bed, tormented, trying for all I was worth to turn the plane just a bit, to miss the peak.

The cantata performance was held as planned, two days later on Good Friday. It was at a large church, near the White House, where Abraham Lincoln had worshiped. The concert became a memorial service, and the audience included other cabinet members, State Department officials, and a large contingent from Commerce. We mourned Ron and the others who died as we listened to Akhmatova's mournful text: "Nothing is left but dusty flowers . . . and tracks, that lead to nowhere."

A few months later Charles and I were in Dubrovnik. We hiked, in a sort of pilgrimage, up St. John's Mountain to the crash site. After a steep ascent we roamed until we found an area marked by charred brush. It was excruciatingly near the top; from the scene of the wreck, we looked up about a hundred feet to the mountain crest.

Charles and I spoke in hushed voices as we filled our light blue pack with stones, then metal and plastic pieces from the wreckage. Back home I glued the fragments onto the stones, creating small remembrances for Ron's and Steve's widows and others closest to them, including Bill Clinton, one of Ron's best friends.

Thinking of all the promise on that plane—talent, relationships, expertise, kindness—I began to cry. Charles came over and sat next to me. He looked into my face, tilted his head, and his eyes softened. With his arm around me, we sat without words in that rocky sanctuary, trying to understand how a brutal rain could cause such immense grief. How in the breadth of a moment, life could simply and utterly disappear.

"It's time to go," Charles said finally. He stood, extending his hand, to help me up.

One of the most difficult aspects of my life as ambassador was the pace. My friends say I've always been a person who feels deeply, who's not afraid to delve into layers of meaning in any situation. But I was running an embassy while raising a family, and I had far too little time to mourn. How could I declare that I was going to simply check out, to take time off to consolidate my feelings? My children needed me more than ever. And the embassy work was more complex than outsiders might imagine.

Part of my job was to deal with the obvious: explaining American policy, examining paragraphs in treaties. But I also spent hours each week dealing with the carefully concealed. In briefings at the CIA, we new ambassadors had been warned about one aspect of diplomatic life, known colloquially as "Spot the Spook." That touch of humor masked the sacrifice of our intelligence staff, the lack of external support they received because of their necessary secrecy, and the life-and-death importance of their success. It was an ironic twist that I, who passed up spy thriller movies with Charles to sit by the fire with the poems of Emily Dickinson, would end up overseeing one of the larger intelligence communities outside Washington.

What a difficult life, the intelligence world. It's easy to see how that culture could drift toward paranoia behind the thick cloak of secrecy. The high pitch of mystery was often preposterous: for example, on our vacation in Greece, I went into the American embassy to send an urgent message to the CIA director about a matter back in Austria. As I typed, I wasn't sure of how to address the director, so I turned to a man watching me carefully from a corner. "What's the official title of the head of the CIA?" I asked.

"I can't give out that information," he said, flatly.

Notwithstanding the micro-silliness (and there was much), my role carried considerable weight. I was the only person with the whole picture of U.S. government activity in the country, and I would have to clean up the mess if an operation went wrong. So I felt more than curious when a high-level intelligence official at State asked to see me the next time I was in D.C. After a few words of catching up, she asked pointedly, "Do you know everything that's going on in your CIA station?"

"How can I know what I don't know?" I replied lamely. Still, I got the drift.

Upon my return to Vienna I began to dig deeper. That same obtuse attitude, I discovered, was hindering our embassy intelligence operation. So I confronted the station chief. "I've been told by reputable sources that you've been keeping information from me, beyond the acceptable withholding of 'sources and methods.' From now on, you need to fill me in or find another job."

"I don't know what you might be referring to. I've always been forthcoming with pertinent information . . ."

"If the only things you're doing are what you're reporting to me, then I can't justify the number of people you have." His trite smile disappeared. Would I possibly cut back his staff? *That* hurt.

But evidently not enough. Over the next days, as the situation heated up, I heard a rumor that the deputy station chief had smirked, "I don't mind lying to an ambassador."

After being supportive, after gentle prods, after explicit instructions —it was time for a showdown. I searched my memory for models with a powerful, confrontational style. My mother? Hardly. John Wayne came to mind—then just as quickly left. Maybe Ray. Just how would I act if I were a man, I asked myself.

Standing in front of the mirror in my office, I pulled back my shoulders, lowered my voice, and rehearsed my confrontation aloud. With feigned confidence, I asked Susan to call the deputy, with his boss, to come to my office. I asked them to be seated across from me, and mustering an unfamiliar sternness, I told them what I'd heard about the deputy's attitude. "I see two possibilities. Either you've been misquoted, and someone is trying to frame you, in which case you have a very big problem." I paused, as the deputy's back stiffened. "Or else you *did* say that, and you have an even *bigger* problem."

The two men looked me straight in the eye. The deputy ardently insisted on his innocence, protesting that after all, he'd been an Eagle Scout. I couldn't believe it. What did he take me for, an idiot? Unimpressed by the protestations of a trained liar, I declared new rules of engagement.

My challenges weren't unusual, I learned, when two other ambassadors wrote scathing reports about station chiefs whom they considered not only uncooperative but working at purposes counter to them.

I don't know how much impact I had with our deputy spy, because within a few weeks he was gone; but I gave a heads-up to the ambassador at the embassy to which my wounded Eagle Scout was rotating. Men like him could be disastrous.

Assisting our station was one of the few requests that could invariably pull me away from evenings with our kids. Diplomatic dinner invitations, after all, flooded into our office. But when a rare request came from the Russian ambassador, I accepted. An unwritten protocol allowed me to match the Russians spy for spy. I wondered what my father would have said if he could have seen me pulling up to the fancy residence with two "aides." He might have smiled. As a way to confront the Red Menace, this sure beat handing out leaflets at the state fair.

We were seated for lunch, my staff on each side, facing the three Russians. After explaining that the doctor had taken him off alcohol, the ruddy-faced diplomat toasted me with a flowery speech, tossing back a jigger of vodka. Exquisite caviar was served with crème fraîche and seafood mousse. Then it was time to toast me again. And again. According to the ambassador, I was the sweetest, most beautiful, most charming diplomat in Vienna. I would also have been the drunkest if I'd kept up with him.

My Russian fancier was suddenly removed from his post a year later, because of an espionage flap. He died not long after, of liver failure. I told his replacement, a likable but more sober fellow, that I'd recently met with Gorbachev, whom I'd found fascinating. The ambassador suggested wryly that since the erstwhile Soviet premier had already overseen the breakup of his empire, perhaps my admiration was a little late.

Late, maybe. But our meeting had provided a memorable moment when Gorbachev asked me to convey to President Clinton his respect. In his current run for the Russian presidency, he explained, he was sometimes making statements critical of the United States. But this was necessary, he said, because, "Some people even accuse me of working for the CIA."

"Mr. President, if that's an offer, we accept." My interpreter, on loan from our netherworld, almost choked. Our relationship with the Russians flourished until we eventually entertained each other in grand style, with torch songs and flowing vodka, as our deputies kicked up a can-can.

But beneath the good times, I'd learned to be less trusting. So many countries had spy operations in Vienna that I was surprised but not shocked when Secretary of Energy Hazel O'Leary, in town for OPEC meetings, noticed a laser dot on her computer screen as it was being monitored from windows across the street.

One incident followed another. A plumber found listening devices in the walls of the VIP suite of an American hotel. Not only the head of OPEC but our CIA director had stayed in the bugged suite. I knew the Austrian president and chancellor hated Vienna's reputation as spy infested, so I took the initiative and called to inform them of the news. "I only *wish* the bugs were ours," I told them.

But despite those episodes, I didn't react when my laptop felt loose after I returned from a briefing at the NATO regional command in Naples. On my way out of our residence, I asked our butler to pick up a screw at the hardware store to replace one that had fallen out. I handed him the computer so he could check the size. "Madame Ambassador, all six screws are missing!" he exclaimed.

"Then get six," I replied impatiently.

Horst chimed in, "Madame, six screws don't fall out."

At the embassy, I began to explain the situation to our RSO (regional security officer), who gestured for me to stop talking, pointing to my sleek gray box that might be transmitting our conversation to parts unknown. My innocuous little laptop was whisked off to Washington for examination.

Our RSO came back with a theory: "It appears, Ambassador Hunt, that a frustrated hacker accessed your hotel room. Not finding your external disk drive, the hacker took the machine apart. Then, tipped off by an accomplice in the lobby that you and your husband had returned early from dinner, he didn't have time to screw it back together before slipping out of your room."

"A highly unlikely scenario," said Charles, when I repeated the saga to him.

I agreed. "I guess the only thing more unlikely," I added, "is that six screws fell out."

Sure enough, fingerprints were discovered on the hard drive. I would have been more incredulous had I not been privy to the astounding number of operatives living throughout Europe, not all of whom were budding entrepreneurs as their business cards claimed. And that was just the Russians.

The terrorist activity that the world discovered in September 2001 was brewing. Our intelligence officers were confronting situations with earthshaking potential. Beautiful, elegant Vienna, with protections against government invasion of privacy, was considered a relatively safe meeting place for bad guys. As a result, I went by CIA headquarters outside D.C. several times a year for highest-level meetings as well as mid-level working groups, and I hosted a steady stream of visitors from Langley (shorthand for headquarters). I demonstrated with ideas and actions that I could help their fight against terrorists. The agency realized my effort was being stymied, and I was assigned a new station chief. "We're sending you our best, Ambassador," assured the CIA director.

"After what I've put up with, I've earned it," I replied.

The new station chief and I got along brilliantly, taking walks in the Vienna sunshine to discuss matters to which no walls should be privy. After a year, he told me he had asked the CIA director, George Tenet, to urge Clinton to have me stay as long as possible in my post, saying that I'd been more help than any ambassador he'd ever worked with.

At least, that's what he said he said.

We're All Mothers

The intrigues of Vienna and the never-ending demands of motherhood clearly could have filled my time. And maybe I'd have had an easier four years if I'd been content to just attend to what was before me. But I've never been very good at near-term focus. My mind's eye keeps looking beyond.

Even as I was pouring attention into Lillian's crisis and trying to manage our complex embassy operation, I was still being pulled by the tragedy right down the road, in Sarajevo. The modern European city had been under siege for three and a half years, for long stretches with almost no water.

During the war I tried to convince intelligence analysts and the U.S.

military that no, the Bosnian Muslims weren't all extremists, and yes, we needed to stop the genocide. Month after month, as the fighting continued, I met with policy makers and military strategists wrestling with how to stop the bloodshed without pulling American troops into another Vietnam. Once the shooting stopped, I frequently, and unsuccessfully, urged President Clinton to instruct the U.S. military stationed in Bosnia to apprehend the war criminals.

Part of my attention was always riveted on the conflict. I worked outside official channels to organize five conferences inside and outside Bosnia, put together an Austria-wide book drive to help restock the shelves of the destroyed National Library, collect eight tons of musical instruments for Bosnian schools, and design a micro-enterprise program for war-affected women, which Clinton announced at the G-7 meeting in Lyon.

The most poignant of my dozen trips to Bosnia was in December 1995, two weeks after the peace agreement was signed in Paris. Charles and I arrived in Sarajevo with dual missions. I'd spend my time finding out how women were organizing to sustain the peace. He would bring the courage of Beethoven and the pulse of Gershwin to a devastated city. His was a bold move; I was only slightly reassured to read "No Weapons on Stage."

We were there for a week, having flown in on a Soviet-built UN cargo plane. (There would be no commercial flights for months.) Before coming I'd called our ambassador to Bosnia, John Menzies, to ask what I might bring for him. Two space heaters. And yes, some Viennese coffee too. Senator Jesse Helms, who referred sarcastically to ambassadors in pinstriped suits, might have been surprised to see how American diplomats read briefings by candlelight, hung their ties on strings between a bookshelf and a window, and slept in sleeping bags on army cots for a year and a half.

Snow had blanketed Sarajevo, covering some of the scars. In the forgiving beauty of that winter, the graceful turn-of-the-century buildings regained a moment of elegance. But just beneath the surface, injury was everywhere: On a father's face as he described how his daughter was shot in her hospital bed. In young and old men hobbling on one leg across the icy streets. In the ravaged carcass of a maternity hospital shelled while unsuspecting patients were inside. In the tears of a refugee grandmother describing six weeks of terror with seven others in her tiny apartment, until gunmen forced them to flee with nothing. In the Olympic soccer field studded like an orderly vineyard with hundreds of wooden grave markers.

My most important work in Bosnia was with the survivors of the Srebrenica massacre. Eight months had passed since Queen Noor's urgent call in the summer of 1995, after thousands of Muslim men and boys were slaughtered in what the UN had declared a "safe zone." The surviving families, some thirty thousand women, children, and old people, were subsisting near Tuzla, their lives in shambles, forgotten by the world. Many were crammed into "collective centers." Others were in flats and houses, ten to a room, paying exorbitant rents. They desperately wanted to return to their homes and farms in territory now controlled by the Serbs. But their efforts met with obstruction and obfuscation by many in the international community, who felt either defensive or shamed by their failure to prevent the massacre in the first place.

Adding to the emotional chaos, there were threads of hope for the women to grab. The *New York Times* carried reports of six Muslim men from Srebrenica who'd been hiding in the woods for nine months and finally stumbled into the safety of a NATO camp. The youngest was sixteen; his mother had given him up for dead. The impact of their reunion reached far beyond his family. Every woman with a missing son or wife with a missing husband hoped against hope that he would come staggering out of the woods. Horrified at the prospect of un-buried remains being ravaged by predators, the women were desperately impatient that of the twelve thousand missing persons on the list maintained by the International Red Cross, fewer than five hundred had been accounted for.

In the spring of 1996, several Bosnians as well as some officials in Washington encouraged me to become involved. But I felt over-whelmed by the immensity of the survivors' needs, especially given Lillian's needs. Lying in bed, I thought how wretchedly ironic it would be if I turned away because the survivors' plight was too dire. I decided to take on some small part: helping the women who were planning a one-year commemoration of their boys' and men's disappearance. (The mass graves had not yet been discovered, so the women refused to say "death.")

I pulled together experts, whose sense of the Balkans I trusted, from inside and outside the embassy. We would respond at practical, political, and personal levels. To determine their practical needs, with phones not working, we dispatched Mirjana Grandits, a former member of the Austrian parliament who spoke Bosnian. The refugees stressed that they "didn't want to live on humanitarian aid," instead asking for specifics such as computers to collect statistics, washing machines for a public laundry, and glass to repair greenhouses.

Our political work was more problematic. I called the State Department to check out a rumor of an effort to quash our plans. A Foreign Service officer confirmed the rumor, saying that international relief workers had been "traumatized" by the "dangerous" refugees who, during a street demonstration, had picked up stones and thrown them at the Red Cross office window. When I pressed for details, he said he'd read about the event in newspapers.

"Dangerous? Were they armed?"

"Well, no, I guess not."

I wasn't put off by the thought of angry women who were at least willing to act. Over the ensuing weeks, we continued to hear of critics within the bureaucracy who ranged from skeptical to adamantly opposed to our work. Some feared that a commemoration might provoke a riot, an unwelcome interruption in what was already a fragile peace process. I took that risk seriously. But to say that diplomats should be prohibited from working with agitated people in a tense situation made no sense.

To address the personal needs of the women, we would let them know they weren't being abandoned. In Bosnia I met with several of the survivors. We spoke not as ambassador to refugee but as woman to woman. A gaunt forty-year-old with stark white hair stood before me. She showed me two napkin-sized squares of fabric, one with her son's name and birth year, 1978; the other, her husband's. As she had embroidered, she'd been overcome by grief and had to be hospitalized. She held the squares with arms outstretched toward me, as if presenting an offering. For each of the thousands of missing boys and men there would be a cloth, much like the bracelets inscribed with the names of Vietnam POWs in the 1960s and 1970s.

The commemoration would mark the hour when the women, a year earlier, had been given minutes to board buses and leave behind their boys and men to be executed. Now buses that the women themselves had hired would carry thousands of refugees from the countryside. I would bring an international delegation, including Queen Noor and the EU commissioner Emma Bonino to underscore the message: You are not alone.

At our planning meeting I tried to maintain a delicate balance, empathizing with the sobbing women whose hands I held in mine, while trying to temper their justified rage. "If I were in your place," I told them, "I'd be out there demonstrating." But I stressed the importance of keeping the ceremony from devolving into a protest rally that would allow the women to be dismissed as troublemakers.

The U.S. military commander who would provide security was concerned that the event would not be "evenhanded." So I asked the women if they could invite Serbs who were also grieving, even though their missing sons might have been perpetrators of the massacre. As soon as the words were out of my mouth, I feared that I was asking too much of women whose losses I would never be able to fathom. But Fatima, one of the organizers, said simply, "We're all mothers."

Our political effort was further complicated, given that war criminals responsible for the massacre were not only on the loose, but in positions of power such as mayor and police chief. How on earth could we expect the women of Srebrenica and hundreds of thousands of other refugees to return home? Yet the peace agreement mandated the right of refugees to return. To pressure policy makers, we mobilized women worldwide to sign an open letter in the *International Herald Tribune*. In only ten days we gathered signatures from more than three hundred monarchs, politicians, bankers, peace activists, business leaders, and celebrities.

At the weekly meeting of our country team, I said that we needed more fax capacity. Offers to help came from embassy employees named Joyce, Jean, and Joy. Women helping women. If we could harness this power, we might have a different world, I thought.

Even Lady Thatcher couldn't stay removed. In her distinctively chilly voice, the former prime minister informed me by phone that she had received our fax. "I generally don't sign these sorts of things, and particularly *this* letter, which strikes me as rather strange. After all you're raising the expectations of these poor women, by overpromising 'concrete help.'"

I told her about the millions in aid that we had accumulated. This didn't satisfy the Iron Lady, who further opined that the political demands in the letter didn't have teeth. I stood at my desk holding the phone, wondering why she'd bothered to call. Then she added that she was faxing her own sentiments, for us to deliver to the refugees. Iron, but with a heart. Margaret Thatcher's letter would join one other in our press kit: that of President Mary Robinson of Ireland. Would that they could have teamed up to solve problems closer to home, I mused to myself.

Valerie Gillen, who was organizing every aspect of the commemoration, went down to Tuzla ahead of me. She brought together U.S. military officers, local government officials, and representatives of the women. Everyone was nervous about security; in a recent campaign, a Bosnian presidential candidate had been hit on the head with a steel bar. As bomb-sniffing dogs and protection teams scoped out the indoor sports arena, our soldiers discovered that a portion of the floor had been ripped up for restoration. Val called to say that the local women had capitulated to the manager of the sports center, who insisted that our event be moved to a gym one-sixth the size.

"Absolutely not," I replied. The manager responded that the floor replacement would take three weeks to complete.

"We'll have our event without a floor," I said.

On July 10, through the night, the grieving women hung their embroidered cloths on every available wall and railing of the center. The next morning I met Commissioner Bonino at the Vienna airport, where our party of sixty loaded onto a flight donated by Austrian Airlines. Among the ambassadors, NGO leaders, members of nobility, CEOs, and media professionals was Laura Bonaparte, a founder of the Mothers of the Plaza de Mayo, who awakened the world's conscience in the late 1970s by protesting on behalf of "the disappeared" in Argentina's Dirty War.

Landing at the military base near Tuzla, we were greeted by several survivors and dozens of soldiers. Queen Noor emerged from her own plane in ecru, a traditional color for Muslim mourning. She carried herself gracefully, a sheer veil draped over her head.

The right people had turned out to do the right thing. But Srebrenica was one of the greatest failures of our generation, and underlying our energy was a sense of dread. Each of the "principals" rode to the stadium in a Humvee with one of the survivors. My escort was Zehra, an engineer. "The only time I'm happy is when I'm dreaming about home," she told me.

The half-hour drive from the base to the sports center was lined with police and soldiers. I noticed a vine with deep-red roses on the side of a burned-out farmhouse. Those roses hadn't missed a summer—despite the murders, rapes, and shelling. But as we entered the arena the air was hot and thick, and the lights were off. Each of the six thousand seats was filled, and people jammed the aisles and doorways. The crowd emitted an ominous hum, like a huge swarm of bees. As our contingent walked in, some applauded. Others reacted with increased agitation, rocking back and forth in their seats, sobbing, or calling out.

We took our places in the front rows on the stadium floor, thirty feet from the stage. Female soldiers from the American base, whom we'd briefed, were positioned throughout the crowd among the grieving women.

The program, planned by the survivors, began with a pre-war tourism film recalling the quiet spa town of Srebrenica. That was followed by news footage of citizens terrified as shells burst around them, a gruesome account of a baby decapitated because it wouldn't stop crying, and unarmed boys and men marching off to execution. A woman recognized her husband and called out his name. Others started to shriek or faint. Commotion was building in the arena as one after another was carried down the steep stairs, unconscious. On the screen, the Serb general was ordering the women to get in the buses. In the arena, cries rang out to stop the film. More and more of the crowd was standing.

A riot was imminent. No one was in control. I grabbed Marijana's hand and bounded onto the stage, calling out for the technician to stop the projector. As a therapist I'd calmed individuals, but I'd never tried to calm a crowd. Taking over the mike, I began intoning in a slow litany, "Please sit down . . . Please sit down . . . Thank you . . . Please sit down . . . I have a message for you . . . Please sit down . . . Thank you . . . Thank you . . . Please sit down." Marijana interpreted my words in a strong but soothing voice until, to my enormous relief, the women nearest the front sat down, then those behind, and those behind them.

Calm was restored. I went on to speak about the international women leaders joining them in common cause that day. And I proclaimed the women of Bosnia the hope for their country's future, describing the help we'd brought, and closing with a letter from President Clinton.

Queen Noor spoke eloquently and regally, delivering an Arabic prayer from the Koran. Her Majesty's words of spiritual comfort were a compress to the women's pummeled spirits. Emma threw away her script. In a scrappy, no-nonsense tone she laid out the European Union's commitment to help. Then Laura Bonaparte, who had the most credibility of us all, took the stage. She recounted the disappearances of six of her family during the junta's reign of terror. As the women wept, she urged them not to relent. When the program was over, as we passed into the ground-level exit, arms stretched toward us from the sides and the seats above.

My heart felt like a stone as I flew in Her Majesty's plane to Vienna. We'd succeeded in our goal of attracting international attention, and consequently support, for the survivors of Srebrenica, who in turn represented two million people displaced by the war. But that day, the first mass graves were being opened. Skeletons and rotting leather shoes would tell part of the story. The women still alive would tell the rest. Thanks to Christiane Ammanpour of CNN and others, the story of the women of Srebrenica circled the globe. The mourning of thousands in the arena became a cry for action articulated by international women leaders and amplified by global media, creating more pressure for political response.

The next day, a different story would lead. But the faces of the women would be with me for the rest of my life. I felt no closure, knowing that they were still waking every morning to face another day, despite their grief. But when I needed strength, I would remember them.

Keeping the Faith

I understood the power of Her Majesty's quoting from the Koran. I too have turned to scriptures for comfort, courage, or healing. My faith provides me some assurance that I'm not crazy to envision a world right at a cosmic level when it is god-awful wrong in reality. But my trust in God doesn't include a belief that everything that happens is part of some divine plan. We are all co-creators, and as such bear responsibility for others' suffering. As a child I'd listened to missionaries urging me to "go ye therefore and teach all nations"; and in a sense my work in the Balkans was a fulfillment of that Great Commission, which compelled me as a teenager to walk down the aisle, dedicating my life "for special service." In the simplest of terms, my work is my ministry.

The core experience of religion exists outside of reason. Emerging into consciousness, it can be fashioned into a cup of cool water—or into a cross, lynching rope, or gas chamber. For millennia political leaders have convinced their citizens or troops that God is on their side. War in the Balkans was no exception. Orthodox and Catholic Christians turned prayers into war cries against Muslims. But religion was also invoked as an excuse by those in the international community who called the genocide a "religious war," providing a reason why they shouldn't intervene. "Those people will always be fighting," the pundits concluded. Others, like me, observed that a "religious war" in a secular, communist country was far-fetched. Milosevic's motivation was political, not religious. Bosnians had celebrated their neighbors' holy days for decades.

Given my background in theology, I welcomed the request from two wise Americans, David Little and Landrum Bolling, that I host two Bosnian leaders from each faith—Muslim, Catholic, Orthodox, and Jewish—for a three-day meeting in Vienna to create an interreligious council. In preparation, I visited each man in Sarajevo, extending a personal invitation for the meeting and asking if he had a special wish. The Muslim imam, trained at the University of Chicago, wanted McDonald's hamburgers and a trip to a theological bookstore. David Kamhi, vice president of the Jewish community, said he'd love to attend a concert, since as a violinist he'd performed in Vienna. I suggested that he bring his instrument, so I could accompany him on the piano. He hemmed and hawed and finally asked if I could borrow one for him, since he might have difficulty bringing his own through customs. (Later I learned that he didn't want to tell a stranger his violin had been destroyed in the shelling.) The strings repairman at the famous Vienna Musikverein lent us one.

The discussions, led by the two Americans, were punctuated by impromptu concerts on our terrace and in the café of the Schönbrunn gardens; I played the piano as David performed for surprised strollers.

As he lifted the bow, joy seemed to flow through the instrument. Finally, David swallowed his pride and asked if he might borrow the violin for six months. The request was startling, but so is war. I bought the instrument and gave it to him with a big red bow. We celebrated with champagne and tears.

The religious leaders identified with opposing forces, but we all knew that if they started indulging in accusations about the war, our negotiation process would implode. My role was to create an environment of trust. I said that we wouldn't observe protocol or use titles; the cardinal probably hadn't been called Vinko in quite a while. Over meals, I intentionally asked personal questions to strip away defenses. We learned that David had put down his violin and taken up a gun to defend Sarajevo, even though killing was an outrage for him, with eighty relatives, friends, and family murdered by Nazis. But everyone had a story. Or stories. The task was to find a balance, not ignoring what had happened but moving on toward hope. In a profound moment, Dushan, the Orthodox priest, united the group, expressing the thought that came to him as he looked out the airplane window: how a God of love must view the travail of creation with enormous pain. On that, we could all agree.

After three days, the men had crafted a joint statement with tedious care so that each could sign. Explaining the successful outcome, they spoke of the family atmosphere. As Dushan kissed nine-year-old Teddy on the forehead, he said to me, "You won our hearts, not just our minds."

Only one key person was missing. The metropolitan (head Serb Orthodox) said he was ill. Instead, I met with him in Sarajevo afterward to enlist his cooperation. The Serb church had been notoriously complicit with Milosovic's aggression, so I felt some trepidation as the metropolitan walked into the lobby of the Hotel Bosna, the no-frills lodging where Charles and I were staying. He was tall and gaunt, wearing black. Although he grudgingly affirmed the joint statement, I felt little rapport as we talked. With his long, white beard and flowing robe, the metropolitan reminded me of the classic God the Father. Given my history, that was a sterile thought indeed.

Soon after their return to Sarajevo, the men held a joint news conference announcing the formation of the Inter-Religious Council and insisting on fundamental human and religious rights. The council would be studied and replicated in other conflicts near and far. Rather than be an excuse for division, faith had fashioned reconciliation.

Religious themes kept seeping into my work, without my looking for them. That was a comfort for me, a private opportunity to remember why, with all the options I had, I've chosen to live a life oriented toward others.

In the fall of 1996 I hosted a dinner for an auction by Christie's of London chaired by my predecessor, Ambassador Ron Lauder. Chancellor Vranitzky called the auction "a sign of reconciliation and of his country's awareness of its moral co-responsibility" for war atrocities. After the Second World War Austria took possession of more than eight thousand paintings and other objects belonging to Jewish families whose homes had been plundered by Nazis. The stolen goods were tucked away in a fourteenth-century monastery in Mauerbach, near Vienna. Owners were located for only four hundred pieces.

Five decades of controversy were the backdrop for this sale of stolen art from stolen lives. Simon Wiesenthal dubbed the auction hall a "gallery of tears." It was packed with private collectors and buyers from Jewish museums around the world; but as if entering a temple, the spectators were unusually silent as they viewed fragments of thousands of lives irrevocably shattered.

Proceeds from the sale went to Austria's Jewish community, 200,000 strong before the war. With sixty thousand put to death in camps and others fleeing, only eight thousand remained. The anticipated revenue from the sale was $3.5 million; but almost all the bidding began above the estimated price, and revenues were fivefold. Even so, this event was about recognition, not compensation.

As I walked through the hall, I thought how each object was both art and memorial, representing moments of home life: a painting that hung undusted over someone's mantel, a sculpture that scampering children almost knocked over a dozen times, a candelabrum that once glowed in a streetside window. I purchased a painting of a young boy, delicate, even pensive, in his gray suit, with an unexpected pink bow tie. He reminded me of Teddy, our Theodore, whose name lineage included Charles's great-uncle Theo, a Parisian banker murdered by Nazis.

My involvement was natural, since Jewish community leaders were in our home frequently, and I attended events in their spaces. I also took it upon myself to encourage the government to establish a Fund for the Victims of National Socialism, providing a lump sum, at least $7,000, to persons who fled the Nazis or were incarcerated in camps. The organizers believed that about half the twenty thousand recipients were living in the United States.

When I visited the office of the fund in old Vienna, I noticed how elderly men and women were pushing open the heavy eighteen-foot door to enter the packed waiting room. More than the money, they wanted a chance to pass on stories, seasoned by decades of remembering. Sometimes, as they overheard each other talk to the staff, the applicants began to interact. "*You* were at Mauthausen *too*? Do you remember . . . ?" Their files were organized by birth years stretching back to the last century, in boxes stacked in every conceivable spot, including a bathtub. The young staff had a great sense of urgency. The clock was ticking. Many of the first recipients were over a hundred years old.

More than the work, the stories themselves took a toll on the staff. Group visits to a psychiatrist addressed the nightmares they were having. I took several hours to talk with the young people, a new generation grappling with the trauma. For both old and young this was a step in the long journey toward healing.

Folding past into present in a way that honors the good and the bad of who we are is a fundamental step for moving into the future. My work with religious communities was laced with reminders not only of my father's narrow social views but also of Mother's religious devotion. Yet when I thought of Mother, I remembered the constraints on her that had left us as kids largely to raise ourselves.

But in Vienna, who was I to criticize? Even after I was in my groove, functioning at full efficiency, my embassy schedule didn't lighten up. There was always another demand, another situation that I could, if I paid attention, help resolve. And so it was both a relief and a concern to see how my husband had dramatically increased his presence in Teddy's life.

I had to push to get back to the residence for dinner by seven, but Charles's office was at home. That meant plenty of father-son time after primary school let out for the day. But my time with my son was relatively truncated.

I didn't recognize the shift in our parenting until one evening, when over soup Charles told me obliquely that we needed to talk after dinner. I looked with curiosity at my husband, trying to guess what was on his mind. When the children had left the table, I picked up my coffee and moved to a chair beside him. Hands folded, he rested his long arms on the white linen tablecloth and leaned toward me.

"Well, Love," he said, in a low voice, "I've been concerned about Teddy's breathing noise during his naps."

I took a sip of coffee. "Teddy still takes naps?"

Charles looked at me with an unwearied smile. "Yes, and when I check on him, his breathing sounds very labored. He's got some obstruction."

"Gee, I guess we'd better take him to a doctor," I suggested, in my best can-do manner.

"I did. The doctor thinks Teddy needs his tonsils out."

"Well, I suppose we should get a second opinion," I offered weakly.

"I already have, and I've made a date with the hospital for the surgery."

I was floored. More than he could have imagined, I appreciated Charles's attentiveness to our son. My husband wasn't socialized for child care. In fact, he was sorely uncomfortable with his frequent role of house-husband. For him to assume that responsibility was a matter of will, not inclination. It was a gift to me; one more time Charles was at my side—coaching me, urging me to reach, and doing whatever was necessary to support me beyond what either of us had imagined when we met.

But though I was appreciative, misgivings plagued me. Teddy and I had more time together when Lillian was hospitalized. But when she was at home and ill, she had to be my highest priority. My little son worshiped his sister and didn't compete with her. He also didn't have, or create, problems to draw my attention. Maybe I was letting him down. A decent mother would know that her child took naps.

I hadn't grown up seeing professional women raising kids. Did they all feel the way I was feeling? Helen and I had hated our mother's distractions. It seemed that she was always at our father's beck and call, or on the phone, or running an hour late. And now, as I moved from one pressing meeting to another, seizing an opportunity here, solving a catastrophe there, I harbored a terrible thought: Perhaps I was replicating what I resented most.

To be honest, I hardly had time to contemplate my shortcomings, never mind how to correct them, given the demands of my work. I was finally able to arrange a meeting between Presidents Clinton and Klestil. As I had with the chancellor, I sat on a sofa in the Oval Office. The presidents moved their heads closer and closer as they warmed up to each other. It was amusing to see how Klestil, unlike Vranitzky from the banking world, knew how to be a good ole boy.

The next day, while Klestil was still in the United States, an official at the State Department announced that Austria had been put on a list of recalcitrant offenders in the global crime network, because it allowed anonymous bank accounts. Neither I nor the White House had been informed, much less consulted. Apart from the dubious merits of the listing, this was an ill-advised move by a State cowboy. But then many would have put me in the cowgirl category.

Given that I didn't take to being corralled, I sometimes wondered how well I fit into the high-level political world. There were many signs of my being trusted, such as having a place on a trip on Air Force One. On my first trip I introduced myself to the man in the next seat.

"Swanee Hunt? I've wanted to meet you. The president's face lights up every time your name is mentioned."

"You're Sandy Berger? I've wanted to meet you too." Sandy was the deputy national security adviser and a long-time friend of the Democratic Party. He'd been with Holbrooke, Harriman, and Albright, keeping the flame alive during the Reagan and Bush years.

In contrast, I wasn't even on the Washington radar. I wasn't an international business leader or foreign policy scholar like some other appointees. And I wasn't a long-time friend of the Clintons. So why I was flying with insiders?

One reason was that certain people liked me. They smiled when they heard that between White House appointments, I blended in among fifty volunteers decorating Christmas trees with clusters of dried hydrangeas, courtesy of Martha Stewart. They appreciated that I brought Viennese chocolates to the White House chief of staff and the secretaries alike. But they also knew that I'd written a paragraph in the story we were all living. In West Wing halls I was met with a grin from staffers two decades my junior now. One recalled the 1992 campaign, how when there was a slump in morale, news of our "Million Dollar Day: Serious Issues, Serious Women, Serious Money" generated a surge of spirit. Another stopped me, saying that she'd come to Denver with Tipper Gore and that the symposium had set a new standard for substantive events on the campaign trail.

"You're family," more than one-high level official assured me.

How, then, to interpret briefings in the Oval Office when "the Man" would hardly look up from his desk, much less express any particular closeness. Maybe that was a signal that I truly *was* family. No formalities needed. But around others, the president seemed warmer. He was quick to compliment me, his arm across my shoulders. "She's doing good work for us in Bosnia," he would tell whoever was in earshot.

So who was I in the high-stakes political world where reputations rose and plummeted within weeks? In Washington, I was a big funder, ambassador to a plum post, Balkan activist, and women's advocate. The first role was a result of my father's and brother's business aptitude. The second was due to the appreciation and confidence of the First Lady. But I dealt with uncertainties over whether I was in or out in Washington, over whether I was insider or outsider, by focusing on the refugees who were counting on me, or the women leaders who spoke of me as one of "their" successes. My activist and advocate roles were my own doing.

There's no question that I was an outsider when it came to State. As a woman diplomat, I knew I was in a minority. Still, I felt disheartened when I walked by pictures of the current chiefs of mission in Europe: dozens of men and four women.

Only one of those women, Ambassador Harriman, had the distinction of being in the nexus of political power. I saw Pamela briefly at Clinton's second inauguration in January 1997. When I suggested that we might get together later that day she sighed, saying that she was on her way to three more parties. We could meet up at one of them, she offered. No, we couldn't. I wasn't invited. That was the difference between my strong relationships and her real connections.

"But what's happening with the family lawsuit that was hanging over your head?"

"It's horrible. I don't know how I got into this mess. I was just leaving the trust management to the lawyers," she sighed, in a manner reminiscent of our conversation three years earlier.

As for her plans, she said that she was returning home, but that she had promised the president she would stay in Paris until her replacement arrived, given the political sensitivities that she was managing with the French. Then, as if it were the next logical thought, she asked what I was wearing to the Inaugural Ball.

"Silk pants? Really?" she lilted. "I wanted to wear pants because they're warmer. Are you sure it's okay?"

Smiling, I reminded her that she set the standard. "If you're dressed more casually, everyone else is overdressed." I was amazed at how self-assurance and insecurity could coexist. We were both, it seems, riddled with contradiction.

Unlike Pamela, I was hoping to stay on. I didn't anticipate a problem, since I'd been repeatedly told by high-level officials that when other ambassadors were replaced for the president's second term, I'd be asked to continue in Vienna or at another post. I was even tracked down by phone on a visit to India to ask what positions I'd find of interest.

Just to dot i's and cross t's, I met with Madeleine Albright. I'd lobbied for her appointment as secretary of state, and we'd had good times together in Vienna and elsewhere. So I wasn't surprised when she responded to my request to stay on with "I want you on my team," before we moved on to a discussion of Saddam Hussein and other troubles.

Melanne, at Hillary's side, was the exception in advising me not to pursue an extension, even though she'd earlier assured me that I'd be asked to remain. But I decided that I had nothing to lose. I would take my request directly to President Clinton.

One more time I showed my identification to the guards on Pennsylvania Avenue and walked up the driveway to the West Wing. Waiting for my appointment, I watched as a sequence of world leaders filed in and out of the lobby. The president was falling farther and farther behind schedule. But his warm-hearted secretary, Betty Currie, had wedged me in. She assured me that I'd still have ten minutes to make my case.

When my turn finally came, I walked into the Oval Office and saw a noticeably tired Bill Clinton. He was recovering from knee surgery, and his back was hurting, but he positioned himself on a tall stool and laid his crutch to the side.

"I know we don't have much time," I said, handing him a piece of paper. At Charles's suggestion, I'd listed on one page the reasons I was a good choice for any of several posts, condensing to sound bites four years of innovation and effort. The president read over the page as I made my verbal pitch. Then he peered over his reading glasses and said, "I'd really like to have you continue. Now, what do you think we should be doing in Bosnia?"

I was taken off guard but managed to rattle off a relatively coherent answer: the most important move right now is to pick up the indicted war criminals. The French are dragging their feet in the quadrant they control, but you're the president of the United States, so you've got to push past their resistance. I know you're getting conflicting messages from State and the Agency. I've seen some of the intel reporting. The CIA is saying that Bosnian Serbs will stage a strong resistance if we pick up their leaders. I've talked to scores of people on the ground who think they're wrong. In fact, the intel you're seeing is often off-base. I'm sure, because I know firsthand some of the people they're writing about, whom the analysts have never met. Meanwhile, if you don't get the war criminals off the streets, refugees will be too frightened to go home. That's half the population. Plus, the fledgling democratic process will stagnate, because extremists will continue to dominate the political parties.

The president listened with a crinkled brow. Then he picked up his crutch. "Thanks. You've done a great job," he said.

"You're so welcome. I'll see you soon."

Grinning, I walked away from the White House and threaded across busy 17th Street. In a café, I was meeting a friend who'd served in multiple foreign policy positions but had recently been unceremoniously ushered out.

"I'm so thrilled. It looks like I'll be staying on," I gushed.

My friend was plugged into D.C. in ways that I would never be. He listened attentively. "What exactly did the president say?" he asked. I recounted our conversation, word for word.

"Be careful. 'I'd really like to have you continue' isn't the same as 'You will continue.'" I was stunned.

Turned out my friend was right. Weeks later I received a memo from the president's chief of staff asking all political appointees to be prepared to depart their posts by July 4. That sterile order was such a stark contrast with the high-flying, over-the-top laudation I'd become used to in Austria. A piece of humble pie, my mother would have said. Adding to the insult, the announcement came after I'd turned over every leaf and gone all the way to the top to try to extend my service into the second term.

On the other hand, although I was terribly disappointed, I wasn't surprised, given the warning I'd received from my veteran Beltway friend, who could cite a long list of people who had done a good job but were now being shoved out. Privately, the chief of staff told me that he appreciated my letter to the president expressing my wish to stay. Of course that wasn't an option, he explained. With very few exceptions, mostly for backroom reasons, the first-term ambassadors were being shown the door so as to let others in. But, the chief of staff thanked me, the page I'd brought to the Oval Office was helpful because it had let the president know that there were some wrong impressions "out there."

So that's where I was. Out there.

Shaping History

Once I knew I was in the final stretch, I began to think of how to wrap up my time, to be sure I made as great an impact as I could. I'd been a good American representative to Austria and helpful in the Balkans. But my work relating to women across Eastern Europe was where I still had the most to add.

My first weeks on the job, I'd made a conscious decision not to focus on women's issues and not to address women's groups, choosing to make my contribution to the feminist cause by establishing myself simply as highly competent. The strategy worked. In my latter two years, when I did engage in women's concerns, I did so as someone whom other women could look up to as well-versed in political issues.

In our own shop, I was appalled at how few professional women were represented at meetings that dealt with hard-core matters like Russia's economic implosion or the metastasizing drug trade. I was determined to do whatever I could so that women wouldn't be written out of the history we were helping to shape. For the hundred or so events that we hosted each year at our residence, I sent a memo to my staff saying that all invitation lists had to have at least 30 percent women. Including women at embassy functions would stimulate fresh ideas, build support for our work in the community, and raise women's professional standing.

The next list I received was from our defense attaché. All men. I sent it back. He said that no women were interested in NATO expansion. I told him that if need be, he would find women in press or nongovernmental organizations. Or he could ask his male contacts for names of their female colleagues. In short, he could find them, or I would. He did.

Secretary Albright was enthusiastic at the effectiveness of this tactic. "Supporting women is not only the right thing to do. It's the smart thing to do," she said on International Women's Day. Still, I was often a lonely voice for women in the foreign policy establishment.

One morning I arrived at my office to find State Department cables spread across my desk. I normally didn't have time to read other ambassadors' mail traffic, but Susan had seen a train going down the track and thought that I might want to throw myself in front of it. The former senator from Colorado, Tim Wirth, was Clinton's undersecretary of state for global affairs. He was considering adding an assessment of women's status to the annual Human Rights Report, which was congressionally mandated and produced by American embassies. The cables from Europe and Canada all opposed including a section on women. One said that embassy staffs were overstretched and didn't have time to gather the information. I was sympathetic. Another said that women could walk the streets of Madrid at midnight, and rape wasn't a problem. I had serious doubts. A third said that to discuss the status of women would trivialize the report. That made me boil.

Susan canceled whatever was on my schedule as I composed a response: I reminded Tim that White House policy articulated by the First Lady at the UN Conference on Women in Beijing was that "Women's rights are human rights. Where the first are respected, the second follow." This was a chance to put that policy into action. Plain and simple.

Tim later told me that based on the other embassies' objections, his colleagues had given up on the idea. But after his team had already left the office, he picked up my cable on his way to their off-site staff retreat. There, when he read my protest, the decision was overturned. Within a couple of years few remembered that the Human Rights Report hadn't always covered women. I was struck by how the stars needed to align: Susan on her toes, I with time at my desk, Tim late to the retreat. This was how a policy affecting millions was made.

The reluctance of the other embassies was distressing but predictable. For four years I'd seen international policies and practices focused almost exclusively on the highest political and corporate leaders —an overwhelmingly male group. The foreign policy establishment seemed not to care that women often had a different way of looking at the world. Nor did they understand how in countries north, east, and south of Austria, women could be the glue holding together fragile societies during transition through rough times. Communist-era quotas to create a political voice for women had been abandoned; females had dropped from 30 percent to less than 10 percent in the parliaments. They'd been the first laid off as economies collapsed. In the new Europe they lacked political and economic power to shape their nations' destinies—or their own.

To support these women, Val (whose boundless energy matched my boundless ideas) and I created the Vienna Women's Initiative. When Charles was away conducting, I moved both children into our bed to free up their rooms for guests. A dozen women leaders from an Eastern European country would spend several days at the residence. One described the post-traumatic stress of victims from Chernobyl; another asked how to save young women from the clutches of sex traders. Croat women from opposing sides of the war refused to speak to each other as they traveled by bus to Vienna. But after three days of our structured activities, they were able to brainstorm joint initiatives for back home.

We visited the women in their countries as well. Our earlier meeting in the backyard of Ambassador Galbraith's residence in Zagreb was the model for another twenty visits across the region: Prague to Moscow, Warsaw to Odessa. Usually I combined family and work: sessions with women in the afternoon, Charles's concerts in the evening. Skopje was typical: the capital of Macedonia, a new state split off from Yugoslavia, it was in turmoil. Women were sharply divided into two camps, as they were throughout post-communist Europe: those faithful to the former regime and those chomping at the bit of democratic reform. I was told that members of each group had refused to attend a reception in the home of Macedonia's new president when they heard that the others were invited.

We began our day in Skopje with a small meeting organized by the American embassy, so that we could hear the women's stories and establish trust. Some of the women were broad-shouldered, with deeply wrinkled faces, testifying to a rural economy and a tough life. Others were slim, wearing fashionable suits and pearls. For both, there was nothing subtle about the heavy makeup and henna-toned hair. But the women's political and social analysis was nuanced, and they were hungry to hear about how organizations in the United States were addressing the same challenges they now were facing in their new, democratic, capitalist reality.

The embassy considered it a coup when the heads of both the communists and the reformers consented to be on the dais for my lecture at the law school. In my address I described how American women donors have united in support of women political candidates, and how we'd crossed ideological lines in the Women's Foundation of Colorado. After fifty years of totalitarian rule, the notion of finding slivers of common ground while not quashing diversity was new.

But the most memorable moment was at Charles's concert that evening. He looked through his scores one last time, and I hung around backstage to give him a report on the audience, straighten his tie, and wish him a lucky "Toi, toi, toi." As the players tuned and he waited in the wings, I was the last to slip into my seat, just in time to clap with the crowd as he strode with deliberative long steps onto the stage.

I always fell in love anew with my striking husband at that moment of a concert, but that evening Charles worked his magic on more than me. Two women, the communist and reformer leaders, approached me during the intermission. They stood with their arms around each other's waist. "The concert is wonderful," they raved. "And we want you to know we're here—and we're sitting *together*."

Our success in Skopje was repeated in visits throughout Eastern Europe. But it took Charles, for the thousandth time my key strategist, to see the pattern and importance of what we were doing. At his urging, Val, her able assistant Sarah, and I created a conference that we named "Vital Voices: Women in Democracy." In July 1997 some 320 of the highest-ranking women in business, government, and law—East and West—gathered to learn from each other's successes and failures.

It was important that our meeting in Vienna bear Albright's imprimatur as the new secretary of state. I sent her the concept paper in March and met with her in April, presenting how this venue would complement her wider European strategy. We scheduled the conference just after a commitment that she already had in Madrid, to facilitate her coming. But State had no funds and the secretary decided not to come, although a member of her staff selected a U.S. delegation. Otherwise, we were on our own.

We put together scores of volunteers and a dozen new hires, found delegates from thirty-eight countries, lined up interpreters and logistics, created background briefings and printed materials, raised $700,000 in cash and in-kind gifts, handled financial accounts, negotiated with governments, designed a logo, and attended to VIPs.

Acknowledging the tough economic and political circumstances burdening many of the delegates, we had a string trio play as they lined up to register, and they found chocolates and cosmetic gifts in their rooms, rare gestures for most of the participants. But the women had come for ideas, not candy. These social activists, judges, educators, politicians, and CEOs were on the cutting edge of democratic change.

At sessions on politics, law, and business, the women discussed the cultural barriers that hindered progress. All the while, they never forgot that they were women. An economist from Bank Austria said, "At dinner we talked about how we wished we had time to iron blouses." The next day she realized that her conversation had been with Elisabeth Rehn, a former defense minister and UN special rapporteur of the Commission on Human Rights in the Former Yugoslavia.

Justice Sandra Day O'Connor gave a strong feminist pitch, and Hillary Clinton paid tribute to the strength of women whom she had encountered in her travels. Once again, we were grappling with serious issues and serious women. But this time, *Hillary* was in a position to bring serious money to the table. She listened to speakers from Lithuania, Bulgaria, and Croatia tell their stories. Then she went to the podium and declared, "We are here to advance the cause of women and to advance the cause of democracy, and to make it absolutely clear that the two are inseparable."

Afterwards the delegates were delighted to learn that we'd arranged for them to have their picture taken with Hillary in the park. The picture would be useful for years in their work back home. Hillary was a star, of course, but I'd grown up with stars and wasn't easily struck, so I flinched as I was pushed and pulled by her advance people, all of whom were professional, competent, and just doing their jobs. We arrived by bus at the park an hour before the picture was scheduled. The advance team wanted to immediately line up the women on bleachers.

"Absolutely not," I responded, unwilling to have the likes of the president of the Polish National Bank, the former prime minister of Lithuania, and a Serb democratic party leader wilting in the hot summer sun. I invited our conference attendees to stroll through the rose garden and held off the advance team for half an hour. After their third request, I asked them to call to see how close to schedule the First Lady was running. Right on time. I didn't believe it but let myself be persuaded. Like dolls on a shelf, Eastern Europe's leading women waited in their high heels and suits in the midday sun for forty-five minutes. Hillary would have melted if she'd known.

Still, the gathering was a success. The cross-fertilization of East and West spawned new legislation, organizations, and a huge boost to the spirits of women forgotten in the postcommunist depression. After my departure, Hillary kept Vital Voices as an initiative of the State Department. We'd created something lasting, not only for the women but also for their communities and countries.

The conference was a turning point in the way policy makers considered women in the changing European political landscape. The powerful journal *Foreign Affairs*, which almost never tipped its hat to women's plight or strength, ran an article I'd written describing the precipitous fall of women's salaries, social supports for their children, and representation in Eastern European government. And the last day of the gathering, the *International Herald Tribune* carried my op-ed echoing the same themes. Dozens of TV, radio, and press organizations covered the meeting. A reporter from Prague took me aside and said: "Thank you for having the impulse for everyday courage."

I realized only later, as I read my journal, that creating Vital Voices was my response to the First Lady's private request to me two years earlier for ideas about how she might support women around the world. As I left diplomatic life, I felt great about her taking on our project as her own. I tried to feel equally generous when *Newsweek* ran an article entitled "Hillary's Vital Voices," describing a forthcoming meeting which they said was part of a movement launched in Vienna in 1997, by Madeleine Albright.

Hillary, with Melanne and Chelsea, stayed on for a week, the longest that the First Lady of the United States, or FLOTUS as she was termed, had spent in any foreign country. The Austrians and I were delighted. But a visit from a principal was a blessing and a curse for embassy staff. While they basked in the reflected glory, for them security, logistics, schedule, and press were just as complicated for a bicycle outing as for a public address.

Seventy people from Washington were involved in the advance work. "Each innie needs an outie," explained my political officer Debbie Cavin, who coordinated the hundreds of moving parts, "wheels down to wheels up." Now, too late, I could see how it felt to others who repeatedly reviewed every detail of arrangements for an event featuring me, only to wait for an hour (for any of a thousand reasons they'd never hear), or learn that I wasn't coming at all.

I thought back on Hillary telling me that White House chefs were flustered when She and He asked for their own jar of peanut butter. After four years of hating that I couldn't pour my own coffee without offending a host, I knew what she meant. So during supper in our residence, I had no wait staff attending. Hillary was serving herself some salad, and a small piece of boiled egg dropped into her glass. When I reached to change her water, she said, "Oh, no, that's fine." So I held myself back for the next hour, watching the egg disintegrating in the bottom of Hillary's glass as she drank the clouded water.

Meanwhile, a crowd of excited Americans had gathered downstairs to share a concert with their First Lady. A member of the FLOTUS advance team politely approached me, saying that he was about to get everyone seated before we came down. "No," I insisted. "She can go down and mingle in the garden for ten minutes, then we'll all move back into the living room."

"It's your house, Ambassador," said the advance man, which I thought was remarkably perceptive.

We descended the stairs. Three steps from the bottom Hillary was surrounded. She could have been dressed in flypaper. We heard whispers: "Take a picture of me with her. Use my camera." The First Lady of the United States was a prop. I remembered how often I'd handed off my own camera, asking someone to take my picture. Now I understood the role of the advance team, and how limited my friend's choices were: either "Make way for the queen!" or bedlam. Watching Hillary's life up close, I ached for her.

We spent the last few days in Salzburg. Across the street from the main entrance of our hotel, crowds waited dawn to dusk behind a barricade, hoping to catch a glimpse of the First Lady. Our comings and goings became the city's latest cultural event. A throng of youth gathered to serenade our hotel. When I leaned out the window, someone pointed up. Thinking that I was Hillary, the young people began to cheer. I waved back. They cheered louder.

Hillary's advance team had asked us to plan several substantive events every day. We arranged a private discussion with Bosnian refugees, and later a lecture that she delivered, without notes, on the failures of the American education system. Another discussion was with Austrian women leaders. The advance team advised that the table should be a certain shape, the flowers in a certain position. Deciding on the invitees required a dozen interactions with the FLOTUS staff, to ensure that we had the women whom Hillary wanted. Some traveled a long distance for the meeting. They were asked to assemble an hour early to plan the spontaneous conversation that would ensue.

I wasn't with them. I was in the car with Hillary, briefing her on the profiles of the women. "And why are we doing this meeting?" she asked.

I looked at her with a hint of a smile. "Because your staff said you wanted it." "*My* staff?" she asked, incredulously. Fortunately the women were fabulous.

The American opera great Thomas Hampson flew in between performances in Geneva to sing for Hillary, accompanied by me on the piano. He sweetly ended with "Swanee River." But for traditional Tyrolean fare I called our friends, the Hauser family, from their nearby country inn. They threw their instruments and children into a van. The family's traditional clothes were a contrast to the hotel's luxurious red silk striped walls and windows. Handsome Balthazar pulled out his guitar, I took the harp, Magdelena played a dulcimer, and Hillary added percussion. We sang to our hearts' content. Eight-year-old Johannes, his father explained apologetically, could play the accordion only without shoes. Off they came, and his bare feet dangled from the chair as he performed.

On her last evening Hillary canceled our dinner plans to stay with Chelsea, who'd had a bike spill. Instead we had tea, curled up on her sofa. As always, Hillary was anxious to hear about Lillian and offered support and advice. As we talked about our pasts and futures, she urged me to write a book while my diplomatic experiences were still fresh. "Take two years," she counseled.

I asked her if she was going to write another. "Oh yes, several," she answered.

"Are you keeping a journal?" I pursued.

"Heavens no," she said. "I wouldn't dare. Someone would subpoena it."

Farewells

During my last conversation with Pamela Harriman, as we reminisced about our time in Europe, she commented, "Well, you've sure pulled your share of the load, Swanee." That was our benediction. The load had become too much for our ambassador to France. Two weeks later, at seventy-six, Pamela suffered a massive stroke as she left the swimming pool at the Ritz Hotel. Her days of dying were front-page news. Leading papers carried one tribute after another to this political insider who had become an accomplished player on the world stage.

I flew to Paris for her memorial service. Standing once more inside the gate of the former Rothschild estate, her assistant said quietly, "When that awful biography came out, your note was the first she got.

She kept it." As we walked up the steps, I remembered how when I'd brought Lillian for a visit, our cab had pulled up as Pamela was walking down those steps, looking smashing in a designer suit, with dark, patterned stockings accentuating her legs. She was so nervous, about to make her first speech in French.

Pamela was some woman. On the go morning, noon, and night, a decade past retirement age. I walked through the house to the yard and took my place on a small stage with a few rows of chairs, facing the back of the mansion. As we waited for the ceremony to begin, I thought of the State official who described to me how Pamela could lock in on a man, making him feel like king of the world. My friend had spoken from experience; she'd stomped out of a dinner when Pamela had focused her penetrating blue eyes on *her* husband.

So I could understand the adoration in the voice of President Jacques Chirac, who came in and stood by the flag-draped casket, eulogizing "*sa charme, sa générosité, sa finesse.*" He clearly appreciated her virtues, but so did two of her former lovers sitting in front of me: the Aga Khan, who oversaw a vast pan-Arabic financial empire; and Gianni Agnelli, head of Fiat and as close to a monarch as modern-day Italy permitted. Another facet of Pamela was represented that day by her son, Winston Spencer Churchill, who spoke with tears of his mother.

The press corps was crowded onto a platform on one side of the yard, their cameras trained on the red-plumed French soldier with horse-hair streaming from his helmet, the U.S. Marines in green uniforms, the flag at half-staff. High officials had flown over from Washington to accompany the casket. "We have come to take her home, where a saddened and deeply grateful president will pay respect," one said.

Even after her funeral, Pamela remained with me every day. From her I'd learned to bridge the policy, personal, and public worlds. A few months later I was in Dallas, a world away from Paris, talking with a relative. A propos a discussion about the limitations of my White House connections, I conceded, "I'm not a Pamela Harriman . . ."

Misunderstanding my intent, my relative responded supportively, "Oh I know that, Swanee. *You* have character."

I thought it ironic that given our family history, we would be judgmental toward my friend's private life. "Pamela was a terrific representative of our country, and a role model for me," I said testily. To my relative's credit, polite silence ensued. But once more, I realized how far I'd moved from Texas.

Preparing to leave Austria, we reveled in a series of feats and fests. I climbed the tallest mountain in the Austrian Alps, with crampons and ropes—in a blizzard, no less. I visited a hospice where a jaundiced woman complimented me that I looked less fat than on TV. And the governments of three Austrian provinces bestowed medals on me. All in all, I was quite self-satisfied.

On Tuesday of my last week at post, I was fêted by the Austrian foreign ministry. Mother flew over with Helen's daughter Kathryn to beam at my side as my hosts expressed appreciation for my work. The setting was one of the world's great hotels, the Sacher. Forty of Austria's leading citizens drank fine wine from stemware by Swarovski. Each setting had eight pieces of silver cutlery. The chocolate on the dessert plate spelled, "*Auf Wiedersehen*, Swanee."

My foreign ministry host toasted me, and with perfect poise I stood and raised my glass in return. Applause. We adjourned. I walked out of the room—into a vortex. As soon as we got into the car, Horst received a phone call and signaled the security in front of us. Sirens wailing, the police forced a lane in the center of the heavy traffic. We pulled up in front of the embassy, and I jumped out as a gurney was being loaded onto an ambulance. One of our Austrian guards, aged twenty-eight, had shot himself in the head in the embassy foyer.

I sent Mother home and pulled together key staff. The guard's heart was still beating, although he was brain-dead. His family had been notified. I let my staff know that I was heading over to be with the family at the hospital. "Ambassador, I don't think that's advisable," I was counseled by an Austrian employee. "The family will be in shock. It's not an appropriate time for you to visit."

I paused. Then I tried to imagine Mother *not* going to the hospital. A few minutes later I was sitting with my arm around the father, answering his questions over and over, and sharing with him the terrible challenges of parenting. Of all the speeches I'd had to make over the past four years, none was more heartfelt than that one. He spoke no English, and I was relieved that for once, my German flowed. "Hans, you respect me, and you believe me, don't you? My child has tried to kill herself. And I'm a *good mother*, Hans. This isn't about you. It's a tragic, terrible mystery. But it's not about you."

Lying in bed that night, I thought about how during my first week as ambassador, I'd toured our four buildings around Vienna, delivering a message sure to inspire: our work ultimately was not about treaties or trade agreements, but people. We had to keep their faces before us every day. Four years later I stared at the ceiling of my bedroom, reviewing how I'd been determined not to focus exclusively on high-profile activities, and instead had spent hundreds of hours trying to connect with our hard-working staff members. That's why every month I'd had lunch with new arrivals, the ambassador's fancy holiday party had become a caroling party with crafts, and we'd made giant Valentine cookies with the names of our employees' children on them.

As I had done in my first week, in my last week I would again gather our embassy employees, this time for a memorial service for Christian, our young guard. Christian, whose first child would be born a few months later. Christian, whom I'd walked by almost every day for four years. Christian, whose name I hadn't learned until after the ambulance pulled away.

A man wrapped up in himself makes a very small bundle.
— *Benjamin Franklin*

CHAPTER 7

Tender Mercies

Hope

The tragedies I encountered throughout my posting were interwoven with Lillian's illness. She was not only depressed or manic but frequently psychotic: One morning I found her stranded, unable to figure out how to step across the hot lava that she saw flowing around her bed. My fears soared when I read that one out of every three cases like hers ends in suicide. So, late in my Vienna tenure, when our doctors had tried every treatment they knew and she wasn't getting better, I flew home to meet with the leading researcher on bipolar illness at the National Institute of Mental Health. Dr. Robert Post met with me in his home for two hours late one night.

I described Lillian's struggle just to get through a day. "Your daughter's system is being poisoned," he told me, his voice clipped with annoyance. "You shouldn't have accepted the debilitating side effects of her medications." He recommended that we start over with an experimental mood stabilizer that had helped 60 percent of his patients who were nonresponders to other drugs.

With a surge of optimism, I asked, "How many have you given it to?"

"Twelve."

I searched his eyes. "How many children?"

"None."

Dr. Post waited as I processed his words. "Do you think it's safe?" I asked nonsensically.

"Safe? You've tried everything else, and your daughter has a potentially fatal illness. It's time to throw the book out the window," he pushed.

No single remedy works magic for every patient. Medication right for one person's brain chemistry may be useless for another. But for Lillian, Neurontin was literally a lifesaver. We were overjoyed when the drug led to an enormous improvement. Although her illness had no cure and she would still have times of high risk, she could now engage with the world around her and not swing out of control so often. It was like watching Lazarus stagger out of the tomb as her wit, sparkle, and keen perceptions were unbound.

Since then we've had plenty of difficult, even excruciating, times. But we both have a blessed sense of being beyond the worst. Maybe that's why I can write about my daughter's past—because I have so much confidence in her future.

Ultimately Lillian united our family in ways none of us could have predicted, eliciting the care and compassion that often stay buried in pain-free circumstances. Charles's resentment changed dramatically once he understood the flood of emotions that Lillian had to manage without a willing brain chemistry. Henry's concern for her was a factor in his earning a master's degree in counseling psychology and then working with troubled adolescents. And Teddy, who adores his sister (he calls her the wisest person he's ever met), developed a profound regard for people with psychiatric problems. Charles, Henry, and Teddy would be the first to understand why, as I look back on my life, I describe Lillian as not only a close friend but also a sage teacher.

One lesson she's taught me is that I must reach high without overreaching. Like all mothers, I've tried to find the balance between trying to safeguard my child and letting her find her own path. But Lillian has reminded me many times that I can't do or be everything for her. I can only offer to be a guide as she takes her own steps. Yes, I could stay at her side when times were roughest. I could get her the best medical care in the world. But I couldn't somehow, by sheer force of will, "make it all well."

Second, my daughter has also taught me that tragedy can be both terror and teacher. Mental illness has followed me all my life. Since my early years I've wanted to alleviate the suffering I saw in the eyes of Hassie and others whose psychiatric diagnoses were emblazoned across their identities. In my breakaway time in Heidelberg, I learned empathy as I experienced the depression that I'd witnessed in my mother. Directing Karis, I was constantly enriched by nursing a cup of coffee with a woman who was trying to hear me over internal voices screaming epithets. And I grew stronger: standing with my arm around the waist of a brilliant pianist so terrified that his future was cut off before it began, I've realized the limitations of talent.

Lillian's third lesson has been the power of others to influence an illness. Her problem wasn't only "chemical imbalance," "dysfunctional behavior," or "genetic predisposition." The reactions of people around her, including me, were in the mix as well. A phone call from a friend, a judgmental scowl, an invitation for tea and conversation. . . . Every act of openness or prejudice shaped her reality. Despite their influence, the people interacting with her have generally had little idea of their impact.

Although with time my daughter has become much more stable, the fear of Lillian's death has never left me. While painful, that fear creates an appreciation for each day that I share this earth with her. That's the fourth lesson. I encounter Teddy, Henry, Charles, my friends, and every other person I touch with a sense of being gifted by their presence. I take no hug, sunrise, kind word, or autumn leaf for granted.

Fifth, as my daughter and I have negotiated a fragile compromise between hope and despair, I've recognized more clearly the essential aid of friends, family, and professionals. Together we laid a foundation of trust and communication by day, only to have night demons rip apart every bridge to sanity we'd built. We all began again the next day, holding onto the promise that failure is an event, not a person.

Similarly, I've realized a sixth lesson—that everyone needs an advocate. No matter how clever, how strong, how experienced, people find themselves trapped. With the same effort I put into finding medical advice for Lillian, I've pressured bureaucracies to help impoverished families. It's not only people on the bottom rungs of the social ladder who need help. My students need to be told when they're brilliant, and women I work with today, who are trying to stop wars, need to be ushered into the offices of policy makers.

Seventh, life with Lillian has taught me not to be afraid of difference. Reality isn't always beautiful, but even when distorted it can dazzle. In my early thirties, Karis and Hunt Alternatives challenged me to appreciate diversity. But those lessons crystallized in my forties when Lillian showed me that life is kaleidoscopic, a turbulent and random recombination of shapes and colors. I came to see the importance of not only a saved soul or healthy psyche, but also a robustly integrated society in which individuals coexist in easy sameness as well as splendid difference. Lofty words aside, I still flinch when an unkempt person approaches me on the street. His mumbling is disturbing. Scary, really. But he could be my child. He is, after all, someone else's.

And a final lesson: Lillian has dramatically altered my perception of success and the value of internal versus external strength. I know plenty of people with exquisitely balanced brains, extensive education, and advanced careers who are miserably unsatisfied with who they are. As I've wondered what I could hope for my daughter, I've constantly returned to the afternoon when Lil, while reviewing her progress with her gentle Viennese psychiatrist, began to ruminate. "It's hard to think about all those years before my illness was diagnosed. Then the months in hospitals, and trying to find the right medications. I imagine: if only I could have had this new drug then. . . . But I guess I really wouldn't want to go back and change anything. After all, every experience is part of me. And I like who I am."

Mental illness isn't a tragedy. It's not an aberration. It's a reality coloring my family's world, adding new shapes and forms. Lillian and I have often discussed how she should pass on this understanding. Should she or I write about it, or protect our family privacy? We thought long and hard, then she decided to craft an article with me requested by *Good Housekeeping*, laying out her experience as a sort of road map for others facing a frightening journey. Bipolar disorder was rarely being diagnosed in children. Lillian said that the article would be her way of turning something terrible into something good for others. As the authors, we could control the tone and content.

When the issue hit the stands, I cringed. It had our text, but the editors' title: "I Couldn't Reach My Daughter." Her courage had been missed by the headline writer. The article was about Lillian, not me.

I'm not sorry we did it, and neither is Lillian. We've helped a lot of people and become more open in the process. But it was a tradeoff.

Tradeoffs

Tradeoff is a subplot in this half-told tale of my life. In my fifties, I've settled the score with Donna Reed, TV's perfect mother in a perfect family, who molded my young psyche every week. Still, trying to balance professional and personal loads, I've made plenty of mistakes. Dragging along three kids as I've gone crusading has been full of challenges, but it's had its beautiful moments too.

The most difficult but also the most striking confluence of work and family life was when my intense involvement in the Balkan War came at a time of almost overwhelming pain for my own family. As innocents fled indescribable horrors, I was trying to ward off legions of devils streaming out of my daughter's mind. But it was our shared vulnerability that allowed the refugees and me to stretch across language, class, and culture—and find each other.

As meaningful as they were for me, those connections weren't necessarily possible for my kids, and I must acknowledge the price they paid in having me as their mother. The cost to them is captured in a memory of a time when I thought that *I* was the one making a sacrifice. Returning one evening from four gut-wrenching days in Bosnia, I walked into the house, straight to Lillian and Teddy at the dinner table. Charles was away, and as the butler brought and took the soup, then the veal, then the strudel, the children didn't say one word about my trip. I finally asked, "Why couldn't you have expressed a bit of interest, after all the phone calls you've overheard, the stories I've told, the political figures you've met?"

"We can't take any more" was the essence of their reply. This was more than compassion fatigue. It was a defense of identity. I'd been so focused on "saving the world" that I'd forgotten a basic principle: my kids shouldn't have to compete with refugees.

I was appalled that I could be so insensitive. It stirred up the self-doubts that plagued me about mothering and career. The mothering pull is powerful, so unrelenting that I think it must be biological—part of the survival of the species mechanism. But rather than observing with some scientific distance, we mothers experience the tension at a visceral level with a sense of overwhelming (and thus secret) guilt.

I figure we have a three-way choice: We can have no children so we can be perfect professionals—and always regret missing out on one of the great joys of womanhood. We can stay home full time trying to be perfect mothers—and wonder if we're using our brains to their fullest. Or we can live with a diminished score on both, career and family.

I haven't trivialized the conflict by ignoring it. Often I've felt I was betraying my children when I left them with someone else so I could go to a meeting. In reality, giving a child space to cope with adversity, to be independent, is solid mothering. Letting a child transfer attention and affection from one person to another teaches an important skill. In my head, I could say my responsibility as a mother was to be sure that every moment each of my children was safe and loved, and that didn't require my constant physical presence. But in my heart, the ache and misgiving were always there. Throughout my childrearing years, the sad contest seethed inside me, at a place no one could see.

Rather than keep the tension in the dark, where it would be most powerful, I've found it's worth taking the time to explicitly stage the internal conversation. Here it is.

One voice lays out the crux: Children need their mothers like they need no one else. They're ours for only a few years, and it's selfish of me to devote myself to my career when I could be with them.

Then another voice speaks up: I love my children with all my heart. And like most working mothers, I often longed to be with them when they were in the care of someone other than me. But I couldn't have become who I was to the world if I'd spent fourteen hours a day with my children. I didn't want to use my time that way. Even so, we had breakfast and dinner together almost every day. I drove my kids to school and curled up in their beds at night to read stories or do math games. I often planned weekend excursions for us or canceled meetings to come home if they were sick.

The third voice isn't internal. It comes from my children, who have let me know, in no uncertain terms, that I wasn't the "unconditionally always there" mother they longed for. I've apologized, with many, many tears, for disappointing them. But when I look back, I'm not sure I could have done it differently. Absolutely, there are specific moments I'd change. But I went to heroic efforts to leave my work behind and enter their worlds, "a thousand times a thousand." That's my mother's expression. My mother, whom I've castigated for leaving me in the care of Franny or just to fend for myself. But now I get it. Now with my own kids, I see my mother differently. She had her life to live, as do I. Maybe children need to have children of their own to understand what I'm talking about.

Rather than seeing my profession and family in competition, as the children did and as I often experienced in a given day, I believe I integrated mothering my little ones and nurturing the world. The desires and demands of those roles blended into a stronger compound.

Certainly, being with my children infused me with love that I turned outward to the world. An hour with my arms stretched out to them opened up my heart to the pain of others. But did being decision maker, visionary, and public personality enrich the lives of my children?

Beyond spending time together, I brought to my children the fullness of who I am as a woman in the world. Now the truth is that they didn't give a hoot about the fullness. They wanted only the mommy part. If I tried to explain the importance of a meeting, they cast it as bragging. If they saw me on stage, they didn't hear the speech because they were focused on the distance between them and their mother behind the podium.

On the other hand, they gained an image of me as a competent person. My favorite reminder of that is when Teddy said, as I tucked him into bed, "Mommy, you should run for president of the United States. I'm serious. Don't smile. There's nothing about the job you couldn't learn. Please, Mommy, do it. *Do* it."

Until they all left home, my ambivalence would persist, and the residue feelings would live even longer. For when guilt is deposited in layers, over hours, months, and years, self-forgiveness happens slowly, also in layers. Ultimately, it's been a spiritual exercise of confession and acceptance. Forgive me, I can say, for not being perfect. I am how God made me. And that must be enough.

Granted, I should have been more sensitive to my children's difficulties being in my wake, given my own difficulty in trying to find a space in a Hunt family brimming over with zealots promoting their causes. That Dallas endeavor was frustrating and painful, but ultimately I found, or created, room for myself. I hope that my kids will too.

Zealots can be blind. We can be narrow. But we needn't be. We can be open to unexpected pressures that rudely reshape our most carefully constructed worldview. I hope I can pass this on to my children and grandchildren. I hope they'll be willing to shake themselves loose from worshipping strength and beauty and give up banishing ugliness, inadequacy, and "inappropriate" behavior to the shadowy margins. I want their kaleidoscopes to have endless hues and patterns, and not all those pretty. And I expect them to be confused and unsettled by some whom they meet; that may include the face each sees in the mirror.

My job is to encourage an openness that will let them realize the connection between themselves and disoriented people at the bus stop, dedicated public servants in the bureaucracy, teenaged Serb warriors, and elegant Middle Eastern royalty.

Ours is a remarkable family, and looking back, I'm grateful for how my sense of mission was spawned as I grew up with people who took great risks for the sake of an ideal. From Lillian I learned the necessity but from the Hunts I learned the art of throwing expectations aside, stretching beyond my knowledge or expertise to engage with whatever reality intruded impolitely on my life.

Dad would be at least bemused to see his role in shaping my worldview. I think he'd take satisfaction in the number of ways I've followed in his footsteps, including by penning this memoir. I've even emulated his syndicated column-writing, albeit as the "liberal voice" for Scripps Howard News Service. Like him I keep churning out books, speaking here, there, and everywhere. However different we are in assessing what the world needs, it was Dad's disregard for boundaries that gave me the gumption to tackle those needs.

Hassie died about a year before this book was published. At his gravesite I read passages from chapter 1. June sang with her guitar. Bunker, Lamar and Norma, and Helen and Harville were there too. I was grateful that they could give their implicit nod to paragraphs Hassie wasn't able to approve. Of all of Mom's four kids, I'd been Hassie's most frequent visitor in his last, bedridden years, often bringing others with me. So Charles, Lillian, and Teddy, Helen's children, and Mark's parents had seen him of late and came to the cemetery. Lillian spoke beautifully, expressing a connection that no one else could fathom.

And then there's Mom, that remarkable woman who let the Thanksgiving turkey get cold while she prayed "for all those in every corner of the world who don't have family to be with." I hope she would recognize a bit of herself in me—if not her creed, at least her passion. A thousand times I heard Mom declare, "I love getting old." In fact she proclaimed 1999, the year of her death, to be the best year of her life—even though she was suffering from cancer. The whole family gathered in her bedroom for her last hours, singing songs from Rodgers and Hammerstein's *Oklahoma!* We were all so into the moment that we didn't notice exactly when she breathed her last, but she entered the pearly gates either to "The Surrey with the Fringe on Top" or "Oh, What a Beautiful Morning."

Dad taught me to launch forth. Hassie, how to give without getting something back. Mom inculcated in me how to care about others. But for fifteen years it was Mark Meeks who convinced me that I should apply that caring to the world, with an insistence on social justice. Putting aside the disappointments of any failed marriage, I'm grateful to him.

And now, as a weathered woman starting to pick my way through the second half of my life, my hat's off to Charles, at once my mentor, partner, naysayer, and cheerleader. Continuing a lifetime of giving, he's created the Boston Landmarks Orchestra, providing free concerts to families. He also spends a chunk of his time on airplanes and in hotels, conducting orchestras around the world, most frequently in Moscow, across Central Asia, and yes, still in Sarajevo. The joy I felt twenty years ago when I first saw him conduct has continued, just as strongly. During more than a few hours of working on this book, I was in the back of a hall as he rehearsed, looking up from my page to gaze at the maestro. Those private moments were like scenes from a movie, complete with soundtrack.

And our kids. As I'm finishing the last commas of this manuscript, for a sweet and rare moment all three of my children like me. And, I should add, I like *them*. Henry is a first-rate husband and dad. He has bloomed as a documentary film producer, leading viewers into the world of a high school basketball team on the Wind River Indian Reservation, then into the Brazilian land equity movement and the accomplishments of a new woman president of war-torn Liberia. Lillian is a talented poet and staunch friend to many. She lives across from her dad's church and at the Columbine Ranch, and she calls me almost daily to discuss some aspect of theology, read to me a passage from a favorite book, or debate a strategy for the Hunt Alternatives Fund. Teddy, bless him, is more than ready to be out from under his parents. He's a deeply spiritual soul and as kind as can be. Now that he's graduated from high school, he's doing his own trailblazing. How much, after all, can I object?

But this is my half-life, not anyone else's. At middle age, I'm more radioactive than ever, hoping to spark some public policy explosions before I decompose altogether. Charles and I are ensconced in Cambridge, Massachusetts, where I wake up every morning relishing the thought of another five decades of organizing, writing, funding, and teaching.

Needless to say, I'm excruciatingly aware of many mistakes that balance my successes, but frankly I feel energized by both. I imperfectly understand and inadequately implement my crystal-clear values, and in true zealot style I can become impatient with people who don't see life as I do. But for all my passion, I'm learning to tolerate, even embrace, a wide range of difference in others. Now, at the half-point of my life, I believe, even if I don't always remember, that only by accepting the complexity and contradictions of other people will I be able to accept the dramatic marbling in myself.

Still at It

When we left Vienna for Cambridge, so did my colleagues Susan, Val, and Sarah. The Hunt Alternatives Fund moved from Denver and was transformed, first under Val's leadership, and now under Sarah's. The fund is going strong, with three initiatives: one global, one national, and one local.

The first, the Initiative for Inclusive Security, works with women waging peace in more than forty conflicts, connecting them to thousands of officials at the World Bank, the United Nations, the State Department, and other halls of power. The women bring a wealth of expertise in law and governance, civil society, academic research, and development. They're involved in hundreds of activities, such as creating a business initiative to stop the civil war in Sri Lanka, organizing mass street demonstrations against the nuclear buildup in Pakistan and India, writing exposés of massacres in Colombia, campaigning for peace referenda in Northern Ireland, reintegrating demobilized soldiers in Rwanda, gathering testimony against war criminals in Kosovo, and training thousands of women to run for office in Cambodia. Ambassador Hattie Babbitt heads our nine-person policy and advocacy office in Washington. I spend considerable time on the road, consulting with women leaders in every corner of the globe, helping them find their voices, as I've found mine.

The fund's national project is called Prime Movers. We support leaders of social movements as they strategize ways to engage millions of citizens to create a more just America. They learn as much from each other as they do from us.

One prime mover is Eboo Patel in Chicago, whose Interfaith Youth Core helps young people share their different faiths while building new houses and feeding the hungry. Another is Sara Horowitz, forming institutions in New York that will ultimately be a model for a "new New Deal," an updated social safety net for the increasing number of workers living without a wide range of basic benefits and protections.

In Massachusetts, the fund has put together a coalition of thirty arts groups through an initiative called ArtWorks for Kids. We link the organizations with our wealthy friends, who become their influential allies, helping to push for political support.

Bring Back the Music, one of our grantees, puts violins, flutes, clarinets, and trumpets into the hands of kids from low-income families. They stepped in when music education was slashed from Boston Public Schools. Urban Improv, another ArtWorks grantee, gets kids talking about peer pressure, violence, racism, homophobia, and substance abuse—all through improvisational acting. Some of our arts programs teach kids entrepreneurship: Artists for Humanity expects its teens to work at least six hours a week and pays them to produce paintings, theatrical sets, photographs, and graphic design for individual and corporate buyers. The young artists' lives are changed as they take control of their microenterprises.

In all these efforts I'm surrounded by talented staff, who endure my constant critique in service to our larger vision. And I don't ever forget that we wouldn't be doing these projects if it weren't for the brilliant stewardship of our family business by my brother Ray, and the support of Helen and June in demanding a funding stream so we sisters could develop our own separate work.

Apart from our foundation, just down the road (ten minutes by bike), is Harvard's Women and Public Policy Program, which I direct. We sponsor research, convene policy makers and practitioners, and shape the experience of thousands of graduate students who pass through the Kennedy School of Government en route to changing the world. Some of those spectacular men and women take my courses in "Inclusive Security," thinking through how they'll bring women into formal and informal peace processes when they are themselves the policy makers in charge.

Over in "the Yard," younger students have signed up for the "Choreography of Social Movements." We examine American movements through a framework of values, vision, leadership, resources, and the ripe moment in time. More important, my zealots-in-the-making meet in small groups to plan movements that they'd be willing to lead. I haven't come across many of the communists that Dad warned were running Harvard, but I've hung on my walls the speech I delivered with him at the East Texas Oil Field, to give them fair warning.

All these activities, whether with our foundation, Harvard, writing, or consulting, feed into a larger aspiration. My vision is a world in which every person is valued. No lives are discarded as statistics. No one is marginalized.

Since I started working on this book eight (eight!) years ago, the landscape of our world has changed dramatically. "Security" is now the leading story. But real security requires more than bombs and bullets. In an increasingly dangerous world, we won't be safe until we cultivate an understanding that every person's tears are the same color (to borrow a Bosnian phrase), and every dream carries the same weight. My life, my passion, my zeal are in service to that vision.

Thinking about overarching vision, I pulled off a shelf the cloth-covered blue journal that I held in my lap as I sat alone on a Himalayan mountain, during my Outward Bound trip in November 1989. Each trekker was told to find a place where no one could see her. There we spent the day alone with our thoughts. Looking down on eagles as they swooped over the folds of velvety valleys, a lake of white clouds, and brilliant fields of snow, I composed this poem. It strikes me as a remarkably fitting summary—and forecast—of my life.

Singla Pass—15,000 feet

Here I am this woman
born into my own intimate moment
of a universe vast and incomprehensible.
In the first half of my living
after heady climbs and disappointing descents
I have learned three lessons:
That although joy awaits discovery
love doesn't come delivered prepackaged or perfect,
no matter what predictions or promises;
That life defies diagnosis, so that
I may bleed without suffering
And other times suffer without bleeding;
And that sometimes, beyond my willing,
my accomplishments far exceed expected limits,
interspersed with times of forgiven mediocrity.

Now, looking out onto the next half of my living,
I am rooting myself in those three lessons
so that, in untamed and verdant response
I will freely give to those closest to me
my brightest and kindest moments, hoping that
from those nearest will extend an ethic to embrace the world.
I will treat myself with kindly care,
earning every wrinkle with worries well-placed
and every leathered crinkle with authentic smiles.
And I will be shoeless nine of ten workday hours,
convince children that rain was part of our picnic plan,
and perform many other hitherto unsupposed feats.
Then someday infinitely soon
I'll wear my grey crown proudly
assumed with graceful dignity and an irreverent chuckle
And I'll willingly, freely, pass on
with the secret delight of passionate memories
and most tender mercies, worthy of my full womanhood.

Index

Page number in *italics* refer to illustrations.

SWANEE HUNT

former U.S. Ambassador to Austria (1993–97),
is the president of Hunt Alternatives Fund, director of the
Women and Public Policy Program at the John F. Kennedy
School of Government at Harvard University, and the
founder and chair of the Initiative for Inclusive Security
(formerly Women Waging Peace), a global policy-oriented
initiative working to integrate women into peace processes.

Library of Congress Cataloging-in-Publication Data
Hunt, Swanee.
Half-life of a zealot / Swanee Hunt.
p. cm.
ISBN-13: 978-0-8223-3875-8 (cloth : alk. paper)
ISBN-10: 0-8223-3875-0 (cloth : alk. paper)
1. Hunt, Swanee. 2. Hunt, Swanee—Family.
3. Ambassadors—United States—Biography. 4. Women
ambassadors—United States—Biography. 5. Political activists—
United States—Biography. 6. Women in politics—United
States. 7. United States—Foreign relations—1993–2001.
8. Vienna (Austria) Biography. I. Title.
E840.8.H87A3 2006
327.730092—dc22
[B]
2006012740